The Bible, Violence, and the Sacred

LIBERATION FROM THE MYTH OF SANCTIONED VIOLENCE

James G. Williams

Trinity Press International
Valley Forge, PA

THE BIBLE, VIOLENCE, AND THE SACRED: *Liberation from the Myth of Sanctioned Violence.* © 1991 by James G. Williams. All rights reserved. Printed in the United States of America. No part of this book may be used or reproduced in any manner whatsoever without written permission except in the case of brief quotations embodied in critical articles and reviews. For information address Trinity Press International, P.O. Box 851, Valley Forge, PA 19482.

PAPERBACK EDITION

Library of Congress Cataloging-in-Publication Data
  Williams, James G., 1936-
  The Bible, violence, and the sacred: liberation from the myth of sanctioned violence/James G. Williams.—1st ed.
      p.   cm.
  Originally published: San Francisco, Calif. : HarperSanFrancisco, 1992.
  Includes bibliographical references and index.
  ISBN 1-56338-116-8
  1. Violence in the Bible.   2. Sacrifice—Biblical teaching.
  3. Jesus Christ—Passion.   4. Girard, René, 1923– . I. Title.
  BS680.V44W556   1995   95-6652
  220.6—dc20   CIP

---

95 96 97 98 99 ❖ 10 9 8 7 6 5 4 3 2 1

Printed in the United States of America

Contents

Foreword by René Girard   v
Preface   ix
Acknowledgments   xv
Note on Translations and Transcriptions   xvi

1. René Girard: A New Approach to Biblical Texts   1

2. Enemy Brothers   33
   Excursus: Folkloristic Approaches to the Bible   68

3. Moses and the Exodus   71
   Excursus: The Great Man Myth: Freud, Heidegger, Mann, and Fascism   98

4. Covenant and Sacrifice   105

5. Kings and Prophets: Sacred Lot and Divine Calling   129

6. Job Versus the "Friends": The Failed Scapegoat   163

7. The Gospels and the Innocent Victim   185

8. Desire, Violence, and the Truth of the Victim   213

9. Conclusion: "A Citty upon a Hill"   241

Notes   259
Index   281

Foreword

Untried ideas and theories should not be criticized in the abstract; they should be put to work. This is how we can find how useful they are. The present book vigorously and most successfully puts to work some largely untried ideas that I was first to formulate.

These ideas are usually referred to as the "mimetic," "scapegoat," or "victimage" theory of religion. We never put labels on our own ideas; other people do, and, in the present intellectual context, it is difficult to think of less appealing labels than the juxtaposition of "scapegoat" and "theory." But labels are unavoidable, and James Williams courageously faces the challenge of these two.

In anthropological literature, the use of the word *scapegoat* goes back to James G. Frazer's *Golden Bough*. If the new "scapegoat theory" were merely an amplification and systematization of what Frazer had in mind, it would deserve not one second of our attention; it would simply make past mistakes worse.

Contrary to what Frazer believed, a scapegoat *theme* is nowhere to be found in his so-called scapegoat rituals. The reason for its absence is not that these rituals are alien to what our modern idea of scapegoating implies; on the contrary, they are too deeply immersed in it to conceive it in any form.

The new scapegoat theory is not Frazer gone mad, therefore; it is not an assimilation or reduction of all ancient religious practices to a still nonexistent *theme* or *motif* of the scapegoat. In many respects it is the very reverse. The modern use of the word *scapegoat*, our own popular understanding of it, is much more interesting than Frazer's. It refers to an intrinsically irrelevant victim—a human being—who is perceived as "guilty" not by a single individual but by an entire human group. A process of mimetic contagion transfers upon this vicarious victim all the fears, hostilities, and other difficulties that this group will not directly confront.

When scapegoating is unanimous, it becomes the almost indestructible "truth" of the scapegoaters. It cannot appear as such, therefore; most religions are too completely dominated by their scapegoat *mechanism* to accede to a scapegoat *theme* in any form.

The main assumption of the new scapegoat theory is that the most intense and primitive versions of the *mechanism* are responsible for the genesis of religion and of the social bond itself. Thematic and structural traces are everywhere, and their pattern is so consistent throughout the world that, in my view, they make skepticism more untenable than direct evidence would if it were available.

Even among us, we modern people who pride ourselves on knowing everything there is to know about scapegoating (and not without some justification), the only scapegoats easy to detect as such are those of our enemies; the scapegoats of our friends are harder to see, and, if they happen to be ours as well, they are completely invisible *as scapegoats*.

The only interesting scapegoat is this invisible scapegoat. Its continued presence in our midst can be guessed from our attitude, we who eagerly denounce the scapegoats of our neighbors but never catch ourselves in the process of scapegoating. This paradoxical dimension of scapegoating, even (and especially) in a world literally obsessed with this evil, is the true reason why the new scapegoat theory remains elusive in its simplicity, why it cannot fail to be widely misunderstood.

The real scapegoat is a hidden generative mechanism, and its theorization has more affinities with the genealogical and deconstructive practices of our time than with the outmoded anthropology of Frazer. The decisive difference is that its effectiveness with religious texts undermines the epistemological nihilism to which other forms of "deconstruction" invariably lead.

As soon as a talented interpreter like James Williams starts experimenting with the explanatory power of the hidden generative scapegoat, the results are striking; they give the lie to the imperative of heuristic impotence that is so dogmatically embraced nowadays.

But if all we reach with this new interpretive tool is the collective violence of scapegoating, have we not merely exchanged one nihilism for another? That would be true if we had to limit ourselves to the discovery of those we may call the "natural religions" of humankind, the ones rooted in arbitrary victimage. But this "naturalism" is only a first phase in the context of which the "unnaturalness" of some exceptional religions can be discovered, the very few religions that forsake the substitute scapegoating of sacrifice and the even fewer that reach back to the victimage origin itself, not to embrace it anew but to repudiate it once and for all.

In the Jewish and Christian Bible, we can see the gradual emergence of scapegoating in the modern and critical sense. It is there and there only that a genuine *theme* or *motif* of the scapegoat can make its appearance and, simultaneously with it, a growing realization that we will not become fully human unless we confront and restrain this unconscious activity of ours by all possible means.

This is the meaning of Jesus' passion in the four Gospels. What God demands is not a sacrifice of his Son, not a perfect scapegoat, but the unconditional refusal of scapegoating, even if the price must be death, even if this very refusal, in a world such as ours, inevitably entails that we must be scapegoated.

Instead of covering up once again the collective ignorance of unanimous victimage, the four texts of the passion disclose it so thoroughly that, in the long run, the hiddenness of scapegoating is everywhere uncovered and its power to persuade gradually undermined.

The most remarkable feature of our world is its loudly advertised repugnance for victimage, which has no equivalent in any other society. Even if our deeds do not match our principles, even if our record of persecution sharply contradicts our language, our awareness of scapegoating is unique, and it cannot be traced exclusively to what Nietzsche calls "resentment" or "slave morality," however pertinent the Nietzschean critique of our world occasionally is.

Like all good things, our concern for victims can be horribly abused, but the very abuse still indirectly testifies to the excellence of the thing abused, which is really a priceless gift to us from Jewish and Christian scripture. Nietzsche was too obsessed with the caricature of this gift to acknowledge the existence of the original.

This so-called scapegoat theory was developed in the context of a general theory of culture. It is essential that it be tested by biblical scholars, working on the original languages of Jewish and Christian scripture. James Williams is such a scholar; he focuses on the Hebrew and Greek of some essential texts in such lively fashion and with such clarity of style that his book greatly reinforces the thesis of a scapegoat foundation of human culture that would gradually come to light in the biblical text. It produces striking new insights in many areas, notably the close mimetic relatedness that underlies the opposition between prophet and king in the preexilic period.

Whenever prompted by the broader interests of his demonstration, the author interrupts his biblical commentaries with uninhibited, sharply polemical, and thoroughly enjoyable discussions of various thinkers whose authority our interpretive nihilists, for all their nihilism, have turned into the most sacred of all sacred cows, notably Freud and Heidegger.

James Williams does not deny the power, even the occasional greatness of these thinkers; he never dismisses them with journalistic dispatch, but he reveals the same flaw in all of them, which is their dismal failure in regard to religion. Regardless of their differences, they all resemble each other in their ultimate reliance upon the impoverished view of religion that we inherited from Enlightenment rationalism. Whether they still denounce their Judeo-Christian heritage as "superstition," or furiously romanticize paganism alone, as Heidegger does, all our revered intellectual gurus cannot help but trivialize religion. With the entire modern era, they fail to grasp the oneness of religion and human culture from the very beginning.

In another passage of highly effective polemics, Williams warns us against the dubious prophecies of Carl J. Jung. His murky archetypes are so ectoplasmic that they fit all phenomena indifferently and cannot really account for the singularity of any.

The current crisis of the modern university began with its failure to do justice to religious texts without conferring upon them some a priori authority. This interpretive failure has gradually spread to all disciplines in the humanities and social sciences, now culminating with a know-nothing nihilism that glories in its own emptiness with unprecedented arrogance and naïveté.

The larger society is finally lending an ear to the strange noises from inside academia, and the always obliging media provide the general public with a picture of unrelieved gloom, as if the only alternative to nihilistic deconstruction were an outmoded rationalism. Lately, of course, the sound and the fury of these twin enemies have been so deafening that their overblown quarrel looks like the sum total of our culture, but there are signs that it will not always be so and the present book is such a sign.

We must not delude ourselves with conspiracy theories; we must not believe that the sacrifice of a few troublemakers will resurrect a dead humanism. Scapegoating does not work any more, and, if we attempt it, it will achieve nothing but only magnify the antics of a few academic operators. Our cultural crisis is too acute for empty rituals.

Rejecting both the old pretense of academic detachment and the more recent affectation that swears never to engage in anything but "verbal play," James Williams honestly grapples in his conclusion with the fundamental issues that most of us prefer to avoid. Can we take our religious tradition seriously without betraying our critical obligation, without surrendering to the forces of superstition? His answer is that the humanism of the future can be broadly religious and still universally acceptable, if only we understand that the real essence of our Judaic and Christian heritage is the value that already unites us all, at least in principle, in the defense of all victims.

My general outlook is perhaps a little less optimistic than his. As I read his book, however, this small difference disappears in an experience of shared intellectual and religious discovery, of joyful solidarity with his message of hope.

René Girard
Stanford University

Preface

I hope that *The Bible, Violence, and the Sacred* (hereafter BVS) will contribute to a new approach in biblical research and biblical theology. I am grateful to Harold Rast and Trinity Press International for putting it out in paperback. All errors called to my attention and that I could find in the hardbound edition have been corrected and some of the bibliographical references have been updated. I will use the opportunity afforded by this preface to respond to critical reviews of the hardbound edition.

1. This new approach to biblical studies must be *interdisciplinary*, taking into account not only ancient Near Eastern texts but also texts from other cultural settings, including the Western intellectual traditions. This is recognized by Charles Mabee and partially acknowledged by James Crenshaw (Mabee: 185–86; Crenshaw: 567).* Crenshaw, however, thinks the critiques of influential thinkers such as Nietzsche, Freud, Jung, and Heidegger are secondary to the book. They are not. It is true that my case for the hermeneutics of the mimetic model must be made from the biblical texts, but these thinkers have affected the course of modern intellectual history and even of popular culture. We need to be aware of the arena into which we have entered as biblical scholars. We are there, surrounded and informed by cultural and intellectual forces, whether or not we know it or like it.

2. The approach I advocate entails a *twofold attitude toward traditional scholarly criticism:* an appreciation of the historical forms of criticism and yet an attempt to modify them in the direction of seeking the generative depth and revelatory character of the texts. Raymund Schwager has touched on this point in his review: "With the exegesis practiced in [BVS] the historical-critical way of putting questions is not bypassed but relativized. Thus the biblical text is not divided up into many hypothetical layers but is allowed to attain, as a whole, to the language by which it is able to address current problems" (Schwager: 340). This more holistic and dialogical approach is not understood or accepted by Neil Elliott, who takes me to task for rejecting both conventional biblical criticism and postmodern methodologies (Elliott: 228–29). He is particularly suspicious of the way I labor "over the difficulty

---

*A list of all works cited is given at the end of the preface.

of sacrificial language in the Gospels. . . ." (ibid., 228) and my refusal to separate Mark's historical background and theological agenda from the historical Jesus (ibid., 229). The question of sacrifice is treated briefly below. As for the biblical criticism, I would refer again to the point made above: the interpreter best fulfills his or her vocation by trying to serve the generative depth and revelatory character of the texts. For whom and what am I—are we—working?

3. The book is a project in *culture criticism*. As Robert Hamerton-Kelly has stated, I show that Girard's theory "is fruitful for the interpretation of texts, and therefore that the texts in turn are warrants for the truth of the theory. This result justifies the use of the theory in the criticism of culture and also justifies the pre-eminent position of the Bible as the standard of the critical truth" (Hamerton-Kelly: 8). In fact, the task of culture criticism led me to devote more than one-third of the last chapter to "The American Pharmacy." Only Mabee among the reviewers caught the import of that discussion. There I argue that "addiction" is what "culture" means and how it operates; it operates through the *pharmakon*, the remedy-poison, whose effect is inseparable from the *pharmakos* or scapegoat. It is only in the context of demythologizing stemming from the Bible and the biblical witness to the innocent victim that we can find our way out of addiction and into the freedom of love elicited by good mimesis, the mimesis of God.

4. The book is intended to be *evangelical*. Bruce Chilton has said that in "his treatment of the Gospels, Girard's analysis becomes openly ethical and programmatic (one might even say, evangelical) in its orientation" (Chilton: 20). Although Chilton's statement refers specifically to Girard, I think that in a general sense "evangelical" is an appropriate word for describing this book. "Pertaining to the gospel," associated with the *euaggelion*, the evangel. At the heart of the book is the conviction that there is good news, that in spite of "our cultural mendacity" there is a power at work in our cultural as well as religious traditions. This dynamic is the Bible, with its message of liberation (Chilton: 20–21). Yes, the Bible is a "mixed text," it often betrays the sacred violence of archaic humanity; but in its distinctive witness it proclaims the liberation of victims and the liberation of victimizers. Are not both Egypt and Israel saved by the mysterious providence at work through Joseph? And are not Jew and gentile, free person and slave, male and female made one in Christ?

Some of the reviews of BVS offer criticisms that are based either on complete misunderstandings or on skewed readings for which I must sometimes take partial responsibility. I would try to make some parts of the book much clearer if I were completely to rewrite it now, and I would want to lengthen and deepen the material on Gospels and on American culture. Meanwhile, there are two criticisms that are quite disturbing to me. One is a distortion and the other is perspectivally limited.

1. The distortion comes from Robert Hamerton-Kelly. He says that I treat "the divine project as a social program for victims, whose flag bearer is righteous Israel"

(Hamerton-Kelly: 9). As Hamerton-Kelly knows, that was not my intention, nor has it been Girard's. In response to the charge of ethnocentrism that one anthropologist makes against Girard, I point out that "only Western thinkers and those who imitate them accuse their own culture of ethnocentrism and victimization of the foreign other" (BVS, 19). This tendency to accuse ourselves of ethnocentrism stems from the Bible, and the New Testament Gospels are the primary foundation of culture criticism in the West, but they cannot be separated from ancient Israel and the Jewish Bible. What I wanted to articulate about the Jewish Bible is that the text both reflects, and reflects on, a struggle to realize the meaning of revelation. I say, for example, that "the disclosure of the innocent victim and the God of victims does not come about quickly and easily. It requires a long and tortuous history with numerous setbacks, for mimesis, rivalry, and violence are embedded in the symbols and institutions of the archaic cultural settings out of which Israel's forebears come" (ibid., 72; see also statements to this effect on pp. 63–64, 78, 126, 187).

I could have been clearer, and there are moments when I come across as defensive—as on page 120 concerning the slaying of Egypt's firstborn sons. I would now revise some passages, and I would certainly give greater stress to the dialectic between the forces of the sacred social order and the demythologizing impulse that stems from Israel's experience of the deep and mysterious grace of the God who cares for his world. But, in my judgment, to say that I tend toward turning "revelation into an ideology by grounding it ontologically rather than by faith" (Hamerton-Kelly: 9) is basically a misrepresentation.

2. The criticism that is perspectively limited comes from James Crenshaw. He writes of my "failure to recognize that violence characterizes the biblical God," whom I describe "as taking the side of all victims" (Crenshaw: 567; cf. Elliott: 228). This is for me a depressing statement from a scholar who has taught on theological faculties educating future pastors most of his professional career. What evangel would he expect them to proclaim? What good news is there if "violence characterizes the biblical God"? Crenshaw has evidently accepted, whether he is aware of it or not, the radical positivist historicism of the "ontology of difference" or "ontology of violence," which is the postmodern problematic stemming from Nietzsche, "the only true master of suspicion" (Milbank: 278). Crenshaw gives the impression of having counted putative instances of a "violent" God as compared to instances of a "compassionate" God of victims and decided on the basis of this count that there is a "dominant understanding" and a "minor tradition" (568). But if we are not to engage in positivist counting of instances—a finally futile way of defending against nihilism—then we must look to the structures and insights and witnesses that are *generative* and *definitive*, that is, that create new insights, perspectives, and commitments and that establish the boundaries and routes for thought and imagination. In the Hebrew Bible we can count and recount many references to violent creation of the world, comparable to creation myths or cosmogonies known among other peo-

ples; but in Judaism, Christianity, and Western culture it is the grandeur of the creation story in Genesis 1 that has set boundaries for our thinking, generated religious thought, and captured the imagination. Gods defeat dragon-scapegoats all over the world and make them part of the cosmic order. But Genesis 1 implies that if there is a dragon-scapegoat, it is not God's doing but our own.

Job is another example. Job is definitely a "minority" figure in the Bible, and the Job of the Dialogue is even a minority figure in his own book. Yet a response to Job, or at least to the questions Job poses, comes in the Servant of Isaiah 52–53 and the Jesus of the Gospels; they are hated without cause and counted among the transgressors and thereby bear the sicknesses and transgressions of others. Do not Job and the Servant and Jesus belong to a history of tradition that is generative and definitive? A history of tradition in light of which to say that "violence characterizes the biblical God" is a sad and misguided comment. Where else and to whom shall we go if not to these Scriptures and to this God who is revealed in the Innocent Victim?

Actually more relevant than the question of whether the biblical God is just and compassionate (the two do not necessarily "cancel one another out," *pace* Crenshaw: 568) is the question as to how God defends victims. "What does it mean for God to be a God of victims?" Is it necessary for liberation movements "to be content with passive non-resistance to violence and victimage?" These are questions raised by Leo Perdue (Perdue: 9). My response to Perdue's excellent questions is based on an analysis of mimesis, which in its basic or originary sense is nonconscious, prerepresentational imitation. There are three forms taken by mimesis, which have not been adequately clarified by Girard and which I did not systematically develop in the book. The highest form is the mimesis of God or the kingdom of God. The intermediate form, in which most of us participate most of the time, is the effective mimesis that enables culture to work on the basis of sacrificial mechanism. The third form is the bad mimesis in which the acquisitive aspect of imitating others breaks out of the bounds of differentiation, the modes of mediation that culture establishes. Great respect should be given to those who are strong and able to fight but who do not reciprocate by imitating the violence of the other. Their witness is absolutely necessary. But it is also sometimes valid to become engaged in the second form mimesis takes, as most of us must, and battle, even physically and militarily, against perceived injustices. There are no easy nonviolent answers in the actual world in which we exist.

I must respond much more briefly to other critics and criticisms. George L. Frear is right that Girard, Hamerton-Kelly, and I should explicate different meanings of the "sacred" (Frear: 116, n.4). The sacred is the primitive power stemming from community violence, but it is also, precisely as violence, generative of differentiations, i.e., order. The biblical tradition moves toward a transformed understanding of the sacred in which it is both supremely numinous and mystical and supremely ethical. The revelation of God and the insights growing from it traverse a long and arduous historical span; it must come into and through human culture and language (*pace* Elliott: 228–29). To give a few examples, I find this transformed understanding in Psalm 51:1–17, Micah 6:6–8, and the transfiguration accounts of the Synoptic Gospels. These texts all witness not only to a transformed understanding of the sacred but also of sacrifice which of course would be closely related to the sacred ("sacrifice" = to render sacred, from the French *sacrifier* and the Latin *sacrificare*). In the psalm, God wants humility, "truth in the inward being," rather than sacrifice; in Micah it is to do justice and love kindness (*chesed*) rather than sacrifice of the first-born; and the transfiguration episodes in Matthew and Mark are intended to introduce the background and necessity of the Son of Man's suffering, death, and resurrection. Reminiscent of the suffering and restoration of the Servant in Isaiah 53, the Gospels tell of the beloved Son who humbly pours himself out to death for the sake of many, thus transforming scapegoating and sacrifice into service in community with others.

Finally, three of the critics do not care much for my attempt in chapter 9 to relate the biblical discussion to contemporary issues in American culture (Crenshaw: 568; Hamerton-Kelly: 10; Elliott: 229–30). The discussion of their dissatisfactions with the last chapter would involve details requiring too much space in this preface. I recognize that the treatment of the issues could take a book or several books. I think, however, that the concluding comments on American culture are important, as recognized by Mabee and as I hear informally from many colleagues who have read the book. My experience with some lay and clerical groups indicates that the last chapter is accessible and interesting to the intelligent general reader. I have already expressed my disappointment that only one of the reviewers (Mabee) devoted any attention to "The American Pharmacy." The theme of the *pharmakon*, the remedy-poison, proposed by Derrida but developed beyond merely intertextual references by Girard, is a paradigmatic concept for understanding our culture if only we do not try to repress or suppress the biblical heritage that can help us understand remedies and poisons, i.e., sacrifices and scapegoats.

James G. Williams
Feast of All Saints 1994

Works Cited in Preface

Chilton, Bruce D., "René Girard, James Williams, and the Genesis of Violence," *Bulletin for Biblical Research* 3 (1993): 17–29.

Crenshaw, James L., review of BVS in *Theology Today* 49 (1993): 566–68.

Elliott, Neil, review of BVS in *Journal of the American Academy of Religion* LXII (1994): 226–30.

Frear, George L., "René Girard on Mimesis, Scapegoats, and Ethics," *The Annual of the Society of Christian Ethics* (1992): 115–33.

Hamerton-Kelly, Robert G., review of BVS in *The Bulletin of the Colloquium on Violence and Religion* 2 (March 1992): 8–10.

Mabee, Charles, review of BVS in *Interpretation* XLVII (1993): 184–86.

Milbank, John, *Theology and Social Theory* (London: Blackwell, 1990).

Perdue, Leo G., Abstract of paper reviewing BVS presented at the conference of COV&R, San Francisco, November 20, 1992, in *The Bulletin of the Colloquium on Violence and Religion* 4 (March 1993): 9–10.

Schwager, Raymund, SJ, review of BVS (and Robert G. Hamerton-Kelly, *Sacred Violence: Paul's Hermeneutic of the Cross*) in *Zeitschrift für Katholische Theologie* 115 (1993): 339–41.

Acknowledgments

The methodological approach in this study is inspired by René Girard, and I wish to acknowledge my debt to him and to thank him for the extracurricular seminar he led from January to April 1990 at Stanford University and for the many conversations we have had. I have found him always kind and generous with his time. I am grateful to a number of my colleagues in the Colloquium on Violence and Religion (COV&R)who have contributed to my research on aspects of this book and are credited in the notes. Besides Girard himself, these include Gil Bailie, Jorgen Jorgensen, Stuart Lasine, Wolfgang Palaver, Thee Smith, Mark Wallace, and two whose critical thinking has sharpened my own in ways far exceeding references in the notes: Robert Hamerton-Kelly and Hans J. L. Jensen. Though not mentioned in the notes, another colleague in the Colloquium on Violence and Religion, Charles Mabee, has been important to me as a conversation partner. Some of these colleagues were active in the now defunct Bible, Narrative, and American Culture Seminar of the Westar Institute (BINAC), which was chaired by Mabee from October 1986 to March 1990. BINAC focused on Girard's work and was fortunate to have him for daylong conversations at three of its meetings.

John Loudon, Noreen Norton, and Virginia Rich of HarperSanFrancisco have done a fine job of working with me to move this book toward publication. My wife Yvonne's love and support have been indispensable, particularly during the exhilarating but sometimes difficult period of my academic leave at Stanford University and the even more difficult period when I completed the writing and revision after having resumed fulltime professorial duties.

This book is dedicated to my colleagues in COV&R.

Note on Bible Translations and Transcriptions of Hebrew and Greek

The Bible version used is the New Revised Standard Version(NRSV)*, unless otherwise indicated. I have also used the Revised Standard Version (RSV)** frequently when I have found it more accurate or more appropriate for my purposes. In some instances, I have given my own translation of passages.

I have tried to approximate Hebrew and Greek words in English transcription without employing diacritical marks. The latter are cumbersome for the non-specialist, while biblical critics familiar with the languages will have no difficulty recognizing the original words behind my transcriptions.

---

*The Holy Bible Containing the Old and New Testaments. New Revised Standard Version. Grand Rapids: Zondervan Bible Publishers, 1989.

**The New Oxford Annotated Bible with the Apocrypha. Revised Standard Version (second ed. of the New Testament, expanded ed. of the Apocrypha), ed. Herbert G. May and Bruce M. Metzger. New York: Oxford University Press, 1977.

1

René Girard:
A New Approach to Biblical Texts

Wee shall finde that the God of Israell is among us.
  John Winthrop, "A Model of Christian Charity"

Fools on both sides, Helen must needs be fair
When with your blood you daily paint her thus.
  Shakespeare, *Troilus and Cressida*

. . . and she bore a son, and named him Seth, for she said "for God has
appointed for me another child instead of Abel."
  Genesis 4:25

A. Biblical Criticism and Its Audience

Very few people now read the Bible. That is a commonplace. I wonder, in fact,
whether Western culture now induces us to ignore the Bible, which is felt by
many to be a sacred museum piece and by others to be a myth or collections of
myths like all the other myths of the world. Whatever the reason, however, it is a
fact that the Bible is not generally part of our reading. In the schools it is out of
bounds because of church-state problems and the dominant inclination to separate religion and public life. The Roman Catholic Church since the Second
Vatican Council has encouraged Bible study, but it is still not part of the agenda
of most practicing Catholics. Most of the mainline Protestant denominations are
actually, if not officially, indifferent to the use of the Bible, as one can see in worship service on any Sunday morning. Even when Bibles are available in the pews,
most worshipers do not open them to follow the reading of the lessons.

There are, of course, various Protestant fundamentalists and evangelical
groups whose doctrines and religious styles put the Bible in the center of daily life
as well as religious ritual. In fact, though the more liberal Protestants and
Catholics attack those who hold that the Bible is wholly or without error the word
of God, I think we owe them a great deal. They have preserved a nucleus of
respect for biblical texts and traditions amid cultural ferment and despite the disdain shown for religion (this usually means Christianity) by both its cultured and
its uncultured despisers.

I am not bothered by "literalism" as such. For one thing, it is often a weasel-word used to dismiss other positions, and in any case, it is not really the appropriate term for most of the fundamentalist-evangelical positions I have encountered. Fundamentalists and evangelicals are just as inclined to use other than "literal" methods of interpretation as other groups on the religious and theological spectrum. However, I do have two problems with a fundamentalist-evangelical approach to Scripture. What bothers me, first, is the usually tenacious fundamentalist-evangelical adherence to a doctrine of *sacrificial atonement,* that is, the necessity of the sacrifice of Christ as the unique and final sacrificial victim offered to God in order to save humans from the violence of God's vengeance. As will become clear in this book, I take a sacrificial point of view seriously, but I hold that, finally, it is not in keeping with the biblical revelation of the God who comes into the world as the Innocent Victim and who defends and frees victims.

The other problem with a fundamentalist-evangelical approach to Scripture is its typical unwillingness to put the study of Bible and religion within a broader context of human history and culture. Failing to do this, it is entrapped in spite of itself in the same rivalries and structures of violence with which the human race has struggled from the very beginning of humanity, since the emergence of humankind from an earlier evolutionary state. The more we claim to be different from others without really knowing those others, the more we will be like them. The sacrificial doctrine of the atonement is a good example of this phenomenon of really being like all the others while striving to be different, indeed unique. The traditional Christian doctrine of the sacrificial death of Christ is purportedly different in that it is a sacrifice made once and for all because of human sin in order to appease a justly angry God, and so is supposed to be the sacrifice to end sacrifice, but it nonetheless preserves the structure of sacrifice at its very core, just like other ancient religions.

Of course, the study of the Jewish and Christian Scriptures takes place in the departments and programs of religious studies in colleges and universities, as well as in the more theologically oriented professional schools for the training of rabbis, priests, and ministers. But here also a negative attitude toward the Bible is preserved and communicated, not in the form of direct attack, but under the aegis of a critical approach that is really dismissive of the importance of religion and particularly of Christianity. In modern intellectual history, religion has generally been dismissed or ignored as unimportant or irrelevant. Supposedly outmoded religious forms and functions such as sacrifice are not taken seriously. It is a telling fact that many institutions offering religious or theological study do not list a single course focusing on sacrifice, which was practiced everywhere in ancient cultures, however one evaluates the question of its centrality in religious life.

As for biblical interpretation, there are not many institutions, outside fundamentalist and evangelical circles, where it continues to hold a preeminent place. And where biblical scholarship is still pursued, much of it is so permeated with overspecialization or intellectual faddishness that it communicates very little to laypeople or even to scholars in other fields. Indeed, much of that very little that it does communicate to the laity is perceived, rightly or wrongly, as destructive, because it appears to negate the value and significance of traditional texts, stories, symbols, and doctrines. One of the primary reasons for this perception is that in the university setting one often finds the point of view that the theologian or the teacher in religious studies is not responsible to any community or circle of people except the academy and its discourse.[1]

The actual situation of biblical studies and public knowledge of the Bible is ironic, both with respect to the Bible's historic role in North American culture and in light of the ongoing concern to find better ways to deal with the human propensity to engage in conflict and violence. Historians of American religion and sociologists of religion now commonly acknowledge and use a term first employed by Robert Bellah in the 1960s: *civil religion.* It is a term that has been called into question,[2] but it is still valuable as an interpretive tool. It refers to that foundational aspect of American society and culture that is informed by the Judeo-Christian legacy—particularly prominent biblical themes—but that is attached more to the "secular" history of the country and pronouncements of political leaders than to the more obviously "religious" institutions of church and synagogue.

Of course, the subject is complicated, because the religious institutions, especially the forms of Protestant Christianity that decisively influenced the English and European background of North American culture, have affected every sphere of life, including public policy and political rhetoric. The "separation of church and state" is a maxim derived from the first amendment of the Constitution, which says, "Congress shall make no law respecting the establishment of religion nor prohibiting the free exercise thereof." Although this has been widely understood as prohibiting any role to religion in politics, it is quite clear that such was not intended by the framers of the amendment in the historical situation.[3] Separation of church and state is a separation of institutions. No religious tradition or institution may become the established religion of the national state, as was common practice in traditional societies and as found still in the United Kingdom and many European countries. But from America's beginnings and even up until the present day, government and politics have been permeated by ideas that have grown out of current interpretations of the Scriptures. As Alexis de Tocqueville observed in *Democracy in America,* written in the 1830s, Christian religion had greater influence over individuals in the United States than in any other country and was quite instrumental in the articulation of public policy, even though no one religious institution could be established as the official religion of the state.[4]

And reciprocally, the perspectives of religious institutions are clearly in the debt of a kind of civil religion, a set of assumptions and a total "story" about the nation and the world that operates more often than not on the unconscious level.

This network of assumptions and narrative motifs has its roots in biblical themes as they were appropriated and shaped by the early Puritans and other groups within the evangelical Protestant spectrum in the first two centuries of European settlement here, beginning with the Puritan and Pilgrim settlers in the early seventeenth century. Of course, there were political, philosophic, and economic currents that had great impact on early American history, so there is no question of tracing all aspects of American culture back to biblical roots or biblical themes. One thinks immediately of the influence of the European Enlightenment, the philosophies of thinkers like Hobbes, Locke, and Rousseau, and the economic theory of Adam Smith concerning the operation of "natural law" in a free market economy. These currents did not directly stem from the biblical and evangelical Protestant traditions, and in a certain regard may justly be viewed as inimical to the latter. In another, and deeper, respect we may ask whether Christianity had certain effects on those aspects of the Enlightenment that sought to liberate human beings from gods, kings, and all sorts of other religious and national symbols that imprisoned people in idolatrous bondage.

American civil religion has its historical roots in what I will call the encompassing archetypal theme of "God's New Israel." I take this phrase from the title of an anthology edited by Conrad Cherry.[5] It is suggested by the epigraph to his preface, which is from a sermon John Winthrop preached to the Massachusetts Bay settlers in 1630.

> Wee shall finde that the God of Israell is among us . . . when hee shall make us a prayse and glory, that men shall say of succeeding plantacions: the lord make it like that of New England: for wee must Consider that wee shall be as a Citty upon a Hill, the eies of all people are uppon us.

What I propose in this book is a nontraditional, interdisciplinary interpretation of biblical texts and traditions that give witness to a revelation and a form of knowledge that have grounded the first principles of our most cherished institutions and traditions in North America, Europe, and everywhere this revelation has become known. The clearest opposition to victimization of all sorts and to concealments of violence, the clearest disclosure of the arbitrariness of selection of victims by the community that has become a mob, the fullest support of the belief that all humans have a voice before the God who creates all and thus in principle a voice that other humans should hear—these biblical themes of witness are the much truer and profounder source of social, political, legal, and religious institutions in the "free world" than what we have inherited from Greece, Rome, and elsewhere. To put it in juridical terms in order to make the point at this introductory juncture, the free world is wherever one is presumed innocent of any charge until and unless proven guilty; it is wherever one may be represented by an advocate who takes the accused's interest as his or her own in the case to be tried; and

it is wherever one's peers are asked to decide on innocence or guilt "beyond a rea-
sonable doubt."

To put it in other terms, the "free world" in my sense here is wherever social,
ethnic, economic, or religious difference is not, *in principle*, a handicap; it is,
indeed, wherever the "handicapped" are not impaired with respect to the *voce*, or
"voice," with respect to the vote or "vow" (Latin *votum*) they make to express
their political choices. Thus it is where even "handicapped" is a category that has
to be reconsidered, revised, reevaluated, for having certain traits that are "deficiencies" or "abnormal" in some way does not mean that one is not accepted ultimately and absolutely, as far as human thought and ability is capable, into the
common weal.

If that all sounds idealistic or visionary, it is. But it is the truth of a deep generative vision in our culture that causes us discomfort, often bringing other problems in its train. It is *in principle*—in terms of first things, starting points, model
points of departure—what biblically informed culture is about. It moves against
scapegoating and toward fuller and fuller liberation from all sorts of victimization.

It is a generative vision that is surely far from what Winthrop had in mind as
he preached to the Puritans, for these settlers sought to establish a kind of theo-
cracy in the new land that was exclusive, intolerant of outsiders (including the
indigenous peoples), and quick to condemn deviation. Nonetheless, the sense of
God's new community contained in the Gospels (Winthrop here alludes to the
Sermon on the Mount) cannot be gainsaid. Wherever texts speaking of a new
form of humanity that refuses to seek vengeance, of those who love their enemies,
of those who serve the Christ in the form of the needy brother or sister (Matt
5:38-38 and 25:31-46)—wherever these texts are preserved, examined, heard,
acted upon, then whatever the intentions of those who hold to narrow definitions
of religion and culture, the texts will have their way; they will work in history.
Moreover, there were movements and groups both in England and in the New
World that sought democratization in the name of Christianity, certain millenari-
ans, for example. The Levellers were influenced by Christian ideals, and, of
course, so was the work of Roger Williams in Rhode Island.[6]

This study will focus on some of the key revelatory moments and stages of
the biblical revelation. The primary aim is to explicate themes of desire, rivalry,
violence, and sacrifice in the biblical context, but in a final chapter I will also
offer some reflections on what I think the biblical disclosure of the innocent victim and the God of victims has to do with America's past and present as a "Citty
upon a Hill."

In order to accomplish the intention of this study I will use, defend, and at
points criticize René Girard's interpretive model of religion and culture. What is
there about Girard's thinking that offers an interpretive key? The only really satisfactory response to this question must await the ensuing sketch of his explanatory

model and its actual employment in the discussion, which moves from Genesis to the Gospels. But to answer in a preliminary way, I think Girard's theory speaks to certain basic problems in a balanced and perceptive way and offers a genuine Judeo-Christian alternative to dominant intellectual doctrine.[7] He is generally respectful of religious forms and institutions; he does not disdain Protestant or Catholic fundamentalism, while avoiding literalism, authoritarianism, and intellectual narrowness in the investigation of religion and culture. He comes out of the context of French critical theory and understands its key figures and doctrines very well, while being very critical of the atheistic, sometimes fascist thrust of modern intellectual history. He is, specifically, severely critical of the anti-Christian thinking that permeates much of European philosophy from Nietzsche through Heidegger to Derrida and addresses himself to precisely those questions of the roots of our most cherished institutions that I mentioned above. His work, radically critical and disconcerting on the side of social theory, conservatively radical on the side of theology, offers, I think, the basis of a new Christian humanism.

B. Girard's Explanatory Model

1. The Model Defined

Girard's thought has been adequately summarized elsewhere.[8] I will not duplicate those efforts by giving a detailed summary but will present the essentials of his theoretical model and indicate how this model may serve to open up the traditions and texts of the Bible, both the Jewish Scriptures, or Old Testament, and the Christian or New Testament, for exciting and religiously relevant new readings.

The fundamental anthropological question as I have heard Girard express it is, "Why is reciprocity fundamental to human existence?"[9] Why do we think and act in terms of tit for tat, giving and getting, always exchanging—and of course, perpetually imitating one another? "What's in it for me?" "One good turn deserves another." "One hand washes the other." "Give and you will receive." All these expressions, which are part of our repertory of ordinary language, point to a fundamental principle of *retribution* that underlies much of human wisdom.[10]

Girard answers that question about reciprocity in terms of mimesis, rivalry, and collective violence; he moves from there to the controlling of collective violence through sacrifice as the beginning of human culture. Before I explicate his model, a brief indication of the development of this model through the stages of his career is in order. He first proposed a theory of mimesis in a study of the novel, *Deceit, Desire and the Novel* (French 1961, English 1965). From there he began to develop the concept of the victimization mechanism in dealing with comparative religion and psychoanalysis, first in *Violence and the Sacred* (French 1972, English 1977), then in *Things Hidden Since the Foundation of the World* (French 1978, English 1987). In the latter book he offers his first extended treatment of biblical texts. Thereafter he sought to validate his model by demonstrating its applicability to a late medieval example of persecution in *The Scapegoat* (French 1982, English 1986). He deepened and extended his argument concerning the scapegoat mechanism and the revelatory character of biblical texts in an important book on Job (1985, 1987), and he has returned now to literature in a book on Shakespeare.[11]

As Girard was led from the mimesis or imitative desire that he found in literary texts back into anthropology and primitive religion, he concluded that culture itself originates in rivalry. As the brain capacity of hominids increased and their mimetic capacity developed and became more complex, they came to the point where living and acting in concert was impossible because of the rivalry that arose from mimetic desire. This rivalry and the ensuing conflict could be managed only by the killing or expelling of a victim.

Perhaps it would be best to clarify Girard's model by putting it initially in narrative fashion. Robert Hamerton-Kelly has stated Girard's model of the origins of culture in the form of a "likely story." To quote the first part of this "likely story":

> Once upon a time there was a group of hominids that found itself unable to do anything in concert because of rivalry among them. Each one [was] inwardly compelled to imitate some other. As the imitation became more successful he found himself a rival of his model, and the more like the model he became the more violent became the rivalry. Co-operation was impossible until one day, [the momentous day human culture began, two] of them discovered that it was possible to agree on one thing, to agree to kill someone else. This was such a compelling possibility that the whole group imitated them, and so the first moment of human solidarity happened as the fellowship of the lynch mob.[12]

Our imagined hominids found themselves compelled to imitate someone else. Concomitant with the development of their enormous imitational capacities was the weakening of powerful instincts to bind and direct them like other creatures; their way of coping with the world was now more dependent on the capacity to imitate. Even the needs that are the necessary condition of desire (hunger and thirst, sexual reproduction, survival against the elements, survival in the face of animal and human predators) are not the *sufficient condition* of desire; that is, it is clear that these needs must be met in some way, but how to meet them is learned through imitation of others. Desire itself becomes informed by a realm of symbols that instruct participants in a given culture how and what they are to desire. Girard's explanatory model argues that the basis of this realm of symbols is the resolution of conflict through victimization, which is both repeated and camouflaged in prohibition, sacrifice, and myth. I will return shortly to prohibition, sacrifice, and myth.

It is important to observe that this fundamental human tendency to imitate does not work simply in a *representational* fashion, representing or presenting again something else; it is also and fundamentally *acquisitive*: it involves learning *what* to desire from the model-rival and *acquiring* what is desired. This is why Girard prefers to use the classical Greek word *mimesis* rather than *imitation*, because imitation usually has the meaning of reproduction or copying without the connotation of acquiring what the other has or being what the other is.

Mimetic desire is such that if the conflict reaches a certain point, then to acquire what is desired it is necessary to displace or eliminate the rival who is felt to have or to be what is most desirable.[13] In other words, the human situation is such that the drive to imitate the feared and respected model results in a double bind in which the model for the subject or group is always a potential rival and the rival is always an implicit model ("peer pressure" is a good example of the latter— "peering at the peer," one might say, in order to know how to present oneself).

Girard's thesis concerning mimetic desire poses a radical challenge to Freud's theory of the Oedipus complex. When Freud dealt with "identification" in *Group Psychology and the Analysis of the Ego* (1921), what he described was basically imitation of the parent (in this case, the loved and respected father). In this essay Freud seemed to hold that sexual rivalry with the parent of the same sex stems from identification, that is, for example, from the son desiring to be like the father and having what he has. But in *The Ego and the Id* (1923) Freud shifted decisively to the Oedipus complex, which makes sexual rivalry primary, something inherent in human biology and human culture. Girard maintains, however, that Freud was on the right track in his chapter on identification in *Group Psychology*. The implied mandate of the model is "imitate me," yet if one were to imitate the model *completely*—and of course the function of culture is to prevent that—one would be and have what the model is and has, therefore displacing the model as rival. So the model is always giving, or giving off, a contradictory message: "imitate me"—but also "don't imitate me (in some basic respect that would change my status, position, or possession)."

Freud's Oedipus theory is more like a myth, with its postulation of something innate, like an "essence," that we inherit in the form of an unconscious part of the self and an inevitable Oedipal rivalry. Although Girard's model of human origins could be termed a "likely story," it is much more "scientific" in the sense that it can appeal to an observation of human acts and relations without resorting to a view of the self that is fundamentally mythical. Freud's myth of the self is expressed most clearly in his concept of the unconscious, which he articulates dramatically by referring to the Oedipus myth. He discussed the Oedipus story as early as *The Interpretation of Dreams* (1900). Freud came to the point of describing a conflict between the life and death instincts, which he presents in a speculative but nonetheless very serious manner in *Beyond the Pleasure Principle* (1920).

In chapter 6 of the latter work he even admits that he is presenting his own version of the Eros myth.

From the standpoint of Girard's mimetic model, rivalry stemming from mimetic desire can reach the point that real difference from the rival is broken down and the rival becomes a *double* of the subject. "When all differences have been eliminated and the similarity between two figures has been achieved, we say that the antagonists are *doubles*."[14] It is this doubling, the confusion of oneself with the other, that lies behind "possession" and being "haunted." For example, as Dionysus possesses Pentheus in The Bacchae of Euripides, Pentheus begins to see double:

> I'd say I see two suns,
> a double city Thebes,
> twin sets of seven gates,
> and a bull seems to beckon me.[15]

The hallucinatory doubling of everything is simply a symptom of a mimetic crisis, the breakdown of cultural forms that manage mimetic desire, and this crisis is dramatically focused on the king, Pentheus. As Girard has commented, "Pentheus associates the double vision with the vision of the monster. Dionysus is at once man, god, and bull."[16]

Now mimesis itself is not *inherently* the acting out of desire determined by rivalry. In fact, Girard has referred to "good mimesis" and "good contagion" when discussing the Gospels and the imitation of Christ.[17] Not all relationships are rivalrous, and we can, of course, imagine other than violent scenarios for the beginnings of human culture. Myths and symbols of paradise are much a part of the history of religions, and doctrines of the end of the world and of states of salvation in the present characteristically resort to this paradisal language, which is the scenario of good mimesis.

Good mimesis in Girard's theory is a situation in which the subject imitates a model who (or which) must of course be related to the subject but which is beyond all differences that are the source of rivalry. This is the situation of *external mediation*: the subject and the model or mediator are too distant from each other's spheres of possible objects of desire to interfere with each other.[18] In other words, the model is not also an *obstacle* to the fulfillment of desire. A *perfect* model or mediator would be completely beyond determination by human differences while caring for all those caught up in the human struggle to establish their differences.

In any case, argues Girard, whatever the *possibility* of good mimetic desire, what is most striking about human society is the phenomenon of mimetic activity that is resolved in differentiation, exclusion, and victimization of *one* so that the *all* (the group or community) may exist in concord. Human beings are universally, if not at all times and necessarily, caught up in the mimetic desire that is potentially destructive. Most of us are entrapped in rivalries of *internal mediation*, a situation in which the subject and the model or mediator occupy common ground or a common center in which objects of desire are contested.[19] In this situation, it appears to the subject that the model must be displaced or eliminated—unless, of course, there are religious and cultural forms that are capable of channeling and deflecting the rivalry and conflict.

Having anticipated myself by touching on the role of the *victim* in Girard's model, I will now give it focus, first by citing the second part of Hamerton-Kelly's "likely story":

> The victim, as the source of the sudden unity and order [i.e., "the first moment of human solidarity as the fellowship of the lynch mob"], was regarded as a savior; and [he or she] was blamed for causing the previous disorder. Thus [he or she] acquired the double valency of the sacred: attraction and revulsion. From the victim came the building blocks of social order: prohibition to control the course of rivalry; ritual sacrifice to reenact and so represent to the group the unifying energy of the founding moment; myth to explain and obscure the violence by covering it up with transformations. The victim became the god, at the stage of the emergence of the gods. Thus society formed in the crucible of religion. Religious feeling [is individual and group awareness of the community, whose power of mimetic violence is represented in the form of gods and the sacred. Therefore, religion is essentially sacrifice— *sacrificare*, "making or rendering sacred."]

The process described in this parabolic narrative of beginnings is basically unconscious.[20] The new human society that emerged from the lynch mob was not aware of what it was doing as it began to view the victim as a savior, just as it had blamed this person for the previous disorder. Human language and culture slowly emerge with the attention given to the one who is "it."[21] The victim is the one who emerges, who makes the primal difference. A double transference occurs of which the hominids becoming human are not fully aware; indeed, the mob-become-society must in some sense "conceal" what is happening from itself, because it feels the necessity to overcome the underlying mimetic rivalry. This double transference consists in attributing the cause of conflict to the victim, but at the same time seeing the victim as an all-powerful bringer of peace and order. So it is that the victim, in the older primitive orders, is deified. Kingship, which originally always invested the king with sacred powers, stems from the primitive attainment of order through selecting and executing a victim.[22]

This double meaning or valency of the victim accounts for the twofold experience of the sacred as described by Rudolph Otto: revulsion and attraction.[23] Otto described this twofold experience as corresponding to the *mysterium tremendum* and *mysterium fascinans* of the sacred. The former repels or keeps one at a distance, the latter fascinates or attracts. In the thought of Girard, this description conceals the centrality of the victim and the victimization mechanism that leads to the killing.

From the victim came the main elements of social order: prohibition, myth, and ritual. Prohibition controls the course of rivalry; it is interdiction of everything that seemed to bring about the crisis in the first place, everything that sows confusion, that effaces necessary differences (murder, incest, gender confusion, etc.). Social order depends upon a system of *differences*. The mimetic crisis is the moment when the drive for differentiation from the rival other (or others) seems to be radically denied in the situation of confusion, of chaos, of *sameness*, for the human mimetic capacity induces human beings to desire the objects that will make them most different from those model-rivals to whom they are most similar.

If the slaying of a victim is the first act of *differentiation*, distinguishing this one from the others (thus creating the group defined vis-à-vis the one), prohibition is logically, though not necessarily chronologically, the next demarcation; it distinguishes the victim's behavior as what led to the mimetic crisis in the first place. The behavior imputed to the victim is the contrary of the behavior that controls rivalry and sustains the group. The emergent social order says, in effect, "We can't do what the victim did to get us into trouble in the first place."

Ritual centers in the sacrifice of a victim.[24] Ritual reenacts and thus represents to the group the unifying energy of the founding moment. It reenacts the crisis in such a way that it is emptied of all real violence in order to arrive at the resolution, the production of peace through the death or expulsion that produced peace in the first place. Ritual is a process in which a community goes into a mock mimetic crisis. It differentiates sacred time—the occasion of the festival or observance— from ordinary time, and within the reenactment of sacred time it represents the necessary differentiations, the threat to these differentiations, and the overcoming of this threat. One way to describe it is to say that ritual undoes prohibition and then reestablishes it. The danger lying behind the prohibition, mimetic desire and mimetic rivalry, is embodied by the victim, whose status as divine validates the community and confirms its identity.

Myth establishes prohibition and ritual but is not temporally prior. Myth represents that stage of language in which the community achieves an explanation of and obscuring of violence by covering it over with narrative transformations. The victim is narrated as the cause of disorder, so the community is justified in its murderous act, so much so that victims are often viewed as willing their own death. The victim is recounted also as the bringer of order and as such is divine. Myth, in sum, is the narrative form justifying the ritual and prohibition. It simultaneously reveals and conceals its own basis.

This social scientific model of explanation coexists with a more "theological" side of Girard's work. He has used his explanatory model to explicate two types of biblical texts. There are those biblical texts that do not seem to be fundamentally different from religious texts in other cultures, but some biblical texts preserve an orientation and a perspective that have worked like leaven in Western culture and opened the way for modern critical theories about human conflict and human rights.

I would put Girard's view of the Bible this way: At certain times in human history there have been disclosures that unmask the victimization mechanism that results in sacrifice and scapegoating. Such disclosures are focused and sustained in the Jewish and Christian Scriptures, though this does not exclude the possibility of other revelations. *Revelation* is a key term, for Girard finds in the Bible the revelation or disclosure of a God who does not want victims, a God who is disclosed in the action of those who take the side of victims.

As revelation is represented in biblical texts, it means, for Girard, the tendency of many narrators to side with the innocent victim rather than with the persecuting figure or community, as in the stories of Cain and Abel (compare the Roman myth of Romulus and Remus)[25] and of the Israelites' exodus from Egypt (compare the later "Egyptian" version of the exodus).[26] He points also to the prophetic repudiation of sacrifice, which is associated with violence in Hosea, Amos, Micah, Isaiah, Jeremiah, and Ezekiel. He emphasizes the innocence of the Servant of the Lord in Isaiah 52–53, and he has devoted a book to Job, who in the dialogues of chapters 3–27 cries out to the God of victims. These latter two texts of the Hebrew Bible he views as prophetic foreshadowings of the Christ of the Gospels. In the Hebrew Bible there remains a certain ambiguity in the relation of the God of Israel to violence. The Gospels, however, disclose both the secret of the mythic camouflage of violence and the way of liberation through a love that refuses violence. The Gospels' story of Jesus as the Innocent Victim reveal the fate of the God beyond differences whose presence in the world so threatens and subverts structures of violence that it cannot be tolerated. "A non-violent deity can only signal his existence to mankind by having himself driven out by violence—by demonstrating that he is not able to establish himself in the Kingdom of Violence."[27]

This God of nonviolence is the God of the oppressed Hebrews in Egypt, the God of the Servant who suffers on behalf of others. This is the God of Job in those lucid moments when Job does not share the language of his friends, whose speeches are the verbal equivalent of a lynching, and turns to the God who is his witness and defender. This is the God of Jesus, whose words and works unveil the mimetic entrapment of the human group that lies behind the image of the demons possessing the man who is kept in chains outside the city, continually crying out and bruising himself with stones so that the people of the city will have a perpetual sacrifice to alleviate their own conflict and violence.[28] The people beg Jesus to depart from their region, but not primarily, as often asserted, because he was ruining the local economy by destroying its herds of swine. No, the reason was much more profound: he was uncovering the sacrificial structure of their social order, which both controlled and abetted the victimization process. A wonderful reversal and transformation thus occurs: the demon-possessed pigs, mirroring the community of lynchers, rush over the cliff into the water like the scapegoat of classical Greece and Rome, while the scapegoat is restored to his right mind. "Imagine," says Girard, "the *Pharmakos* [scapegoat or person being lynched] forcing the inhabitants of a Greek city, philosophers and mathematicians alike, over a precipice. Instead of the outcast being toppled from the height of the Tarpeian rock it is the majestic consuls, virtuous Cato, solemn juriconsults, the procurators of Judea, and all the rest of the *senatus populusque romanus*. All of them disappear into the abyss while the ex-victim, 'clothed and in his full senses,' calmly observes from above the astounding sight."[29] The Gospels tell, of course, not only of the healing of the demon-possessed who are the slaves of mimesis but above all of the event whereby God, in and through Jesus, enters fully into the sacrificial structures of human culture, which must have its demoniacs out among the tombs, and takes the fate of the demoniac upon himself.

To summarize what has been said so far about Girard's thought, his understanding of human culture is based on a theory of the Bible's significance that is supported by a social scientific model of explanation. (1) The explanatory model has a number of parts and refinements, but basically it includes these elements: society and culture are (*a*) rooted in a nonconscious process that begins with mimetic desire, which in turn leads to (*b*) mimetic rivalry and conflict. The outcome of mimetic rivalry and conflict is (*c*) collective violence against a victim. (*d*) The originating event of collective violence is managed and concealed in prohibition, ritual, and myth. (2) The Bible witnesses to a God, above all the God of Jesus Christ, who is "beyond differences," that is, beyond the differences established by the victimization mechanism. He is loving and just and does not intend the structures of violence (or sin) that human beings perpetuate. He thus reveals that he sides with victims and intends a final reestablishment of his rule of love.

Finally, this sketch of Girard's model should include clarification of the phrase "explanatory model." I am using this term as a clear and, I hope, less provocative way of presenting what Girard himself has called his "scientific" theory. It depends, of course, on how one construes science, but the prevailing usage of words like *science* and *scientific* emphasizes investigation of observable phenomena and proposal of falsifiable hypotheses. Girard might fairly claim that his theory is scientific in that sense if his claim is located in "an essentially analytic rather than positivistic understanding of the methodology of the human sciences."[30] It is not falsifiable in the sense proposed by Karl Popper,[31] although it certainly can be ranged against other theories and compared for adequacy in clarifying the data in question. Robert Hamerton-Kelly suggests his methodology "might . . . be called an heuristic model . . . to be tested by its analytic power on the raw material to be interpreted."[32] In adopting Hamerton-Kelly's suggestion I am not proposing that Girard's theory be judged on the basis of whether in a strict sense it is factually accurate concerning original "hominization" (that is, the process by which the creature we know as *homo* emerged from a prehuman or primate state), a process that obviously cannot be factually duplicated. Nor do I think the question is whether it accounts for *all* the basics of human culture in every detail, for Girard himself has discussed the manifold variations that emerge, particularly as traditions begin to develop new layers around the original victimization mechanism. The question is whether the model has great analytic power in interpretation of the data. Will it make sense in response to certain questions about religion and culture in a way that other models do not?

2. Theories of Sacrifice

It would be helpful, I think, to compare Girard's understanding of sacrifice with other theories, in order, by way of contrast, to get a better sense of what he is about. It would not serve the purposes of this book to offer a discussion of these alternative theories in great number or detail; however, the outlines that follow give a good sampling of the beginnings of hypotheses about sacrifice in anthropology and history of religions and reflect some of the contemporary intellectual currents. After presenting them I will give a Girardian response to them.

Edward Burnett Tylor drew an analogy between prayer and sacrifice. As prayer "is a request made to a deity as if he were a man, so sacrifice is a gift made to a deity as if he were a man."[33] There is a progressive "spiritualization" of sacrifice from gift to "homage" to "abnegation." In other words, sacrifice begins with a principle of exchange, *do ut des*, and tends to evolve away from that to a ceremony that centers in spiritual or moral effect on the worshiper.

W. Robertson Smith viewed certain offerings as essentially gifts, but he emphasized that sacrifice was originally a communal act.[34] The generic root of sacrifice among the Semites is expressed in the root *zbch* (*zebach* in Hebrew). In the *zebach* the worshiper eats part of the holy flesh offered to the god, so it is in origin a communion meal. The god is the personification of the society, the empowering principle that enables it to be. The basis of the efficacy of sacrifice lies in acceptance of this principle.

Because the conscious beliefs of worshipers characteristically misconstrue what is actually being represented in sacrifice, Smith stressed the primacy of praxis, of ritual action rather than conscious belief.

James George Frazer's work was done independently of Smith.[35] His point of departure was the grove of Diana Nemorensis (Strabo). The priest of the site, known as the king of the wood, was "an incarnation of the spirit of the woodlands." Insofar as he is "the embodiment of the spirit of fertility, the priestly king is a human god." When the king shows signs of decay he has to be killed or deposed in order to protect the spirit he embodies. His death is at the core of primitive sacrifice. It is also the origin of scapegoating in that the ailments of the community are transferred to the dying god. Frazer described this as a "pathetic fallacy" that confused things physical and things mental. His implication is that a correct understanding of these distinctions would enable us to avoid the nasty practice of scapegoating. Frazer was in general very contemptuous of the "superstitious" ideas and practices he studied.[36]

Henri Hubert and Marcel Mauss attacked the eclectic methods of Smith and Frazer, although they credited Smith with being the first researcher to give a "reasoned explanation of sacrifice."[37] They started from representative ritual texts, particularly the Bible and Hindu Vedic texts, and developed a schema that was supposedly universal. Unlike Robertson Smith, they were interested in the typical rather than what was temporally prior.

They held that sacrifice functioned to modify the condition of the person for whom it was offered or the objects of that person's concern through the consecration of a victim. They assumed that the purpose of sacrifice was to establish communication between the profane and the sacred world, and the model they employed was that of rites of passage. The significance of the sacrificial victim is that it becomes progressively divine until the climactic point is reached in its death, which procures the benefits of the sacrifice.

Hubert and Mauss were influenced by Émile Durkheim, although his great work on religion was published subsequent to their essay.[38] Although Durkheim did not place sacrifice at the center of his theory, it is quite clear that he viewed it as one of religion's important functions in unifying society. He gave a more systematic form to the idea that sacrifice is the metaphorical extension of a moral reality, namely, the interdependence of individual and society. Sacrifice of a victim is both communion and oblation; worshipers commune with their god and make an offering to this god. The gods are nothing other than a symbolic expression of the social order.

E. E. Evans-Pritchard viewed the sacrifice as a gift of expiation and propitiation whose purpose is to separate the sphere of the supernatural from the sphere of nature; its object is not to unite God and human beings but to keep them apart.[39] The god or the spirit represents a danger. An ox is offered that is identified with the offerer. The victim offered appeases the spirit, which then withdraws from the offerer's life.

Jean-Pierre Vernant is a structuralist who studied with Claude Lévi-Strauss and published an important book with Marcel Detienne.[40] According to Vernant, sacrifice "consecrates, in the very ritual that aims at joining mortals and immortals, the insurmountable distance that will henceforth separate them. By bringing alimentary rules [ritualized cooking] into play, it establishes man in his own status, between beast and gods, at just the right distance from the savagery of the animals, devouring each other raw, and the unchanging bliss of the gods, ignorant of hunger, fatigue and death because they are nourished by nectar and ambrosia."[41]

Finally, there is Luc de Heusch, a structuralist whose formation, like that of Detienne and Vernant, was under the tutelage of Lévi-Strauss.[42] In general de Heusch understands sacrifice as a reenactment of death and rebirth. More specifically, sacrifice depends on the principle of debt to the god. "It is more particularly when the stakes of a sacrifice are of a collective and cosmological nature that the preferential victim is none other than man himself." Concerning the Lugbara people he says, "Whereas in family sacrifices the sacrifier[43] pays his debt to the ancestors with an animal, in former times an innocent man was disemboweled on top of a hill in order to end a catastrophic drought. Today the rite is carried out with a ram abandoned alive to God by the rain priest after the territory concerned has been 'encircled' by the animal."[44] With respect to sacrificial substitution, he says that the benefits of a man-god's primordial immolation is repeated in every sacrifice.

The purpose of performing a sacrifice is to try to outwit death. "Human sacrifice represents the outer limit which many rites—in which the sacrifier is seen to project himself into the animal victim, losing a part of his 'having' in order to preserve the essential—strive to reach. This limit is indeed reached when the king, the epitome of 'having' and 'being,' is doomed to immolation for the good of the community."[45]

Now what would a response informed by Girard's approach be to the main points of the theories of sacrifice that I have presented?

He would agree with Robertson Smith, Hubert and Mauss, and Durkheim in particular that sacrifice stems from the awareness of the overwhelming importance of the social order and the individual's continual dependence on the community. It is partly disguised in myth, ritual, and prohibition, but the social order is the actual "transcendent" that is confirmed and reenacted in these foundation blocks of culture. Durkheim articulated this with great power, although sacrifice is not as prominent for him as for the others.

Even though Smith, Hubert and Mauss, and Durkheim identified the primary reality of the social order, they still do not really get at what lies behind sacrifice. After all, why would killing a human or animal victim emerge if groups simply wanted to commune with the divine, to affect their moral and spiritual condition, and so on? If worshipers sacrifice for the purpose of affirming and participating in the transcendent reality of the social order, which is disguised in the persona of deity, then they must have first conceived the idea or mental picture of that order, unconsciously disguised it to conceal its tenuousness, then conceived of killing an animal or human victim in order to actualize and affirm it. Durkheim suggests precisely that, and the beginnings of religion can be understood in that way—but is it likely? Is it likely that the thought or idea precedes the act in this manner? On the basis of Girard's model, one would say that the act precedes the idea, and to take Girard's model seriously it is necessary to accept the precedence of action and concrete situation over intellectual formulations thereof.

So to repeat, why is immolation or lynching the best means of communicating with the divine? Or the best means of appeasing the divine Spirit, as Evans-Pritchard proposes? Or the best means of joining the mortal and the immortal, as Vernant holds? Or the best means of paying a debt to the divine and outwitting death, as de Heusch says? How can one answer this basic question without simply appealing to some principle of sacrifice itself? That is, if one replies that human beings wish to give over what belongs to God or the sacred, if they wish to surrender their very life for the sake of communion, atonement, propitiation (appeasement of the divine), or expiation (removal of sin or stain), one is merely explaining sacrifice by appealing to the preconceived notion that there was *already* a metaphysics or theology that induced our human forebears to engage in the immolation or lynching of a victim. We know, of course, of the power of thought—and since Marx we often say, of ideology—to determine action, and in fact ordinary experience betrays a chicken-and-egg relationship of thought and action. But here we are talking about what determines our basic structures of self and society both in their origin and at their deepest roots. When dealing with this question, the tendency of intellectuals is to give primacy to thought and idea, the mental activity that distinguishes them. The tendency of the lay public is to give primacy to myth and symbol, which convey thought and idea in more compact, emotionally laden form. But the question is, Is the primacy of thought and idea itself a fiction that covers up the primary role of those acts that involve unifying the community through a substitute or surrogate victim, someone or something that is "it," that is killed or expelled for the good of the all?

As for the structuralists, two remarks about a Girardian response to them. First, Vernant. He and Detienne may be right about a system, a transformative structure that operates in the cuisine of sacrifice, for example, to maintain human order, to preserve the status of human beings as between gods and beasts. But the problem with most forms of structuralism is that they do not get behind or beyond the structure, they content themselves with an appeal to the binary oppositions that are endemic to the human mind and that take definite forms in given cultures. For example, if the Oedipus myth stems from a basic human propensity to distinguish between order and disorder, life and death, and so on, which here takes the form of kinship too close versus kinship too distant and health or wholeness versus infirmity, then what do we find out? We learn that there are basic polarities that conflict with each other and so must be mediated. But how are they mediated or reconciled? According to structuralism, they must be reconciled through change or transformation already operative in the system. We therefore can never get behind or beyond the system itself. Sacrifice and expulsion are really left unaccounted for. Structuralism is another example of finding a mental code enshrined in the myths and symbols of culture, which are manipulated by the inquirer without reference to real events.[46] By contrast, the Girardian model is based on the premise that real human beings, real human relations—indeed, real events of violence—have generated myth and ritual. In other words, according to this model, sacrifice is not a mere metaphor of the social order but a primary sign of the original signifier, the primal sign-bearer in which language begins, the victim of collective violence.

In Shakespeare's *Troilus and Cressida*, Troilus says, "Fools on both sides, Helen must needs be fair / When with your blood you daily paint her thus."[47] Girard has commented on these lines, "This is better than any anthropologist could ever tell you about the origins of religion." [48] I think he may have had the structuralists particularly in mind. In other words, do the Greeks and Trojans have a prior concept, "Helen," that leads them to kill each other for her sake? Does the attempt to represent and resolve conflict begin with a mental operation?

A Girardian comment on the struggle over Helen would be that the story of belligerent rivalry between Greeks and Trojans begins in real rivalry, no matter how opaque it may seem either to figures in the story or to subsequent interpreters of the story. Shakespeare's poetic insight and dramatic analysis bring to light that real events (whether they can ever be historically reconstructed or not) and real relationships lie behind the code of the Helen myth in its various versions. What Shakespeare tells us, in effect, is that it is as if the Greeks say, "We have to besiege Troy because the Trojans have Helen and we want her" (because they have her), and as if the Trojans say, "We have to fight to keep Helen because the Greeks want her" (and we want her because the Greeks are fighting to get her).

Next, I will say a little more about de Heusch and his criticism of Girard. He engages in three escalating levels of attack on Girard. He charges first that Girard propounds "a vulgarised Durkheimian theory, based on the symbolic prevention of crime."[49] Obviously crime continues, so Girard's speculation is supposedly silly. But of course Girard has not claimed that sacrifice prevents all crime. His claim is, rather, that it, with its attendant elements of prohibition and myth, channel and control violence, so preventing a return to mimetic crisis. And with respect to Durkheim, his influence on Girard is great, but mimesis and the victimization mechanism play no part in Durkheim's theory.

Even worse than "vulgarised Durkheimianism" in Girard's model is that "ethnocentrism again rears its ugly head."[50] All of Girard's categories, particularly the distinction between sacred and profane and the understanding of sacrifice as "that which makes sacred," are simply drawn from Western assumptions and distinctions. The problem with this charge, which is very common, is that only in the Western tradition of philosophy and social science have certain critical questions concerning the nature and function of religion been raised and treated. In fact, it is only in Western modes of thought and their sphere of influence that the question of ethnocentrism itself is posed; only Western thinkers and those who imitate them accuse their own culture of ethnocentrism and victimization of the foreign other. If to ask certain critical questions and to propose an analysis or a theory of religion is to be ethnocentric—well, then perhaps we are unavoidably ethnocentric. But perhaps it is sounder to conclude that Western thought has uncovered a universal problem through critical categories that cannot be avoided. Is the interpreter of religion and culture to use Nuer or Navajo categories and address only a Nuer or a Navajo audience? One might ask about the adequacy of the interpreter's mediation between the subject studied and the cultural context of the contemporary audience, but surely the charge of ethnocentrism is here an inflated rhetoric of rivalry.

Ending with a grand flourish, saving the most damning accusation for last, de Heusch charges that Girard's theory is really—*Christian theology!* This has become serious indeed. But not only is it "a neo-Christian" theology, it is even a "somewhat heretical . . . theology"![51] De Heusch's rhetoric implies that it is really offensive to hold a Christian theological position, but if one commits that offense one should at least be orthodox. It is true, of course, that, for Girard, the Gospel witness to the unmasking of violence and mythology introduces into human history the possibility of recognizing the victimization mechanism for what it is, and so, in this sense, Christianity (the Gospel basis of Christianity) is the foundation of all forms of thought that call the authority of mythology and sacrificial institutions into question. This influence of the revelation made known in the Gospels is, for Girard, the main reason the critical awareness of ethnocentrism and victimization has arisen in Western thought. I will return to the coexistence of culture criticism and Christian theology in Girard's thinking. Suffice it to say here that granting a place of privilege to Christian theology in the construction of a theory would not rule it out unless one had already decided that Christianity is false in the first place—false, or intolerable in some way. But in my view, if one found Christianity or Christian theology intolerable, it would have to be for reasons similar to Nietzsche's. Nietzsche found the Christian God insufferable as the imposer of a "slave morality." He proclaimed the "murder of God" and proposed Dionysus as the divine model and the Overman as the human model.[52] But as I will propose in this book, Nietzsche was wrong, and the modern intellectual tradition has gone awry.

De Heusch says that Girard "reduces all forms of sacrifice to a theory of the scapegoat, instead of questioning the exact place of that ideology within the field of sacrifice." He continues by saying that his own research group in Paris "tried to situate sacrifice within the general system of 'offerings.'"[53] A Girardian response is that as long as you try to situate sacrifice within a system, it's just like language or whatever you're dealing with, you will always presuppose and return to the system, but you will never discover what generates it; without this discovery, you are simply doomed to repeat and justify the system. That is all a structuralist approach can do[54] unless it accepts a model that supplements it and modifies all its assumptions.

3. The "Emerging Exception," Language, and Culture

A model that is different from the structuralist paradigm is "the model of the exception that is . . . in the process of emerging" (*le modèle de l'exception en cours d'émergence*). That is, if in the mimetic crisis the all (the point zero) turn against one, we have a generative model that posits an event prior to binary oppositions. Girard has described this model as one that focuses on

> the single trait that stands out against a confused mass or still unsorted multiplicity. It is the model of drawing lots, of the short straw, or, of the bean in the Epiphany cake. Only the piece that contains the bean is truly distinguished; only the shortest straw, or the longest, is meaningful. The rest remains indeterminate. . . .
> . . . It seems clear that this model served as the basis for the invention of what are called games of chance.[55]

It is this "model of the exception . . . in the process of emerging" that will, I think, offer a way out of the endless play of bipolar oppositions in structuralism and the endless differentiating process of deconstructionist thought. The way Girard describes the sacrificial crisis is similar to the way Derrida and others describe all of reality. There is a kind of continual sacrificial crisis in which all differences are effaced (*différance*).[56] By contrast, structuralism tends to content itself with the play of differences within given cultural systems, as though human cultural codes did not have their beginning in real events. Girard basically agrees with the tradition of thought that may be traced back from Derrida and Lévi-Strauss to Rousseau (and ultimately to Hobbes): culture is something added to nature, a "supplement" that, in keeping with the connotations of the French *supplément*, both adds something to and substitutes for some origin or original. However, Girard departs from the recent critical tradition in postulating an actual starting point that generates culture. Lévi-Strauss is content to focus on the supplement as cultural code, and Derrida takes every cultural form back to its previous *pharmakon* (poison/remedy) or scripture or supplement, but he does not believe in starting from a center, a full presence of some original reality; he engages rather in methodological play within the difference between thinking that represents origin and presence and thinking that affirms the world of signs that have no center or origin.[57] From a Girardian perspective the Derridean method could be viewed as a continual ritual process that engages in a "mock mimetic crisis" with every text and every subject by undoing it in order to arrive again at this position of difference, that is, at *"différance."* The model of the exception in the process of emerging accounts for culture and language as a system of differences (structuralism) and for the human drive to differentiate without ceasing (deconstruction), while offering a real theory of origins that is simultaneously a theory of human relations.

This model also offers considerable insight concerning the origin and function of language. Girard's explanatory model of religion and culture attaches language to the victim, the one who is "it," who emerges from the human group's mimetic desire and rivalry and its need for unity. In the same context as the discussion of the model of the emerging exception in *Things Hidden Since the Foundation of the World*, Girard says that the original sign for emerging humanity is the victim. According to modern linguistics, the sign includes the signifier (the word or sound that indicates an object) and the signified (the object, or concept of the object,[58] that is indicated). In commenting on this distinction between signifier and signified, Girard states,

> The signifier is the victim. The signified constitutes all actual and potential meaning the community confers on to the victim and, through its intermediacy, on to all things.
>
> The sign is the reconciliatory victim. Since we understand that human beings wish to remain reconciled after the conclusion of the crisis, we can also understand their penchant for reproducing the language of the sacred by substituting, in ritual, new victims for the original victim, in order to assure the maintenance of the miraculous peace.[59]

In the given tradition as it develops, the signifying activity that is at the center of language and ritual comes to the point where "the original victim, rather than being signified by new victims, will be signified by something other than a victim, by a variety of things that continue to signify the victim while at the same time progressively masking, disguising, and failing to recognize it."[60]

This model of the victim—the exception in the process of emerging—explains why certain functions (or "tropes") of our language are so slippery, so difficult to pin down. Metaphor, for example, has become important again not only in literary criticism but also in philosophy and other fields. It is usually distinguished from metonym and synecdoche. But what, really, is the difference between metaphor, metonym, and synecdoche? Here are standard dictionary definitions.[61]

Metaphor: "a figure of speech in which a word or phrase denoting one kind of object or action is used in place of another to suggest a likeness or analogy between them (as in *the ship plows the seas* or in *a volley of oaths*)." Also "an implied comparison (as in *a marble brow*) in contrast to the explicit comparison of the simile (as in *a brow white as marble*)."

Metonym: "a word use in metonymy." *Metonymy:* "a figure of speech that consists in using the name of one thing for that of something else with which it is associated (as in *spent the evening reading Shakespeare; lands belong to the crown;*

demanded action by City Hall). . . . Use of one term for another that it may be expected to suggest."

Synecdoche: "a figure of speech by which a part is put for the whole (as *fifty sail* for *fifty ships*), the whole for a part (as *the smiling year* for *spring*), the species for the genre (as *cutthroat* for *assassin*), the genre for the species . . . or the name of the material for the thing made."

These definitions seem to be *different*; that is, they seem to define or demarcate boundaries between distinct functions in speech and literature. However, they are all obviously based on two things: (1) a figure of speech, which is a form or image that is not an exact replica of a word or a thing but suggests the word or thing by similarity, association, or analogy, and (2) a substitution of some sort—for metaphor, "one kind of object or action is used in place of another"; for metonym, "using the name of one thing for that of something else with which it is associated"; for synecdoche, "a figure of speech by which a part is put for the whole." In fact, if we look at it closely, we see that "figure of speech" itself is an operation of substitution. I tried to avoid expressing this too baldly in the definition above by saying "suggests . . . by similarity, association, or analogy."

But it is clear that the form or image that is similar, associated, or analogous must *stand for* something else. The figure "suggests" something or someone that is not directly present, but then that is the very foundational characteristic of language itself: it furnishes a substitute for what is not present.

If we probe the matter of substitution further, we find that with careful scrutiny the distinctions that appear at first so clear in the three definitions begin to get very fuzzy. Consider metonym and synecdoche. All the quoted dictionary examples for the two are interchangeable. That is, *Shakespeare* is a metonym of the literary works of the great playwright and poet, but is it not also synecdoche? Shakespeare here means the total *oeuvre* (and even that, his corpus of works, is a kind of synecdoche for the person Shakespeare in all his creative efforts), so the whole stands for the part, the specific play or sonnet. The crown that signifies the king (and as such functions already as a kind of metaphor) is associated with the king, but it is not just any old thing like a beard or a nice belt; it is rather a "kingly thing," and in this case it is the part for the whole, the crown for the king, his family, and so on. As for the synecdoche of *sail* for *ship*, no doubt it is part for the whole, but no one will doubt either that it is metonymic, in the sense of an object that expresses something significant about the thing or being with which it is associated.

With metaphor we have what seems to be a clear distinction. A ship is not normally associated with a plow, nor are expletives with the shooting of a gun. Nevertheless, it is not hard to see that unless there is at some point an association of one thing with another or of a part for the whole (or vice versa), metaphor is not really possible. In English the hard-driving action of cutting through the soil in order to prepare it for planting comes to stand for the entire act called plowing, which in its so-called literal meaning would include a person pushing or driving an apparatus (formerly with oxen or asses) that has a handle or handles, shafts to hold the blade, and so on. Without that synecdochic association, there would be no derived metaphors of plowing.

Nonetheless, metaphor appears to be a kind of imaginative leap in which certain essential qualities or features of something in one context point to the meaning or action of something in another context. But in spite of this appearance of "leaping" from one context to another, it is important to stress that the metaphor does nothing else than *stand for a greater or lesser series of substitutions.* In this resides its appeal, its power, but its appeal and power depend on a concealment. With the plow-ship relationship, there is a series of surrogate associations that would have to be linked on a spectrum between a blade cutting through material and a ship's prow cutting through water, making furrows.

Now let us see how the three kinds of figure are related to the victim as sign. First, we may summarize the ordinary, lexical understanding in this way:[62]

Synecdoche: A–a. A is understood in terms of its part *a* and vice versa.
Metonymy: A–A'. A is associated with A'.
Metaphor: A–B. A is understood in terms of B.

If we look at these tropes from the perspective of the model of the emerging exception that focuses on the victim, the substitutionary nature and context of their functions will be illuminated. No doubt one cannot "prove," by appealing to ordinary criteria based on sense experience or falsifiability, that the functions of substitution in language stem from a primal substitution of the victim for the group torn by rivalry. However, and to repeat, we can ask whether the hypothesis makes better sense of the evidence we have than other hypotheses. At any rate, here is how the model looks if applied to the operations of metaphor, metonym, and synecdoche:

- Convergence upon a victim that is part of the group and that the group unanimously agrees to eliminate: *sign as part for the whole and whole for the part;* A *is understood in terms of* a (synecdoche).
- Conferral of meaning, so that the excluded victim, as associated with the group, becomes the signifier of the group (gives it its unity and identity): *sign as distinct from the group yet associated with its meaning;* A *is understood in association with* A' (metonym).
- Establishment of differentiations in prohibitions, mock undermining and reaffirming of prohibitions in ritual (which centers in sacrifice of victim), and emergence of narrative concealment in myth. The victim as divinity, as sacred power, is now truly distinct from the community. A,

the group, is understood in terms of the separate reality B, the god
(metaphor).

As I have already indicated, synecdoche and metonym are so closely related that it is difficult to distinguish them clearly. Therefore, if the sign-creating process is understood more or less as sketched here, it is very difficult to unpack and distinguish the first two moments, the synecdochic and the metonymic.

From my standpoint, one way in which an explanation like this is more satisfying is that it offers a better accounting of verbal concealments, euphemisms, and things that go without saying. I remember my maternal grandmother speaking of a baby "brought by the stork." It is obvious that a series of substitutions lie behind the expression, which is a metaphoric phrase for the birth of a child. One can easily identify these substitutions (stork brings child—mother gives birth—mother and father have sex [already a metonymic or synecdochic euphemism]), which arise in a setting in which sex and reproduction are taboo subjects. And why are they taboo? A structuralist answer takes us at least this far: with sexual relations we are dealing with the problem of exchange and differentiation; if proper differences are not observed, then confusion and conflict ensue. The purpose of the taboo is to avoid or control rivalries. But we cannot go further than this on the basis of a structural model, which assumes that actual conflict takes place only when ontologically prior codes have been transgressed.

The Girardian model proposes that on the basis of our mimetic capacity we need both to imitate a model and differentiate ourselves from it. Sexual relations are one of the important spheres of life in which conflict and violence may occur at a number of levels; for example, the subject may vie with a rival for the same sexual partner *because* the rival desires that sexual partner (the rival could also be a sexual partner if important differences are not operative, or a peer); or the subject may desire the economic or political benefits that come with a certain sexual partnership (again, some sort of model-rival is in effect for the subject); or the subject may physically mistreat or violate a sexual partner, who exists for the subject as a substitute for the rival or the rival's object of desire; the subject may be viewed as inferior for not having children; and so on. Various life situations connected with sexual desire, sexual relations, and child bearing have been the occasions of real violence. *Behind the prohibition lies the awareness of confusion in social order that stems from actual events of violence.* Violence is the ultimate confuser, the chaos maker, the overturner of differences, the upsetter of systems.

And ritual is a mock mimetic crisis that replays the threat of undifferentiation, the undoing of differences that leads to the central crisis that has been resolved. We can see this ritual replay not only in ordinary religious ritual but on those occasions of social ritual when within the acceptable boundaries of relationships (kind of friendship or type of social gathering), people make jokes about otherwise taboo subjects. There is a kind of conventional license to engage in a little "bawdy" talk about sex that may include "perverted" forms of sexual contact and incest. But the ritual character of this kind of conversation is confirmed in the participants' acceptance of the premise, whether true or not, that these sexual dangers do not apply to them or that they know how to deal with them. Talking about them in a jocular manner is already a ritual of resolution.

The prohibition, whatever form and application it may take, *is therefore due to real events of conflict and violence,* and from the standpoint of the model argued here, it is directly a function of the core event of collective violence against an arbitrarily chosen victim. It is this primary crisis that gives rise to language, because it gives rise to culture, to human being as such.

C. Brothers in Conflict: An Initial Step into the Subject

In the Bible we find an uncovering of this primary crisis, a revelation or "unveiling" of the victimization mechanism in which the narrative and the God of the narrative side with the innocent victim. To conclude this chapter I discuss two perspectives on this revelatory discovery from the Book of Genesis. At the same time, the discussion of these texts will give the reader an initial sense of how I use the Girardian model of explanation.

There is a noteworthy tension between the story of Cain in Genesis 4 and the Priestly genealogy in Genesis 5. Adam, who is created in the likeness of God, begets a son who "is in his own likeness, after his image" (Gen. 5:3). In other words, this son, Seth, perpetuates the divine likeness, which has not been effaced. The Priestly[63] version of the beginnings of the world and of humankind thus moves directly from creation to the continuity of the generations without a hitch. The Priestly writer affirms the likeness of Seth to his father and sets up no rivalries, like that between Cain and Abel.

Seth is the firstborn of Adam, his only son as far as Genesis 5 is concerned. Cain is not there; he does not belong to the generations of Adam. There is no violence, no conflict, no problematic beginning of human culture. Likewise, the Priestly account of beginnings is vague about the reason for the great flood. Whereas the J or Yahwist account (see also below on Cain) relates the mating of divine beings with human women, leading evidently to evil deeds and thoughts (Gen 6:4–5), the Priestly narrative states only that "the earth was filled with violence" (Gen 6:11). The word *violence,* Hebrew *chamas,* is important to note. Violence is precisely the key to understanding human beginnings. My point, however, is that in its concern to witness to a redeeming alternative for Israel and humanity, the Priestly account shies away from specifics, from concrete instances of violence, and thus the Priestly story of Israel acknowledges but does not account for violence. But the earlier Yahwist account does give a kind of narrative explanation of the flood—the confusion caused by the transgression of divine-human boundaries—and, of course, the course of human civilization has already been set by the acts of Eve, Adam, and Cain. Here let us focus on the story of Cain and Abel.

When we come to the genealogy in chapter 5 of Genesis, we know, as the Priestly writer knew, that the story of Cain and Abel is already there. Cain became angry because his brother Abel's offering was accepted by the LORD and his was not. The form of acceptance is expressed by the verb, *shaah* (to look or gaze upon). "And the LORD had regard for Abel and his offering, but for Cain and his offering he had no regard" (Gen. 4:4b–5a). Cain becomes angry, and his "face falls," as the Hebrew expression has it. The face "falling" is a commonly recognized sign of anger and depression. It is a sign of the feeling, whether momentary or sustained, of the dissolution of one's personal center, thus of chaos. One's person is manifest in one's *persona*, Latin for face or mask (note also the Greek *prosopon*, face, mask). Not to be regarded by the one whose favor is sought or needed is to be *persona non grata*. The focus of the text on this inner turmoil of Cain is indicated in the repetition of the phrases in the LORD's question: "Why are you angry, and why has your countenance fallen?" (4:6). The LORD continues, "If you do well, will you not be accepted? And if you do not do well, sin is lurking at the door; its desire is for you, but you must master it" (4:7). But Cain proceeds to invite or lure Abel out into a field and kill him.

The LORD punishes Cain by condemning him to be a fugitive and wanderer in the earth (4:12). Cain cries out that he will be defenseless, and everyone will try to kill him as he killed Abel. His state of extreme vulnerability is the exterior manifestation of his inner dissolution when God's first differentiation, the regard for Abel's offering, turns Abel into a rival that he must eliminate. So now God has another sort of regard for Cain by putting a mark or sign on him that will protect him from that very process of rivalry that has made him defenseless. The mark is a reminder that differentiates Cain: God will avenge him if anyone murders him, while for the narrative itself the mark is also a reminder that Cain is a murderer. Cain then goes to live in the land of Nod (Wandering) and builds the first city. A chain of differentiations is established: the favored brother (the one whose sacrifice is acceptable) and the unfavored brother (the one whose sacrifice is not acceptable)—the murderer and the victim–the sign of the protected murderer and the others (who would kill him)–the city and the presence of the LORD. The story of Cain is one version of human beginnings, commonly considered part of the J or Yahwist Source in biblical scholarship, a version that associated civilization with violence and the control of violence. The sign of the victim is the beginning of language; it is the "it," the "that," that marks the community as distinct from, yet dependent on the "exception in the process of emerging." In one sense Abel is the beginning of human culture as the first victim, but Cain displaces him and becomes the victim-progenitor of subsequent humanity. Girard has commented that he sees in the Cain and Abel story "the establishment of a differential system, which serves, as always, to discourage mimetic rivalry and generalized conflict."[64]

From this perspective our problem is that we are too much alike. As alike, we imitate one another as rivals who are model-obstacles to one another. We learn what to desire mimetically by desiring what we perceive or imagine the other person desires. This is a confusing and potentially violent situation unless differences can be established that will demarcate functions and spheres of desire.

The differentiating mark is also a sign confirming that Abel was innocent. Cain did not kill him because Abel deserved to die but because he could not tolerate his own inadequacy before God. The story is a condemnation of the murder, which is highly significant when contrasted with comparable stories like the Roman myth of Romulus and Remus. Livy gives two versions of the twins' struggle. In one, Romulus kills Remus "in a fracas" (in turba);[65] in the other, Romulus slays his brother when he transgresses the limits he has established for the walls of the city. Although Livy presents Romulus as morally ambiguous, in neither version is he blamed for the killing, and the question of Remus's innocence does not come up. In other words, although Livy has some distance from the older stories, he still preserves the point of view of the myth, which basically takes the side of the founder of the city of Rome.

Girard acknowledges that although Genesis 4 is very different from other myths in its focus on the innocent victim and its condemnation of the slayer, it is also like other myths to the extent that it conceals another sequence of events behind the story we have in the present biblical text. The story he deciphers behind the received text is that of Cain killing his brother; Cain's murder of his brother is then explained by reference to the respective sacrificial offerings in a new, later version of the story. But in the hypothetical earlier version, Abel, offering the firstlings of his sheep in what was evidently a burnt offering, possessed an appropriate outlet to control violence—animal sacrifice. Cain, however, "does not have the violence-outlet of animal sacrifice at his disposal."[66] Cain's jealousy brings about a mimetic crisis because he does not have a real sacrificial outlet, a suitable victim to which the mimetic conflict could be transferred. Therefore, the real import of this story behind the story would be that Abel as the victim of murder becomes the first sacrifice for the descendants of Cain; the subsequent events in the story then relate the mechanisms of prohibition and linguistic differentiation that control victimization.

The narrative in Genesis 4 tells of the descendants of Cain, the development of tools, and the mushrooming of vengeance in the song of Lamech (4:23–24). The narrator takes us then back to Adam and Eve, who have another son, a son named by his mother. "And Adam knew his wife again, and she bore a son and called his name Seth (shet), for she said, 'God has appointed (shat) me another child instead of Abel, for Cain killed him'" (4:25).

The story in Genesis 4 therefore leaves us with the juxtaposition of the two surviving brothers: Cain, who replaces Abel in the sense of *eliminating him*, and Seth, who replaces Abel in the sense of *compensating for him*. The morally ambiguous reality of Cain, which is at the heart of the story of the beginning of civilization, is not denied. At the same time, the birth of Seth signals an alternative to the bloodstained foundation of human society that Cain represents.

The Priestly story of beginnings does not eliminate the Cain material, and to that extent it does not do violence to the older story. But when we compare the genealogy in chapter 5 to 4:17–26, we see that there is a sense in which the Priestly view of beginnings *replaced Cain and Abel with Seth*. It is not that the Priestly narrative is unaware of Cain, any more than it is unaware of Genesis 2 and 3 in presenting a different view of creation in Genesis 1. What the Priestly narrative does is offer a "re-vision," a new vision of humankind and Israel in the postexilic period. We can thus see a real difference between the Priestly interpreter of Israel's past and the predilections of many modern and contemporary interpreters of the human heritage. Consider, for example, Claude Lévi-Strauss: his unwillingness to deal with the undifferentiated in myth and his low opinion of ritual (to the point that we find almost nothing about ritual in his writings) contrasts sharply with the Priestly enfolding of the ancient texts while bringing a new point of view to bear. Girard has described the reading of mythical texts by Lévi-Strauss as a new expulsion, much like ritual expulsion. The act of expelling is expelled, but it simply reinforces the ancient taboo.[67] The Priestly approach is not radically ideological (or sacrificial) in the sense that it completely censors the primordial expulsion of Adam and Eve from paradise and Cain from the vicinity of paradise. The story and tradition of the innocence of Abel and the guilt of Cain are too strong and vital and serve to mediate between the original emergence of the slain brother–expelled brother and the renewal of life represented in Seth. Nonetheless, *the Priestly story is concerned to represent human nature as nonviolent, for the image of God continues unmarred in humankind until the great flood.*

In the Priestly creation story, Genesis 1, the world is created nonviolently. There is no doubt that the writer or writers knew not only the story in Genesis 2, but myths of violent creation such as we find in Psalm 74:12–17 and in Mesopotamian mythology. Traces of such knowledge may be discerned in the divine control of the watery chaos or *tehom* in Genesis 1:2, which brings the cognate name Tiamat to mind,[68] the goddess of the salt waters that Marduk defeated and slew in order to establish the ordered world and the Babylonian cult. But there is no battle in Genesis 1. The dragon-scapegoat is removed from the creation. Even after the flood, the Priestly perspective does not posit violence as necessary among human beings. It holds, rather, as a kind of substitute for human warfare, that human beings will engage in warfare with the animals and will be allowed to eat their flesh as long as they do not consume the blood (Gen 9:1–7). And even this consumption is brought under the control of sacred regulations. As Norbert Lohfink states, "In the world of the Priestly historical narrative one normally eats only meat which previously was offered to the divinity in cultic ritual. And vice versa, the ritual of which P thinks is not conceivable without animal sacrifice." As Lohfink points out in his important essay, "The Priestly historical narrative thinks of a society, and so also of a world construction, which functions and could function, at least, among human beings, without the interference of violence. It is a world that has become peacefully maintainable through the cult and the power of ritual." In the interim, between the Priestly completion of the Pentateuch in the postexilic era and the war and conflict that lasted from the time of the Maccabees into the second century C.E., "this community living non-violently had its basis in the Pentateuch."[69]

There is a certain grandeur in the Priestly perspective, as we find in the creation account, Genesis 1–2:4a, which is marked not only by the transcendent majesty of God but also, as I have noted, by the absence of violence in the creation of the world. As Girard has remarked, "In the story of the creation of the world, the founding moment comes at the beginning, and no victimage is involved."[70] The Priestly intention of minimizing violence reflects the effectiveness of the sacrificial system and the Priestly concern to encourage Israel to act responsibly and to hope for the future after the Babylonian Captivity in 586 B.C.E. We shall return to the sacrificial system in subsequent chapters. The absence of violence in Genesis 1 has endured as a revelatory model of nonviolent creation of the world.

In sum, it is not my intention to say anything derogatory about the Priestly way of handling the story of Cain and Abel, for the replacing of Cain and Abel with Seth belongs to the Priestly vision of a nonviolent society. What I would like to stress here is that in spite of this grand vision, the Priestly narratives do not afford the best sense of the *process* by which Israel struggled to realize its own particular revelation and its specific identity. This deficiency is signaled in the willingness to pass over the earlier story of mimetic rivalry, even though (unlike modern totalitarian ideologues) the Priestly writer does not suppress the Cain material. The Cain and Abel story is a paradigm of human desire and violence that tells us much about how we are and how we have become how we are. It also tells us much about the God who cares for the murdered brother, who marks the murderer but cares for him also.

What we read in the Yahwist narratives is more indicative of the process by which Israel came to understand itself, its God, and its world. We see in the Yahwist narratives an Israel becoming ever more conscious of "the exception [the innocent victim] that is still in the process of emerging." Israel began to perceive its own origin and destiny in the light of the innocent victim.

Israel's story as a people begins with its emergence from the nations. Israel does not appear at the founding moment, at the time in the beginning, as is typical in the myths of most peoples. Babylon, for example, is founded as the result of procreation and battle in the primordial "time before time." In Egypt, mythogra-

phers evidently struggled to surmount the problem of violence and partially succeeded, as indicated in the texts of "The Creation by Atum," "Another Version of
the Creation by Atum," and "The Theology of Memphis."[71] But the success is only
partial. For one thing, polytheism is a mythological theology presupposing rivalry
among the gods. Rivalry and conflict either come to the fore or are referred to in
these texts. In "The Creation by Atum" the pyramid builder, King Nefer-ka-Re,
has to be protected from evil, "from all gods and all dead." In the other version of
Atum's creation, not only are the death and transformation of Horus and Osiris
presupposed, but the enemies of Osiris must be annihilated in order that his son
Horus may rule. Finally, in the Memphite text, the domain of Upper Egypt is
removed from Seth and given to Horus. Although the text asserts that Horus and
Seth were reconciled, the conflict among Seth, Horus, and Osiris is clearly recognized. For the Priestly account in Genesis, there is no divine battle in the beginning (or subsequently), and creation comes about through the divine word of
command. The Yahwist has a "chaos and conflict" perspective, depicting human
beginnings as the result of an expulsion (Gen. 3) and a murder (Gen. 4).
Nonetheless, *Israel* is not founded on an expulsion or murder committed by its
ancestors but is created *through a process of becoming exceptional vis-à-vis the violent structures in the midst of which it came to be.*

It is not as though the biblical texts present Israel as morally unambiguous in
the person of its ancestors and leading figures. The ironic and critical recognition
of participation in victimization and violence is, as a matter of fact, the most distinctive quality of Israel's literature among ancient texts. What I would emphasize
here is its insight into scapegoating, into the mechanisms that serve to justify victimization and violence in most cultures.

What I wish to do in this study is to explore this revelation, this uncovering of the
victimization mechanism and the favoring of the innocent victim that the biblical
heritage ascribes to the God who sides with victims. The Yahwist account offers us
the insight that Cain replaced Abel in the sense of murdering him and the LORD
replaced Abel with Seth in the sense of compensating Eve for her loss. The Priestly
story of beginnings, acutely sensitive to the human predicament of rivalry and violence, tries to replace Cain and Abel with Seth, who perpetuates the divine likeness in humankind. But the basic thrust of the biblical texts is not to let us ignore
Cain and Abel, even while asking us to think in terms of a nonviolent social order.

By taking a point of departure from two biblical perspectives on the rivalry of
Cain with Abel, we have encountered the major themes of the biblical witness to
revelation. This story, the narration of a struggle against mimetic desire and for a
good mimesis, God's will for nonviolent human community, will lead us through
the Law and the Prophets to the Gospels, where we find a radical articulation of

the revelation in the story of the Innocent Victim. I hope to weave the biblical texts and contexts into a tapestry displaying the full biblical picture that forms the basis and background of the words attributed to Jesus in the Passion story, "They hated me without cause," and, "He was numbered with the transgressors."[72] This exploration will then lead us to consider the biblical revelation in relation to contemporary American culture and to ask, What is "good mimesis" for us—mimesis that frees us from or drastically diminishes rivalry, conflict, and violence?

2

Enemy Brothers

Beloved enemy is no rhetorical expression; it is exactly what Caesar is to Brutus.
René Girard, *A Theatre of Envy: William Shakespeare*

Angry words ensued, followed all too soon by blows, and in the course of the affray, Remus was killed.
Livy, *The Early History of Rome*

For truly to see your face is to see the face of God.
Genesis 33:10

In the texts about enemy brothers we encounter revealing stories of mimetic rivalry and violence and ways of dealing with rivalry and violence. These are master texts, paradigm cases for understanding the problem of desire and rivalry in general. They are associated with founding events in the traditions of ancient Israel, and each offers penetrating insights concerning processes of victimization, the role of sacrifice, and the status of the innocent victim before the God who does not recognize human differences.

A. Once More Cain and Abel: The Slain and the Expelled

When the LORD says to Cain, "Where is Abel your brother?" he answers, "I do not know; am I my brother's keeper?" (Gen 4:9). Cain's claim of ignorance is viewed in the story as a deceptive pretense, but this pretense may be construed in another way when read in context. Abel's *blood* cries out to God from the ground. The spilling of blood was a feature not only of murder but of sacrifice, and attempts have been made to relate this aspect of the text to rituals of sacrifice.[1] Cain's murder of Abel is not a sacrifice in the strict sense, but three matters should be noted: (1) The issue that occasions the rivalry is precisely sacrifice. (2) A case can be made that the spilling of blood in any sort of killing and the offering of blood in sacrifice stem from the same pattern of meaning and practice in ancient social and religious institutions. Even if ostensibly different in a given people's folk wisdom and mythical or ideological rationalizations, they share a common core of meaning. (3) Prohibition is the concomitant of sacrifice and has a dialectical[2] relation to it, so as a rule one should look for the presence of sacrificial processes wherever basic prohibitions or taboos are in question.

The blood of human beings and animals was sacred, reserved for God only. According to the Priestly account of beginnings, mankind was allowed to eat meat after the Flood, but blood could not be consumed, for in it is life (Gen 9:3–4). In the Levitical doctrine of sacrifice it is *atoning* when offered upon the altar (Lev 17:10–11). According to Deuteronomy, the blood of animal flesh that is used for ordinary consumption is to be poured out on the earth, while the blood of sacrificial offerings is to be poured out on the altar of the LORD (Deut 12:23–24, 27). From the standpoint of the Girardian model employed in this study, the sacredness of the blood is itself a sign of the victim, whose violent death is assigned a divine value once the killing has occurred. The identification of blood with life retains a trace of the original killing without full recognition of the *homicide* that lies behind it. The Priestly source recognizes that eating blood and shedding blood are related (Gen 9:4–6), but the exact nature of this link remains somewhat obscured, in part because the Priestly narrative goes to great lengths to present a nonviolent picture of human nature and human dealings. The theological reason given for interdiction of human bloodshed is that *Adam*, humankind, is made in the divine image (9:6). For the Priestly writer, the image of God supersedes the mark of Cain as the point of differentiation that is intended to protect human beings from violence.

Abel's blood on the ground is a feature of the story that coalesces with one of the cultic stipulations, that the blood of animals killed for meat should be poured out on the ground. According to Leviticus 17:13, this blood is to be covered with dust, whereas no such injunction is given in Deuteronomy 12:23. In sacrifice as such, the blood is poured out on the altar, as already stated. The altar is both the primary place of ritual enactment and the ritual dividing point between prohibition and confusion. The altar is a concrete, spatial reminder of the prohibition, in this instance, "Thou shalt not kill," and the point where the community may transgress that prohibition through offering a substitute victim. At the same time, as the community blesses God in offering the sacrifice it likewise gives collective support to its common life and the power to overcome conflict.

The Cain and Abel story is "originative" or "generative" in the sense that it moves behind or beyond the altar, so to speak, in order to lay bare the beginnings of human culture. The difference between this text and ordinary mythical texts is that the latter typically justify the murder, presupposing the existence of the community that must not let itself be subverted by taking the side of the victim. Nothing like an altar appears in the Cain story—but the *sign or mark on Cain functions as a prohibition:* "so that no one who came upon him would kill him" (Gen 4:15).

At this point let us return to Cain's initial declaration of ignorance of Abel's fate. Once we have shown the lines of connection between Abel's blood and sacrifice, we are in a position to see that *Cain attempts to present himself as without knowledge in a manner similar to participants in ritual sacrifice.* Cain's denial of knowledge about what happened to his brother could be construed as a universal ritual phenomenon. If ritual is a kind of expelling or exorcising of the original act, then the Genesis text discloses that very process. Of course, it does not allow Cain to get away with it. If we placed the text in a wider ritual context, we might even give Cain the benefit of the doubt and suppose that he really believes his own denial. Nonetheless, the text forces his confrontation with God, who brings the deed to light and announces the curse that expels him from the arable soil into the land of Wandering.

The outcome of Cain's murder of Abel is the beginning of civilization, which is built upon mimetic desire. Because Cain had been able to see himself only through his brother, his brother became his *double*, the rival other whose authority and power effectively take on divinity, which Cain then internalized to the point that he could not properly distinguish himself from the all-powerful other. In order to differentiate himself once this happened, what was left for him to do but to kill the other or kill himself? One modern option for someone caught up in the predicament of the double is to become "insane," but that does not seem to be an available option in founding stories, which require a decisive exteriorization of mimetic desire.

The LORD had said to Cain, "If you do well, will you not be accepted? And if you do not do well, sin is crouching at the door; its desire is for you, but you must master it" (Gen 4:7, RSV). Sin is portrayed as an alien force in the image of a wild beast "crouching," lying in wait for its prey. The Hebrew verb, *rabats*, means "to lie down" or "to crouch," (e.g., the leopard in Isa 11:6). Gaster notes the "croucher," *rabitsu*, in Mesopotamian demonology.[3] This alien character of sin is very much like that in its embodiment in the serpent at the beginning of Genesis 3. In fact, I think Hamerton-Kelly is right in explicating the serpent as a metaphor of mimetic desire,[4] and surely the same holds for Genesis 4:7: "sin" or "going astray"[5] not only has desire for Cain but *is* desire. In the confusion or chaos of undifferentiation, when rivalry reaches its height of intensity, it is a power that seems to come from outside the human subject and the community. It is the experience of *pandemonium*, the state brought about by the Pan-demon. Since *pan* means "all" in Greek, *pandemonium* means the contagious experience of a community that becomes a mob, everyone caught up in undifferentiated rivalry with everyone else. This kind of turbulence in a festival setting is described by Euripides in *The Bacchae*, in which Dionysus becomes everyone's double and rules the city. As Girard has aptly put it, "[T]he Dionysiac elimination of distinctions rapidly degenerates into a particularly virulent form of violent nondifferentiation."[6] Abel is Cain's double, a substitute for God, and as deity's substitute Abel is Cain's god. Cain undergoes a kind of inner pandemonium, which is expressed in his anger and fallen face. God's words have no effect on him; it is his brother Abel with whom he is concerned. Then, after he kills Abel, he listens to God. The LORD's assertion that he is cursed from the ground because of his brother's blood gets his attention. Behind the prohibition, the sign protecting Cain from murder, lies the curse, and behind the curse lies the murder, and behind the murder lie mimetic desire and mimetic rivalry.

Desire, rivalry, and violence lead to Cain's expulsion. He is "driven" from the ground, "hidden" from God's presence, a dweller in the land of Wandering. One might well ask whether behind the Cain story lies a scapegoat tale in which an innocent person, represented in the present text by Cain, was expelled from the community in a time of crisis. In the present text of Genesis 4, God would be, in that case, the divine symbol of the offended social order. There is no way to assert absolutely that the biblical text does not conceal such a narrative, but it is crucial to observe that it is precisely certain biblical texts, not mythic sources from other contexts, that articulate so acutely this question of a concealed victimization mechanism. Beyond this consideration, it is quite clear that in the present story of Cain *he is protected from punishment by the sign.* This feature makes the story much different from the archetypal expulsion myth, one like the story of Oedipus. When Oedipus recognizes his crime, he confesses and blinds himself, thus complying with the sacrificial process at work in the community.[7] Another example of the expelled scapegoat is the Gerasene demoniac in Mark 5:1–20, briefly discussed in chapter 1. The outcast possessed of an unclean spirit lives among the tombs, "always crying out, and bruising himself with stones" (Mark 5:5). Acting berserk, crying out, injuring himself—this was exactly what the community wanted. As long as he was possessed by an unclean spirit, the others were safe, there would be no pandemonium. He served as a continual sacrifice on their behalf. It is therefore no wonder that they begged Jesus to leave when he healed the demoniac by exorcism.[8]

But God protects Cain from this cycle of victimization, and in so doing, in giving him the mark, he makes him sacrosanct, "set apart."[9] At one level Cain has got what he wanted, for now he himself is a kind of god whom others may not harm. He is protected from the effects of vengeance, from being a scapegoat, wherever he wanders. But this protection from others in the world "outside," east of Eden, is simultaneously a sign distinguishing him from Abel and so preventing him from being "haunted." In conflictual mimesis, the rivals are *too close,* too much alike. The death of the rival could make the subject's enactment of the model-obstacle as double even worse unless there are means of reestablishing the subject as distinct, as different. The other who is the criterion by which one judges oneself, and yet from whom one can no longer distinquish oneself, is no longer physically embodied; as invisible in the realm of the dead, the other becomes positively dangerous. Inasmuch as the subject has wished for the elimination of the model-obstacle, he or she experiences the guilt of desiring the disappearance of the one who obstructs the path to fulfillment of desire, but who is at the same time the one whose superior being makes the object of desire worthwhile. It is no wonder that the subject experiences conflicting feelings and often severe depression and death wishes when the model-obstacle dies. How much more so if the subject has actually killed or murdered the model-obstacle!

The universal structures for accomplishing this differentiation of the subject are sacrificial. The one who is executed as a victim is a substitute for the model-obstacle. In terms of the social order, this means that the victim embodies the danger that humans experience in their network of mimetic rivalries. A society, in other words, is made up of a complex web of relationships that in certain crises become model-obstacle relationships. If sacrificial ritual is effective, it detoxifies and so ameliorates the mimetic conflict.

Abel is the first scapegoat, but then Cain, as the one who is "signed"or "marked," is the substitute for Abel. He in turn would be murdered if it were not for the sign. The sign is thus a substitute for the victimization process that averts a new sacrificial substitution through the prohibition (i.e., "thou shalt not murder Cain as he murdered Abel").

Theodor Gaster has collected some interesting material on the mark. A mark or brand has in various social contexts been employed to identify devotees of gods, slaves owned by certain masters, and criminals.[10] Even more interesting are the examples in a long excursus reproducing Sir James G. Frazer's discussion in *Folklore in the Old Testament*. I will not make a detour to give extensive citations. It will suffice to quote two statements. The first is a summary of Frazer's inference concerning the mark of Cain. "The mark of Cain . . . may originally have represented a mode of disguising a homicide or of rendering him so repulsive or formidable in appearance that his victim's angry ghost would either fail to recognize him or be scared of haunting him."[11] The practices then described include banishing the homicide, sometimes for a limited period of time. The second statement is Frazer's conclusion to the material he has arrayed:

> We may smile at these quaint fancies of vengeful ghosts, shrieking gore, and Earth opening its mouth to drink blood or to vomit out her guilty inhabitants; nevertheless it is probable that these and many other notions equally unfounded have served a useful purpose in fortifying the respect for human life by the adventitious aid of superstitious terror. The venerable framework of society rests on many pillars, of which the most solid are nature, reason, and justice; yet at certain stages of its slow and laborious construction it could ill have dispensed with the frail prop of superstition.[12]

Here we have a typical example of Frazer moving so close yet remaining so far from the truth of the texts that fascinated him but with which he dealt so arrogantly. He recognizes the phenomenon of haunting, but he never arrives at its rootage in mimetic rivalry. He notes "superstitious terror" (which in this context could be translated as "the sacred"), but his dogmatic attachment to notions of nature, reason, and justice blinds him to the possibility that the mechanisms at work in tribal and archaic societies are not absent even in "enlightened" Western culture. Ruth Mellinkoff remarks, for example, on the badge laws of Nazi Germany, which are one offshoot of the mark motif. Badge laws "began officially with Innocent III in the thirteenth century, but [their] real genesis can be laid to Augustine and his ancient allegorical comparison of Cain and the Jews—and more specifically to his comparison of the 'sign' of the Jews and Cain's unknown, mysterious mark."[13]

In the event, Cain is protected both from being haunted by his double and from the vengeance of others. But Cain is protected from vengeance *at the price of vengeance*. "If any one slays Cain, vengeance shall be taken on him sevenfold" (Gen 4:15). The biblical narrative gives no indication of further troubles for Cain as he sires a son and builds a city and names it after his son, Enoch. However, one of his descendants, Lamech, sings boastfully of the vengeance he has exacted:

> I have killed a man for wounding me,
> a young man for striking me.
> If Cain is avenged sevenfold,
> truly Lamech seventy-sevenfold.
> (Gen 4:23b–24)

The narrator evidently intends to indicate that the violence that begins with Cain is now growing out of all bounds. For the Yahwist narrator this situation is the backdrop of the confusion of divine and human beings in the time of the giants, when the LORD recognized the wickedness of humankind (Gen 6:1–8). God then sends the Flood in order to dissolve the old creation and start anew.

It is, however, important to recognize that insofar as Cain's murder of Abel is a founding act, thus sharing in a universal mythical theme, it is not concealed or given any sort of justification in the biblical narrative. Nor is it the act that founds the people Israel or any of its great institutions. It is the human act of one who is typical in the measure that he desires what his brother has, and when he cannot perceive himself as different from his brother as his equal or superior, he kills him. He cannot tolerate the differentiation that God has made, so he slays his brother.

The cycle of desire, rebellion, and violence continues through the scattering and confusion of Babel to the call of Abraham, Genesis 12:1–3. In the story of Abraham and his descendants, the people who emerge out of the peoples as the divinely chosen exception, God's promises begin their work in history, which is the story of victimization and sacrifice.

B. Jacob and Esau: Israel and His Other

Since enemy brothers are the primary focus in this chapter, we will move over the Abraham story to the story of Jacob and Esau in Genesis 25–35. Jacob and Esau are twins, twins "with a vengeance," so to speak, for their birth is all but simultaneous (Gen 25:24–26). Esau comes forth first, but Jacob immediately follows holding Esau's heel. This heel-holding is the occasion of a wordplay: the word *heel*, Hebrew *aqev*, is construed by the narrative as the basis of Jacob's name, Hebrew *yaaqov*, probably suggesting "taker of the heel" or "supplanter." In the Israelite tradition the prophets Hosea and Jeremiah viewed the name as meaning rivalry. Hosea (who prophesied about 740–720 B.C.E.) juxtaposes the birth account and the struggle with the divine adversary at the Jabbok: "In the womb he took his brother by the heel, and in his manhood he strove with God" (Hos 12:3, RSV).

Clearly the events are similar from the prophet's standpoint. In both instances Jacob holds on in a *contest*. Hosea has already announced the LORD's indictment against Jacob (12:2), and he identifies Jacob with contemporary Ephraim in the figure of a swindling merchant (12:7) and compares him unfavorably to Moses (12:12). There is thus no doubt that Hosea uses part of the Jacob story to make a negative statement about Israelite society.

It may be that Jeremiah (who prophesied about 626–585 B.C.E.) refers to the Jacob tradition when he warns of the evil in Judean society:

> Let every one beware of his brother,
> and put no trust in any brother;
> for every brother is a supplanter
> (*kol ach aqov yaaqov*),
> and every neighbor goes about as a slanderer.
>
> (Jer 9:4, RSV)

It reads like an allusion to Jacob, and at any rate it fits in the prophet's warning about the brother who cannot be trusted, who tries to oust or eliminate his brother.

The narrator wants to ensure that the reader understands Jacob and Esau as so close, so much alike, that they are not only twins but struggle already in their mother's womb for superiority (Gen 25:23). An attempt is made to show how different they are in a number of respects:

- Esau was red (*admoni*) and hairy (*sair*). Both these words play on Esau as the ancestor of those named Edom (*edom*), whose land was also called Seir (*seir*). We find out eventually, however, that Jacob has skin that is "smooth" (*chalaq*, 27:11), a word that may also mean "tricky, deceitful."
- Esau became a hunter and an outdoorsman (25:27). In the same line Jacob is identified as a tent dweller, an "indoorsman," who is "quiet" (*tam*). The word *tam* is ambiguous. Normally it means either "whole" or

"innocent." It is used, for example, in Job's asseveration in Job 9:20:21: "I am innocent," that is, not guilty of any crime that deserves the punishment I am undergoing.

- Esau was favored by his father (in Hebrew, literally, "Isaac loved Esau because [his] game was in his mouth," 25:28), but Jacob was favored by his mother.

But for the Israelite tradition in which the Jacob story was composed, redacted, and transmitted, *proper* differentiation could only be the process in which Jacob emerges as the ancestor of the chosen people, the people whose forebear Abraham had received the promise from God that his descendants would be a great people and a blessing to other peoples. There are three moments in the Jacob story where this differentiation process is at issue: Jacob's purchase of Esau's birthright, Jacob's theft of Esau's blessing, and his encounter with God and then with Esau. I view the encounter with God at the ford of the Jabbok River and the meeting with Esau as two sides of the same event, as will be explicated below.

1. The Birthright (Genesis 25:29–34)

Esau comes in famished from the field and exclaims that he must have some of the pottage, or stew, Jacob is boiling. Esau describes the stew as "that red, red stuff" (in Hebrew, literally, "the red the red," *ha-adom ha-adom*). "Therefore," the text explains, "his name was called Edom" (*edom*). Jacob agrees but only in exchange for the birthright, *bekorah*, literally "(rights and privileges) pertaining to the older brother," who is the *bekor*. The birthright was evidently a status or place of authority in the family having to do with religious duties and inheritance. As such, for the elder son, the status of having the *bekorah* would probably not have been distinct from receiving the *berakah*, or blessing of the father, which is what is desired by Jacob and his mother in Genesis 27 and which I will treat below.[14] David Daube suggests the incident of the birthright and the incident of the theft of the blessing are two versions of the same event, because they are "centred upon the same ideas or idea."[15] This is an important observation whose relevance will be taken up shortly. When Esau accepts the exchange, Jacob makes him swear an oath to transfer the birthright to Jacob. This done, Jacob gives his brother "bread and lentil stew."

This is a strange little tale. It is much more difficult to comprehend than the theft of the blessing in chapter 27. Of course, it could be viewed as fun at the expense of the Edomites, whose ancestor is portrayed as primitive and slow of wit. Daube and others have pointed out that the verb Esau uses when he asks for the red stew, *laat*, "swallow" or "gulp," suggests "bestial wildness."[16] But whether or not a comical note is intended, the transaction is serious. As a result of the

exchange, stew for birthright, Jacob has the birthright, or right of the elder brother. The oath then establishes a line of demarcation that cannot be transgressed.
The structure of the resulting situation is that of sacrifice and prohibition, namely, the exchange of food consumed by Esau transfers the birthright without violence; the oath implies, at the least, this negative imperative: "You shall not take
any step, violent or nonviolent, to do what your brother has done in getting the
birthright from you."

Now if one maintains that there is more than a connotation of the sacrificial
in this tale, can this possibility be pursued and supported in any way? At this point
it is relevant to mention Daube's comment that when Esau saw what Jacob was
cooking, "It must have been the colour of blood that struck him and roused his
desire." He goes on to say Esau "thought that Jacob was preparing a blood-broth, a
dish to which antiquity ascribed special powers of reviving a tired body and the
fare, it may be recalled, of the Spartan warriors."[17] It certainly rings true, given
what we have been told about Esau, that he would have been more aroused by a
dish with meat or blood in it than by lentils. What Daube does not discuss is why
a descendant of Abraham would eat something made of blood: the Priestly pro-
scriptions of blood must surely have been rooted in ancient practices. If Daube's
comment is on the right track, then the biblical text presents Esau as wishing to
violate a taboo. Did the sight of the prohibited blood "rouse his desire"? If so,
then Daube's suggestion would lead to reading the episode in the following way:

1. Esau, hungry, is aroused by the sight of prohibited food being prepared
   by Jacob. The prohibition associates blood with life, which cannot be
   taken. But Esau, as a hunter, is already involved in the shedding of animal blood, that is, a generally accepted practice of violence.
2. Jacob offers the prohibited food in exchange for the birthright. The
   exchange is therefore sacrificial.
3. The oath Esau swears prohibits a violent retaking of the birthright. The
   oath thus has the effect of the prohibition, "You shall not kill," as
   applied to the specific matter of the birthright.
4. Jacob does not give Esau blood-broth but a soup of lentils. A deception
   has occurred. The lentil soup has replaced the blood-broth. Esau accepts
   this because of his hunger, dull wit, or both.

In other words, in terms of structure the movement is from transgression of prohibition through blood, to sacrificial exchange, to renewed prohibition, and finally
to substitution for the sacrificial substitution (blood). If viewed in this way, the
selling of the birthright is a ritual occasion and, like so many other stories in the
Scriptures, a model of how ritual works. In many instances, as we have seen in the
accounts of Cain and Abel and will see in the story of Joseph and his brothers, the
substitutions of the ritual are uncovered and the victimizers are not allowed to

perpetuate their (knowing or unknowing) deceptions. In this little tale, however, the exchange of birthright for food is allowed to stand without criticism; in fact, it is justified, for the narrator comments, "Thus Esau despised his birthright" (29:34). But then this is a kind of cover-up justifying Jacob by comparison with Esau, as if to say, "Well, Jacob may have tricked him, but after all, Esau didn't really give a hang about his birthright. He was really more concerned about his stomach."

2. Theft of the Blessing (Genesis 27)

A meal is also at the center of this series of events. Isaac was old and nearly blind. He requested of his older son a meal of wild animal meat before he died. Then he would bless him. It could be read simply as a request to indulge the elderly father before he dies, but I think the text makes more of it than that. For one thing, the blessing to be given involves conferring real power and status not only in the family but for the future of the family. For another thing, the Hebrew text presents the meal as the *precondition* of the blessing: "and bring it to me to eat, so that (baavur) I may bless you before I die" (27:4). The phrase baavur, "so that" or "to the end that," must be translated as a purpose clause.[18]

So the meal is not an ordinary meal. It functions evidently as a kind of medium of exchange—the meal in exchange for the blessing. Because its main dish is a preparation of wild game, it entails hunting and killing animals that live outside the domestic sphere. What the meal and blessing involve, then, is a series of acts that may be expressed in purpose clauses: hunting and killing game *so that* a meal may be prepared for Isaac *so that* he will bless Esau *so that* he will be lord of the family (see 27:29). But these purpose clauses may be reduced to a series of substitutions: meal for killing of game, blessing for meal, rule of family for blessing. If these exchanges or substitutions are seen as sacrificial, one can understand why the blessing is of such great moment. It is obviously an object of desire and could be the cause of chaos in the clan if rivalry is not controlled. The killing and cooking of an animal is a substitute for actual sacrifice and, in fact, a bare substitute: it is scarcely concealed at all.

The series of substitutions exemplifies the process of the sacrificial mechanism: victim killed (game killed), ritualization (meal prepared), (prohibition [struggle for power and murder prohibited]), myth (the success of God's chosen one). I have put prohibition in parentheses because it is implied rather than spelled out—but implied pretty clearly, I think, in Isaac's blessing (27:29):

> Be lord over your brothers,
> and may your mother's sons bow down to you.
> Cursed be every one who curses you,
> and blessed be every one who blesses you!

In other words, the force of the word of blessing is to prevent rivalry and conflict in the family and to assure success for the family through the one who is blessed.

The sacrificial situation of the blessing is triggered, of course, by Isaac's impending death. The death of the patriarch in tribal society is comparable to the death of a king; it has the same effect within a clan or tribe. Hence Isaac's impending death is a mimetic crisis. The proof of that is the deception perpetrated by Jacob and his mother and Isaac's reaction to it.

The account of the deception has much in it that has been compared to ritual practices. Frazer discusses various rituals in which sacrificial skin is placed in some form somewhere on the sacrificer or the person on whose behalf sacrifice is offered: adoption, new birth, circumcision, and expiation in a situation of evil or pollution. His general conclusion concerning sacrificial skins is that their use is for "investing a person with a portion of a sacrificial skin [in order to] protect him against some threatened or actual evil, so that the skin serves the purpose of an amulet." Concerning the relation of Genesis 27 to practices of new birth, Frazer conjectures that the text "contains a reminiscence of an ancient legal ceremony of new birth from a goat, which it was deemed necessary or desirable to observe whenever a younger son was advanced to the rights of the firstborn at the expense of his still living brother."[19] Frazer does not have direct evidence of the advancement of a younger son from any other culture but relies instead on the analogy of the ritual of moving into a higher caste in India.

That the skin of a sacrificed animal may serve as an amulet of some sort there is little doubt. Probably the amulet function is also one of the factors in Frazer's new birth-rebirth material, for the animal victim is a kind of protection against any conflict or violence that prevents the "birth" from taking place. What Frazer typically does not see clearly is how all his data are centered in sacrifice and the attempts to ward off a mimetic crisis. Girard's brief comment on the deception in Genesis 27 goes immediately to the point: "Two sorts of substitutions are telescoped here: that of one brother for another, and that of an animal for a man. Only the first receives explicit recognition in the text; however, this first one serves as the screen upon which the shadow of the second is projected."[20] He goes on to compare Jacob's disguise in Esau's clothing and goatskin on his hands and the smooth part of his neck to the ruse Odysseus used against the Cyclops in the *Odyssey*. Odysseus escapes the Cyclops's cave by clinging to the underside of one of the rams leaving the cave; the Cyclops, in a gesture similar to Isaac's, runs his hand over the back of each animal to make sure it carries no passenger. "The two texts are mutually revealing: the Cyclops of the *Odyssey* underlines the fearful menace that hangs over the hero (and that remains obscure in the Genesis story); and the slaughter of the kids in Genesis, along with the offering of the 'savory meat,' clearly implies the sacrificial character of the flock, an aspect that might go unnoticed in the *Odyssey*."[21]

In addition to the factors of Isaac's impending death and the two substitutions of Jacob for Esau and an animal for a man, another sign of the crisis—and the most telling indication of its impact—is Isaac's *confusion*. To understand this we must be aware of the father's role as model of authority. We have focused so far on enemy brothers as rivals, but obviously any parent-child relationship may be the matrix—or vortex—of rivalry, and father-son rivalry is certainly a classic situation of conflict. Jacob and Esau, as twins, have not sufficiently differentiated, but Isaac, who "loved Esau, because he ate of his game" (25:28, RSV), now becomes "too close"; he is too much like the son he would bless. That is understandable, after all, when a patriarch approaches death and sees himself and the future of his clan (which bears his name) in the son to be blessed. He sees himself through his son's object of desire, which is patriarchal authority and its attendant benefits. His blindness is a symptom of his inability to differentiate; he is easily fooled, for someone not caught up in the blindness of mimetic rivalry would be more than a little suspicious of the goatskin on Jacob (how hairy *was* Esau, anyway?). "The voice is Jacob's voice, but the hands are the hands of Esau" (27:22).

Isaac cannot see, but he feels and hears *double*; the twins are still undifferentiated for the father, whose status is supposed to assure the efficacy of mediation—and mediation entails differentiating the sons into their proper roles and destinies. Isaac reacts, of course, to a trick that is played on him, and to this extent, the doubling is something objective, working on him from the outside. Objectively considered within the text, the masquerade is that of a *monstrous* being: Jacob's voice, Esau's hair, and the skin of a goat bringing the two together. But one may ask whether the mask, the disguise, both evokes Isaac's desire and affords him the opportunity to conceal it with impunity. In my reading it is ironically significant that Isaac so quickly and easily accepts the allaying of his suspicion, for his only test is to pose a halfhearted question, "Are you really my son Esau?" (27:24). When Jacob says yes, Isaac accepts the answer and gives the blessing. Perhaps he is fooled, but perhaps part of him prefers Jacob. A bit of textual evidence for this latter possibility is the use of the third person in 27:25: "Bring it to me, and I will eat of *my son's* game, that (*lemaan*) I may bless you" (my translation). Notice Isaac does not say, "your game," but "my son's." And once again we observe the purpose clause, indicating that the blessing is predicated upon the consumption of the meal.

The consequences of the "stolen" blessing display the confusion that still reigns: (1) Isaac seems to react with shock and dismay when Esau shows up with a meal of game. Nonetheless, when Esau cries out for a blessing, Isaac is able to tell him immediately, "Your brother came deceitfully, and he has taken away your blessing" (27:35). ("The voice is Jacob's voice, but the hands are the hands of Esau.") (2) In spite of Esau's pleas, the blessing cannot be retracted. The commentaries conventionally point out that Isaac's refusal or inability to cancel the first blessing is based on the ancient Israelite and general Semitic understanding of language; words create and destroy, and when spoken by a person with authority and power, they have a potency in their own right. The word of blessing, like the curse, works as an independent reality in its own right. This is undoubtedly correct as far as it goes. What is usually neglected, however, is the total sacred context of the blessing and curse. Both are ritual utterances presupposing the prohibition and sacrificial substitution. A quick survey of blessings in the Hebrew Bible will show this to be the case. For example, God blesses Noah after the Flood after Noah has built an altar and offered burnt offerings (presumably of animals from the ark, Gen 8:20–22; 9:1–7). The interdiction of blood plays a significant role in the blessing beginning at Genesis 9:1. The promises to the ancestors are blessings and are typically connected to altars and sacrifices. Abraham builds an altar after God promises him that the land will belong to his descendants (Gen 12:7–8), he offers sacrifice in conjunction with the reiteration of the promises (Gen 15), and he is blessed by the LORD's angel after a ram is substituted for Isaac on the altar (22:9–19). The Blessing of Moses in Deuteronomy 33 belongs to a ritual setting that includes the offering of firstfruits and the announcement of blessings and curses in Deuteronomy 25–31. Therefore, when Esau asks, "Have you not reserved a blessing for me?" (27:36), the answer has to be negative. The consumption of the meal as a sacrificial substitution has sealed the matter. Isaac has only a kind of curse for Esau, which is modified by the promise that he will finally liberate himself from servitude to his brother (27:39–40). The sacrificial process has worked, but it has worked by excluding Esau. (3) So it was that "Esau hated Jacob because of the blessing" (27:41), and he resolves to kill his brother when Isaac dies. Esau, torn with bitter envy over the loss of the blessing and knowing that Isaac had charged Jacob not to marry a Canaanite woman, married an Ishmaelite woman because he "saw that the Canaanite women were evil in the eyes of Isaac his father" (28:8, my trans.). The result of the mimetic crisis for Esau is the desire to kill his brother and the transgressing of his father's prohibition. (4) The result of the mimetic crisis for Jacob is flight, which amounts to a kind of expulsion. Although his father is strangely passive, a character quality of Isaac that has appeared before,[22] Jacob has deceived his father and infuriated his brother, and so would be properly subject to revenge in the context of the patriarchal social order. His departure is an important moment in the story of Israel's origins, for here the ancestor who will bear the name Israel begins to become differentiated; he is in the process of becoming the emerging exception by leaving the blind and confused father, the envious, hostile, and vengeful brother, and the doting mother who did his thinking for him. But the differentiation of Jacob and Esau and the beginning of Israel will not occur until Jacob returns and encounters God and his brother.

3. Jacob's Encounters with God and Esau (Genesis 32–33)

a. The Encounter at the Jabbok.   The mimetic crisis was abated only by Jacob's flight or expulsion, and as he returns to Canaan from Aram, Jacob knows that he must still deal with its consequences. Esau has reason to hate him and seek revenge, even though twenty years have passed. From Jacob's standpoint the messengers he sends to Esau only confirm his worst fears, for Esau approaches to meet him with four hundred men. "Then Jacob was greatly afraid and distressed" (32:7), dividing his people, flocks, herds, and camels into two companies in the hope that if Esau attacked the one the other would escape. Jacob prays to his God for deliverance from his brother, reminding God of the promise made at Bethel (32:9–12).

Now Jacob conceives a strategy of "softening up" Esau by sending ahead animals at intervals as a present to his brother (32:13–21). As is well known to Hebrew Bible specialists, the word *face* (Hebrew *panim*) in some form occurs six times in this passage. Some of them, as isolated occurrences, would simply belong to colloquial expressions and so would carry no special meaning. However, taken together, they form a kind of litany that prepares the way for Jacob's struggle with the Adversary at the spot that he would name Face of God. The first occurrence is, in truth, rather isolated, so it is arguable whether it belongs to this configuration: "Pass on before me [*lefanay*, 'to my face'; the *p* sound becomes like our *f* after a vowel], and put a space between drove and drove" (32:16). But there is no doubt about the pattern in verses 20–21:

> And you shall say, "Moreover your servant Jacob is behind us." For he thought, "I may appease him [*akapprah fanayw*, 'cover or atone his face'] with the present that goes ahead of me [*lefanay*, 'to my face'], and afterwards I shall see his face (*fanayw*); perhaps he will accept me [*yissa fanay*, 'lift my face']." So the present passed on ahead of him [*al-panayw*, "on or to his face"]; and he himself spent that night in the camp.

The Hebrew expression "atone his face" is particularly interesting. The ordinary way of saying "appease" someone would be to "find favor in his eyes," or some expression of that order. The wording here is much more serious and fraught with tangles of meaning. The noun related to *kipper*, *kofer*, has the common signification of "ransom" or "price of exchange" (so Exod 21:30). Hartmut Gese discusses various occurrences of this root, *kpr*, and concludes that *kofer* and its Greek translation *lutron* bear the basic meaning of "means of exchange for release" (*Lösegeld*), that is, "what comes in as the price of a life, what can stand in for my life." The verb then denotes to find a *kofer*, and in relation to God this means to "release from death-guilt, and from the human side only total surrender can be adequate to that."[23]

The sequence of occurrences of the word for face makes it appear that ritual process is being described in 32:20–21: (a) finding release from death-guilt for his face (b) by means of the gift that goes to my face, (c) and afterward (i.e., so that) I will see his face; (d) then perhaps he will lift my face. By the logic of this process, if he lifts my face (accepts me, is reconciled with me), then I will have atoned for or propitiated his face. Then—and it remains to be seen precisely what this could mean—we both will have our proper face.

In this situation of acute anxiety for Jacob in which he agonizes over "facing" his brother, he does a very strange thing: he sends the remainder of his party—his two wives, his two maids, and his eleven children—across the fording place of the Jabbok River and spends the night alone on the farther side. Is it his fear that prevents him at this moment from taking another step toward meeting his brother? Or is it a literary device, not smoothly employed, to have Jacob alone for the ensuing struggle? Because I think the author is both cunning and profound, I find it hard to accept the notion of an awkward literary device, but this question need not detain us.

Jacob's struggle with the strange assailant is narrated in 32:24–30. (Verse 30 is not part of the contest episode as such, but as the text stands it relates the object of the narrative, so I will include it in my comments here.) The literary richness of the passage has often been noted by the commentators.[24] Only two of the literary elements interest us here: the repetition of the word *name* (*shem*) and the movement toward the naming of the spot Face of God. I will come to these shortly.

The adversary who attacks Jacob is called initially a "man," in Hebrew, *ish*. Whether this is to be taken as an actual male human being, or God, or an angel in the form of a man is not clear. The God of Israel and of the ancestors could appear in human form, as could his messengers (see Gen 18:1–15; 19:1–23; Judg 13), and in the early Israelite tradition the prophet Hosea called Jacob's adversary "the angel" (Hos 12:4). Of course, in popular mythology there was a fine line between God and angels, and the appearance of both as the subject of the same passage probably indicates not a contradiction, but an expression of the same reality viewed from a slightly different angle.[25]

As it turns out, this "man" cannot defeat Jacob, whose strength is evidently superhuman (so his feat of rolling the stone away from the mouth of the well, Gen 29:10). He has strength and staying power. As he had held on to Esau's heel at birth, so now he holds on to his opponent and will not let him go.[26] The opponent even puts Jacob's thigh out of joint, but still he holds on, until the adversary says, "Let me go, for the day is breaking" (32:26). But Jacob refuses to release him unless the opponent blesses him. This demand of a blessing shows that Jacob views his opponent as divine.

> And he [the opponent] said to him, "What is your *name*?" And he said, "Jacob." Then he said, "Your *name* shall no more be called Jacob, but Israel, for you have striven with God and with humans, and have prevailed." Then Jacob asked him, "Tell me, I pray, your *name*." But he said, "Why is it that you ask my *name*?" And

he blessed him. So Jacob called the *name* of the place *Face* of God (*Peniel*), saying, "For I have seen God *face* to *face* (*panim el-panim*), and yet my life is preserved."(32:27–30, RSV modified; my italics)

I italicize *name* and *face* in order to highlight the significance of Jacob's new name and the naming of the site. We find in this fascinating episode simultaneously a recognition of rivalry and a disclosure of its emptiness. The disclosure of emptiness is a subversion of the ritual process of substitutions for the original victim. Jacob had been anxious about encountering Esau and had sent expensive gifts ahead to pave the way, hoping that he could "atone his face." But with his mind on that he is encountered by an adversary who is, in effect, Jacob's true opponent, his Other, who wrestles with him but renames him and blesses him. The name and blessing are gained for no other reason than his strength and persistence: he holds on until dawn. There is no question of an exchange of anything. The adversary will not disclose his name, which means that Jacob cannot have power over him (see Exod 3:13–14 and Judg 13:18). What Jacob can give or ascribe to him *makes no difference to him*. Jacob's differences do not matter to the Other, but the new name and the blessing make all the difference to Jacob.

Jacob has won; he has prevailed—over Esau, Isaac, and Laban, and now over his Other, over God. Or at least this is what he concludes: "I have seen God face to face, and yet my life is preserved." Something like a substitution *has* taken place, of course—the name Israel for the old name of Jacob. But it is not actually a sacrificial substitution, for there is no concealment or denial of the old name, which he continues to use and which is employed more frequently than "Israel" in the remainder of Genesis.

But the Jacob story does not break *completely* with the cultic context. Ancient Israelite readers undoubtedly understood the naming of the site as an etiology, or tale explaining how a cultic sanctuary got its name, and at the surface level of the text such is the case. Furthermore, the injury of Jacob's thigh (32:31–32)—or perhaps penis or groin[27]—is related to a cultic taboo. The injury is related to the universal motif of the hero's injury.[28] And the hero's injury or disability is conventionally a sign of his outsider status and an indication of his fate as a victim. But the figure of Jacob is now basically different from the expelled hero or sacred king. Unlike the blindness of Oedipus, Jacob's limp is a sign of his success, a *sign that he has been victorious without scapegoating or being scapegoated*. The great disorder he has endured has resulted in *sight*, not blindness: "I have seen God face to face." He no longer must live away from his land but is now prepared to return. *Rival* comes from a Latin root meaning "other side, river bank." Now Jacob knows who his real rival is, the Other who lets him win. Now he can cross the river.

Some years ago the structuralist-poststructuralist critic Roland Barthes presented a very interesting reading of Jacob's struggle at the Jabbok. His overall approach, which he calls textual analysis, "seeks to say neither *from where* the text comes (historical criticism) nor *how* it is made (structural analysis), but how it undoes itself, explodes, disseminates—by which coded routes it *departs*." Most of the essay is devoted to "sequential analysis," which is an inventory and classification of actions. The most striking result of his sequential analysis is the observation that the personage delivering the supposedly "conclusive blow" (*coup décisif*) is not the winner: the adversary, angel, deity, or whatever it is, delivers the blow that injures Jacob's thigh, but he is blocked or stymied and so enters (must enter?) into negotiation with his human opponent. But even though the weaker combatant stymies the divine adversary and wins new name and blessing, he is "marked," that is, injured: "the weaker defeats the stronger, *in exchange for which* he is marked (on the thigh)." Barthes goes on to observe that just as Jacob had earlier "marked himself," as it were, in grasping his older brother's heel at birth, so he accomplishes an analogous feat here. "One may say in a sense that [God] is the substitute for the older brother, who once more submits to defeat by the younger brother: the conflict with Esau is *displaced* (every symbol is a *displacement*; if the 'struggle with the angel' is symbolic, then it has displaced something)."[29]

As for Jacob's new name, it is part of the pattern of "mutations" that are discernible in the narrative. That is, "the entire episode . . . functions as *the creation of a multiple trace*: in Jacob's body, in the status of the brothers, in Jacob's name, in the name of the place, in dietary practice." The sequences analyzed are instances of *passage*: "of place, of parental line, of name, of dietary ritual, all of which remains very close to an activity of language, to a transgression of rules of meaning."[30]

After a few further comments on a structural, rather than textual or sequential, analysis of the passage, Barthes concludes that what really interests him "are the frictions, the ruptures, the discontinuities of readability, the juxtaposition of narrative entities that to a degree escape an explicit logical articulation: one has to do here . . . with a sort of *metonymic montage*." The logic of this metonymic montage is that of the unconscious, and it is this that should be the focus of the reading of the text, of its "dissemination," rather than the question of its "truth." "The problem, at least the one I pose to myself, is really to succeed in not reducing the text to a signified, whatever it may be (historical, economic, folklorist, or kerygmatic), but in maintaining its open meaning."[31]

The lucidity of Barthes's reading, in conjunction with the appeal of structuralist and poststructuralist approaches since the early 1970s, has resulted in the high status accorded this essay in the recent history of biblical studies. The paradox of Jacob's "victory," the function of symbolizing as substitution, and the description of metonymy are interpretive insights that are deservedly esteemed. I have, however, two primary objections to his reading. One is an issue at the level of assumptions and philosophical perspective. The appeal to the unconscious and to the work of Freud on rivalry and displacement is an appeal to a myth that sucks up the meaning of the text into a dark abyss where all signifieds, all objects of signifiers, disappear. One then does not have to deal with real things, with real events, with "truth"—because the "truth" is foreclosed by the "truth" of the unconscious, which is the origin and end of all attempts at signification. The ethical issue, as I see it, is that one does not have to assume responsibility for the text in the context of its tradition or relations with other persons. Or to put it another way: one assumes responsibility only to show continually how the signifier—the text, the sequences and functions of the text, the words, the sounds of the words, and so on—refers always to another signifier in a metonymic chain.

Second and concomitantly, the reader of the text does not then have to become engaged with the question of real conflict and violence. I think this is the surest proof that a reading like Barthes's is still caught in the myth of Oedipus, accepting the blindness that the community demands but attributing it to the unconscious. The displacement into nonviolent resolution of the conflict of brothers becomes simply a signification of a different sense, a different language. Violence and scapegoating cannot really be a subject of concern because to lift this to the light of day would be to call the reading, along with the power and prestige of the reader, into question in light of an interpretive consensus that signifiers deal with nothing real but other signifiers. What Jacob sees, the God beyond differences, is only a difference thrown up by the unconscious, and this difference or meaning, this "truth," can only lead into other differences that come from the unconscious. It seems very similar to a chain of victims or victim substitutes offered in sacrifice so that the community will not have to confront why it offers sacrifice continually.

b. The Meeting with Esau.   After the encounter at the Jabbok, Jacob must still face Esau. As he sees Esau approaching with four hundred men, he anxiously arrays his women and children, with his favored ones, Rachel and Joseph, at the rear where they will presumably be safer. Jacob leads the way, "bowing himself to the ground seven times, until he came near to his brother" (33:4). Jacob is overwhelmed with Esau's enthusiastically affectionate greeting. When Esau asks him about the "camp," or company of animals, Jacob replies that it is all for his older brother, "to find favor in the sight of my lord" (33:8).

We as readers are not prepared for Esau's generous welcome of the brother who had tricked him out of the blessing. After the notice that he had married Canaanite women to displease his father, we hear no more of him until he comes within Jacob's horizon once more. Has he changed? Has the divinely guided process of differentiation been at work in his life also? Or has he simply received the message that the cattle and sheep and other animals were intended as a peace offering to him? In that case, he approaches Jacob with some guile in his own right, although the story intends us to understand that he and his men could have easily destroyed or captured Jacob and his company.

However that may be, the next three verses are crucial for understanding the reunion of the brothers: "And Esau said, 'I have much (*rav*), my brother; keep what is yours.' And Jacob said, 'No, please, if I have found favor in your eyes then take my gift (*minhati*) from my hand, because (*ki al-ken*) I have seen your face, [which is] like seeing the face of God, and you have accepted me. Please take my blessing (*birkati*) that is brought to you, because God has dealt graciously with me and because I have everything (*kol*).' And so he urged him, and he took it" (33:9–11, my translation).

Esau, pretending perhaps not to desire the gift, says "I have much." The usual translation is "I have enough" (so the RSV and NRSV). The word in question is *rav*, which in context may mean "enough," or simply "much" or "a lot." It is also used for other distinctions. In the oracle to Rebecca before the twins were born, the LORD told her that "the one shall be stronger than the other, the elder (*rav*) shall serve the younger" (25:23). The *rav*, the older brother, now tells the younger, "I have *rav*," but the younger then tells the older, "I have everything (*kol*)"! This phrase, "I have *kol*," is usually taken as having the same sense as "having *rav*," but this rendering is to miss the comparison Jacob is making: Esau has a lot, but he, Jacob, has everything!

That is not all, for the "gift" that Jacob offers turns out to be a "blessing"! The Revised Standard Version and New Revised Standard Version render this also as "gift," but again, translators have had difficulty with this word because they did not comprehend what is at stake in the story. Of course, in the sphere of the sacred, giving a gift and giving a blessing are distinct but closely related ritual acts. In ritual or a highly ritualized situation, the gift is a substitute for sacrifice; the blessing is the ritual word that confers the peace and welfare that form the obverse of the disorder the prohibition seeks to avoid. Nonetheless, in ordinary speech they have the appearance of being quite different from each other, so Jacob's use of the word *blessing* comes as a surprise here. It may be a slip of the tongue, as Michael Fishbane maintains (see below), but deciding the question does not really matter. What matters is the outcome of Jacob's thought, "I may propitiate or atone his face with a gift." Jacob is returning the blessing that he had stolen, and in so doing he is asking his brother for forgiveness. He is asking, indeed, for release from death-guilt, and in requesting this release he compares his brother's face to the face of God ("because I have seen your face, which is like seeing the face of God").

A number of years ago Michael Fishbane already discerned some of what I have set forth here concerning Jacob's meeting with Esau. Two passages in his essay are worthy of quotation. The first concerns the blessing. "What [Jacob] says, in effect, is 'Take [back] the blessing which I have tricked from you.' Esau does, in fact, accept it from Jacob. By such an external transaction the internal guilt of a misappropriated blessing is 'atoned' for."[32] The other has to do with Fishbane's interpretation of the relation of Jacob's struggle with the adversary and his meeting with his brother.

> The wrestling scene thus appears to be part of Jacob's dream-work, whereby he "works through" the anticipated struggle with Esau by fusing it with earlier wrestlings with his brother—in the womb and at birth. The use of the wrestling image not only underscores the *agon*-struggle which Jacob anticipates with Esau, but effectively discloses the psychic core of the event (also indicated by the tongue-slip [saying "blessing" rather than "gift"]). Compounded by guilt, the anticipated fraternal strife is fused with an earlier one, allowing Jacob to resolve the conflict raging within him. In the "night encounter" Jacob wrestles with the "Esau" he carried within him. The "rebirth" Jacob achieves by his psychic victory in the night had still to be confirmed in the light of day. . . . Having seen Elohim face to face at Penuel, Jacob can prepare to meet Esau face to face as well.[33]

I find Fishbane's reading quite perceptive. For my purposes it does not matter whether Jacob is engaged in "dream-work," although in general I would want to avoid the connotation of psychological processes that stem from an "unconscious," a kind of mythical place of the psyche that determines psychic life.[34] But I agree with Fishbane on these specific points: (1) Jacob says to Esau, in effect, "Take back this blessing that I tricked from you." He thus atones Esau's face with the gift-blessing in the sense of releasing himself from death-guilt and renewing his relationship with his brother. (2) The contest at the Jabbok recapitulates Jacob's previous struggle with Esau (in the womb, for the blessing) and represents what he anxiously anticipates as a conflict-ridden, if not violent, meeting with his brother. (3) Jacob himself, perhaps by analogy to his mother carrying twins, struggles with the "Esau" he bears within him, and in successfully carrying this through he experiences "rebirth." I would want to emphasize, though, that a rebirth for Jacob is in some sense a rebirth for Esau.

Fishbane's analysis of the Jacob story need only be supplemented and strengthened, first, by the recognition that sacrifice, blessing, and prohibition are rooted in mimetic desire and rivalry.[35] The Jacob story is told within this ancient structure of the human condition but seeks to disclose a liberating alternative, a good mimesis in response to the ancient structure of the sacred.

Jacob and Esau desired the same object, the patriarchal blessing (that is, patriarchal status and power), because their father had it, and each knew the other wanted it. But the sacrificial substitutes (the meals), prohibition (not to kill, not to displace the rival who has the blessing), and myth (the tradition of the chosen one who will prosper) have not sufficed to differentiate the enemy brothers and settle their differences. At the Jabbok, Jacob "forces" the divine adversary to bless him and "accepts" the blessing that attends a new name. The name Israel signifies that he is no longer "Jacob" in the sense of "Jacob struggling with Esau," but is now "Israel" in the sense of "Jacob the ancestor of God's people of the future." As such, as this "new Jacob" that is "Israel," he is ready to become the ancestor of a great people.

Moreover, in my reading, the Face of God plays a more significant role than in Fishbane's. Fishbane speaks of Jacob's face-to-face encounter with God as a preparation for his encounter with Esau. I think it is much more than that. The Face of God is the gracious power that differentiates properly and appropriately. The encounter with the *Panim* has done what birth and sacrifice and patriarchal blessing could not do: separate the rival twins so that they could be brothers and not enemies. When Jacob says, "Because I have seen your face, which is like see-ing the face of God," he clearly means that Esau's face is a *reminder* of the divine countenance, of the Face that settles differences because it is not caught up in human differences. Esau is no longer god to Jacob, but he is a reminder of the God that accepts both brothers as distinct.

In a sense, it does appear that Esau is a kind of "god" to Jacob, for the plot line of the story indicates Jacob's fear of Esau. Moreover, Jacob humbles himself as if he were Esau's subject, not only bowing to him but also calling him "lord" (33:8, 13, 14, 15) and referring to himself as "your servant" (33:5). This is also probably an ironic touch in the narrative in light of the oracle to Rebecca ("the elder shall serve the younger") and Isaac's prophecy of Jacob's dominance (27:29, 40). But if at the narrative surface Jacob appears to grovel, at a deeper level the significance of the transformation at the Jabbok has taken away his need to contest anything with his brother. He can "return" the blessing and politely grant Esau the title of lord on Esau's turf because now his own destiny is clear, his own "lordship" has been affirmed.

The aftermath of the meeting with Esau could be viewed purely and simply as Jacob up to his old tricks. Esau wants Jacob to come with him to Seir, and Jacob promises to join him there after he makes a slower journey so that his children and the flocks will not be overtaxed. But when Esau leaves, Jacob journeys on to Canaan and builds an altar at Shechem, an altar that he calls "God, the God of Israel" (33:20). Again, even though this is deception at the narrative surface, we are prepared by now to accept the differentiation of Jacob and Esau that has taken place. They will henceforth be properly distinguished, Jacob in Canaan and Esau in Seir. Each must go his own way.

To conclude concerning the story of Jacob and Esau, the relation of the brothers is a model of mimetic desire and rivalry precisely because the brothers are twins, a factor that intensifies the rivalry and the need to differentiate the two. This need for differentiation functioned in Israel's traditions as a story of Israel's differentiation from its ancestral stock and relationships. At the same time it discloses that separation and identity can and should take place without violence. As already noted, in the Jacob model of origins, the hero's injury or disability is not primarily a sign of his outsider status and an indication of his fate as a victim. The figure of Jacob is basically different from the expelled hero or sacred king. Unlike the blindness of Oedipus, Jacob's limp is a sign of his success, a *sign that he has been victorious without scapegoating or being scapegoated.* The truth of the revelation to which the text bears witness (which, because of its debt to the myth of the unconscious and of endless signification, an analysis like Barthes's will not touch), is that there is an Other whose providential reality is necessary to liberation from victimization because this Other is beyond differences and accepts human creatures in spite of the differences they make between God and man and between each other.

C. Joseph and His Brothers: The Triumph of the Innocent Victim

Joseph's father Jacob doted on him "because he was the son of his old age" (Gen 37:3). This sounds as if he was the youngest of the sons, although we know that Benjamin was also born to Rachel before she died. The story probably intends, at this point, to set the context in terms of the older brother–younger brother conflict that we know from the Jacob story and can detect in the story of Isaac and his older half-brother Ishmael.

In any case, Jacob gave Joseph a long robe with sleeves, the kind of robe that was worn by Tamar and other royal princesses, according to 2 Samuel 13:18–19. Given that Joseph "brought a bad report of them to their father" (37:2) and received a robe from their father that was associated with royalty, it is no wonder the brothers hated him as much as Jacob loved him!

We do not know, of course, whether the unfavorable report was well founded. Probably the narrator intends for us to understand that it was. The Genesis narratives have already given more than an intimation of conflict in the family. Simeon and Levi had taken vengeance on the Shechemites for Shechem's rape of their sister Dinah (Gen 34). The anger of Simeon and Levi and the subsequent slaughter they committed were undoubtedly fueled by what they perceived to be lack of concern on Jacob's part. The reason was that Simeon and Levi, like their sister Dinah, were children of Leah, the unfavored wife (29:31–35). Another one of Leah's sons, her firstborn, Reuben, lay with Bilhah, concubine of Jacob (35:22). And in chapter 38 of Genesis, the parenthetical narrative that follows the opening of the Joseph story, we see that yet another son of Leah, Judah, married a Canaanite woman and was involved in an unseemly way in the life of his two sons Er and Onan and his daughter-in-law Tamar. The "blessing" of Jacob probably reflects a tangle of violence and criminal acts by some of the brothers.[36]

Nonetheless, the sense we get from the beginning of chapter 37 is that Joseph himself fed the rivalry among the brothers. The ill will brewing is brought to a crisis point when Joseph reports his dreams to them (37:5–11). In the first, they were all binding sheaves in the field; Joseph's sheaf stands upright, and the brothers' sheaves bow down to it. In the second, the sun, the moon, and eleven stars bow down to him. It is no wonder, then, that the brothers "envied him" (37:11). In other words, they began to see from his point of view. They not only desired the same object, namely, to rule the family, but they began to accept the truth of his dreams—that Joseph himself would be the ruler. So the plot of the story is known to the brothers, Joseph's rise to power and status, but they seek to abort it by expelling Joseph.

But before we turn to the expulsion once again, let us look further at the rivalry within the family. If Joseph's dreams precipitated the mimetic crisis, they certainly did not cause the rivalry and acquisitive mimesis that prevailed. The model of authority in the family is, of course, the father, the patriarch. His favoritism is obvious. By doting on Joseph and giving him a robe with royal connotations, he has already given a message that the dreams do nothing but confirm. Joseph is the one he has chosen. The dreams confirm that and probably suggest, in context, that he is God's chosen. Jacob rebukes Joseph for having or relating such dreams (37:10), but the narrator adds a note indicating that Jacob was not very displeased: "but his father kept the matter [the report of the second dream] in mind" (37:11).

Jacob sees himself—the future of Israel—in Joseph, and as a consequence this is what Joseph sees; he is simply imitating Jacob. And the brothers imitate Jacob and imitate Joseph in understanding their destiny as determined by Joseph. Joseph has indeed become their "god." Their own language comes close, at least, to identifying him as divine: he is a *baal ha-halomot*, a "lord of dreams," but his dreams will be ended if he is slain (37:19–20; the Hebrew "lord of dreams" is rendered simply "dreamer" in RSV and NRSV).

It should be remarked, however, that at least one of the brothers, Reuben, has maintained enough distance from the mimetic rivalry that the sacrificial crisis has not overwhelmed him. He persuades the others not to murder Joseph but to cast him into a pit. He expected then to rescue him. In what appears to be another version of how Joseph's life was spared, Judah persuades the brothers not to murder Joseph but to sell him to traders traveling to Egypt. It is Judah who later pleads for Benjamin and offers himself as a surrogate for their youngest brother. These attempts by Reuben and Judah show that the brothers do not form a unanimous lynch mob and that they are aware on some level that mob violence is wrong. Judah, of course, still wishes to expel his brother by selling him into slavery in a foreign land. Reuben's intervention, however, prevents the expulsion from being all against one. At the same time, it is another indication of the discord among the brothers that is the basic presupposition of the story of Joseph's expulsion.

But even if the brothers' intentions do not all amount to all against one, the effect is the same: "and they [the Ishmaelites] took Joseph to Egypt" (38:28). We have already observed in chapter 1 the similarity between sacrificial ritual and the brothers' strategy in communicating Joseph's disappearance to their father. Here I would pause to emphasize what a good example it is of the model of the exception in the process of emerging, which in turn clarifies the origins of language in the basic tropes of synecdoche, metonym, and metaphor.[37] (1) Joseph is the victim, the *synecdoche*, the part for the whole. If the master of dreams is eliminated, his dreams will not come to pass. The brothers, who otherwise would have been in conflict over the favor of their father, can now be secure through eliminating Joseph. (2) "Then they took Joseph's robe" (38:31a): the robe is the *metonym* both of Joseph, for it was associated with his person, and of the brothers as a group, for its connection with Joseph represents also an expression of the patriarchal favor by which they identify themselves. (3) "[A]nd killed a goat, and dipped the robe in the blood" (38:31b); the goat is a substitute for Joseph, and the blood is a metonym of the goat that is a substitute for Joseph. The robe dipped in goat's blood is now a *metaphor*; that is, a transfer of meaning has occurred that is based on a series of metonymic substitutions (Joseph–goat–blood–robe). The robe dipped in a goat's blood now "is" (i.e., carries the transferred meaning of) Joseph as the expelled brother.

Literally speaking, the brothers do not tell a story to Jacob. By the strategy of asking a certain kind of question, similar to the strategy of the serpent with the woman in Genesis, they elicit the answer they want from their father without putting their deception into words. They bring the bloodstained robe to their father and say, "This we have found. Please look at it. Is it the robe of your son or not?" (37:32; my translation). Jacob does exactly what the brothers request: "He looked at it and said, 'It is my son's robe'" (my translation). He then draws his own conclusion: "A wild animal has devoured him; Joseph is without doubt torn to pieces" (37:33). Jacob then tears his garments, puts on sackcloth, and mourns for his son. The outcome of the series of events from Jacob's point of view is that Joseph is torn to pieces, and he now mourns for Joseph. Insofar as Jacob and his sons are the Israel of the future, what Jacob believes about Joseph's fate *could* have become one more example of how myth, ritual, and prohibition typically work. A typical myth could have emerged. Joseph, the divinely gifted brother, was attacked and torn to death by a wild animal, and the "evidence" is the robe stained with his blood. In the course of the hypothetical ritual that reenacts the slaying, those playing the part of the brothers find the robe and take it to their father, who then begins the process of mourning. The ritual ends with an affirmation of the slain brother's divinity and the continued benefits he confers on the community. Since prohibition is the concomitant, and in some respects obverse, of sacrifice, the ritual undoes the taboo against murder and fratricide, then reaffirms it.

The Joseph story thus takes the side of Joseph in showing how Israel came to dwell in Egypt, but it also presents an Israelite version of collective violence, namely, the brothers against Joseph. A Girardian view of what lies behind mythic narrative is a schema like the following:[38]

1. A stable order prevails; there are no transgressions of prohibitions, and structures are intact. *All under one* (king, established order).
2. A crisis arises, whether enemy attack, plague, famine, transgression of prohibitions—in short, any denial or confusion of differences. The result is conflict and a mimetic crisis. *All against all.*
3. Exclusion or elimination of a victim. *All against one.*
4. Crisis is resolved; plague or whatever it is disappears. A new order is established. *All for all.*
5. The new order (whether identical or not with the old order), new ruler or ruler reestablished. *All under one.*

In the Joseph story this series of moments is enacted, but the narrator's sympathy is with Joseph, the expelled one, and clearly indicates that God stands with the innocent victim. This identification with the innocent victim entails a significant modification of moments 2, 3, and 4 of the structure, as follows:

1. Jacob and family are at peace in Canaan. Jacob is ruler of the clan under his God, the God of Israel.
2. A crisis of fraternal rivalry occurs that is occasioned by *(a)* Jacob's favoring of Joseph and *(b)* Joseph's dreams, which are interpreted by Joseph to mean he will be the ruler of his family. Joseph and his brothers are the same to the extent that they desire favor with the father and power over one another. And each desires this because the others desire it. We already know that Joseph is one of the two sons of Rachel, Jacob's favorite wife, and that two of the sons of Leah, Simeon and Levi, have caused trouble in the land of Canaan. In a subsequent crisis in Egypt, Joseph is cast into prison on a trumped-up charge of attempted rape. However, in both instances of expulsion we know quite definitely that the narrative point of view assumes that we will side with Joseph against his persecutors, *for the victim is really innocent.* The all against all is recognized in the story rather than being concealed.
3. The expulsion-sacrifice of Joseph and resulting peace in the family of Jacob. There is also, of course, a kind of peace in the family of Potiphar after Joseph has been imprisoned. But in both instances God enables Joseph to extricate himself and rise high in another setting, first in the family of Potiphar, then in the Egyptian court. *The one is liberated from the all-against-one that would destroy him.*
4. The family crisis is resolved, Joseph and his brothers and Joseph and his father are reunited. The situation is now all-for-all, but *it has been brought about by the innocent victim, who has become the one-for-all.*
5. There is a new situation in Egypt after the family reconciliation, Israel prospers, and Joseph is head of the family.

To review the Joseph story (Gen 37–50) with an eye to emphasizing its genera-tive model of the emerging exception who is the innocent victim that God favors, I would stress three points. First, mythological conventions would tend to exoner-ate the brothers and side with them in the initial conflict, just as they would blame Joseph in his relationship with Potiphar's wife.[39] The basic structure of the Joseph story is the same as that of well-known myths such as Oedipus the King—with the significant difference, of course, that the latter takes the side of the community against the victim–tragic hero. But Genesis 37 definitely holds the brothers to blame, with a partial exemption of Reuben and Judah, who at least want to spare their brother's life. Likewise, the accusation of rape made against Joseph is false.

Second, when Joseph uses trickery to accuse and arrest his younger brother, Benjamin, Judah offers himself in place of the lad, stating in a moving speech that he pledged himself to Jacob for the boy's safety and could not "see the evil that would come upon my father" (Gen 44:34). His willingness to become a victim as an act necessary to achieve the welfare of the community shows that Judah has come to grips with the violence of the family's past and is now willing to do something that runs counter to the all-against-one of collective violence that brought them to this moment of confrontation. In some respects the act of Judah anticipates the Suffering Servant of the Second Isaiah and Jesus as the Crucified in the Gospels.

Third, and finally, Joseph attempts to nullify the deification process. He for-gives his brothers, affirming instead God's hidden design, and he attempts to reunify the family by demanding that the brothers bring Jacob and the rest of the clan to Egypt (Gen 45:1–15). Later, after Jacob's death, the brothers fear that Joseph will want revenge for expelling him. Will the cycle of mimetic rivalry and vengeance continue? They present themselves to him and fall prostrate before him. In a revealing word of reassurance, Joseph says, "Fear not! For am I in the place of God? But as for you, you meant evil against me, but God meant it for good, in order to bring about the survival of a great people, as it is this day" (Gen 50:19–20, my translation). "*For am I in the place of God?*" Joseph's denial that he is in the place of God breaks, in principle, the victimization mechanism.[40] If in mythology the victim is deified as the sacred victim, this is not the case here. He is simply their brother—with power and status, indeed, but not a god. As such, as the brother whose dreams have come true, "he reassured them, speaking kindly to them" (Gen 50:21).

Joseph, then, is an important instance of the model of the emerging exception. He is the signifier and signified, the point of differentiation, inasmuch as he was the scapegoat for his brothers' conflict, subjected to their collective violence, cast into the pit, and "expelled" or "exiled" by being sold to Ishmaelites or Midianites who "took him down" into Egypt. The brothers' ruse of taking his magnificent robe and dipping it in the blood of a goat they killed is a perfect example of an act that is parallel to a ritual substitution, but in this case, of course, the substitution does not work. The brothers want to present the death as an accident, and the bloodstained robe is evidence thereof that they present to their father. The presentation of the robe and the story that attends it are an obvious cover-up, but if viewed from the standpoint of ritual, this combination of robe and story amount to an "expelling of the expulsion" of their brother, a narration that removes deliberate elimination of Joseph and leaves an accident in its place. It is therefore doubly ironic when they eventually see him as a kind of god and he has to reassure them that he is human and has good intentions toward them.

The strategy of the brothers is structurally comparable to any conscious or unconscious procedure, whether religious or scholarly, whereby one focuses on the *substitutes that by their very mode of expression conceal as much as they reveal*. But the biblical text itself, as in the tale of Cain and Abel, stands as a continuing witness to thwart such attempts to conceal a lynching. It both thwarts such attempts and points to a renewed human community whose necessary condition is the unveiling of the victimization mechanism.

How would the Joseph story look from an "Egyptian" perspective? There were references to Moses and Joseph in the works of Egyptian authors writing in Greek in the Hellenistic period. We have, in fact, much more of such material on Moses and the exodus than on Joseph, and this exodus material will be discussed in the next chapter. It is instructive, however, to take note of the two references to Joseph. Pompeius Trogus, writing evidently at the turn of the eras about the Seleucid monarchy, speaks of Joseph as a "master of the arts of magic" and as "the first to establish the science of interpreting dreams; and nothing indeed of divine or human law seemed to have been unknown to him." His knowledge was so great "that his admonitions seemed to proceed, not from a mortal, but a god."[41] The tendency to divinize the victim is precisely what happens when the sacrifice—in this case sacrificial expulsion—is successful. It is likely that Egyptian and Greek authors, reading the ancient Judaic tradition through their own mythical lens, unconsciously changed the Joseph story by placing it within their own frame of reference.

The other reference to Joseph in this late literature is made by the Greco-Egyptian writer Chaeremon (first century C.E.). He makes reference to the people, 250,000 in all, whom the king of Egypt banished in order to purge Egypt of its contaminated population. Their leaders were two sacred scribes, Moses and Joseph, whose Egyptian names were Tisithen and Peteseph, respectively.[42]

The tradition on which rest Pompeius's and Chaeremon's references to Joseph shows the tendency of a culture to appropriate an expelled victim-deity for its own mythical tradition. Joseph the victim of his brothers was a sacred scribe, perhaps even a god; therefore, he must have been an Egyptian! We will see the same tendency in the Greco-Egyptian version of the exodus.

In other words, from the standpoint of mythic structure, the "Egyptian" mythical perspective is that (1) the kingdom was united and stable under the king until (2) the social and political order was contaminated by a group of marginal people,

(3) who had to be banished. (4) When this expulsion occurred, peace returned, and (5) all were united under king and government again. In this Egyptian version the quality of divinity attaches particularly to Joseph (more than to Moses) because of his ability to practice magical arts and to interpret dreams. Joseph is thus an Egyptian gone awry, and although the Egyptian version does not divinize the entire group of Hebrews, Joseph is retained in the mythical tradition as a kind of divinity-victim.

By contrast, behind Israel's image of Joseph and his triumph lies Israel's struggle with its own identity based on a particular revelation of the God of justice who sides with the victim—an identity that had to be hammered out on the anvil of history. Joseph's own ability to understand the story-history of which he is a part and to accept the wisdom of the guiding God enables him to forgive his brothers and reunite the family of Jacob in Egypt.

D. Patterns in the Brother Stories

In the Torah and elsewhere in the Hebrew Bible there are many brothers who are significant in ancient Israelite traditions. In some instances they figure only in passing, although reference to them usually indicates some issue or conflict that is being treated. Besides the brother narratives on which readings have already been given there are also Isaac and Ishmael, Perez and Zerah, Ephraim and Manasseh, Moses and Aaron, Nadab and Abihu (replaced by the younger Eleazar), and David and his brothers. The narratives do not generally focus on their relationship in the same intense manner as the stories of Cain and Abel, Jacob and Esau, and Joseph and his brothers. The one exception to this is the relation of Moses to Aaron, but I will comment on that in the next chapter.

When one looks at all the brother narratives and references in the Hebrew Bible, certain elements stand out and form a pattern. These elements are the younger brother as a shepherd, the younger brother as favored by one or both parents and by God, and the displacement of the older brother followed by the ordeal of the younger and some sort of reconciliation or reintegration of the two.

1. The younger brother is a shepherd (Abel, Jacob, Joseph [although his brothers are also presented as shepherds], Moses, David). The older brother may be a farmer (Cain) or a hunter (Esau) or function as a warrior (David's brothers), but the younger brother is a shepherd. This is one of those typical elements that signal to the reader-hearer that the personage is divinely favored.[43] Why a shepherd? According to the Genesis tradition of the ancestors of Israel, they were seminomadic sheepherders and cattle herders, so it could be a way of asserting the priority of the patriarchal way of life. It is also a fact that in the ancient Near East "shepherd" was a common title, so the word may be a code term for the favored one who is destined to rule. The presence of such a code is particularly evident in the Jacob-Esau narratives.

2. The younger brother is always the favored one—the "chosen." That is, the narrative point of view sides with the younger, and God prefers him. This element was so deeply imprinted in the Israelite tradition that it undoubtedly was felt necessary to include it even in stories where order of birth was not a primary issue in the account. For example, in the narrative portions of Exodus, Leviticus, and Numbers one cannot tell and it does not seem to matter which is the older, Moses or Aaron. However, the priestly genealogy lists Aaron first (Exod 6:20), implying that he is the elder.[44] Their respective age status is confirmed in Exodus 7:7, where it is noted that when Moses and Aaron first appear before Pharaoh, Moses is eighty years old and Aaron is eighty-three. Putting Aaron's name first in the genealogy was probably a conventional response to Moses' pride of place in the story of Israel's beginnings. Another likely instance of the conventional use of this literary device, though in this case more deliberately done, is found in the birth of Perez and Zerah. According to Genesis 38:27–30, Zerah was actually the firstborn, in the sense of the one making "the first opening of the womb" (*peter rechem*, see Exod 13:2, 12, 15). He got as far as sticking out a hand, around which the midwife tied a scarlet thread. But he drew back his hand, and his twin brother came out. This brother who was not the *peter rechem* was named Breach, Hebrew *perets*. This is a strange little account in which undifferentiation reigns.[45] Concerning the scarlet thread tied to Zerah's hand, the word in Hebrew is simply *shani*, "scarlet." It could be used by itself for material dyed in scarlet, as in 2 Samuel 1:24; however, the usage here is reminiscent of *ha-adom ha-adom*, "the red, the red," as stated by Esau to Jacob (Gen 25:30). As "the red, the red" signals the sacrificial nature of the transaction between Esau and Jacob, so, I would suggest, the scarlet in Genesis 38:28 is probably a metonym of blood and a sign that Zerah the younger is to be exchanged for Perez the older. This development appears to be an attempt to turn the brother known as the older into the younger. In Numbers 26:19–22 Perez is listed before Zerah, which, as I have said, is a probable sign of seniority. I suspect the Genesis tale makes of him the younger because he was known as an ancestor of David (Ruth 4:18–22), and someone who figures importantly in the genealogy of the great king has to meet conventional requirements. So, according to mythical type, Perez must have really been the younger.

3. As the chosen one, the younger brother typically displaces the older as the recipient of God's favor and, in the stories of the patriarchs, the recipient of special blessing and the promises made to Abraham. The displaced older brother is, however, still shown to be enfolded in God's care, as in the promise that Ishmael will become a great nation (Gen 21:18), in Jacob's transfer of the gift-blessing to Esau (Gen 33:11), and in the final reconciliation of Joseph and his brothers. This connection of the older brother to God's care and to the life of the chosen one is very important, for otherwise the older brother would be simply an innocent victim of literary and theological determinism. This reading of texts is not based on structuralist or deconstructionist premises, so my inference is that such determinism

both reflects and affects historical reality. Since the motif of the youngest son as the favored one is so deeply embedded in the tradition, the oldest son would be simply a sacrifice to the youngest in Israel's interpretation of its history if it were not for the qualifications of this tendency that appear in the narratives.

The motif of the victory or achievement of the younger brother is well known in myth and folklore.[46] Hans J. L. Jensen has observed that this motif in biblical literature could be construed as a variant of the younger brother's achievement of the difficult task that his older brothers are not able to accomplish.[47] I think there is no question that a universal mythic motif has been employed, but how and with what import for understanding the biblical stories?

The response in general must be that the motif of the younger brother's accomplishment has been enlarged and modified to serve as the vehicle of the history of Israel's foundations as God's covenant people. The younger son's glory does not lie simply in the reversal of fortune or the surprise that the youngest could win out;[48] it resides rather in a powerful vision of the human condition and God's revelation of a new form of community through Israel. The unlikelihood of the younger son's accomplishment undoubtedly plays a part in this vision, as Israel is identified with those who are weak or marginal or are outsiders. But this substratum of the common mythic motif is expanded and deepened through narrative insight into mimesis and the expansion of God's promises into the center of the plot and the national destiny.

The enemy brother narratives of the Hebrew Bible begin to open up the meaning of mimetic desire, which can only be understood in connection with the disclosure of the innocent victim. This is not done, of course, in the form of abstract definitions, but is articulated in the drama of interactions between the characters in the stories. The two clearest instances of the revelation of mimetic desire in Genesis appear in the Cain and Abel tale and at the beginning of the Joseph story.

When Cain is in the midst of anger and depression over his rejected sacrifice, God tells him, "Sin is crouching at the door; its desire is for you, but you must master it" (Gen 4:7).[49] The connection of this image to the pronouncement of the women's fate in Genesis 3:16 is patent. There the woman is told, "Your desire shall be for your husband, and he shall rule over you." Desire in this sense has to do with mastery or rule of what is desired by the rival other, but the object of desire is really secondary to identifying oneself by the criterion of the other, who governs the subject's view of himself or herself. If one becomes attached to the other in a relation of mimetic desire, conflictual mimesis results. That is, in seeing oneself mimetically through the other's eyes, one must try to be what the other is while maintaining the insurmountable "otherness" of the other that allows one to gauge oneself, to attain differentiation. The greater the preoccupation with the other as model-obstacle, the more one is ruled by the other. In 4:7 this desire is personified as *chattat*, "sin," whose etymology is a root meaning to miss a goal or way, to err, to go astray.[50] Going astray is like a beast or demon that "desires" the subject, but that must be mastered lest it completely overcome one. But this metaphorical personification describes something that is real only in relationships, and in this context it is the rivalry of Cain with Abel. If Cain does not rule it, he will be conflictually subject to the other as the woman is to the man in Genesis 3.

The Joseph story may be viewed as a series of self-fulfilling prophecies that are produced by conflictual mimesis. Of course, the reader is to understand that God is working through human mimesis to bring about a good end, but seen at a human level each event produces another in a mimetic series. Jacob dotes on Joseph, which angers the brothers. Joseph relates his dreams in which *he rules* his brothers and parents. The dreams could be construed as presupposing and reversing the brothers' desire to dominate him and have the favor of their father. Even Jacob worries about Joseph's dreams, for it is quite clear that his son believes he will displace his father as the head of the family. As a result of the dreams, which are the final straw for the brothers, Joseph is cast into a pit and is taken to Egypt as a slave to be sold. But of course, if the father had not been doting and the brothers jealous, Joseph would not have ended up in Egypt and finally in a position to save his clan!

The outcome of mimetic desire is that Joseph *does* rule his brothers, but the process of conflict and expulsion is ended in two ways: (1) Joseph reveals himself after an initial reconciliation occurs when Judah offers himself in place of their youngest brother, Benjamin. (2) Joseph twice forgives his brothers and breaks the spell of the brothers' tendency to deify him, which had been in effect from the beginning of the story. "Fear not, for am I in the place of God?"

This conflictual mimesis is at the root of culture; it dominates human relations. But from the standpoint of the Torah it has to be placed in the context of the story of Abraham and his descendants. The promises of God to Abraham (Gen 12:1–3, 7) become the frame of reference for working out a new human destiny that would witness to the revelation of the God of Israel who is the God of victims. Cain's rivalry with Abel is a paradigm of the human condition, but the outcome of the stories of Jacob and Joseph show the way of a good mimesis that is enacted through the story of the promises.

It is not as if the displaced or excluded older brother is simply sacrificed to the way of the chosen one; he is rather redeemed or "won back" for the larger story. The reconciliation of Jacob and Esau and Joseph and his brothers is a model of the process of reintegration of what has been excluded. The Hebrew Bible does retain, it is true, a certain degree of exclusion of the other and a line of differentiation between Israel and non-Israel. Within these limits, however, the biblical text achieves a remarkable degree of reintegration of the "unchosen one." Ishmael, though expelled, is to become a great people in his own right; Esau likewise. And even Egypt is recognized more positively in the tradition than is commonly noted.

There is, for instance, no hint of aspersion cast on Joseph's sons Ephraim and Manasseh, even though their mother is Egyptian (Gen 41:50). In fact, according to the later Jewish law that the child's identity is taken from its mother, these two Joseph tribes would be Egyptian! One of the outcomes of the struggle with the question of Israel's identity vis-à-vis the foreign or enemy other is the statute in Deuteronomy 23:7: "You shall not abhor an Edomite, for he is your brother; you shall not abhor an Egyptian, because you were a sojourner in his land. The children of the third generation that are born to them may enter the assembly of the LORD" (RSV). This is far from a warm and immediate welcome of the Egyptian and the Edomite into the assembly of the God of Israel. The community has its lines of demarcation that give it identity in relation to other peoples, and quite clearly a sort of genealogical "purification" process must take place before these two peoples may become members of the holy people. Nonetheless, the relationship of Israel to Edom and Egypt is recognized and affirmed, and exclusion on the basis of genealogy or race is undercut.

It is important also to emphasize that the favored brother is not exempt from the sacrificial structures that the world imposes. The younger son must also go through the scapegoating ordeal. Isaac is placed on the altar; Jacob is beset by the divine adversary; Joseph is expelled and enslaved; Moses is attacked by the LORD; David faces Goliath: these are endangerments that the chosen one must undergo. As I have intimated in the comment on the Joseph story in this section of the chapter, one way to construe the endangerment of the chosen younger brother is to see it as a necessary aspect of the mimetic process in which he himself participates and for which he must pay a certain price of redemption. It is no narrative accident that Abraham is commanded to sacrifice Isaac (Gen 22) after the expulsion of Hagar and Ishmael (Gen 21:8–21) or that Jacob wrestles with the divine adversary before he meets Esau and reenters the land of Canaan. After Jacob's gift of the long-sleeved robe and Joseph's dreams, Joseph must undergo a threefold "descent": into a pit, into Egypt, and into prison.

In other words, if the older brother is displaced or eliminated from the genealogical line in which the promises are transmitted, still the younger brother must undergo a sacrificial ordeal. The similarities between the ordeals of the younger brothers and ritual sacrifice have been pointed out in the stories of Jacob and Joseph. The connection is also quite evident in the binding of Isaac (Gen 22) and the divine attack on Moses (Exod 4:24–26). In the former, Abraham is stopped from sacrificing his son at the last moment, and a ram caught in a nearby thicket is offered in Isaac's stead. In the little tale relating the LORD's attack on Moses, Moses is saved by his wife, who circumcises their son and touches Moses' "feet" (perhaps genitals) with the foreskin.[51]

A narrative poetics of these texts and any similar to them must deal with a ritual process. That is, at certain points in narrative time before the next series of significant events can occur, the authors felt it necessary to subject the chosen one to an ordeal that had a ritual character. This is not to say with the structuralists and deconstructionists that we are dealing here only with codes and traces behind which there is nothing, an absence, the lack of a center. Nor is it to say with the mythicopsychologists, whether of Freudian, Jungian, or some other variety, that the events narrated are fantasaic projections of psychic life. These two positions convey certain insights, but they are doubles of each other; their upshot is historical irrelevance and, usually, the expulsion or displacement of the Holy Scriptures.[52] Although I do not think most of our stories are "historical" in the usual modern sense—pertaining to a series or narrative of events that are "factual," that are derived from witness according to sense perception—I believe that the reader can trust that real events, real people, and above all a real involvement with divine disclosure of justice and victimization lie behind the text. This struggle with God's revelation in human history has been arranged in a certain way, and this way includes a kind of ritual of storytelling, writing, and reading.

In order to clarify this point, I would first repeat the definition of ritual given in chapter 1:

> Ritual reenacts and thus represents to the group the unifying energy of the founding moment. It reenacts the crisis in such a way that it is emptied of all real violence in order to arrive at the resolution, the production of peace through the death or expulsion that produced peace in the first place. Ritual is a process in which a community goes into a mock mimetic crisis. It differentiates sacred time— the occasion of the festival or observance—from ordinary time, and within the reenactment of sacred time it represents the necessary differentiations, the threat to these differentiations, and the overcoming of this threat. One way to describe it is to say that ritual undoes prohibition and then reestablishes it. The danger lying behind the prohibition, mimetic desire and mimetic rivalry, is embodied by the victim, whose status as divine validates the community and confirms its identity.

As a sort of ritual process, these moments of endangerment of the chosen one are a kind of mock mimetic crisis for the community. They "undo the prohibition" (i.e., You shall not murder the founder or deny the divine promises the founder embodies) and reaffirm the promises of God as the foundation of the sacred community. The status of the promises and the struggle to overcome the victimization mechanism means that the foundation of the covenant people is not established, in principle, on the death of victim who is deified. The victim–chosen one survives his ordeal, and even the displaced older brother has a significant place within divine providence and in relation to Israel.

It is true, of course, that the Israelite tradition was aware of ancient murders that in some fashion had a founding significance. The story of Cain and Abel bears all the signs of just such a founding story, but we must stress that the beginnings of civilization as related in Genesis 4 are quite clearly distinguished from the emergence of Israel from the nations. Whatever the ancestors of Israel may have known and experienced historically, the total story of beginnings witnesses to the attempt to master mimetic desire, rivalry, and scapegoating. In addition to the story of Cain and Abel, the strange little account of the death of Nadab and Abihu (Lev 10:1–7) may reflect a struggle for priestly power that was marked by violence (see chapter 4). But this event was not allowed to become a founding moment for Israel, and it was hedged about with substitutions that sought to minimize the effects of violence and human sacrifice.

E. The Prodigal Son and the Faithful Son

The New Testament preserves an account of brother rivalry in the parable of the prodigal son, Luke 15:11–32. It is worth pausing here to look at this story, not so much to clarify the situation of the younger son as to understand the reaction of the older son and the father's response to him.

The Christian tradition has focused on the younger son, and in English the parable is usually titled "the Prodigal Son." German Bibles and scholars are accustomed to calling it "der Verlorene Sohn" (the Lost Son).[53] As many recent commentators have pointed out, it could well be called "the Loving Father" or "the Forgiving Father," for the father's responses to the two sons dominate the parable. The Christian tradition has also been inclined to see the two sons as an allegory of Christianity and Judaism; whatever Jesus' intention in some original form of the parable, it does appear that Luke uses it to comment on the relationship of the Jewish tradition to the new religion (note also Luke 16:19–31, the parable of the rich man and Lazarus), but that point need not detain us. The primary concern in the present context is to show how one source in the early Christian tradition handles the ancient theme of rivalry between brothers.

The parable may be divided into three parts: (1) the younger son's departure with his inheritance and his life abroad, verses 11–19; (2) his return and the father's welcome, verses 20–24; (3) the older son's angry reaction and the father's reassurance, verses 25–32. The traditional focus on the younger son is understandable in that the Christian tradition was concerned with repentance and identified Christianity with the younger son.[54] The older son has been viewed as churlish and as a typical picture of the Pharisee who does not rejoice over the one who "was lost, and is found" (15:32). Nonetheless, this son who is angry and refuses to enter the house to celebrate with the others is not condemned by the father. His father goes outside to entreat him, in a gesture parallel to running to embrace the lost son who returned. The older son complains that he has served the father faithfully and has never disobeyed his command. He has, in other words, observed the positive side of the prohibition of parricide by remaining obedient to his father's commands. Yet—yet he has never been rewarded with a big party that included the preparation of a young goat to eat.

It is striking that the older son emphasizes the animal prepared for the banquet. There were other things that could be mentioned: for instance, the nicest robe and the signet ring given to his brother, which are signs of restored status. He speaks of a "kid" that was never prepared for him, but it is the "fatted calf" that the father orders for the wayward son (15:23, 27, 30). One gets the impression that the older son is saying, "You never had *even a kid* dressed for me." In this comparison arising out of conflictual mimesis, there is probably both a trace of sacrificial practice and an allusion to the brother stories in Genesis. The fatted calf (*ho moschos ho siteutos*) was a young bull, widely known as an animal used for sacrifice (Heb 9:12; see the Greek translation of Judg 6:25; note *moscharion* in Gen 18:7). On the other hand, the word for kid or young goat, *eriphos*, is also used in the Greek translation of the stories of Jacob and Joseph. In the first instance Jacob takes Isaac the meat of two kids and wears their hair on his hands and neck; in the second case the brothers kill a kid, smear its blood on Joseph's fine robe, and take it to Jacob as evidence that he was slain by a wild animal. Since the older brother is angrily expressing his disappointment, which is emotionally synonymous with having been deceived,[55] this allusion becomes even more likely.

The trace of a sacrificial crisis and the ritual of sacrifice undoubtedly remains in the father's act of ordering immediately that the fatted calf be killed. The kind of celebration involved in this dinner or banquet probably has its origins in sacrifice, which may have been the primary occasion for eating meat for our human ancestors.[56] If the younger son had directly rebelled against his father, which the parable does not actually say, then we would have little trouble identifying the banquet upon his return as part of a sacrificial ritual of receiving him back into the family with full sonship status. As it is, the willingness of the father to let him leave with his portion of the inheritance and his true joy over his return home overwhelm all but a barest trace of the sacrificial aspect of the feast. But the older brother wants to hold on to that trace of sacrifice, which is never, after all, very far away from the exchange of gifts. If the father had offered the gift of a fatted calf, why had he never been offered an animal as an exchange that would symbolize *his* worth in the father's eyes?

To revert to a point made at the beginning of this discussion of the parable, it is crucial that its center is the father. The brothers are called sons on every occasion except two: when the servant informs the older son about the celebration and when the father makes his final pronouncement. The older son is so furious he cannot speak of the younger son as his brother, but says to his father, "But when this son of yours came, who has devoured your living with harlots, you killed for him the fatted calf!" (15:30, RSV). He is on the verge of imitating his younger brother by doing something drastic that will sadden his father; the rewards are clearly great, as witness what happened when the younger son returned home! But the father himself does not act mimetically. He does not retaliate for the older son's anger against him, just as he does not punish the younger for having left home and wasted his inheritance. Instead, he tells his older son, "Son, you are always with me, and all that is mine is yours" (15:31).

The father is not one who makes differences, who establishes categories of reward and punishment, who sees his sons as rivals for his affection, his prestige, his property. The differences of rivalry, of comparison, of exclusion are in the mind of the older son. He thought he could earn his father's good graces and the family property by acting as a servant to his father ("these many years I have served [*douleuo*] you"). The Greek verb has the same root as *doulos*, "servant" or "slave." The younger son's mimetic burden was just as great as his older brother's, for he thought that his wastrel escapades had probably earned him, if his father received him back at all, the lowly status of a *misthios* or hired day laborer.[57] In other words, he would deserve the revenge or retaliation from his father. As the parable ends, the focus is on the older son, but both sons have a basic choice to make: will they see themselves in terms of their father's love or not?

Excursus: Folkloristic Approaches to the Bible

In the first two chapters I have made a number of references to extrabiblical myth and folklore, especially as collected and treated by Frazer, Gaster, and Propp. Stith Thompson's indexes of motifs and types of folktales is also quite helpful in looking for tales and narrative elements comparable to biblical stories. Using this rich array of material enables the interpreter to determine how and where the biblical texts draw upon common, sometimes universal motifs and modify them in various ways as they are adapted to the concerns of the biblical writers. It goes without saying that this process of borrowing and adaptation is of enormous interest not only to anthropological but also to literary approaches to biblical texts.

The problem is that these anthropological and literary approaches typically share in the general critical ignoring or denying of the sacrificial function of religion and, concomitantly, of the distinctive contribution of the Bible. In the last twenty years biblical scholars interested in comparative religion and folklore are not usually "positivists" like Sir James G. Frazer, who collected evidence he viewed largely as rank superstition; for researchers of his ilk, the authority of the Bible is undercut if it can be shown that comparable material is to be located outside the Bible. Many recent biblical scholars tend instead to be "structuralists," in the sense that they focus on types, conventions, and codes and eschew the validity of the search for origins. The empirical and historical reality of the victimization mechanism and its sacrificial outlets cannot be allowed to surface as a significant focus of inquiry. One cannot get behind the code—which, when all is said and done, is a mental or symbolic reality that is posited as prior to act and event.[58]

A case in point is a book that is excellent in its own right: *Underdogs and*

Tricksters: A Prelude to Biblical Folklore, by Susan Niditch.[59] Niditch surveys the important work in comparative folklore, particularly with reference to the "trickster," and brings it to bear in a reading of the wife-sister, Jacob, Joseph, and Esther stories that is richly textured and illuminating. Nevertheless, her argument flounders for two reasons.

First, her understanding of trickster mythology is determined by modern anthropology, which is generally unwilling to deal with the question of the role of sacrifice in culture. The trickster is a "gross deceiver, crude prankster, creator of the earth, a shaper of culture, a fool caught in his own lies."[60] The trickster is a liminal figure, "undifferentiated" in that he is often depicted as man-woman or human-animal; he is typically a wanderer.[61] "The trickster is a subtype of the underdog. A fascinating and universal folk hero, the trickster brings about change through trickery."[62] She is undoubtedly right in maintaining that trickster myths become available for use in entertainment and in subverting social systems for those who are "underdogs." But what she fails to see is the roots of trickster mythology in the victimization mechanism and scapegoating. All the trickster traits and functions can be adequately explained by the Girardian model. The trickster represents "the paradox of the god who is helpful because he is harmful, a force of order because he creates disorder. Apart from the gods who do evil unwittingly and the gods who are forced irresistibly to do evil, there is inevitably a third solution, the god who enjoys doing evil and is amused by it. Although he always helps in the end, he is delighted when things go badly and continues to enjoy it. He is known for his games . . . he justifies every *effort to correct* and, by virtue of these efforts, he is transformed into a benefactor."[63]

The trickster embodies "one of the two great theologies to evolve as a result of the sacralization of the scapegoat: the theology of *divine caprice*. The other theology is *divine anger*." The latter is more profound than the former in that "it introduces the rare idea [to communities] that their scapegoat is not the only incarnation of violence. The community shares the responsibility for evil with the god; it begins to be guilty of its own disorders."[64] Profound as it is, however, the theology of divine anger still does not succeed in unraveling the persecution at the heart of the scapegoat mechanism.

Second, Niditch's treatment leads to "cultural assumptions" and "cultural expectation," where the scapegoat mechanism is concealed or denied. "[W]e look to composers at home in a tradition, weaving tales out of familiar narrative threads for audiences who identify with the same set of cultural assumptions. The interest in composers leads away from composite sources and to the treatment of narrative wholes as they now stand. Folklore, biblical form-criticism, and composition-criticism thus meet on a boundary marked by the signpost of literary creativity circumscribed by cultural expectation."[65] What one learns is something about cultural assumptions and cultural expectation. "Literary creativity"—the only value of biblical texts that really remains—is what affords the texts a certain distinctiveness.

Niditch goes on to ask important questions and to make significant observations. In fact, in my estimation her sort of "structuralism" could be very creative if it were modified and combined with a model that postulated the generation of mythic and cultural codes from real acts and experiences of human beings.[66] As it is, Niditch's work is circumscribed by the boundaries of cultural assumptions and cultural expectation. The "search for Ur-forms" is eschewed.[67] The subject of study and the conclusions drawn show connections and differences, but have no center. This becomes strikingly clear in her concluding paragraph:

> Tales of underdogs and tricksters ultimately deal with fundamental aspects of individual and group identity, such as authority and empowerment, stasis and change. The study of traditional narrative patterns points to interconnections between the layered material of story and the patinas of human behavior. Israelite tales of unlikely heros reflect the worldviews of a variety of authors and audiences but also provide options for modern readers and appropriators. Folklore, the field of study and the material studies, sensitizes us to the complex webs of content and meaning linking our stories and ourselves.[68]

In this interesting paragraph I surmise two contestants for bedrock reality: structural realities that are encoded in various ways (individual and group identity, stasis and change, empowerment and authority) and ourselves. These two realities are put against the backgroup of "human behavior," but it is clear that the encoding transmitted in story is foundational in relation to "the patinas of human behavior." However one utilizes the word *patina*, its core meaning has to be that of a surface reality, a film, an encrustation—almost a parasite in relation to the host material. The "linking of our stories and ourselves" is a human task at the core of our work in biblical studies, theology, and the humanities. But insofar as it is merely providing "options for modern readers and appropriators" it seems to be the same thing as providing differences—of reinforcing the sacrificial reign of *différance*.[69] The human chaos, the problem and fear of undifferentiation that myth and ritual convey, are lost to this perspective.

The enemy brother stories, permeated though they may be with universal folklore motifs and functions, raise a question about all processes of sacrifice, including the reign of *différance*. To ignore that is to ignore or expel our origins.

3

Moses and the Exodus

It was
Murder that brought the plague-wind on the city.
Sophocles, *Oedipus the King*

Ah, the net
Of incest, mingling fathers, brothers, sons,
With brides, wives, mothers: the last evil
That can be known by men.
Sophocles, *Oedipus the King*

I have seen the affliction of my people who are in Egypt, and have heard
their cry because of their taskmasters; I know their sufferings, and I have come
down to deliver them out of the hand of the Egyptians.
Exodus 3:7–8

In this chapter I will first survey the story of Moses and the Israelites from the
beginning of the Book of Exodus through the exodus itself and the initial period
in the Sinai wilderness, focusing on mimesis and violence. (The covenant and sacrificial worship will be taken up in chapter 4.) Then I will deal with an "Egyptian"
mythic view of Moses and the Exodus, discussing in particular the interpretation
of that great modern mythmaker, Sigmund Freud. The tendency to mythicize
persecution or to revert to myth in coping with conflict is such a powerful human
tendency, I felt obliged to highlight this tendency, which may be extracted from
both ancient and modern intellectual history.

A. The Exodus: Crisis and Liberation

1. Introduction: The Sacrificial Crisis

The story of Joseph comes to a happy ending of sorts at the end of the book of
Genesis, but soon there arises an Egyptian king "who did not know Joseph" (Exod
1:8). The Hebrews had prospered in the age of Joseph, but then, as they increased
in number, they were perceived as a threat to the Egyptians. The Egyptian king
decrees a policy of oppressive labor and even goes so far as to try to kill all newborn males of the Hebrews. The infant Moses is hidden by his mother and discovered by the daughter of the king, who raises him as her son. Moses becomes the

leader of the Hebrews, and after a series of plagues, which reach a climax in the slaying of Egypt's firstborn sons, the Hebrews are allowed to leave. Thereupon they are pursued by the Egyptians, who have changed their mind about releasing them, and they escape miraculously through the Sea of Reeds. They ascribe their liberation to the God who revealed himself to Moses, the God who says, "I have observed the misery of my people who are in Egypt; I have heard their cry on account of their taskmasters. Indeed, I know their sufferings, and I have come down to deliver them from the Egyptians, and to bring them up out of that land to a good and broad land" (Exod 3:7–8a). The people's journey through the wilderness is punctuated with conflict and rebellion, but finally they arrive at Sinai where YHWH God of Israel reveals his law to Moses and a covenant is enacted between YHWH and the people.

The traditions layered and intertwined in this story are many and complex, but there are discernible threads that enable us to grasp its unity. One thread is the outbreak of oppression and violence against a non-Egyptian minority people perceived as a security threat (Exod 1:10). Why an Egyptian king would decree the policy of slaying all Hebrew newborn male children is difficult to understand. My hypothesis concerning a historical core behind this story is that there was an actual experience of oppression and violence that has been shaped in this way in order to achieve total symmetry in the exodus story. The reigning monarchy, caught up in envy of a growing minority population perceived to be rivals of Egyptian power, no longer observed the ancient differences of law and order, which means that the order of things established in sacrifice, prohibition, and myth was threatened by change of some sort. The Egyptian government probably executed some "Hebrews"; we surmise in any case that the indigenous people were affected tremendously by the invasion and rule of the "Hyksos" about 1725–1575 B.C.E. John Wilson has noted "the real change which this foreign domination made in the national psychology: the real change from a confident sense of domestic security to an aggressive sense of national peril."[1] The exodus tradition probably preserves at its core the endangerment of some of the ancestors of Israel that occurred as the result of the anxiety and insecurity that characterized Egyptian culture and government after the Hyksos period.

The Exodus text as we have it narrates a process of struggle to witness to the revelation of the innocent victim. The plight and the liberation of an oppressed people, and first of all their little ones, the newborn male children, are at the heart of the story. The innocent victim, if not recognized as such by the political powers, must have a defender, an advocate, and that defender in Exodus is the God of Abraham, of Isaac, of Jacob, and of Moses. But the disclosure of the innocent victim and the God of victims does not come about quickly and easily. It requires a long and tortuous history with numerous setbacks, for mimesis, rivalry, and violence are embedded in the symbols and institutions of the archaic cultural settings out of which Israel's forebears come.

2. Mimetic Rivalry and Plague

But would the Egyptians have resorted to infanticide? That may seem unlikely historically, although we know that in myth, literature, and ritual, plague is associated with complete social and religious breakdown, of which the slaying of infants is one manifestation.[2] What we find pictured in the exodus story is a situation of chaos, of undifferentiation, in which various mimetic rivalries run through the accounts like wild electric currents.

a. Israel (or "the Hebrews") Versus Egypt. The text presents the rivalry between Israel and Egypt as based in the new king's desire to dominate at least the land of Egypt, if not also foreign states, "lest [the Israelites] multiply, and, if war befall us, they join our enemies and fight against us and escape from the land" (Exod 1:10). From the standpoint of the story, this arch-rivalry produced the opposite effect: the Israelite population increased even more, and the Egyptians were in dread of them (Exod 1:12).

b. Moses Versus Pharaoh. The rivalry of Moses and Pharaoh is parallel to that of Israel and Egypt. Moses, raised as an Egyptian, kills an Egyptian who was beating a Hebrew (2:11). "When Pharaoh heard of it, he sought to kill Moses" (2:15), which is the occasion of Moses' flight and attachment to the Midianites. Later, as the leader of the oppressed people, he confronts Pharaoh in the plague narratives, which culminate in the slaying of Egypt's firstborn (chaps. 7–12). The king's refusal to release the Hebrews is ascribed over and over again to the hardening of his heart by the LORD. What occurs in chapters 7–12 is a process that has its counterpart in ritual: the total fabric of social order is rent; the prohibition that protects the network of differentiation is to be, in dramatic fashion, completely and utterly undone. This prohibition could be articulated in the words of the apodictic law that applied to Israelite society: "You shall not revile God, or curse a leader of your people" (Exod 22:28). The authority of gods and king is called directly into question. The story says, in effect, that the God of Israel sustains the Pharaoh's refusal until the full process of dissolution takes place. At this point the narrative does not rise above a "theology of divine anger" (see the excursus on folkloristic approaches to the Bible at the end of chapter 2). But there is no doubt that the king's reaction to the Hebrews must be traced back to the king's desire to subject the Hebrews completely, as stated in Exodus 1:8–21.

c. Moses Versus the Court Magicians. Another rivalry, that between Moses and the court magicians, is an offshoot of Israel versus Egypt and a form of the confrontation of Moses and Pharaoh that focuses on rivalry as an out-and-out contest. Pharaoh will demand a sign, which is translated in the Revised Standard Version as "miracle": "Prove yourselves by working a miracle" (7:9). The Hebrew phrase literally rendered is "Give for yourselves a sign" (or portent). The Hebrew word *mofet* evidently meant "sign" with the connotation of wonder or prediction of a future event.[3] The staff cast down by Aaron turns into a serpent, and the court sages and sorcerers pull the same trick "by their secret arts" (7:11). However, "Aaron's staff swallowed up theirs" (7:12). Then the magicians respond tit for tat with the first two plagues; as Moses and Aaron produce blood in the Nile (a portent of sacrificial crisis and death) and frogs in the land, the magicians do the same. But when the pair bring gnats upon the land, the magicians are not up to it by their secret arts and admit defeat, telling Pharaoh, "This is the finger of God" (8:19). The magicians perceive that this is a crisis of a magnitude that they cannot handle. The gnats, as well as the subsequent flies and locusts, represent a full-fledged divine or demonic *attack*. Animal packs and insect swarms are metaphors of collective violence that probably originate in the action of a *mob* falling upon a victim.[4]

But the king refuses to heed his sacred counselors, and the plagues continue: flies, cattle pestilence, boils, hail, locusts, darkness, and finally the slaying of the firstborn. Everything has been affected; the welfare of the society has been totally destroyed.

d. Moses Versus God.   On his way back to Egypt, Moses and his family stop at a lodging place, "and the LORD met him and tried to kill him" (4:24). The incident is reminiscent of Pharaoh's attempt to kill him (2:15), and even the wording is strikingly similar. I have two comments on this confrontation. First, the endangerment of the chosen one is an element in narrative pattern of founding figures, as has already been pointed out in the explication of the brother stories. If the older brother is displaced, the younger brother in turn undergoes an ordeal that is the narrative analogue of ritual process in initiation and sacrifice. Although Moses' status as younger brother of Aaron is not a dominant factor in the traditions of the exodus and the covenant, his role as mediator is a sufficient reason in its own right to make him subject to the narrative necessity of trial or endangerment. I think therefore that Martin Buber was justified up to a point in making the following statement about the attack on Moses: "This is no survival, no 'primitive fiend' which has entered, as it were, by mistake from earlier polydemonism into this purer sphere, but it is of the essential stuff of early Biblical piety . . . . The deity claims the chosen one or [*sic!*] his dearest possession, falls upon him in order to set him free afterwards as a 'blood bridegroom,' as a man betrothed and set apart for Him by his blood . . . . [As with Jacob] the wanderer has to go through the dangerous meeting, in order to attain the final grace of the leader-God."[5] The point of the narrative ritual is not only to qualify the founder or leader for his new role but to undo the divine promise, so to say, in order to reaffirm the divine providence and the blessings. The threat of violence and dissolution of leader or community is reenacted in order to arrive at an equilibrium that will provide a basis of trust in the destiny of God's people.[6]

Second, Buber passes over too lightly the glaringly violent and sacrificial character of this episode. In chapter 2 I focused on the sacrificial aspects of the stories of Cain and Abel, Jacob and Esau, and Joseph and his brothers, but the Moses episode is different with respect to the connotation of "divine demonism" and the graphic recounting of the circumcision ritual. Zipporah cut off her son's foreskin "and touched Moses' feet [perhaps genitals] with it." She said, "Truly you are a bridegroom of blood to me!" (4:25).[7] The son, who may be Moses' firstborn Gershom (2:22), is evidently a substitute for Moses, and the foreskin is a substitute in turn for the son on the principle of a part for the whole. The result is that the deity "let him alone" (4:26). The passage thus has nothing to do with drawing a moral from Moses' failure to have his son circumcised.[8]

In my reading of the passage, the mimetic crisis is so great that God is drawn into it from the narrative point of view, just as he is made responsible for the continual hardening of the king's heart in the plague narratives. The crisis in Egyptian cultural and political life and consequent oppression of the Hebrews has led to the dissolution of differences. The cycle of revenge is a series of attempts to overcome the mimetic crisis that are doomed to intensify this very crisis: the Egyptians murder Hebrew children, Moses murders an Egyptian, the king seeks to take Moses' life, and so on. Moses the leader-designate of the Hebrews is an Egyptian by adoption and culture, according to the biblical story, and as such subject to being scapegoated by the Hebrews. In fact, the two Hebrews in Exodus 2:13–14 do not accept his judgment, and there are numerous instances in the Torah of Israelite rebellion against Moses, beginning already prior to the plagues (Exod. 5:20–21; see below, "Moses Versus Israel" and the section "Sacrificial Crisis in the Wilderness"). It may be that an attempt to lynch Moses is a hidden historical event behind the account of the divine attack on Moses' life. The episodes of conflict between Moses and his people in the Sinai wilderness undoubtedly reflect such an attempt, if not an actual lynching of Moses (see below, "Moses Versus Israel"). In fact, Moses has all the features of the scapegoat as king or leader, but an examination of kingship will be postponed until the beginning of the Israelite monarchy is treated in chapter 5.

In any event, the mimetic fury of the situation requires differentiation, and that means sacrifice. The crisis of sameness reaches such a height that Moses the "Egyptian" must be differentiated from the Egyptians and Moses the bearer of the divine presence and the divine speech (3:12; 4:12) must be differentiated from the God who is with him. Eric Voegelin saw this point, although without adequate attention to prohibition and sacrificial ritual in religion and symbolic thought: "Perhaps it was the Egyptian in Moses, the old Son of God, who rose for the last time and had to be 'killed' in order to establish the new Son of God."[9] Thus even God, in the sense of the deity who can be expressed in narrative form, cannot avoid entanglement in the crisis. The LORD's violent act represents that power of differentiation that *is* the sacred. Again, the text is here working at the level of a theology of divine anger, as in the accounts of the ten plagues. The attack on Moses is resolved by sacrifice in a twofold substitution: the life of the son for the life of Moses, and the foreskin for the life of the son. The struggle is part of the attempt to realize the meaning of the new revelation and become liberated from sacrificial violence, in that a minimal sacrifice with no loss of life, not even an animal life, is exacted. But the process of realizing revelation will be a long and hard one.

e. God versus Pharaoh.   "God versus Pharaoh" means essentially "God versus the Egyptian gods" (see the comments on Egyptian culture and mythology in the second section of this chapter). Now of course the God of Israel and the gods of Egypt do not confront one another in an "immediate" sense; Moses and Israel are YHWH's representatives, and the gods of Egypt are mediated through a divine hierarchical order that is symbolically centered and embodied in the king. The model of this confrontation between the old sacral order and the emergent Israelite vision is captured in Exodus 4:22–23, where the LORD commands Moses to go to Pharaoh: "And you shall say to Pharaoh, 'Thus says the LORD, Israel is my first-born son (*beni bekori*), and I say to you, "Let my son go that he may serve me"; if you refuse to let him go, behold, I will slay your first-born son'" (RSV). Eric Voegelin was the first, as far as I know, to relate this passage to the symbolic order expressed in Egyptian mythical texts. He points out that in the Pyramid Texts part of the coronation ritual was the greeting of the gods to the new king: "This is my son, my first-born."[10] It is a sign of the poverty of modern biblical scholarship that this confrontation is ignored or denied. This is the case with respect to even the best of biblical critics. For instance, Gerhard von Rad, in his *Old Testament Theology*,[11] does not deal with such questions. Brevard Childs is aware of such considerations, but rejects their relevance. Concerning the king in Exodus 1:8–14, he says, "The Egyptian king is not presented as the incarnate Son of Re, who rules with absolute sovereignty over a nation, but as a clever despot who sets about to convince his supporters of his plan."[12] I find it difficult to accept that the Israelite writers were unaware of the role of kingship among surrounding nations. The depiction of the king of Egypt in Exodus 1 no more suggests lack of awareness of Egyptian myth and culture than the realistic view of David and his court in 2 Samuel indicates the irrelevance of the Israelite sacral order of kingship (2 Samuel 7) for understanding the narrative events. The ultimatum to release the people Israel therefore "means more than the loss of a working force; the Egyptian ruler has been spiritually demoted and must surrender his position as Son of God to Israel."[13]

The crisis is approaching its full extent, so the demand of God to release his firstborn son Israel only increases the king's desire to maintain power over the

Hebrews. They are his pool of marginal people, his scapegoats in a period of inse-curity (see the comments at the beginning of the chapter). When Moses and Aaron report the divine command to hold a "feast" in the wilderness and to offer sacrifices in the wilderness in order to ward off divinely sent pestilence or war (Exod 5:1, 3), Pharaoh becomes even more adamant in his refusal. "Who is the LORD, that I should heed him and let Israel go?" (5:2). He goes so far as spitefully to withdraw the supply of straw so that the slaves would have to gather their own straw to make bricks (5:7); in addition he increases the work quotas (5:8–9).

In Exodus 4:22–23 the symmetry of the cycle of violence and revenge has already been signaled in sacrificial terms by the opposition of Israel as firstborn son and the king's firstborn son. If captive Israel is not set free, then the king's firstborn will be slain. The firstborn of the king is put in the singular in 4:23; we know from chapter 12 that all the firstborn of Egypt will be killed, but the use of the singular here reinforces the language of sacrificial substitution. The firstborn of the king represents the king and all of Egypt. The outcome is the murder of Egypt's firstborn as the price of Israel's release.

Violence permeates the exodus story, but it should already be quite clear that the sacred is a metaphor of violence. It is characteristic of modern modes of thought not to deal with it, either by decrying it without examination or by ignor-ing it. One spin-off of this modern and contemporary misunderstanding of—or contempt for— religion is an extremely negative attitude toward the Bible, espe-cially some of the unsavory parts of the Hebrew Bible and the New Testament that tell about God killing off people. Many intelligent people who find this vio-lence and concern for history distasteful turn to archaic myth and theosophical forms of religion that are nothing more than the double of a reigning scientific-technological view of the world. The religiosity attached to ancient myth and forms of theosophy (literally "god-wisdom") functions to confirm the reign of sci-ence and technology and allows them to go their own way unchallenged. This is the price or "ransom" of a religiosity that gains its ability to maneuver by accept-ing social and historical irrelevance.

But this mode of religiosity is both simplistic and entrapped in modern myths. It is crucial to see the *struggle to realize the revelation* in the Book of Exodus and elsewhere in the Scriptures. It is not a simple matter to become disentangled from sacred violence; in fact, who succeeds completely?[14] The gift of Israel is to show the insight of revelation and inspiration at work in the midst of actual human experience, historical events, and cultural institutions. The mimetic conflict and violence in Exodus should not be minimized. Nonetheless, it is important to note three textual facts in the story of Israel's beginning as God's covenant people: focus on the innocent victim, a sacrificial modification of violence done to the Egyptians, and a series of substitutions that diminish violence.

1. The Exodus texts exhibit a focus on an oppressed people that is without parallel in the ancient world. One may point out, to be sure, that the Israelites were doing nothing other than taking their own side and glorifying their own account of origins. But if their story of disreputable beginnings as Hebrew slaves is historically accurate, why preserve a core of historical accuracy like this? If the truth were known, there were probably many mean, dirty doings in the formative period of all the peoples of the world, and certainly some of the ancestors of some of these peoples must have suffered oppression at some time or another. But Israel holds on to its earlier status as an alien people oppressed by its masters like a mother bear to her cub. Why? It must have to do with the conviction that the very basis of Israel's history is created by relationship to the divine reality that is just and compassionate, that intervenes on their behalf.

2. In spite of everything, the narrative relates a sacrificial modification of violence done to the Egyptians. It is important to observe that the royal policy was to execute all newborn Hebrew males. In keeping with the sacrificial terms set up in Exodus 4:22–23, only the firstborn of Egypt were to be slain. This sacrificial resolution would have ended the struggle if Egypt could have accepted it. Unfortunately, Pharaoh's heart or mind is "hardened" again (Exod 14:4, 8), and with his army he pursues the escaping Israelites to the Sea of Reeds, where the Israelites cross over and the Egyptians are overwhelmed by the waters. This action of Egypt's, which is ascribed to divine agency (like pandemonium; see chapter 2), is a way of talking about human decisions and acts that are made and understood within the sphere of sacred violence. The king had already implicitly announced his intention to pursue Israel by saying, "They are entangled in the land; the wilderness has shut them in" (14:3, RSV). In context, the narrator feels obliged to ascribe this to the LORD's agency.

3. Within the framework of awareness of conflict and violence and the pressure of its own dawning insight concerning the God of victims, the tradition tries, vainly or not, to put in place of series of substitutions that will minimize violence, particularly violence done to those who are innocent. The firstborn sons of Egypt and the firstborn of the cattle are taken in place of all of Egypt; the firstborn of Israel are spared through the blood of the lambs touched on the doorposts (12:21–27) and later by sacrifice of lambs (13:4–16). These matters will be treated more at length in the section of chapter 4 entitled "The Struggle over Sacrifice."

This process of holding mimetic rivalry and violence within very limited bounds is very different from the rejection of sacrifice in the prophets and by Jesus in the Gospels. But it is already based on the experience of the Voice that says, "I have seen the affliction of my people who are in Egypt . . .; I know their sufferings, and I have come down to deliver them out of the hand of the Egyptians, and to bring them up out of that land to a good and broad land" (3:7–8).

f. Moses versus Israel. In the sacrificial crisis narrated in Exodus 1–12 Moses is inevitably the focus of anxiety and frustration on the part of his people, and the reports of conflict between Moses and the people increase after the exodus itself. As already noted, the situation of oppression produced a cycle of violent vengeance in which the main actors in the drama were caught up in a kind of "musical chairs," assuming the role now of the victimizer, now of the victimized. The situation is similar to what Girard describes in the cycle of conflict in Sophocles' *Oedipus Rex:* "The only distinction between Oedipus and his adversaries is that Oedipus initiates the contest, triggering the tragic plot. He thus has a certain head start on the others. But though the action does not occur simultaneously, its symmetry is absolute. Each protagonist in turn occupies the same position in regard to the same object."[15] In the Book of Exodus, up to a point, we find the same thing: Egypt oppresses the Hebrews and slays their newborn males; Moses slays an Egyptian; the king seeks to kill Moses; God seeks to kill Moses; God sends the plagues, which from the standpoint of the model of victimization and scapegoating are a symptom of Egypt's mimetic crisis; the Egyptian firstborn are slain; Israel is released to leave Egypt, but Egypt pursues in order to regain them as slaves; Egypt is overcome at the Sea of Reeds. This is all very much like the mythic structure that is set forth as paradigm in the Oedipus story. But there is one *exception:* the victims of oppression do not wish to retaliate, but to leave, to travel to a new order of existence under the guidance of the God of the ancestors and of Moses. Moses is the mediating figure through whom a break with the endless cycle of mimesis and vengeance comes to light.

Moses' career in the Exodus story begins as an Egyptian who recognizes his kinship to the Hebrews. The episode in Exodus 2:11–15 presents his feeling of kinship and so suggests that the reader or hearer should sympathize with Moses' action of killing the Egyptian; nonetheless it is quite clear that what Moses does is a form of murder. "He looked this way and that, and seeing no one he killed the Egyptian and hid him in the sand" (2:12). On the basis of this verse alone, it is hard to decide whether the killing should be called manslaughter or murder in the second degree. The reason for killing the Egyptian rather than intervening in some other fashion seems unclear enough that the later tradition, both Christian and Jewish, was exercised to explain and justify it.[16] In any event, Moses' desire to intervene in this way is thrown up to him the next day as he tries to break up a fight between two Hebrews. "Who made you a ruler and a judge over us. Do you mean to kill me as you killed the Egyptian?" (2:14). Moses knows then that he has been found out, and he flees when the king seeks to kill him.

Therefore the chaos of the mimetic crisis extends to the Hebrews, who are subjected to slavery and infanticide. Moses tries to intervene violently, and though the text of 2:11–15 is not explicit about this, his twofold intervention has the effect of separating Hebrew and Egyptian and distinguishing the Hebrews who were fighting from one another. The verb used for their fighting, *nitsim*, is in the form of a stem often employed to indicate reciprocal action, and in this form of the verb the struggle is always physical. This very basic physical level of rivalry signals the dissension among the Hebrews or Israelites, and Moses' failure to mediate the conflict signals the opposition he will meet in the future. Moses is the main human figure who is to bring degree or difference into the crisis:[17] his role is to establish right order by separating Israel from Egypt and bringing to the Hebrews the divinely given distinctions that would protect them from the sameness or undifferentiation that results in violent struggle.

It is therefore not surprising that the leadership of Moses and Aaron is not accepted without question; indeed, given the situation depicted, one might expect more murmuring and dissension before the exodus itself. As the text stands, the only such instance prior to the Passover occurs at the beginning of Moses and Aaron's visits to entreat the king. His stubbornly cruel response—increasing quotas and requiring the laborers to gather their own straw—has two results. One is that the foremen of the Israelites, in understandable exasperation, go to appeal to Pharaoh in person rather than letting Moses and Aaron serve as their representatives (5:15). It is common for source critics to attribute this to an earlier layer of the tradition in which Moses and Aaron had not yet appeared. But to approach the text in that manner is to betray a narrowly focused historical positivism, for the situation makes good dramatic sense when construed in light of the motif of Moses versus Israel.

The other result of the king's response is that these work crew leaders confront Moses and Aaron and accuse them in the form of a judgment oath: "The LORD look upon you and judge! You have brought us into bad odor with Pharaoh and his officials, and have put a sword in their hand to kill us" (5:21). Slaves are forced to see themselves through the eyes of their masters, and conversely, masters, though usually not aware of their own enslavement, see themselves in terms of recognition from their slaves.[18] The master, Pharaoh, has brought extreme pressure to bear upon the Hebrews, so it seems everything in the state of affairs mitigates against their seeing themselves through the eyes of Moses and his message.

Now Moses, whose previous conversations with the LORD have taken the form of resistance and argument (see Exod 3–4), turns against God with complaint and accusation: "O LORD, why have you mistreated this people? Why did you ever send me?" (5:22). This is as if to say perhaps the foremen are right: the master (Egypt) defines the situation in which Israel must see itself through its master's eyes as slave. Indeed, the outcome of Moses' leadership has been nothing but a strengthening of the king's cruel policy toward the Hebrews (5:23). So the mimetic strife spreads in every direction. It does not end when the people make their escape.

3. Sacrificial Crisis in the Wilderness

Prior to the covenant at Sinai there are four other instances of conflict between Moses and the people he leads: Exodus 14:10–18, the people's fear as the Egyptians pursue them; 15:22–27, complaint about the bitter water of Marah; 16:1–30, cry for bread and meat in the wilderness; 17:1–7, outcry for water. The latter three belong to the wilderness narratives, and that alone would suggest a close relationship among them.[19] There are, however, certain patterns that join all four and that represent the deeper narrative level that operates both with and against the victimization mechanism.

a. Mimesis. The problem is the *Egypt* that still dominates the Israelites' hearts and minds. Three of the four narratives refer to this. The pursuing Egyptians have the power of life and death over the Israelites (14:10–12); they ate bread and meat in Egypt (16:3); they had plenty to drink there (by implication in 17:3). If the God of Israel could have become "Egypt," so to say, and if Moses could have become his king-mediator providing the necessities of life, they would have been glad to exchange—one slavery for another!

b. The Mob. The three wilderness episodes are quite explicit about the shifting of the "people" into a "mob." Although a Hebrew word for mob is not used, the word *murmur* is the key to a mimetic contagion that suggests unruliness and potentially dangerous action.[20] In two of these passages Moses "cries" to the LORD in reaction to the murmuring (15:25, 17:4). The latter verse pictures a desperate Moses: "they are almost ready to stone me."

c. Differentiation. The wilderness journey is a figure of the spiritual process of the people emerging as an exception among the nations where sacred violence prevails. A process of winnowing, sorting, defining occurs that will continue even beyond the destination of the journey, the promised land. New boundaries are established as the people-mob is led to become the people Israel. This differentiation process is expressed twice by Moses' use of his staff and twice by the giving of a statute. In 14:16 God commands Moses to "lift up your staff, and stretch out your hand over the sea and divide it, that the people of Israel may go into the sea on dry ground." This division is an act of creation (see Gen 1) that will be Israel's salvation and Egypt's downfall. The sea as destructive force, as chaos, will roll back over the Egyptians, and it is a fitting symbol of the mimetic crisis that has occurred. But the work of the God of Israel brings an order, a differentiation in the chaos—and Israel, the innocent victim, is the primary sign of this new order. In 15:26 the LORD makes a pronouncement that is called "a statute and an ordinance" but is actually a conditional promise: if Israel obeys its God, he will not afflict the people with the diseases that came upon the Egyptians. Lying in the background of this conditional promise is a prohibition against turning to other gods, an act of rebellion that by implication would bring the plagues that befell Egypt. Plague as a figure of radical disruption and disorder is stayed by prohibition. The manna and meat episode in chapter 16 reads as though it is centered in the instruction concerning the Sabbath (16:22–30; see 16:4–5). The question of whether the people "walk in my law or not" (16:4) has to do primarily with whether they will obey the command to gather twice as much bread from heaven on the sixth day in order to remain at rest on the seventh day. In other words, the Sabbath is the institution that provides the central point of differentiation. From the Priestly standpoint, observing it faithfully is what distinguishes Israel from other peoples; to celebrate it is to obey the God of Israel who is the Creator God (see Exod 20:8–11 and Gen. 2:2–3). In Exodus 17:5–6 Moses is to strike the rock with the staff with which he struck the Nile. The reference to the Nile means there is a quite deliberate contrast between the water that comes forth from the rock and the water of the Nile turned into blood. The differentiating function of Moses' act is basically the same as that of dividing the waters at the Sea of Reeds. Water has many attributes in patterns of symbolic language: undifferentiated, life-giving, dangerous and dark if it is deep. Egypt's water is death—is violence as murder and violence as the offering of sacrifice. Israel's water, as given by God, is life, is the overcoming of violence. The place is named Testing and Dispute, in English transcription Massah and Meribah (17:7), names that serve to condemn the attitude of the people who put the LORD to the test and are ready to lynch Moses. The implication is that they are still not sure about what distinguishes them from Egypt and their former life in Egypt.

   d. Sacrifice.   In the journey out of Egypt and into the wilderness, Moses does not offer sacrifice (in the sense of offering a victim at an altar) prior to the arrival at Mount Sinai. The altar Moses builds (Ex 17:8–16) and the sacrifice offered by Jethro (Ex 18:12) are exceptions, but in neither instance is Moses (or Aaron) described as a sacrificer. That Moses does not offer sacrifice in the more formal sense is probably deliberate on the part of the narrators, for sacrifice as such was to be instituted at Sinai. Nevertheless, sacrifice in the sense of the operation of the victimization mechanism in sacrificial substitutions is quite evident. First of all, the destruction of the Egyptian army in chapters 14–15 highlights the depth of the mimetic conflict between Israel and Egypt. No event of sacrificial substitution has sufficed to join the rivals or at least bring hostilities to a halt. In a final violent outburst the Egyptians pursue the escaping Israelites. The pursuit and imminent attack of the Egyptians is analogous to the all-against-one of collective violence. An army in the time of battle is an organized mob, and if the group attacked is small in number or has no military defense, the structure of the situation is comparable to that of a lynch mob turning on a victim. The annihilation of the Egyptian army thus comes across as the tragically fatal outcome of the desire for power.

But Israel has its own internal problems, which now become the focus of the narratives. Having seen themselves in terms defined by their oppressors, the Israelites are now torn among three alternatives: (1) to continue viewing themselves as their Egyptian overlords had done, (2) to view themselves in terms of their opinions of one another, or (3) to view themselves as the people of the God of Israel under the leadership of Moses. If the first alternative were to prevail, they would return to Egypt. But they are in a state of transition from the first to the third alternative, so the second alternative, the intensification of group rivalry, continually comes to the fore in the narratives. The result is that the people turn into a mob. And a mob needs a sacrifice in order to avoid a "plague," that is, self-destruction. As the dissatisfaction with their lot reaches a head, they turn on Moses. In the episode of the bitter water, 15:22–27, the bitter water (whatever the historical reality lying behind the story) functions to reflect the people's bitterness, their fear of disease, of poison. The LORD shows Moses a tree, which he throws into the water. The water then becomes sweet. The commentators generally connect the miracle to the magical properties believed to inhere in trees or their leaves, bark, or fruit.[21] Childs comes close to what I view as the correct way of construing the passage in relating it to the plague tradition, but he finally resorts to the common exegesis: "the help was mediated to Moses in the form of a divine disclosure of the special properties of a tree."[22] That trees in part or whole were thought to have magical, healing properties, I have no doubt; however, as Derrida shows so strikingly, the very concept of medicine or remedy (*pharmakon*) is rooted in a primary notion of substitution for or supplementation of an original reality.[23] Since the Greek *pharmakon* meant "poison" as well as "remedy," *pharmakon* as medicine could be construed as antidote or antibody, which is actually the disease or poison copied and used *for* the patient and *against* the original condition. One can thus easily see the logic of the *pharmakos* or scapegoat, which Derrida treats only very briefly.[24] Crucial to Girard's project, besides explaining the function of mimetic desire, has been to show the centrality of substitution, the victim (*pharmakos*) executed as remedy for the dissolution of the community, which is at the heart of human culture.[25] The *pharmakos* is the provider of the *pharmakon*. So the tree Moses casts into the water is a substitute. A substitute for what? Undoubtedly for Moses. "The people murmured against Moses" (15:24, RSV). He is the most available *pharmakos*.

The episode of the bitter water is quite typical of scapegoat stories around the world. There is a general crisis that evolves into an all-against-one situation. The poisoning of water is common, certainly in European medieval scapegoat stories, although the Exodus tale does not ascribe the poisoning of the water to the scapegoat, as is usual. This is probably because its point of view will not allow Moses to be at fault, and in any case it is part of a narrative struggling to pull away from victimization and sacrificial thinking. But Moses *does* have the power to bring the mob out of its crisis. However, instead of bestowing benefits through being lynched, he is able to displace the energy and attention of the people to the tree. What I have said here about Moses as *pharmakos* offering a *pharmakon* or remedy as substitute for himself is simply a variation on what Girard says: "The universal execration of the person who causes the sickness is replaced by universal veneration for the person who cures the same sickness."[26]

It may seem strange that the leader is the potential scapegoat, but see my discussion of the king as sacrificial victim in chapter 1. Girard points out certain "stereotypes of persecution." One is an accusation that violent crimes have been committed against authority figures who represent the social order and its prohibitions. Another is a community in a state of undifferentiation, which can easily turn into a mob. A third is the choice of victims who are marginal either as outsiders or insiders in a group or social system. Marginal outsiders are the foreigner, the poor, the physically handicapped. Marginal insiders include not only the extremely poor, children, and prostitutes but also the rich and powerful whose position is *enviable*, and as objects of envy they may, if the conditions are right, become subject to scapegoating.[27] The fourth and final stereotype is that of the ultimate measure, murder, justified as an execution necessary because of the evil nature of the victim.

So Moses as the leader is the potential scapegoat. From the standpoint of his motley group, he is not simply the mediator of power but the *source* of power. Whether he *is* the medicine or provides it is a distinction they are not prepared to make. The threat of a lynch mob becomes even stronger in the Massah and Meribah incident, 17:1–7. The medicine or remedy is water, which Moses is supposed to provide. In the plight of extreme thirst, the power of mimetic desire and rivalry rivets on Moses and Egypt as the two great sources of power, of life. It was *Moses* who brought them out of Egypt, as though it was not really their idea, and it is in Egypt that their needs could be met (17:3). "So Moses cried to the LORD, 'What shall I do with this people? They are almost ready to stone me'" (17:4). There is a sense in which the water from the rock is a surrogate for Moses. Rather than shedding his blood, which would be a reversion to the violence of Egypt (see above on blood in the Nile), the people drink the life-giving water.

In the struggle to overcome the victimization mechanism through revelation of good mimesis, the question remains, "Is the LORD among us or not?" (17:7). The covenant tradition underwrites a conditional yes to this question (see chapter 4 on the covenant).

4. The Relation of Moses and Aaron

In the events narrated prior to the Sinai covenant there is no conflict between Moses and Aaron. There are some passages where Aaron assumes a more prominent role, which may well be due to Priestly redaction of the text. This will be taken up below in the subsection on the interpretation of Moses in the tradition.

Even later on in the golden calf episode, Exodus 32, Aaron escapes with startling impunity. At other points where strife over leadership and prestige could break out, conflict is utterly absent. Consider, for instance, Exodus 40, a Priestly passage in which Moses is denied entry into the Tent of Meeting, whereas according to Exodus 33 Moses entered the tent and was addressed by the LORD "face to face, as a man speaks to his friend" (33:11). There is only one episode, in which Aaron, with Miriam, attacks Moses. In Numbers 12 Miriam and Aaron speak against Moses because he married a Cushite woman. Even there, it is Miriam who is afflicted with leprosy. The implication is that Aaron too would be punished if he did not repent, but again it is as if the narrator deliberately avoids any action taken against Aaron.

I would propose two reasons for this avoidance and mitigation of conflict between Moses and Aaron, who are not explicitly a model of "brothers in conflict." (1) They are not founding fathers or ancestors of tribes like Abraham, Isaac, Jacob, and Jacob's sons. The historical reality and symbolism of family conflict do not have the same role as in the Genesis stories. (2) There is a sense that the disclosure of the good mimesis of the God of the oppressed people must prevail between Israel's leaders in the narration of the exodus and the covenant. Of course, the final Priestly redaction of the Torah, with its concern for the authority of Aaron and his sons, could have created conflict and established Aaron as triumphant over Moses. The Priestly writers inserted blocks of material that undergirded their own authority (for example, chapter 40 of Exodus, already mentioned). That they did not attempt such a triumphal reconstruction is probably rooted in two factors: the authority of Moses in the tradition and the Priestly tendency to avoid violence or to do deal with it through a series of substitutions (see chapter 1 on Cain, Abel, and Seth).[28]

5. The Interpretation of Moses in the Torah Traditions

As indicated in the earlier discussion of Cain, Abel, and Seth in Genesis 4 and 5, I accept the basic critical consensus that different traditions with different perspectives and concerns are represented in the Torah. There it was a matter of a writer or school, perhaps the earliest of the Israelist traditionists, whose work is designated as the "Yahwist" or "J" and a writer or school of priestly affiliation who brought the Torah into its final form during or after the Babylonian Exile. Observing differences in "sources" or "layers of tradition" may often be most instructive, particularly if it does not interfere with an engaged reading process or with disengaging the powerful generative vision from which the Bible as a whole stems. By "engaged reading process" I mean that whether one is a committed Jew or Christian, a religious inquirer or an agnostic or atheist, the reading should take place within the frame of reference of a great drama; the issues are of life-and-death importance, the characters are our spiritual and cultural forebears, so no one should read without absorbing interest. As for "disengaging the powerful generative vision" of the Bible, that is what this book is about: the power of some biblical texts in unmasking the victimization mechanism that results in sacrifice and scapegoating. An adequate criticism, or "science" if one prefers a classical term, will meet these two conditions.

Moses, I think, was doubtless a historical person. Why would Israel have invented a leader like him, someone who had an Egyptian name and may have been Egyptian?[29] As we shall see in the following section, Sigmund Freud had reasons, not entirely clear to himself, for not only making of Moses an Egyptian but also for making of Jewish monotheism a religion of Egyptian origin. However, the tendency of the tradition in Genesis and Exodus moves the other way: to explain Israel's connection with Egypt but at the same time to *differentiate* Israel from Egypt. If the tradition were engaged in a real cover-up on Moses, one could imagine a story of a figure like him born elsewhere, outside of Egypt, and then sent in to lead his people out. Whether or not the tradition is right about Moses' Israelite ancestry, it certainly has not invented him.

Of course, this does not mean that Moses appears in the same light, with the same status and functions, everywhere in the Torah. There may have been tales in which he was inserted later. One of the tenets of form criticism, which focuses on isolable units of speech and their life-setting, is that Deuteronomy 26:5–9, supposedly the oldest cultic recital of the LORD's saving acts, mentions neither Moses nor the Sinai covenant. (Joshua 24:2–13 includes Moses and Aaron, but not Sinai.) The form critical assumption, as represented especially by Gerhard von Rad, is that the Pentateuch or Hexateuch was developed out of these compact cultic recitals of God's saving acts. The omission of Moses and Sinai is thus, from a form critical standpoint, an indication that they were subjects that had a different life-setting from the exodus-conquest themes and were joined to the latter at a much later time than the earlier oral stage of the tradition. There is nothing particularly troubling about this approach as long as it does not interfere with an engaged reading process and can be utilized to identify and clarify the generative level of the biblical text. To the extent that it might share in the rationalist bias of the structuralists and infer that the Bible has its origins in forms of speech, it is caught up in the deadly "expulsion of origins" with which I will deal in the next section of the chapter. As for the omission of Moses and Sinai in Deuteronomy 26:5–9, a purely literary approach, apart from any other considerations, would indicate two things: (1) Moses is the speaker in Deuteronomy. His status is so great that he tells the story. What would be the point of including himself in the compact recital of God's deeds on behalf of Israel? (2) The recital focuses on going in and coming out, on God's providence in leading Israel. God's Torah and the covenant are not the subject.

In any event, it is agreed that in the final form of the Torah, Moses is the central figure in the four great traditions of interpretation upon which modern scholarship has come to a general consensus, but he is viewed somewhat differently in each of them. The primary result of modern critical scholarship that is of interest in this context is that Moses assumes a more and more important role in the history of tradition, although with the Priestly redaction of the Torah, Moses' priestly prerogatives are rendered subservient to those of Aaron and his descendants through Eleazar and Phineas.[30] A concomitant of this result that is not recognized in critical scholarship is the different ways Moses is depicted as a sacrificial surrogate for Israel in J, E, and D, while in P the control of violence is shifted away from Moses and Aaron to the total sacrificial system.

In J Moses has a prophetic commission (Exod 3:7–8, 16–20) and appears as an actor in the narrative whose work is subordinated to the LORD's. For example, in 8:20–32 the swarm of flies is entirely the work of God. Moses does not act with his staff, and there is a question whether the staff is part of the J tradition. It seems that if and when E can be disentangled from J, Moses' prophetic status in E is higher and more theologically weighted (e.g., Exod 3:10–15), his agency is more prominent vis-à-vis God and his brother Aaron, and his intercessory charisma is such that it is almost a powerful substance: God takes "some" of the Spirit that is upon Moses, who bears the burden of the people, and transfers it to seventy elders (Num 11:17–25).[31] In D or Deuteronomy Moses attains such a status that he has not only been a participant in the story; he *tells* the story as the LORD's narrator. In Deuteronomy he is the paradigm of leader and mediator. In P he continues to be the key figure as the receiver and mediator of revelation, but he gives way to Aaron's role as ancestor of the high priestly line. Moses himself cannot enter the Tent of Meeting when the cloud is over the tent (Exod 40).

If this overview of the traditions of interpretation is approximately correct, one outcome is that the tendency of the traditions, as they came together and were reshaped, was to elevate Moses more and more to the level of sacrificial surrogate for the people, while simultaneously removing him from involvement in mimetic conflict. In other words, to refer to Girard's terminology, Moses becomes more and more an *external mediator* who is not involved in rivalry with those for whom he is mediator and model.[32] The higher his status and prestige, the more he becomes explicit sacrificial object.

In the Yahwist or J perspective he is clearly the potential surrogate victim, and one may sense that an actual scene of violence may lurk closely behind a scene like those of Marah and of Massah and Meribah (Exod 15:22–27; 17:1–7). By the time we get to D, Moses is not only the object of collective violence, he is also, as von Rad has put it, "a suffering mediator."[33] Whether E represents a transitional stage, it is very difficult to tell, because the problems in disentangling J and E sometimes threaten to make a mockery of source criticism and redaction history. In Exodus 32:31 Moses offers to have himself blotted out of the LORD's book because of the people's sin, and according to Numbers 11, as we have remarked, he bears the burden of the people. Both these passages have been read as Elohist (so von Rad), but many commentators take them as J or JE. However, the final form of Deuteronomy depicts Moses as the mediator who is the narrating voice for God and who takes the divine wrath upon himself. The consequence is that Moses is not allowed to enter the land of Canaan. Of course, Deuteronomy also includes the tradition that Moses acted rashly against God (Deut 32:51; Num 20:1–13). If Numbers 20:1–13 is Elohist, it may be a good indication of a halfway stage between Moses the prophetic leader of J and Moses the suffering mediator of D. In E Moses is of such sacral importance that he is somehow caught up in the conflict and disorder of the people. In D his mediatorial, scapegoat function is clearly recognized. "The LORD was angry with me also on your account, and said, 'You also shall not enter there'" (Deut 1:37, RSV). "Furthermore the LORD was angry with me on your account, and he swore that I would not cross over the Jordan" (Deut. 4:21; see also 3:26, RSV). This picture of Moses as mediator who suffers on behalf of the people is similar to what is said in Psalm 106:23:

> Therefore he said he would destroy them—
> had not Moses, his chosen one,
> stood in the breach before him,
> to turn away his wrath from destroying them.

What we find, then, is the growth of the portrayal of Moses as servant of God who is the suffering intercessor for his people. He has been differentiated from the people and their propensity to become a mob. As such, he is not affected by the mimetic desire and conflict of the people, as in the earlier tradition, and in that respect he is a precursor of the Christ of the Gospels.

At the same time that Deuteronomy portrays Moses as suffering mediator, its actual thought world is separated from the concrete sense of violence, sacrifice, and revelation that many of the narratives in Exodus communicate. It makes of Moses a sacrificial object, but it does not account for mimetic crisis and the need for mediation or a surrogate. The Israelites are simply declared to be disobedient and rebellious. Everything takes place in the sphere of the *word*, God's word of command and Israel's obedience or disobedience of that word as spoken through Moses. Moses as word-bearer in Deuteronomy becomes the complete focus of Israel's attention and of God's attention. The collective dissatisfaction with Moses (Deut 1:9–12) is presented in a remote fashion, and there is no inclination in Deuteronomy to give a graphic description of mob action against Moses, just as there is no indication that God requires any sort of human sacrifice. Nonetheless, Moses is posed between God and people as the object of divine wrath for the sake of Israel.

B. An "Egyptian" Point of View: Manetho, Apion, and Freud

The Book of Exodus, even though a multilayered, highly interpretive work far removed from the events of Israel's beginnings, is a wonderful text not only for finding Israel's interpretation of these beginnings, but for finding the traces of a struggle that must surely take us back into the issues at stake in Israel's formative period. Israel's religious revolution shines through the text: although many features of the ancient sacred order and sacrificial violence remain in the narrative, the narrator's sympathy lies not with the dominant social order, that of the Egyptians, but with *those who are expelled*. Whatever the problems of mimetic desire, rivalry, and sacrificial violence that remain in the Book of Exodus, as in the Bible as a whole, a breakthrough has occurred here.

Now one could ask what an Egyptian version of the same events would be. We have no historical records from the fourteenth and thirteenth centuries B.C.E. that give an Egyptian point of view. However, we do have later Egyptian versions of the exodus from the Hellenistic period. They indicate that from the Egyptian standpoint the departure of the Hebrews from Egypt was actually a justifiable expulsion. The main sources are the writings of Manetho and Apion, which are summarized and refuted in Josephus's work *Against Apion*. There are also fragments from other writers.[34] Manetho was an Egyptian priest in Heliopolis. Apion was an Egyptian who wrote in Greek and played a prominent role in Egyptian cultural and political life. His account of the exodus was used in an attack on the claims and rights of Alexandrian Jews. Although these writers incorporated later traditions and legends and may have had some bare acquaintance with the Book of Exodus in Greek translation or through oral sources, what they present affords a glimpse into the typical perspective of the dominant community promulgating a myth. From these sources the Hellenistic-Egyptian version of the exodus may be summarized as follows: The Egyptians faced a major crisis precipitated by a group of people suffering from various diseases. For fear the disease would spread or something worse would happen, this motley lot was assembled and expelled from the country. Under the leadership of a certain Moses, these people were dispatched; they constituted themselves then as a religious and national unity. They finally settled in Jerusalem and became the ancestors of the Jews.[35]

The details vary on how the decision to expel came about and exactly what the nature of the crisis was (fear of epidemic? divine punishment? lack of piety? foreign rule?). There are varying reports as to whether the people in question were originally aliens or native Egyptians. Manetho identifies Moses as the later name of Osarsiph, a former priest of Heliopolis, and Apion repeats part of this account. Another Greco-Egyptian writer, Chaeremon, a contemporary of Apion, also identifies Moses as an Egyptian priest and sacred scribe who, with Joseph, led 250,000 infected people who were expelled from Egypt. Apion's account is distinctive in "portraying the Mosaic cult as an offshoot of Egyptian religion."[36]

But all these variations are typical for the myth of the scapegoat. To illustrate this with the Girardian schema for mythic narrative, here are the main moments in the Egyptian-Hellenistic myth:

1. A stable order prevails.
2. A crisis arises that threatens the social order with disease and confusion.
3. Those to blame are a group of people who are either foreigners or Egyptians who suffer from various diseases. A sacred source (whether oracle or popular consent, as *vox dei*, voice of God) prescribes the expulsion of this group. The implication is that the Jews descended from this sickly, trouble-making group are just like their ancestors (and are a plague to Egypt once more).
4. The threat to the social order is resolved by expelling the offending people, and by implication
5. the old order is reestablished.

Thus the "Egyptian" or at least *an* Egyptian point of view on the Jews' escape from Egypt! In a reversal of the biblical account, they are *blamed* for the plagues. Aside from questions of historical reconstruction of events in Egypt, it is certainly credible either that certain diseases were rampant in Egypt or that there was a cultural and political chaos that was made concrete by attaching it to plague legends, for plagues are frequently associated with social and moral chaos.[37] This Egyptian mythical perspective amounts to saying that the Hebrews were expelled for good reason, for they brought trouble in their train, very much as Oedipus' murder of his father and marriage to his mother threatened the existence of Thebes. Even before Oedipus comes to the "discovery" that he is the criminal, the parricide and committer of incest whose presence is deadly, Creon reported from the oracle at Delphi what must be done:

Creon: The god commands us to expel from the land of Thebes
          An old defilement we are sheltering . . .
Oedipus: What defilement? How shall we rid ourselves of it?
Creon: By exile or death, blood for blood. It was
          Murder that brought the plague-wind on the city.[38]

The Hellenistic-Egyptian sources do not, of course, accuse the expelled people of having committed murder. However, Manetho implies something just as bad in one of his versions, describing the Jews as the descendants of the ancient Hyksos, outsiders who dominated Egypt during the second millennium B.C.E. (see below) and thus disrupted the sacred political and cultural order of Egypt. From the mythical perspective, any basic disruption of the sacred order is a transgression as evil as murder.

The Egyptian perspective delineated in the histories of Manetho, Apion, and the others is perfectly in keeping with ancient Egyptian mythological traditions, which legitimated the sacred social order centered in the divine king. At the center of Egyptian myth and ritual was the great god Osiris, father of Horus and the divine form of the king of Egypt when he died. Osiris had three aspects: the dead god, the dismembered god, and the reconstituted and resurrected god.[39] Egyptian society was founded upon the death and rebirth of the sacred victim, the victim incarnate in its sacred power in the person of the king, who was Horus during his reign and Osiris in the realm of the dead. With a myth and theology of sacred kingship, it is necessary, in a time of critical instability to the regime and social order, either to make a sacrificial offering of the king or of a surrogate for the king. Powerful kings usually manage to find surrogates, like, for example, the Hebrews in the Exodus story. But it is more accurate to say that the power of kingship is based upon the king's ability to refer his victim status to surrogates.

By contrast, the ancient Israelite social order, as articulated in the tradition of the ancestors and the exodus, began to free itself from the old sacred realm and move into a realm of freedom associated with covenant in the wilderness. Sacrifice and sacred kingship did not completely die out any more than their source, mimetic desire and conflict, was remedied. Nonetheless, a breakthrough occurred; a set of insights emerged; a discovery or "un-covering" happened that I am calling *revelation*.

A modern point of view that argues for the Egyptian origins of Moses and the Egyptian inspiration of Israel's ethical monotheism is that of Sigmund Freud.[40] His argument is worth surveying as an instance of a modern mythical interpretation of Moses and the exodus that both denies and conceals the revelation of the God of the innocent victim. Drawing his evidence from the work of certain Egyptologists and biblical historians (particularly Sellin) but filtering it through his own interpretive screen, Freud argued in *Moses and Monotheism* that Moses was an Egyptian noble who himself was both inspired by the religious revolution of Akhenaton (Amenophis IV, c. 1364–1353 B.C.E.) and very ambitious to exercise power over a community of his own making. He became the leader of a sizable group of "Jews," who "were to be a better substitute for the Egyptians he left behind."[41] This Egyptian Moses gave the Jews a high monotheism that prohibited images of God and required integration of the community on the basis of a treaty and a set of precepts that were to be accepted as divinely ordained. Circumcision, which was practiced by the Egyptians, was to be obligatory for all males as a sign of belonging to this new people. But the people, who were after all "savage Semites,"[42] revolted against this new commander and his high-handed ways and killed him. Subsequently there arose another leader in Midian, the son-in-law of a

Midianite priest. He regrouped the people under the violent volcano god Jahweh and led them in conquest of the land of Canaan. The stories of the original Moses and the anonymous figure of Midian and Qadesh became fused together in the tradition. Although the violent, polytheistic (or henotheistic) energy of the second "Moses" tradition dominated the Jewish tradition until the Babylonian Exile and continued to make itself felt in Jewish history, it is the work of the original Moses, the Egyptian "great man," that enabled the Jews to survive and make their distinctive contribution to civilization.

Freud's model of interpretation in *Moses and Monotheism* remains consistent with *Totem and Taboo*, published over twenty-five years earlier: "religious phenomena are to be understood only on the model of the neurotic symptoms of the individual."[43] One interpretive criterion of this model is that long forgotten traumatic events that occur in the formative years of an individual and return later on in the form of neurotic symptoms (the "return of the repressed") are construed as analogous to evolutionary and historical stages of the human race. These later symptoms contain a personal or historical truth even though it may be concealed to consciousness. The application of this model to the early history of Israel entails seeing it as a crucial instance of the general principle that human social organization begins when the sons in the primal horde who are gathered around a father-leader revolt, kill him, and eat his body in order to gain his power—his being. The murdered father-leader becomes a divinity. The clan, in reconstituting itself, eventually substitutes an animal for the father-god, and this animal becomes the basis of the *totem*. The concealed and forgotten event continues to return, however, in the form of fixation and compulsion that is denied in prohibition ("You shall not kill—above all not your father") and acted out in ritual where concealed forms of the murder are repeated and resolved in order to allay guilt.[44] Freud understands the origin of Christianity as a series of events and circumstances in which the repressed material could not be checked by prohibition, ritual, and myth, and so a new religion came about. The primary agent in the development and spread of this new religion was the apostle Paul. It was Paul who understood the death of the crucified Jesus as the saving event revealing both the Father and the Son. Jesus as the Christ is a symbolic representation of the slain Father and likewise of the Son as the embodiment of the brothers who murdered the Father. By identifying with the Son, believers can be absolved of the primordial guilt generated by the original slaying.

Freud holds that the monotheism of the Jews brought them certain advantages. These include the grandeur of a new concept of god, the conviction that the Jews are "chosen" and destined to enjoy divine favor, and a motivation, even compulsion, to progress in spirituality. This progress in spirituality "opened the way to respect for intellectual work and to further instinctual renunciations."[45]

This "Mosaic religion" is the "Father religion" par excellence from Freud's standpoint. Its spiritual and moral greatness is simultaneously its oppressiveness, and this paradoxical combination of qualities is a paradigm of the effect of civilization on human beings. Murderous hatred of the father could not be directly expressed in the religion of Moses; what emerged instead was a reaction to this hatred in the form of guilt and a bad conscience. Guiltiness became part of the religious system and was concealed under the illusion that the Jews were God's chosen people; in this manner "the consciousness of guilt because they were such sinners offered a welcome excuse for God's severity." But the need to satisfy this sense of guilt was insatiable, coming as it did from a much deeper source than transgressing the laws placed upon the chosen people. The result was that they rendered "their religious precepts ever and ever more strict, more exacting, but also more petty." The twofold effect was that on the one hand, the Jews subjected themselves to greater and greater instinctual renunciation; but on the other hand, this moral asceticism enabled them to attain intellectual heights far exceeding those achieved by other ancient peoples. The origin of guilt in repressed hostility to God "bears the characteristic of being never concluded and never able to be concluded with which we are familiar in the reaction-formations of obsessional neurosis."[46]

As for Judaism's heir Christianity, there is a sense in which Freud sees it more as a "slayer" of its parent religion than as an heir, for Christianity repeats and regresses to the slaying of the original Father and blames those who have remained Jews for not committing themselves to the same myth and ritual. The Jews have suffered this reproach from the new religion: "They will not admit that they killed God, whereas we do and are cleansed from the guilt of it." The emergence of Christianity had the appearance of Egypt coming back "to wreak her vengeance on the heirs of Ikhnaton."[47]

It would be inappropriate to discuss in detail what motivated Freud in completing his latest book and allowing it to be published. Obviously Nazi anti-Semitism, from whose virulent expression he had fled, was something that preoccupied him—along with anti-Semitism in general, with which he had dealt all his life. The other side of this concern was deep ambivalence about his own Jewish identity, deeply imbued as he was, both as a social scientist and creative thinker and writer, in the intellectual history of the Western world. His own views and investigations did not support a positive view of religion, but then the very intellectual presuppositions of the dominant philosophies and theories of the nineteenth century were shot through with anti-Christian and anti-Jewish assumptions and conclusions. However, evidence has come to light that Freud did receive religious instruction, learned to read biblical and liturgical Hebrew in primary school, and did not have a completely irreligious home.[48]

Now it could be, of course, that the historical Moses was an Egyptian. That is not the point. Our concern here is the effect of Freud's interpretation and its relation to the subject of this study. However one evaluates Freud's concern for truth, as expressed in the disclaimer at the beginning of his study,[49] the effects of his reading of Jewish origins are three: (1) *It is ambivalent in that it partially communicates a basis for a derogatory attitude toward the "Jews."* (2) *It expels the Jewishness of Jewish origins.* (3) *It eliminates the oppression of Israel and its innocence as a victim of Egypt.* These three effects are all related to the mythical point of view presented by Manetho and Apion.

The original Jews or Semites were not, according to Freud, responsible for the creative breakthrough in religion and morality. They were primitive, savage, worshiping a dark, violent volcano god. This god "is an uncanny, bloodthirsty demon who walks by night and shuns the light of day."[50] The descendants of those who were formed into a people by a combination of the work of the Egyptian Moses and the Midianite "Moses" did, to be sure, attain great moral heights, but the view of the typical Jew that emerges from Freud's reading is that of a compulsive, obsessive person who sees his people as superior to other peoples and must always strive to find ways to obey an impossible law because of guilt that can never be made conscious and resolved. He is, in other words, a cross between the Egyptian and the Midianite, the monotheist and the polytheist, the moralist and the sensualist, always having to keep himself in check, always obliged to control his Jewishness or Midianite-Semitic urges for the sake of the Egyptian-Gentile law that is imposed upon him.

It should be noted that Freud achieved a kind of compromise in portraying his Gentile model of authority. The German intellectual tradition not only reflected a residual anti-Semitism that embittered Freud as he struggled to gain recognition but also was enamored of classical Greek culture. Friedrich Hölderlin was especially important in the intellectual apotheosis of everything Greek.[51] Freud's compromise was, on the one hand, to reject his Jewish past by the way he dealt with Moses as a non-Hebrew or non-Jew while, on the other hand, aggrandizing a great figure who was *not an Indo-Aryan.* Whatever his motives, conscious or unconscious, the result has a certain creativity about it. Moses is not an Indo-European, but a Gentile nonetheless, and in this fashion Freud could identify with the Gentile world without submitting to the Aryans. And Moses was the great leader of the Jews, who were a motley lot—but by identifying thus with Moses he could recover what he viewed as best in the Jewish heritage, the Mosaic contribution of ethical monotheism.

Freud's reading of Jewish history may be construed as a kind of replay of Freud's doctrine of the superego and the id, with the ego struggling for a bit of freedom and breathing space between these two great powers. It is fruitful to view his myth of history as containing the deep, generative structure of his theory of the psyche, a theory whose roots he struggled to express toward the end of his life. His psychology is little different from old theologies of fate, and that means a theology of the sacred social order, very similar to the theology of Oedipus myth except that fate and the gods become the Unconscious with its forces and counterforces. But Freud recognized, as we see in *Totem and Taboo* and particularly in *Moses and Monotheism*, that human beings are determined by their own actions in rivalry with others. There is a definite conflict between these two tendencies in his thought, between appeal to the Unconscious and recognition of mimetic rivalry (although he did not finally comprehend the principle of mimesis).

In *Moses and Monotheism*, Freud *attempts to expel his Jewish origins*. This may seem like a strange claim, particularly because he mounts an argument for Jewish contribution to civilization and is obviously a foe of fascism in the form of National Socialism and its European anti-Semitic heritage. Yet one can only wonder how Freud could have been insensitive enough to publish his work at a time when Jews were being vilified and persecuted by the Nazi regime. Murder had already begun.[52] His act of publishing his *Moses* is strange in light of the contemporary theology of the German Christians, who asserted that Jesus was not Jewish but an Aryan. Was Freud imitating his anti-Semitic foes? In any case, we know of his career-long struggle with the "Aryan" overlords who made his life as a Jew at times so miserable. Indeed, Freud was preoccupied with the "Aryan" world. As early as 1908, in the context of the developing friendship with C. G. Jung, he confided by letter to Karl Abraham his sense of the importance of gaining a "Christian and the son of a pastor" for psychoanalysis, thus saving it "from the danger of becoming a Jewish national concern." In other letters he complained that "if my name were Oberhuber [a common Austrian name], my innovations would have found . . . far less resistance," and he warned him "not to neglect the Aryans, who are fundamentally alien to me." Freud worried, in fact, "about the 'hidden anti-Semitism of the Swiss.'"[53]

The Egyptian Moses seems to be a way for Freud to work through the problem of his Aryan double. The double is the model-obstacle who has such mimetic influence on the subject that one can no longer distinguish oneself from this model and rival other. Freud, to the extent he was tied to an ancient myth of fate that perpetuates the father's supremacy, could not have been prepared to ascertain the status of the Aryan in his thinking. He did not see that the model-obstacle was not necessarily a father or a father substitute; it could be anyone who is potentially a model, a rival, a double. As noted already, he did shift toward the latter insight in *Totem and Taboo* and *Moses and Monotheism*, but he had too much invested in his doctrine of the Unconscious to modify it in light of his own observations concerning desire, conflict, and primordial lynching.

The reactions, sometimes horrified, of Jews and Christians to *Moses and Monotheism* correctly intuited the danger posed by the expulsion or scapegoating of the foundations of the two religions—an expulsion promulgated by one who fled as an exile from probably the most horrible outbreak of ritualized persecution and violence in human history. But even these usually very conservative reactions did not perceive the really radical nature of what Freud had done.

Freud held that the genius of the Jews is really the genius of the great man Moses. This is another aspect of Freud's debt to his intellectual heritage: the "great man" myth of nineteenth- and twentieth-century Occidental thought. It stems from the heritage of Romanticism, but here, too, the ancient tragic hero and the theology of the sacred social order have left strong traces. Freud develops his particular form of it on the basis of the work of his former student Otto Rank, *The Myth of the Birth of the Hero*, although the foundations of his thinking may have been influenced by the Philippsohn Bible that was used in his home. Ludwig Philippsohn was a Jewish scholar influenced by the Romantic pietism of early nineteenth century Germany.[54]

The great man Moses is a mediator of the Ikhnaton revolution in religion. If one were to view the writing of a book as a kind of ritual process, then I think Freud's *Moses* is an undoing of the prohibitional foundation of Jewish identity (i.e., in effect, You shall not bring about a crisis in Jewish identity by denying its god, its chosenness, the truth of its divine law, etc.) in order to reaffirm the insights of psychoanalysis and their contribution to sanity while justifying his own ambivalence about being Jewish. He says, as it were, "I know I'm Jewish and I'm not ashamed of this, but to be Jewish is finally to be Egyptian (i.e., Gentile, specifically non-Aryan Gentile) and so I affirm my oneness with the non-Jewish world." However, though both sides of the dialectic are present in his interpretation, it is the Egyptian that is superior. The Jews, "were to be a better substitute (*ein besserer Ersatz*) for the Egyptians he [Moses] left behind." They were to be better—but they were to be a substitute, and in Freud's view they were really never the equal of the Egypt they left behind.

The implication of the Jews as a substitute for the Egyptians is missed by Marthe Robert in her generally very helpful book *The Psychoanalytic Revolution: Sigmund Freud's Life and Achievement*. She says, "The fact is that except for the thesis that Moses was an Egyptian, an idea which the orthodox consider blasphemous and archaeologists and historians think highly disputable, the book retraces a spiritual epic in which the figure of the law-giving prophet radiates power, intelligence and light . . . . Moses, with only the help of his stupendous vision of man, transcended time and founded the moral civilization from which a whole world was born. The mysterious perenniality of the Jewish people is his achievement."[55] To say "except for the thesis that Moses was an Egyptian," in the context of Freud's total argument, is like the famous question, "Other than that, Mrs. Lincoln, how was the play?" Robert recognizes the probable analogies between Freud and Moses from Freud's conscious or unconscious point of view,[56] but she fails to recognize the expulsion of origins and the undercutting of the distinctiveness of the Hebrew Bible that he undertook.

Susan Handelman's portrayal of Freud's work in *Moses and Monotheism* is more accurate: Freud "undoes Moses" or "slays Moses." Moses is a "father figure . . . whom he needed simultaneously to murder, identify with, and replace." Freud's "interpretation makes Moses into an Egyptian, as if both to deny and affirm Freud's link to the covenant of his forefathers: to restore Judaism and demolish it; to affirm himself as a Jew and deny it, to destroy the giver of the Law, and then himself give the new law of psychoanalysis."[57]

Handelman's acceptance of the myth of the Oedipus complex in explicating Freud's obsession with Moses is debatable. She views Freud's work very positively in the context of poststructuralist thought and deconstruction, which she appropriates and legitimates by interpreting it as a modern extension of rabbinic midrash. However, her simplistic contrast of ancient Hebrew and Greek thought and the linking of rabbinic interpretation, particularly midrash, to the "open" and "metonymic" modes of deconstruction cannot withstand the light of historical and literary investigation.[58] The deconstructionist mode actually contradicts the basis of rabbinic interpretation and has the effect of expelling origins and denying the distinctive testimony of the Bible.

It is a great paradox that a creative thinker like Freud who recognized the tendency to expel origins by denial and concealment uses his very model and analytic tools to disassemble Jewish origins and make them Egyptian. This allowed him to "save his identity," so to speak, but it also meant that he undercut it by his partial identification with the mythology of the foreign oppressor. Although he eschews any accusation against the Hebrews or Semites in Egypt as troublemakers or lepers or spreaders of plague, he deracinates the tradition by denying the gift of revelation that the Bible claims. This does not mean that in a simplistic theological sense he did not believe in God and the Bible as holy scripture; it means much more radically that the real uniqueness of Israel's witness is thrown out, for *he eliminates Egyptian oppression, Israel's innocence, and Israel's witness to the God that stands with the innocent victim.* The Hebrews, or "Jews," as he would say, were simply there, descendants of the Hyksos, or "shepherd-kings." Their ancestors had indeed disrupted the continuity of Egyptian rule and culture, but Freud does not dwell on that after the pattern of Manetho and Apion. Nonetheless, the latter-day heirs of Manetho and Apion had disturbed him, and he seems to have become engaged with them as rivals whom he opposed but whom he finally imitated in the most basic way possible: the Egyptians had enlightenment—to the extent one could have it in the world, especially in the remote past—and the Jews were imitators. Egypt, in the form of the great man Moses, becomes God. The very basis for unveiling the victimization mechanism is thus demolished in spite of Freud's great insight into the human condition. The ancient Israelite journey of increasing disclosure of the effect of desire, mimesis, and victimization is turned into a struggle to allay the guilt of the victimizers who murdered their great Egyptian leader. Through his reconstruction of Moses, which was simultaneously a "deconstruction" and a "destruction," Freud joins the victimizers against himself and his ancestry!

Ancient myth appears ever again in new forms. As I view modern intellectual history, there have been three great myths responsible for intellectual and social change and stress: the myth of history and social harmony, the myth of the chosen people destined to rule the world, and the myth of the great man. These three myths cannot be neatly separated from one another. The first two emerged more out of Christian or Judeo-Christian foundations, although the Nazi form of the chosen people myth was really an amalgam and perversion of Christian and non-Christian symbolic thought. The great man myth was probably primarily pagan in origin, stemming from the preoccupation with human potential and classical sources that began with the Renaissance. Freud was enamored of this myth, as his correspondence shows.[59] Yet at the same time he was engaged in a lifelong battle with the myth of the chosen people, which affected him in two ways: he was always conscious of his Jewish heritage and the "mark" of the male Jew, namely, circumcision, and at the same time had to confront the appropriation of the chosen people theme in the German world by those who turned it against the Jews. Although he opposed racist mythology, his preoccupation with it seems to have mesmerized him, as we can see in Moses. The danger of mimetic desire is that the rival is a model. If the rival becomes a double, one can try to slay this "god" over one's life, but if one succeeds in killing it, literally or figuratively, one simply supplants the god and acts in the very way that seemed so threatening in the beginning. To differentiate, to establish order in chaos by the ultimate chaotic act, is simply to continue the chaos. In Moses and Monotheism Freud slays Moses the Jew (= Freud) in order to liberate Moses the Egyptian (= the non-Jewish great man = Freud).

Excursus: The Great Man Myth:
Freud, Heidegger, Mann, and Fascism

There is much evidence for the power of the great man myth. To go into it fully, one would have to look at Hegel (the philosopher as possessing "absolute knowledge"), Carlyle, Nietzsche, Rank, and, of course, Heidegger and the National Socialist myth of der Führer. The historical background would include German nationalism, whose intellectual adherents looked to classical Greece as the primary model. It would also include features of romanticism in the nineteenth century.[60]

Concerning Martin Heidegger, it is interesting that in the very period Freud began writing his essays on Moses, Heidegger delivered a lecture, "Introduction to Metaphysics" (1935), which conjoined the great man theme to the theme of the people with a transcendent destiny.[61] When the lecture was published in 1953 Heidegger changed "inner truth and greatness of National Socialism" to a phrase about technology and modern man.[62] Particularly important in this lecture, in my estimation, is Heidegger's statement about the poets, thinkers, priests, and rulers who create the *polis*: "[T]hey are without rules and limits, without structure and connections, because *as* creators they are obliged to establish all these things first."[63] These creators are engaged in a struggle or battle, Greek *polemos* (whose older meaning is struggle or debate in rhetoric). Heidegger argues that *polemos* and *logos* (word, reason, discourse, structure) are the same; from a higher point of view, concerning the work of god and creative humans it can be said that "they cast the project against overwhelming power to rule and exorcise (*bannen*) thereby the world opened up."[64] Notice how Heidegger here uses a language of ritual. Heidegger's concept of "Being" is a concept of the sacred, which is always rooted in and justified by the sacred social order. And like the sacred social order, it must achieve itself through violence.

Heidegger states that for the Greeks, beauty is mastery (*Bändigung*). "Gathering together of the highest conflict is *polemos*, struggle (*Kampf*) in the sense of coming to an expressed understanding" (*besprochenen Aus-ein-ander-setzung*, literally, "discussed or debated conflict or controversy"). He also says, "Because being as logos is original gathering, no shuffle and mixture (*Geschiebe und Gemenge*) where everything means indifferently much or little, rank (*der Rang*) belongs to being, to sovereignty (*Herrschaft*)." A concern with rank, degree—*difference*—is another expression of Being as the sacred social order. Also, "Since being is [logos, harmony, truth, nature, manifestation], it therefore is shown to be far from pleasing. The true is not for everyone, but only for the strong."[65] That is, it is for the elite, those who belong to the *Führung*, the leadership, of the sacred social order.

In the same context he states that the logos of the New Testament is not the being of beings, as for Heraclitus, not the gathering together of what is in conflict, but a particular being, the Son of God. Heidegger says that the Septuagint translation of the divine word of command in the Old Testament by *logos* is simply replaced by *logos* as proclamation of the Cross or the crucified one in the New Testament. The crucified one is the logos of eternal life, of redemption. As two sides of the same coin, so to speak, law and gospel, command and redemption, the biblical logos is a restricted and restrictive concept far removed from the all-inclusive logos of Heraclitus. Heidegger would therefore exclude from his chosen people, his city or state, the idea of the logos as the God who takes the side of the innocent victim (Hebrew Bible), the logos as the God who becomes the innocent victim (New Testament). The logos as being of beings has no truck with the innocent victim. Heidegger in his own way, like Nietzsche in his, asserts the priority of the strong man, the great man, who affirms *polemos*, strife, battle, debate and who understands the work destiny has given to certain peoples and cultures.

Heidegger's philosophical language, certainly in *Introduction to Metaphysics*, is an expression of the will to power. One could argue that it is not fair to compare Freud's self-expression in *Moses* with Heidegger's philosophical defense of National Socialism, but I think that Freud's preoccupation with his Aryan double led him to come up with some of the same results: the work of the great man is exalted, the biblical foundations of Judaism and Christianity are denied, and Israel and Christ are excluded—once more!—from the "Egypt" of high civilization. Once more and once again there are those who would "afflict them with heavy burdens" (Exod 1:11). Once more and once again Jesus is made to suffer "outside the camp" (Heb 13:11–12).

Similar comments could be made also about the German Christians who denied Jesus' Jewish ancestry and sought to understand the gospel in terms of pagan mythology. The crudeness of the Aryan Christians and of Hitler's Nazi ideology may seem far removed from the philosophical sophistication of Heidegger and the psychoanalytic penetration of Freud's essays on Moses and monotheism. They are closely linked, however, as rival interpreters of the same myths.

Thomas Mann's novella about Moses, *Das Gesetz (The Law)*, published in 1943, shows that he was more sensitive than Freud to the problem of Jewish identity in relation to oppression and victimization. We know, of course, that Mann was an admirer of Freud and influenced by his thought. Indeed, Mann's tribute to Freud, which was published in *Vossische Zeitung* in 1931, shows that his own view of Freud was permeated with the great man myth. Using Nietzsche's words about Schopenhauer, he describes him as "A man, a knight, with the steely look who has the courage to be himself, who can stand alone and waits neither for the orders of those who went before nor signs from on high." Mann writes, "I am happy to have had the opportunity to profess to him my faith."[66] If Mann's Moses narrative is any indication, Freud's influence was still strong, but he intended partially to remedy Freud's *Moses*.

As the original German title indicates, Mann was concerned to view Moses in terms of the law as an accomplishment that was "the condensed will of God, the bed-rock of all good behavior and breeding."[67] Moses is born of a brief sexual encounter between a Hebrew slave and an Egyptian princess. The princess initiates the encounter, and the Hebrew is murdered by her overseers immediately after the dalliance. She gives the infant to a Hebrew family to be nursed and cared for part of the time. In early adulthood he learns of the God of the Midianites, has a number of religious experiences, and concludes that this "Yahweh" is the God of the Fathers. He was particularly impressed with Yahweh's invisibility, which he considered "so full of incalculable implications." As identifiable with the God of the Fathers, Yahweh was also the God "of the poor benighted folk" who "were enslaved, their traditions forgotten, their worship utterly disorganized."[68] With the help of his Hebrew adoptive brother Aaron and the young man Joshua, he leads the Hebrew slaves into the wilderness and gives them the law. The miracles of the biblical story are explained naturalistically, and Moses' God is an idea, a vision that moves him in his thought, meditation, and solitude to create the law as the foundation of his people and of a better humanity in the future.

This summary leaves out many details of Mann's version of the Moses story, of course. What I wish to emphasize here is the extent to which it is caught up in the myth of the great man, even though it is sensitive to some important aspects of Jewish identity and the Jewish Scriptures. In appearance this Moses is quite different from Michelangelo's Moses, which so fascinated Freud, but ironically Mann modeled his Moses after the artist, Michelangelo![69] This artist Moses is a man whose personal strength and inner intensity are almost too much for his body and his use of language.

> When he returned to Egypt, filled with his discovery of God and with his mission, he was a robust man at the height of his powers; with flattened nose, prominent cheek-bones, a beard parted in the middle, wide-set eyes, and wrists that had a striking breadth about them, as one could see particularly when he covered his mouth with his right hand, musing, as he often did. He went from hut to hut and work-shed to work-shed, shook his fists alongside his thighs, and spoke of the Invisible, the God of the Fathers expectant of the Covenant. But although he talked much, at bottom he could not talk. For his was altogether a pent-up, inhibited nature, and in excitement he inclined to be tongue-tied.[70]

The Hebrews are expelled finally after the last plague, which kills many Egyptian children, especially the firstborn, in the area of Goshen and in the cities of Pithom and Ramses. However, it is at bottom Moses' connection with the court of Pharaoh that allows him an audience with the king and enables him to get permission finally to depart with the Hebrews. In other words, it is Moses' status as an Egyptian on his mother's side that enables the exodus—from the Egyptian standpoint, an expulsion—to take place. Theologically, of course, there is no reason why one could not see the work of God in Moses' Egyptian circumstances, but the author's point of view seems to focus on the qualities and connections of the man Moses, whose personal virtue and insight far surpass that of all the motley Hebrews, including that of his chief lieutenants, Aaron and Joshua.

The effect of Mann's "great man" point of departure is to highlight the *achievement* of the law and to relegate to a marginal position in the story the *revelation* of the God of victims who stands with his people and delivers them. No doubt the commandments, the statutes, blessings, and curses of the covenant are an implied comment on the barbarism of fascist totalitarianism, and as such they represent Mann's view of the sort of regime that fosters violence and sacrificial thinking. However, Mann comes perilously close to throwing out the baby with the bathwater, for the relation of law to the innocent victims is not developed in the story, and the supreme feature of the God of Israel is his invisibility and mobility, not his will to eliminate the difference of slavery and establish a community of peace and righteousness. Moreover, Moses gets his ability to serve as mediator and lawgiver from his status as half-Egyptian. There is nothing wrong with this speculation as such, if one takes Moses' Egyptian acculturation as historical. In fact, as half-Egyptian and half-Hebrew, speaking three languages but confused by them and by his own intense spirituality, Mann's Moses has a marginal status that is quite appealing and true to the thrust of the biblical traditions. Finally, however, the story emphasizes the advantages of Moses' Egyptian education and connections, while the locus of his discovery of Yahweh is the religion of the Midianites. The benighted Hebrews in Egypt don't fare much better than in Freud's account. The source of Jewish greatness is not the Hebrews (=Israelites=Jews) but the contributions of Egypt and Midian.

Moses is the leader, the mediator figure for the Israelites from the very ealiest traditions of the Exodus story. His position is subordinate to the total event of the exodus, although he assumes more and more prominence in the ongoing tradition of interpretation. With Deuteronomy he becomes a prophet and legislator far removed from actual mimetic crises of the people. He is the "external mediator" of Israel's understanding of itself in tradition, covenant, and law. In P, as stated, his role as sacrificial leader-victim is superseded by the total sacrificial system.

As mediator, Moses' position is inherently ambiguous. He is the focal point of Israel's struggle to come to terms with the revelation it has been vouchsafed, the revelation of the God who cares for the world and takes the side of the victims. He is the servant of the God who is not subsumed by human differences, even the differences established between human beings and God. But the knowledge of this God is continually attacked and thwarted, usually covertly, by the age-old human languages, institutions, and symbols that are caught in the web of the sacred, with its structure of violence. It is easy, therefore, for the people to slip back into nostalgia for Egypt and its gods, or to exalt Moses and turn against him. Exalting the leader and attacking him is inherent in the universal human process of making gods and kings.

Whether or not Moses was an Egyptian, it seems clear that these interpretations of Moses and the exodus that are motivated by mythic impulses are weighted toward seeing him as Egyptian. Why? Because from the mythic standpoint of the sacred social order this makes his crime even greater, for it is a crime against his own order, a kind of parricide and matricide. This may have attracted Freud, for the model of a non-Jewish, yet non-Aryan great man who tried to shape the miserable Jews could have fed his own profound ambivalence.

From the mythic standpoint the "exodus" of Hebrew victims is "expulsion" of diseased aliens who have brought disorder and divine wrath into the social order. As for Freud, at the surface level he does not describe the Hebrews as criminal or sinful in this usual mythic manner, but I have contended that the effect of his reading is the same, for without Moses and the high ethical monotheism he shaped out of the Akhenaton movement, the Semites Moses led would have been simply savage Semites worshiping a bloody deity.

4

The Covenant and Sacrifice

But [God's] command is plain: the parricide
Must be destroyed. I am that evil man.
　　　　Sophocles, *Oedipus the King*

. . . and each of you kill your brother, your friend, and your neighbor.
　　　　Exodus 32:27

. . . you shall have no other gods before me. . . . Honor your father and
your mother.
　　　　Exodus 20:3, 12

A. The Covenant

In the long, sometimes arduous process of realizing the revelation of the innocent
victim and the God of victims, the covenant and the commandments represent
the center and the periphery of a circle, the circle of the people of God.

It is the covenant that forms a new community in its "commonness," its
Gemeinschaft, its sharing of a common past, a common hope, an identity based
on relationship with the God who brings Israel "out of the land of Egypt, out of
the house of slavery" (Exod 20:2). But those who share their life in common, in
community, impinge upon one another mimetically in their similarities and differences. They are impelled to imitate one another, but if the imitation goes too
far and the differences melt or are destroyed, then a sacrificial crisis of huge proportions erupts—the mimetic being must have a model or rival to imitate, else he
or she will be utterly lost. The dissolution of differences impels the rage to find
new differences, and in human culture the most economic way of doing that is to
establish the scapegoat as the new point of differentiation. The commandments
represent a sort of periphery, an outer edge of the circle that cannot be transgressed without the danger of undifferentiation, of chaos. The covenant is the
center, the motor, the motivating force, the point of departure. The commandments are the boundaries forestalling the kind of mimetic crisis and violence that
the story of oppression in Egypt and liberation recounts.

Here I will focus the discussion by commenting on the text of Exodus, chapters 19, 20, and 24:1–14. Although biblical critics tend to see in these chapters
some combination of the J and E sources (with 24:15–18, at least, belonging to P),
I will read them as a unity.

1. Exodus 19:1–6

The people Israel arrives at Mount Sinai, and God speaks to Moses on Sinai. The primary differentiation between Israel and Egypt and between Israel and the nations is "I bore you on eagles' wings and brought you to myself." This divine statement is to be repeated as an affirmation of Israel's beginnings and God's character. As such, it anticipates the "first word" or "first commandment" in the Jewish tradition of the Decalogue: "I am the LORD your God, who brought you out of the land of Egypt, out of the house of slavery" (Exod 20:2). In context, it is the basis of the covenant and Israel's sacral status, for the people Israel is to be "a priestly kingdom and a holy nation." The minimal meaning of this national priesthood is that Israel is to be consecrated and set apart for God. The inner dynamics of the priesthood is a series of substitutions. The priests are consecrated to God and as such are holy victims. The priests are a pool of victims standing in for the firstborn of Israel. These victims are, in turn, redeemed by animal sacrifices. (For further discussion and documentation, see the second part of this chapter, "The Struggle over Sacrifice.") Therefore, part of the meaning of Israel as a kingdom of priests has to be that the structure of its social and religious order is a series of sacrificial substitutions, and, as we shall see, these substitutions seek to ameliorate the structure of sacred violence that sacrifice maintains.

The *maximal* meaning of a kingdom of priests and a holy nation would be that Israel is God's mediator among the peoples of the world. As the sacred mediator, Israel would be, in principle, the sacred victim of God whose life would be offered unless redemption were made. This maximal meaning is not developed in the Exodus context, but it is in keeping with God's promise to Abraham, "and in you all the families of the earth shall be blessed" (Gen 12:3). This promise is a motif at work in Abraham's intercession for Sodom and Gomorrah and for Gerar (Gen 18 and 20), Jacob's offer of "blessing" to Esau (Gen 33:11), and Joseph's rescue of the Egyptians and his own people through his gift of dream interpretation.

2. Exodus 19:7–15

The people are to be prepared for God's revelation on Mount Sinai. The center of this passage is the command "And you shall set bounds for the people round about, saying, 'Take heed that you do not go up into the mountain or touch the border of it; whoever touches the mountain shall be put to death'" (19:12, RSV). This warning and the penalty of death by collective execution ("he shall be stoned or shot [with arrows]") show that the mountain represents that primordial point, the primary difference or line of demarcation between order and disorder, between peace and violence. As such, it is the "original" of which the altar is a copy. To pass over that line, to confuse the divine and the human in some way (undifferentiation of God and humans, of parental and ancestral authority, of sexual partners, etc.) is to force a repetition of the mimetic rivalry and violence that necessitates the sacred in the first place.

Moses is the narrator of God's words in the text that is the narration of Moses narrating God's words. We obviously have a series of representations or substitutions in which the "text," the text that I or any given reader uses in a specific situation, is the most recent instance. Moses is the stand-in for Israel and for God; the narrator is the stand-in for the author or writer; the text as I have it through whatever traditions[1] is the stand-in for earlier texts—for the writer, for the narrator, for Moses, for Israel, for God. This series, from the standpoint of the logical or mathematic infinity of differentiation, could go on and on, with no center, no starting point. That is, in the abstract realm of logic and mathematics, the starting point is always arbitrary and utilitarian, and the only reality is scale, ratio—*difference.* Difference is part of the structure of our mental operations, but what I would emphasize here is that *the people Israel existed and still exists* and *they have had boundary experiences* that are more real than the modes of interpretation by which they have been understood. The power of the text lies in its ability to lead us through the series of substitutions to the point where we discover that standing at the mountain we cannot touch and preparing for the divine disclosure is more real than the illusory forms of criticism that seem to bear the mountain-experience away in an infinite regress of substitutions. Illusion, like idols, is real, but its reality is ephemeral and subordinate and must be subject to the Voice of the covenant tradition.

3. Exodus 19:16–25

The next passage is focused on the danger of the mountain, in effect a kind of ritual undoing of the order established by the erection of an altar. God commands Moses to bring Aaron up on the mountain with him, "but do not let either the priests or the people break through (*yehersu*) to come up to the LORD; otherwise he will break out (*yifrats*) against them" (19:24). The verb *parats* is a strong one that predicates an act of overthrowing, breaking down, or tearing down. It suggests how close the revelation of the control of violence is to violence itself, which is always a potential just scarcely on the "other side" of the boundary or of the altar, so to say. The people are (always) close to "breaking through" and "breaking down" the lines of difference in the chaos of violence. When this happens, God is experienced as the source of counterviolence. The "breaking out" of God against the people expressed by *parats* should probably be construed as divine wrath in the form of *plague,* as recounted in Psalm 106:28–30:

> Then they attached themselves to the Baal of Peor,
> and ate sacrifices offered to the dead;
> they provoked [the LORD] to anger with their deeds,
> and a plague broke out (*wattifrats*) among them.
> Then Phineas [son of Aaron] stood up and interceded,
> and the plague was stopped.

Phineas's act of interposing or intercession is reminiscent of Moses' act as related in the same psalm: he "stood in the breach (*bapperets*) before [God], to turn away his wrath from destroying them" (v. 23). The psalm is helpful to read in conjunction with Exodus 19, both for the light it sheds on the subject of sacred violence and as a reminder that in the biblical traditions the mediator-scapegoat overshadows the altar as the protective representative and line of differentiation between order and violence. He can readily become caught up in the outbreak of divine wrath whose social meaning is collective violence.

4. Exodus 20:1–17 (the Decalogue)

The Ten Commandments as they are known in Christianity and Western culture are called the Ten Words in the Jewish tradition. (The Hebrew word for commandment, *mitsvah*, is used neither here nor in Deuteronomy 5 where the other form of the Decalogue is found.) No sanctions are given for disobedience. Elsewhere, similar commands carry the penalty of death, for example, Exodus 21:15–17; 22:19–20. The command not to revile God or curse a ruler does not include a penalty (Exod 22:28), but probably the death penalty is assumed. In context, I would infer two considerations about the absence of sanctions in the Decalogue: (1) A spatial boundary has been set that points to the divine presence on the mountain that the people are not to touch. The commandments are the verbal expression of the boundary between covenant order and the danger of disorder, divine wrath, and violence. In other words, there is a situational sanction. The people know, or are supposed to come to know, the boundary Moses has set. On the other side of the boundary loom disorder and death. (2) The commandments are given as if there is a healthy, dialogical relationship between speaker and hearer that does not require the mention of sanctions. Israel is addressed in the second person singular in the Hebrew text ("thou shalt [not]") as though it is one person, but allowing the sense that each individual among the people is addressed.

   a. "I am the LORD your God, who brought you out of the land of Egypt, out of the house of slavery" (20:2).   In the Jewish tradition of interpretation this prologue is the First Word, and this is quite appropriate, in that the commandments should be placed in the context of the story of the saving acts of the God who takes the side of his oppressed people.[2] God's self-identification is central to the meaning of the biblical revelation and biblical theology: what finally and absolutely differentiates YHWH God of Israel from other gods is that he leads his people out of slavery and into the freedom of the covenant. The freedom of the covenant requires, in turn, the discipline of boundaries for the control of mimetic desire and mimetic rivalry. The commandments articulate these boundaries.

b. *"You shall have no other gods before me" (20:3).* You shall not *confuse* any other god with the God of the Covenant, who leads you out of the land of Egypt, out of the house of slavery.

c. *"You shall not make for yourself a graven image, or any likeness of anything that is in the heaven above . . ." (20:4–6, RSV).* The second commandment is simply an extension of the first commandment. Making and worshiping a graven image is the exteriorization and ritualization of the act of overturning the covenant order by denying the God of the Exodus and the Covenant or confusing him with another god. The LORD as a God of "jealousy" or "zeal" (Hebrew *qanne*) has been dealt with, in effect, in the comment above on Exodus 19:16–25. In the movement from the controlled sacred violence of sacrifice to the beginning of a new order based on law, sacred violence has not been completely overcome. In fact, sacrifice and law will continue to coexist, but the later prophets and the Jesus of the Gospels will radically differentiate sacrifice from the covenant order. Even the basis of law would be called into question, particularly by Jeremiah, the Second Isaiah, and the Gospels—for finally, a system of law, though it diminishes the role of sacrifice in offering a developing set of regulations for social discipline and the control of vengeance, is based on the sanction of the sacred social order. The sacred social order as such does not witness to the true God, or does so only opaquely—for the true God is not a God of vengeance and violence. But to the extent that a given tradition has not yet attained to or received this disclosure, the sanction of law is collective violence regulated in various degrees by representatives (judges, advocates, executioners, etc.). In a clan or tribal situation the execution pronounced might actually be performed by a crowd, as presumably death by stoning often was. The rationalization of this collective violence, which is more or less regulated in different social settings, is the divine anger, the divine wrath, the divine zeal for the welfare of the people. And this is what we see here in Exodus 20:4–6.

d. *"You shall not make wrongful use of the name of the LORD your God, for the LORD will not acquit anyone who misuses his name" (20:7).* It is not entirely clear whether this commandment is intended to proscribe a wide range of acts that involve false or deceitful use of the divine name in order to attain one's own ends or is directed to the specific abuse of a false oath whose purpose is to bring evil on another.[3] Probably the former alternative is to be preferred. In any case, the Name (YHWH, perhaps pronounced "Yahweh," though that is conjectural) represents the very being of the God of Israel. The prohibition of vain, empty, or deceitful use of the Name brings to a sharp focus the function of the commandments: as the Ten Commandments are the verbal expression of the boundary between covenant order and the danger of disorder, divine wrath, and violence, so the Name represents that boundary that the mountain stands for in the spatial images of the narrative setting. The Name, which the people know and have and may call upon, is the perpetual Word that separates order from disorder, life from death, peoplehood from slavery. It is to be used and thought carefully, with greatest respect, even with fear, for from it Israel begins. When the people start out again on their wilderness journey (Num 11:12, 33), they leave Sinai, but they go forth with the Name.

e. *"Remember the Sabbath day and keep it holy . . ." (Exod 20:8–11).* The Sabbath is the main division or boundary of time. To remember in the biblical sense is normally much more than a mental operation; it is an act that involves behavior and consequences. The form of the fourth commandment in Deuteronomy 5:12, "Observe" or "keep the Sabbath day," says the same thing with greater ritual specificity. So to remember the Sabbath is to keep or observe the seventh day, which differentiates periods of the lunar month and which functions here to establish temporally the same boundary that the mountain sets spatially and the Name fixes verbally.

The reason given for Sabbath observance in 20:11 is a rationale that connects the commandment with creation. God, in creating the world and then resting on the seventh day, sets a divine model. In remembering the Sabbath, Israel remembers God and creation, and the creation itself is made real once again in time and ritual. In celebrating God's creation through the Sabbath, Israel regains, at least partially, the divine image in which Adam was created. In Deuteronomy 5:12–15 the explanation is based on the exodus from Egypt. There, keeping the Sabbath is a redoing of deliverance into freedom and the covenant.

f. *"Honor your father and your mother, so that your days may be long in the land which the LORD your God is giving you" (20:12).* As the Name is the verbal expression of the boundaries that make Israel distinct and as the Sabbath is the temporal expression of this distinction, so the fifth commandment is the fundamental demarcation of social authority that maintains tradition, order, and respect. One could find a certain hierarchy in the Ten Commandments, in the sense that the second, third, and fourth commandments may be read as the extension and specification of the first, "You shall have no other gods before me"; the fifth commandment is the point of departure for the sixth, seventh, eighth, and ninth commandments. The tenth commandment, then, is an expression of the generative principle of commandments six through nine (see below).

There is no crime worse than patricide or matricide or any of its correlates, such as regicide (see Exod 22:28). Anyone who strikes or curses mother or father

shall be put to death (Exod 21:15, 17). "But [God's] command is plain," says
Oedipus: "the parricide must be destroyed. I am that evil man." Conversely, to
honor father and mother is to maintain the lines of authority of the tradition; it
involves respecting all those who have a "parental" role: ancestors, rulers, teachers,
judges, and so on.[4]

In honoring parents those addressed are given a sense of the connection of
time and place. The fifth commandment is the only one that includes an explicit
promise (although 20:6b, "showing steadfast love to thousands," etc., implies a
promise): "that your days may be long in the land which the LORD your God gives
you." Honoring parents is the point of differentiation connecting the covenant
God to social life and is presented as the basis of Israel's long continuation in the
land promised to the ancestors. Time, as continuation of the generations, and
place, as life on the land, are linked together through father and mother.

Although the Ten Commandments imply a basis for questioning or rejecting
the authority of parents in the name of the LORD, whose worship logically entails
the rejection of any instruction or practice involving worship of other gods, making idols, and so on, even if perpetrated by a parent or parent figure, nonetheless
the context does not assume there will be conflict between allegiance to God and
allegiance to parents. In the Gospels, however, with their radical demystification
of the sacred violence lying at the heart of sacrificial institutions and the law, allegiance to family and parents became a problem and was subverted to some
extent.[5] Disrespect for parents is nowhere recommended in the Gospels and the
New Testament, but parental authority was so bound up with a system cohering
in Temple and Torah that questions of allegiance and continuance of relationships evidently came up frequently.

*g. The commandments against killing, stealing, adultery, and false witness (Exod
20:13–16).*   These commandments, all in the form of prohibitions, presuppose
the fifth, which is the basis of social order and the link between covenant relationship with God and social order. "Killing" means here the taking of life that is
motivated by hatred and malice, although at an earlier time the verb *ratsach* indicated a slaying that would call forth blood vengeance.[6] "Adultery" is primarily the
breaking of the sanctity of marriage. It evidently entailed greater restrictions on
the woman, who was forbidden any sexual relations except with her husband,
whereas the man could have intercourse with an unmarried or unbetrothed
woman (so Gen 38 and Judg 21:16). "Stealing" has no object in the formulation of
the commandment. This omission may be deliberately intended to cover a wide
scope of cases from secretly and unlawfully taking someone else's possession to
the kidnapping of a person. "False witness" is lying in court or making a false
accusation that could lead to trial and unjust punishment. In the Israelite tradition there was a tendency to broaden this commandment so that all instances of

injuring a person by abusing his or her reputation are prohibited (see Hos 4:2 and Lev 19:16).

One could understand these four commandments as extensions and even applications of the first five in terms of the right to life and prevention of blood vengeance, the maintenance of marriage and family, the ordering of relationships pertaining to property (including the person as property), and the right to protection against unfair accusation.

h. "You shall not covet your neighbor's house . . ." (Exod 20:17).   In Hebrew Bible scholarship there has been a dispute over how to construe *chamad*, which is customarily translated "covet." The verb seems usually to express a desire that strongly impels one toward acquiring the object of attraction, although some modern studies have raised questions about this. Brevard Childs' judgment on this discussion seems judicious: "The emphasis of [*chamad*] falls on an emotion which often leads to a commensurate action."[7] Good examples of this usage would be Exodus 34:24, foreign peoples desiring (i.e., seeking to acquire) Israel's land; Micah 2:2, land-grabbers desiring (i.e., plotting to seize) fields and houses; and Genesis 3:6, Adam and Eve desiring the fruit of the tree to be desired (i.e., that attracts one to eat it) in order to become wise.

The Hebrew word, therefore, is a key aspect of *envy*; it is characteristically the movement of envy toward acquiring an object for which a rival must be overcome, displaced, or eliminated. The use of *chamad* in the Garden of Eden story (Gen 2:9; 3:6) indicates precisely this acquisitive character of envy, for in the story God informs his council that the pair must be expelled from the garden before they go even further and eat of the tree of life (Gen 3:22–24). The tenth commandment thus deals directly with mimetic desire and mimetic rivalry. In my reading it functions as a conclusion that sums up and states the general ethical principle behind commandments six through nine, whereas the fifth commandment, to honor parents (ancestors, tradition, etc.), is the primary social regulation protecting against envy. The relation of mimetic desire to the prohibition of false witness may not seem immediately apparent, but if false witness is understood as false accusation that may involve a legal case, then quite obviously *acquisitive desire* is the motivation of the perpetrator. The latter envies the rival's property, prestige, or power, or, in imitating the rival, seeks to gain the same property, prestige, or power that is the object of the rival's desire. With regard to commandments six, seven, and eight, the relation of envy or acquisitive mimesis to killing, adultery, and stealing is patent. Our paradigm case is the story of Cain and Abel, discussed in chapters 1 and 2.

To summarize my reading of the Decalogue in outline form:

First: Allegiance to the God of the Covenant (positive statement in preface, 20:2, prohibition in 20:3).

Second: Prohibition of confusion of gods.

Third: Prohibition of language confusion or indifference (undifferentiation).

Fourth: Keeping the time difference for remembering God and God's creation.

Fifth: Allegiance to the social order ("father and mother") governed by the Covenant God.

Sixth: Prohibition of disorder/undifferentiation as expressed in killing.

Seventh: Prohibition of disorder/undifferentiation as expressed in adultery.

Eighth: Prohibition of disorder/undifferentiation as expressed in stealing.

Ninth: Prohibition of disorder/undifferentiation as expressed in false witness.

Tenth: Prohibition of mimetic desire and rivalry (the ethical principle underlying the sixth, seventh, eighth, and ninth commandment(s).

5. Exodus 20:18–26

The boundary situation of the Decalogue is now brought to completion. As the people were warned in 19:16–25 not to approach the mountain, the people now tell Moses that if God spoke to them directly they would die. Moses must serve as the mediator; he is the representative of (substitute for) God who translates or adapts the divine Voice. God's own speaking, insofar as it is the sacred basis of law, endangers human life (see discussion above of 19:16–25 and 20:4–6).

Earlier the people had tested or "proved" the LORD when they were on the verge of collective violence against Moses (Exod 17:1–7; see 15:22–27). This violence was averted by the sacrificial substitute of a tree that sweetened the waters of Marah and of the water from the rock at Massah (Testing) and Meribah (Dispute) that replaced the blood spilled in Egypt. An anticipation of the Decalogue is the "statute and ordinance" requiring that the people, who are about to become a mob, heed the voice of God in order to avoid disease (15:25–26). Now at Sinai God tests the people. The danger they perceive in God is the dark underside of their own potential for collective violence, an underside that haunts the Torah in all its greatness.

Now the mediated words of Moses reiterate the sacred differentiation that lies behind the first and second commandments: "You shall not make gods of silver alongside me (itti), nor shall you make for yourselves gods of gold" (20:23). An altar of earth is to be made; it is a substitute for the mountain and the ritual locus of the prohibition of worshiping other gods. The command to make it of soil, or of unhewn stones if stones are used, reads like an imperative to make the altar resemble the mountain. The altar is not to have steps so that human nakedness not be exposed on it. This, again, is an attempt to avoid confusion or undifferentiation. "Nakedness," Hebrew arvah, is evidently that reality associated with the person that ordinarily cannot be seen or "acquired" by another without confusion. It is closely connected to sexuality, of course, but what must be understood is that sexuality, next to language, is the sphere where mimetic desire and rivalry has the greatest potential to damage human community. This concern for human community lies behind the focus on nakedness in the Levitical laws proscribing sexual relations with near relatives (Lev 18:6–18). To "uncover the nakedness" of another is a joining or a uniting that must be carefully regulated in order to keep conflict and violence at bay. In other words, this restriction on nakedness over the altar is a reinforcement of the altar's differentiating function in service of sacred prohibition. The restriction is nothing other than the ritually oriented expression of the command to honor father and mother—to maintain allegiance to the divinely given and guided social order.

6. Exodus 24:1–14

God commands Moses to come up again to him with Aaron, Nadab, Abihu, and seventy elders. In this command a hierarchical differentiation is made: Moses alone will come near to the LORD; the others ascending with him shall not come near, and the people shall remain below. This command is fulfilled in verses 9–14. Moses and his company eat and drink in the presence of God; then Moses ascends further to receive the tables of the law. (Verses 15–18 are a Priestly introduction to chapters 25–31.)

But before the new ascent occurs, Moses reports the words of the LORD to the people and leads them in the actual ceremony of the covenant. He builds an altar at the bottom of the mountain along with twelve pillars for the twelve tribes of Israel. "Young men" or "youths" (naarim) of the people of Israel are chosen and delegated to offer the burnt offerings and peace offerings of oxen to the LORD. Martin Buber made the interesting conjecture that these youths were firstborn sons who "were apparently devoted to YHVH for the term of their youth as a substitute for the common Semitic sacrifice of the firstborn; and who were afterwards redeemed by the Levites [Num 3:12]."[8] Buber's observation makes sense, given what we know about sacrifice and its logic, but of course there is no way to demonstrate it empirically from the text.

Moses takes half of the blood collected to throw it against the altar, and the other half he casts on the people after the covenant book is read and they vow an oath to obey it. On the one hand, the blood is a symbol of the life they share together and with their God. That binding of people and God is the front or top side of the altar, so to say. The underside is the divine wrath as collective violence that is reenacted and overcome in the killing of the animal victims. The blood of the oxen or bulls is a substitute for the people caught up in mimetic violence. As already amply discussed, this is the danger and problem of the law that is still associated with sacrifice and thus rooted in the sacred social order. However, the series of substitutions or supplements that are actually present are signs of the dawning awareness of the contradiction involved in sacrificial worship of the God of victims. The blood of the bulls substitutes for the young men, and later for the Levites, who substitute for the firstborn, who substitute for the people. The series of substitutions, which are not concealed at all in the biblical texts, are an attempt to "repair" the sacrificial order, but the sacrificial structure remains.

That Moses writes "all the words of the LORD" comes as something of a surprise, since all communication has been oral until now. The *written* divine words will function analogously to the Name: the "words" or "commandments" (*devarim*) and the "judgments" (*mishpatim*) extend the prohibition maintained by the altar, where order and disorder are differentiated, into a mobility that transcends the altar. In fact, the "book" (*sefer*, literally, "scroll") will eventually become a substitute for sacrifice. In the prophetic tradition, a tension arose between obedience to the divine word, to which the book gives witness, and the duty of sacrifice. "Behold, to obey [the voice of the LORD] is better than sacrifice" (1 Sam 15:22, RSV). This tension between obedience to the Word of God and sacrifice becomes an open conflict, perhaps even a contradiction, in the messages of Amos, Hosea, Isaiah, Micah, Jeremiah, and the Second Isaiah (see chap. 5).

The factor of obeying the divine word cannot be emphasized too much. "And they said, 'All that the LORD has spoken we will do, and we will be obedient'" (*nishma*, "we will hear"; 24:7).

The people take an oath to hear, to obey what YHWH says, which means to obey what Moses has written. Although they are "covered with blood," as it were, the words and the writing are already beginning to take precedence over the blood of sacrifice. It is quite clear here that book and sacrifice coexist, but obedience to the divine word is beginning to replace sacrifice and, as such, may be viewed as a substitute for it. To the extent that there is a point to the poststructuralist talk about text and writing as a "wound" and equivalent to an act of violence, we find its real basis here. Primary and primordial differentiation involves exclusion for the sake of inclusion. It involves, as in some of our games, making someone or something "it" in order to achieve orientation, order, and rules to keep the game going. To this extent, viewed formally and in terms of ritual processes, Moses' book is an inscribing of the blood on the altar, and the people's vow to obey is a speaking of the blood that binds them to God and one another.

But poststructuralist deconstruction, like its philosophical point of departure, structuralism, gives the impression that nothing ever comes out of actual experience and real events, the process of thinking and symbolization being instead an endless game of substitution that we humans play. Human chaos and the actual process of scapegoating is not of interest to this perspective; nothing is at the "center" or at the "origin" of anything except the human fate of determination by differentiation and substitution. Jacques Derrida, for example, has moved back and forth continually within his concept of difference (*différance*—which he would call a nonconcept!), and when he is addressing himself to the question of God, the book, and writing, it becomes quite clear that everything for him originates in difference and differentiation. He asks, for instance, "if God was an *effect of the trace?* [that is, of the primary or archetypical difference, supplement, or substitution] If the idea of divine presence (life, existence, parousia, etc.), if the name of God was but the movement of erasure of the trace in presence?"[9] Derrida seems able only to repeat in endless variations the idea of the trace, of difference, of substitution; everything for him is finally a mental operation, a substitutionary game that people play, and the worst offender is Christianity and its theology of the Logos as divine presence. No less than Freud he seeks to hold on to Scripture, though unlike Freud he does not overtly seek to expel the Jewishness of Jewish origins. However, he in effect eliminates the oppression of Israel and its innocence. Neither the reality of historical events and circumstances nor the reality of the God of victims can have meaning except as a meaning that is continually erased or effaced. With this mode of thought, one always has one's cake and eats it *and* has one's cake and doesn't eat it *and* doesn't have one's cake and eats it, and so on in an infinite progression or regression. We can see this clearly at the beginning of Derrida's essay on Edmund Jabès and the question of the book. Jabès says the Jews are a *"race born of the book."* Derrida reflects that history is a reflexive/reflective folding, and "this fold, this furrow is the Jew." Jabès says that *"Judaism and writing are but the same waiting, the same hope, the same depletion."* Derrida reflects that the "exchange between the Jew and writing" is "a pure and founding exchange." He goes on to say, always in commenting on Jabès, that when a Jew or a poet proclaims a site, which is freedom, then "this site, this land, calling to us from beyond memory, is always elsewhere. The site is not the empirical and national Here of a territory. . . . It is tradition as adventure."[10]

Land, history, oppression, the disclosure of the God of victims who is the God beyond differences, events of deliverance, covenant community: these are real only as "folds" and "traces." For Derrida, "God" is Difference. Or, insofar as all his words for the "trace" or "pharmakon" are nonconcepts, one could as readily say God is Indifference. In any event, the innocent victim is not a factor in his thinking, for the only victims are words and texts and substitutions. A theology of liberation—which is to say, any adequate theology based on the biblical witness to revelation—cannot become enamored of such a perspective or method. It must rather, in order to be faithful to its sources and responsibilities, interpret on the basis of a model of the exception—an actual person, group, or event—in the process of emerging (see discussion in chap. 1). I would insist once again on what I said earlier: *the people Israel existed and still exists* and that *they have had boundary experiences* that are more real than the modes of interpretation by which they have been understood.

The covenant is an event and a model of existence in which Israel's beginnings in God's act of deliverance is reaffirmed. Its enactment requires awareness of and preparation for the danger of the "other side" of the differentiating line marked by mountain, altar, and prohibition. In the Ten Commandments both the entire people and each individual are addressed and instructed in boundaries that must be maintained; these boundaries are marked out in terms of allegiance to the God of the Covenant, allegiance to the covenant order, and control of mimetic desire and rivalry. In the binding of people to God, the altar and the words of God in Moses' book are formally equivalent, but obedience to the divine word here begins the process of displacing sacrifice. The covenant is finally an alliance or binding of Israel to the God "who brought you out of the land of Egypt, out of the house of slavery."

B. The Struggle over Sacrifice

1. Slaying of the Firstborn

In the fourth section of chapter 2, "Patterns in the Brother Stories," I presented a brief overview of the narrative convention that has the younger brother replacing the older brother in God's favor and receiving of the promises of God that inform the Torah narrative. I pointed out that even though the older brother is excluded from the line of promise to Abraham, he is nonetheless blessed and shown to be deeply related to the younger brother in the larger story of God and the world. Moreover, the younger brother must also undergo a kind of sacrificial ordeal, for he is not exempt from the victimization mechanism and sacrificial structures that the world imposes.

Now one of the striking patterns in the Torah is the relation of the foundational stories of older and younger brother and the sacrificial legislation requiring offering of the firstborn son, the *bekor*. Just as the *bekor* is always displaced by the youngest son, so the *bekor* must be sacrificed to God. In the Covenant Code God stipulates, "The firstborn of your sons you shall give to me" (Exod 22:29). Exactly what "give" means in this verse has been disputed. There can be no doubt, however, that, on the basis of a study of both the history of religions and the Girardian model developed and employed in this book, the Israelite tradition represents strong traces of earlier practices of child sacrifice. The references to child sacrifice are quite clear not only among foreign nations (2 Kings 3:27) but also among Israelites (2 Kings 16:34, Hiel of Bethel laying the foundation of Jericho "with Abiram his firstborn" [my translation]; 2 Kings 16:3, Ahaz offering his son or "making him pass through fire"; see 2 Kings 23:10; Jer 7:32; 19:11–12; also 32:35, on child sacrifice in the Valley of Hinnom). It is prohibited in Leviticus 18:21; 20:2–5 and Deuteronomy 18:10, and condemned in Deuteronomy 12:31.

Now although the biblical narrative is very negative about Hiel and Ahaz, it is interesting that the king of Moab's act of sacrificing his firstborn son in order to avert an Israelite attack is reported matter-of-factly. When he performed the sacrifice, "a great wrath came upon Israel, so they withdrew from him and returned to their own land" (2 Kings 3:27). The Israelite narrator accepts this sacrifice of the firstborn as a matter of course. Deuteronomy condemns such practices (Deut 18:10), and so presumably the historians influenced by Deuteronomy who did the final editing of Kings would condemn it also.

The point is that the tradition knew of child sacrifice as a phenomenon not merely of the remote past and was forced to come to grips with it. Mark Smith has recently argued that it was a phenomenon of royal, urban religious practices.[11] His conclusion, however, does not deal with the divine command to offer the firstborn that we find in Exodus 22:29. Even if by the historical period (from the time of the Judges on) this was understood as a principle of God's rightful ownership for which a substitute could be made (so, for example, Exod 34:20), the point is that the *principle* of the sacrifice of the firstborn was not challenged in ancient Israel except by the great prophets.[12]

Israel inherited from ancient Near Eastern cultures the principle of a foundational slaying; some of its clans and individuals, understandably, reverted to this practice in times of crisis. It may have been more widespread than the biblical texts indicate. The main thrust of Israel's sacrificial legislation is to overcome child sacrifice through a series of substitutions, which will be discussed shortly.

In any case, the right of the God of Israel to Israel's firstborn sons is certainly acknowledged in principle. We may note also the commandment in Exodus 34: 20: "The firstborn of a donkey you shall redeem with a lamb, or if you will not redeem it you shall break its neck. All the firstborn of your sons you shall redeem." Here, as well as in Exodus 13:13, the ritual evidently involves presenting the firstborn son at the altar and redeeming him with an animal substitute.

In Exodus 13 the consecration of the firstborn of humans and animals (vv. 1–2) is connected, as a primary sign of devotion to the God of Israel, to the exodus and the acquisition of Canaan (vv. 3–20). This substitution of an animal for the firstborn is replaced in the priestly tradition by the Levites, who stand before the altar in the place of Israel's firstborn (Num 3:11–13; 8:14–19; 18:15). In turn, the firstlings of the Levites' cattle are to be sacrificed in place of the firstlings of the cattle of Israel for the firstborn (Num 3:41, 44), and for the number of Israel's firstborn beyond the number of Levites a monetary redemption is to be offered (Num 3:44–48).[13] This system of one-for-one representation, a Levite for a firstborn son, is ideal and probably was never realized historically, but the important thing is the understanding of representation as sacrificial substitution that we find in the priestly materials.

As stand-ins for the firstborn the Levites are "to make atonement for the Israelites, in order that there may be no plague among the Israelites for coming too close to the sanctuary" (Num 8:19). The offering of the firstborn through the Levites as surrogates averts the plague, the disorder of mimetic conflict and rivalry that in a theology of divine anger is ascribed both to God and to the responsibility of the community (on the theology of divine anger, see the excursus at the end of chap. 2).

In the next subsection of this chapter I will offer a hypothesis on how the Exodus narrative understands the process by which the Levites became priestly surrogates. Meanwhile let us focus on the relation of the consecration of the first-born sons and the slaying of the Egyptian firstborn. The connection made by the narrator in Exodus 13:14–15 is quite clear:

> And when in time to come your son asks you, "What does this [act of redeeming the firstborn] mean?" you shall say to him, "By strength of hand the LORD brought us out of Egypt, from the house of bondage. For when Pharaoh stubbornly refused to let us go, the LORD slew all the first-born in the land of Egypt, both the first-born of man and the first-born of cattle. Therefore I sacrifice to the LORD all the males that first open the womb; but all the first-born of my sons I redeem." (RSV)

It does not matter how the sacrifice of the firstborn and the interpretation of the exodus came to be connected in the tradition; the primary thing is that they *were* connected, that the tellers of Israel's story understood the connection between the creation of a new people, the slaying of victims, and the sacrificial rite that was probably more important than any other, for the offering of the firstborn son stood in principle for all other forms of sacrifice. To offer the firstborn male is the chief representation for offering the life of the family and the group, as expressed also in sacrificing firstfruits and the firstlings of the cattle.

We have seen that the Exodus story has a historical core rooted in actual oppression of Hebrews, which may have included infanticide. The Israelite narra-tors shaped the earlier accounts to serve their own theological and ritual ends, but right at the center of their web of tradition, clear and constant, is the tale of oppression and the affirmation of the God who takes their part. The slaying of the Egyptian firstborn, whatever factual basis it may or may not have, is the narrative climax of the chaos, of the plague that besets the oppressor at the height of his mimetic crisis. Egypt loses its firstborn sons, and the foreign slaves are expelled. The Exodus narratives attribute this, of course, to the design of the God of Israel, for in them a theology of divine anger that has not completely realized the mean-ing of the God of victims affects the understanding of the God of the Fathers and the God of the Burning Bush. Israel as represented in Exodus has not extricated itself completely from the mythical camouflage of the victimization mechanism, in which the scapegoat becomes the god who is responsible for the community's blessings after the slaying of a victim, to whom is attributed the disorder prior to the murder.

From the standpoint of the biblical narrative, the slaying of Egypt's firstborn sons and all the firstlings of the cattle is a *limitation* of the disease and disorder that a massive plague could produce. As long recognized in biblical criticism, all the plague narratives have a ritual cast, as though Israel's beginnings in the exodus are being translated into the ritual language whose significance could be understood and communicated in the tradition. A plague-event is thus translated into sacrificial terms, and as a sacrifice it has a positive and negative side for Egypt. The negative side is the culmination of warnings to release the Hebrews; the positive side is that the slayings are intended to end the conflict and violence already breaking out in Egypt. In this latter regard, the death of the firstborn of Egypt is not for the sake of Israel but for the sake of Egypt. Israel has its own sacrifices and its own problems in struggling with sacred violence.

So we see two things quite clearly in the slaying of Egypt's firstborn. (1) Egypt has brought it on itself through policies of oppression and violence. (2) The chaos could have ended with the slaying of the Egyptian firstborn if the king had been able to comprehend the event as sacrificial. He could not or would not, he pursued Israel with his army (an organized mob), and they ended up covered by the sea, sinking down in the waters to the "floods" and the "deeps" (Exod. 15:8). The undifferentiation of Egypt's mimetic violence rejoins the undifferentiation of the cosmic chaos of the deep waters.

In conclusion concerning the slaying of the firstborn sons, the preeminence of the sacrificial institution of the offering of the firstborn, at least through surrogates, and the pattern of the displacement or replacement of the oldest son in the stories of founding figures shows that both the cultic sphere of sacrifice and the narrative sphere of founding stories were deeply imprinted with a substitutionary code that attempted to deal with and ameliorate the victimization mechanism that is endemic to culture. This substitutionary code took form in multiple developments and variations and could be ended only by a truly divine innocent victim who discloses the God of victims and unmasks the disguises of religion and culture. We shall take note of the movement toward this disclosure in the Servant of the LORD. The psalmist, at the edge of this disclosure, calls upon God, "Deliver me from murder [Hebrew *damim*, blood], O God" (Ps 51:14, my translation), and he affirms,

> For you have no delight in sacrifice;
> were I to give a burnt offering,

you would not be pleased.
The sacrifice acceptable to God is a broken spirit;
a broken and contrite heart, O
God, you will not despise.

(Ps 51:16–17)

Likewise the prophetic voice that asks rhetorically whether God wants sacrifice of one's firstborn for one's transgression (Mic. 6:7); the answer:

He has told you, O mortal, what is good;
and what does the LORD require of you
but to do justice, and to love kindness,
and to walk humbly with your God?

(Mic 6:8)

2. Rebellion and Brothers in Conflict

The incidents in Exodus 32 and Leviticus 10:1–3 offer a number of clues as to how Israel understood the origins of the sacrificial cult and the Levitic priesthood. These clues are presented dramatically and in some respects opaquely; however, certain basic matters come through with startling clarity. Substitution and displacement, anchors of sacrificial thinking, are illuminated in an unusual manner.

Following the lead of Stuart Lasine[14] in reading the text of Exodus 32 with a literary consistency, the following issues emerge:

a. When Moses asks for volunteers for YHWH, all the sons of Levi gather about him. Moses commands the Levites to take up their swords and to "slay every man his brother, and every man his companion, and every man his neighbor" (32:27). They kill three thousand men, and Moses commends them, "Today you have ordained yourselves for the service of the LORD, each one at the cost of his son and of his brother, that he may bestow a blessing upon you this day" (32:29, RSV).

Although "the people" are the object of the attack (so 32:25), only three thousand are slain. What is the basis of this selectivity, or is there any criterion at all? Are only fellow Levites slain?—such could be allowed by a literal reading of the text. And why is Aaron exempt from punishment?

b. Moses will reascend to the LORD in order to make atonement for their sin. He asks God to forgive their sin—"but if not, blot me out of the book that you have written" (32:32). The LORD replies, "Whoever has sinned against me will I blot out of my book" (32:33). He then promises divine judgment, which comes in the form of a plague upon the people.

Why does Moses not first offer himself as a sacrifice of atonement rather than having the Levites take up the sword? And concomitantly, once the judgment or division has taken place with the slaying of the three thousand, why does the LORD send a plague?

c. Earlier, before Moses came down from the mountain to see the golden calf and the celebration, the LORD had informed him of what was talking place below and had promised to destroy the people with his wrath. Moses interceded, and God repented of this. Why then the series of incidents that follow?

I think the strange features of the mustering of the Levites can be accounted for adequately by the argument of Gil Bailie: Exodus 32 represents, from the standpoint of the Israelite tradition, "the formal institutionalization of the sacrificial cult," whose genesis comes about when the three thousand are slain.[15] Lasine infers along similar lines that "the installation of the Levites in Exodus 32:29 begins a process of ritual duties and identity for the tribe which culminates in the book of Numbers after Korah's rebellion."[16]

In collective violence the primary pattern is all against one. One variation can obviously be the many against a few, and another is a group of superior strength (due to numbers, weapons, or some other factor) against a weaker group. The Levites are of superior strength because they have swords, and the Torah traditions ascribe to them a violent nature. Levi and Simeon attack the Shechemites (Gen 34) and are condemned in Jacob's final pronouncement on his sons: "Simeon and Levi are brothers; weapons of violence are their swords" (Gen 49:5). The Levite Phineas's vaunted act of zealotry in Numbers 25:1–15 involved killing not only the Midian woman Cozbi but also her lover, the Simeonite Zimri. Because Simeon is a brother-tribe (both Levi and Simeon are sons of Leah), Lasine comments that Phineas's act "appears to be another case of sacrificial fratricide," one comparable to the incident in Exodus 32.[17] Finally, in Judges 19 it is a Levite who cuts up his dead concubine into twelve pieces as a message to the tribes of Israel. The concubine had been raped and killed by men of the tribe of Benjamin. Her dead body, in turn, becomes a means of uniting Israel against Benjamin. The Levite "offered" her to the mob as a substitute for himself and his host. The Levite's contact with the dead body under Levite statutes would have defiled him (Lev 21:1–3), and he defiled as well the body of the dead person. In fact, in hacking up the body he has the ritual appearance of a sort of sacred executioner, as does Saul at a later time (1 Sam 11:7).

One of two hypotheses must therefore be held concerning the origins of the Levites: either they committed acts of violence in the name of their God and were set aside for the priesthood because of this, because they were contaminated by sacred violence and posed a threat to the tribes unless they were controlled; or there were acts of violence committed by others, and the Levites were set aside as a kind of scapegoat tribe to which the other tribes could turn for redemption. A third alternative, that Israel's traditionists completely fabricated a violent history for the Levites, is unlikely. However, if such a history of violence had been fabricated, which I doubt, it would still imply the association of violence with the priests as guardians of the sacred.

The effect of all the alternatives is the same, of course: the Levites become scapegoats for the atonement of Israel, and they in turn are redeemed by animals or money. The foundation of this Levite role is represented in the narrative of Exodus 32.

As for the identity of those the Levites kill in Exodus 32, I have already mentioned the possibility that they are fellow Levites. The alternative reading of "brothers" and "neighbors" is that of fellow members of the new covenant society. In any case, with the Levite aspect of the narrative we encounter a sort of ritualization of mob violence whose object is to show how the Levites came to be set aside for priestly service, "each one at the cost of his son and of his brother."

Whether or not the slaughter takes place among the people as a whole, the Levite passage, verses 25–29, serves to highlight the foundation of the Levite priesthood. The people's condition and punishment is related in that general symbolic catch-all, the plague. The plague is the undifferentiation that the people have already fallen into with the worship of the calf idol. In terms of how things work socially and historically, the condition of contagious mimetic conflict first prevails before the violence occurs and the sacrificial institution comes about. The narrator makes just a brief, vague, anticlimactic reference to the plague, a likely sign that the narrative focus is placed on the institution of the Levite priesthood.

It is noteworthy that Moses offers himself as a sacrificial ransom on behalf of the people. He says, "perhaps I can make atonement (*akapperah*) for your sin" (32:30), and asks that he be blotted out of God's book if God will not forgive the people. Presumably the death of the three thousand and the deaths in the plague remove the necessity of Moses' death as a sacrificial ransom. Underlying the first part of the account, verses 1–6, is the motif of Moses as scapegoat that we found in Exodus 15:22–27 and 17:1–7. Moses is the absent leader, and the gods the people demand are clearly to replace Moses: "Come, make gods for us, who shall go before us; as for this Moses, the man who brought us up out of the land of Egypt, we do not know what has become of him" (32:1). The people are reverting to their old mimesis, to the reenactment of slaves seeing themselves through the eyes of their Egyptian masters. Aaron takes advantage of the situation in assuming leadership. Not a little mimetic rivalry between Moses and Aaron must lurk under the surface of the story. The probable intention of the narrative tradition is to maintain "damage control" on conflict between Aaron and Moses in order to avoid confusion concerning models of authority. The confrontation of Moses with Aaron and Miriam in Numbers 12 is an exception, but even there, interestingly, it is Miriam, not Aaron, who is punished with leprosy.

Now let us take note of the strange incident in Leviticus 10:1–3. The two old-est sons of Aaron, Nadab and Abihu, are slain by a divine fire because they offered "unholy fire before the LORD."[18] The context is the ordination of the sons of Aaron in Leviticus 8–10. In the narration of what immediately precedes the pas-sage in question, a primitive streak of catharsis or purification may be seen in the ritual whereby the animal victim dies and God makes his presence known. "And Aaron lifted his hands toward the people and blessed them; and he came down after sacrificing the sin offering, the burnt offering, and the offering of well being. Moses and Aaron entered the tent of meeting, and then came out and blessed the people; and the glory of the LORD appeared to all the people. Fire came out from the LORD and consumed the burnt offering and the fat on the altar; and when all the people saw it, they shouted and fell on their faces" (Lev 9:22–24). The formal elements of the purification of the community in the primitive setting are still quite visible here. (1) The sacrificial victim or victims are offered, in this case a number of animals (Lev 9:3–4). (2) The deity, which at an earlier stage was the apotheosized victim, appears in "glory" or "honor" and is associated with the fire from the altar. It is likely that one of the really archaic elements of the ritual is rep-resented in the fire—the death of the victim produces the effective presence of the life-giving god. (3) The community is united in the thrill of unanimity brought about by the succession of the death of the victim and the flaring up of the fire ("they shouted and fell upon their faces").

What immediately follows, the incident of Nadab and Abihu, lacks a satisfying explanation. One could view it as a displaced way of getting at Jeroboam and his sons, as already mentioned. But even if that is one of the motives of the story, the manner of death is peculiar, and even more peculiar in context. A reason for the killing of the priestly pair is given, but their offering of "unholy fire" is reported vaguely. I suspect, following Bailie, that communal violence lies behind the tale. As the report of the ordination of the Levites in Leviticus 8–10 moves toward its conclusion, the story includes a juxtaposition of sin-offering and the brothers' unholy act. It is possible that the sin offering is a substitution for the people com-mitting violence. If we recall that God's punishing wrath is the concealed form of collective violence, then the fire from God could be a cover for mob action. If this hypothesis is correct, it would be another part of the picture of the beginnings of the Levite priesthood. The Levites were victims or have mythically replaced actual victims who were murdered in acts of collective violence.

A partial confirmation of this hypothesis is the narrative connection that is drawn between the death of the brothers and the narrative of the scapegoat in Leviticus 16. It would have been simple enough, and more common narrative pro-cedure, to have begun, "The LORD spoke to Moses"; the following adverbial phrase, "after the death of the two sons of Aaron," appears to connect what follows to the previous event in Leviticus 10. What we find in Leviticus 16 reads as though the scapegoat ritual is a further differentiating procedure, this time substituting animals for humans in order to avoid the offering of human victims in the control of violence. Aaron is told he will die if he comes into the holy place before the ark except at the appointed time when he makes atonement for the entire people. He engages in a ritual of dress, purification, and sacrificial offerings. The latter include one goat to be immolated and one to be sent into the wilderness to Azazel, a demon of the desert. I read the demon as an extension of the victim, who potentially "haunts" his victimizers, and as such is an attempt to separate the victim further from the God of Israel and his involvement in any kind of collective violence. If, as Gil Bailie argued, the priestly class who established the scapegoat ritual was thrown into a double bind because they knew what they were doing in connecting the death of Nadab and Abihu with the sacrifice of the two goats,[19] then it became even more important to dissociate YHWH from the violence of Levite beginnings.

One other detail in Leviticus should be noted, the silence of Aaron according to Leviticus 10:3. "And Aaron was silent" is an intriguing narrative notation. The Hebrew verb, *damam*, "to be or grow silent," is usually employed with a connotation of being forced to say nothing under hostile circumstances (e.g., Amos 5:13). It may even be synonymous with perishing (Jer 8:14; 48:2). Its occurrence here suggests that Aaron was either disturbed about Moses' leadership or distressed over the death of his sons. Perhaps both. We see later in the chapter that Moses becomes angry because the two younger sons of Aaron, Eleazar and Ithamar, have not eaten the goat of the sin offering. Although Moses' reprimand is evidently directed to these two sons of Aaron, it is Aaron who replies. The upshot of his reply in Leviticus 10:19 seems to be his fear that the LORD would be unwilling to accept his or their atonement for the people, and the unstated reason must be the sin of Nadab and Abihu. Surprisingly, Moses is content with this response (10:20). One can only surmise that in a situation of rivalry Aaron has humbled himself and Moses has acknowledged and accepted Aaron's statement about the deficiency of Aaron and his sons as the leaders of the priesthood.

The slaying of the priest brothers in Leviticus 10, taken as a narrative continuation of the Sinai episode in Exodus, reads like a reassertion of the primitive power of the act of sacrifice as it flows over its prescribed bounds and erupts in violence. It may also be viewed as a partial and covert representation of the origins of the priesthood. The association of the event with the congregational ecstasy over the glory of the LORD and the fire in 9:22–24 and with the conflict between Moses and the Aaronite priesthood in chapter 10 points, as I have proposed for Exodus 32, to the killing of Levite brothers and kinfolk as the act of collective violence from which the priesthood begins. At the same time, the priesthood that begins in violence is also the agency for controlling it.

The same sort of thing could be said about the Korah rebellion in Numbers 16–17. Again there is rivalry, this time much more open, in the form of rebellion. Again "brothers and kinsmen" are slain, in this case Korah, a descendant of Levi, and his followers. And as in Exodus 32, a smaller group is executed, and then the whole congregation is punished with a plague from God for having sided with the rebels. One of the most interesting things about the account from the standpoint of a theory of sacrifice is that the censers of the Korah group are to be hammered into plates as a covering for the altar (Num 17:36–40). The plates will serve as a sign, as a reminder to the children of Israel that only the priests who are descendants of Aaron through Eleazar may approach to burn incense before the LORD. The rebellious, rejected priests are thus represented on the altar itself. Their destruction confirms the differentiation of the priesthood into the Aaronites and the rest of the Levites.

There is no doubt then that whatever the precise historical core of these accounts, Israel was well aware that the beginnings of its priesthood were associated with violence, as were also its beginnings as the people of covenant with YHWH. But just as the God of innocent victims is revealed to Moses as one who delivers the oppressed and gives them covenant bonds and a law to live by, so also the authority of Moses and the exodus event ameliorates the sacrificial mechanism, the structure of sacred violence, which conceals persecution and elimination of victims. A structure of sacred violence is formally maintained both in law and in priesthood, but it is qualified by various substitutions that seek to put violence at a distance, and it is bounded and informed by the conviction stated in Leviticus 11:45: "For I am the LORD who brought you up out of the land of Egypt, to be your God; you shall therefore be holy, for I am holy."

Stuart Lasine observes that the rhetoric of the biblical narrators took into account and addressed an audience they assumed to be actually *related*, as kinfolk and descendants, to the Levites and other biblical personages. He points out that "this aspect of biblical rhetoric acts as an oblique way of leading readers to acknowledge their own potential to act as scapegoaters. In this sense biblical rhetoric transcends the tendency to scapegoat those we regard as scapegoaters."[20] The biblical narratives themselves document human failures and resist all attempts to camouflage and mythologize these failures completely.[21]

The failures are in part due to the weight of archaic cultural traditions in which mimetic desire, rivalry, and conflict are managed through victimization, scapegoating, and sacrifice. In Exodus, Leviticus, and Numbers we find many signs of these archaic survivals, not only in the murmuring against Moses, but also in the slaying of the three thousand (Exod 32), the death of Nadab and Abihu (Lev 10), and the rebellion of Korah (Num 16–17). One must add to these texts others indicating the Levites' reputation for violence (Gen 34; 49:5–7; Num 25:6–13). Violent deeds there are, but a "covenant of peace" is purchased by the violent acts (Num 25:12–13), which are not to be repeated. The Levites themselves are to be substitutes for Israel's firstborn males; the Levites' cattle is to be offered in place of the cattle for the firstborn, and the remaining firstborn, beyond the number of corresponding Levites, are to be redeemed by monetary payment. The Levites as substitutes are already sacrificed, in principle, in that they belong to the LORD (Num 3:44). The series of substitutions is striking. Its purpose is to mitigate violence. But it could continue indefinitely in an endless chain of substitutions.

The revelation struggling to make itself known in the covenant, commandments, and cultic texts reaches a new stage of clarity with the great prophets, to whom we now turn. As I pointed out in chapter 1, the main pillars of the social order are the religious realities of myth, ritual, and prohibition. Myth may be viewed as the primary narrative and symbolic expression that legitimates both sacrifice and the obsession with differentiation that prohibition or primitive law reinforces. The prophets subverted the primitive, universal foundations of religion and culture that continued to have considerable influence in ancient Israelite institutions. But in order to understand the origin and vocation of the prophets, it is necessary first to examine the institution of kingship.

5

Kings and Prophets:
Sacred Lot and Divine Calling

. . . but the goat on which the lot fell for Azazel shall be presented alive before
the LORD to make atonement over it, that it may be sent away into the
wilderness to Azazel.

Leviticus 16:10

And I heard the voice of the LORD saying, "Whom shall I send, and who will go
for us?" Then I said, "Here am I! Send me."

Isaiah 6:8

They on the other side that had conspired his death compassed him in on every
side with their swords drawn in their hands . . . and [Caesar] was hackled and
mangled among them, as a wild beast taken of hunters. For it was agreed among
them that every man should give him a wound, because all their parts should be
in this murder.

Plutarch, *Lives*

. . . and the whole rabid pack were on him. There was a single, universal howl:
the moans of Pentheus (so long as he had breath) mixed with their impassioned
yells. One woman carried off an arm, another a foot, boot and all; they shredded
his ribs—clawed them clean. . . . His body lies in pieces.

Euripides, *The Bacchae*

Forthwith the whole company fall on the victim [a camel] with their swords,
hacking off pieces of the quivering flesh and devouring them raw with such
wild haste, that in the short interval between the rise of the day star . . . and the
disappearance of its rays before the rising sun, the entire camel, body and
bones, skin, blood and entrails, is wholly devoured.

W. Robertson Smith, *The Religion of the Semites*

A. The Calling of Prophets and Kings

The conflict between ancient Israelite prophets and kings is apparent, and the
conventional wisdom is that they had a completely separate origin and function.
The great prophets who were independent critics of the monarchy stood in the
traditions of the old Israelite tribal confederacy with charismatic leadership; the
kings based their rule either on the sanction of military power or on a dynastic
principle. In fact, the great dynastic ideology of the descendants of David in

Jerusalem was rooted in a symbolism of kingship that became intertwined with the traditions of Zion, so that for a period even well before the Babylonian Exile one can speak of a David-Zion tradition.[1]

The biblical writers, however, understood the basis of kingship and of prophecy to be essentially the same. Samuel was divinely guided to choose Saul as the first king, and Saul's selection was not completed until he "prophesied" with a band of prophets (1 Sam 9–10). The text narrates a kind of ritual process in which Saul first becomes "prophet," then king. David was also selected by the agency of Samuel (1 Sam 16:1–13). In Nathan's oracle to David concerning building a "house" for the LORD (temple) and a "house" for David (dynasty), the LORD says, "I took you from the pasture, from following the sheep to be prince over my people Israel" (2 Sam 7:8). The wording is strikingly similar to that in Amos's account of his calling: "and the LORD took me from following the flock, and the LORD said to me, 'Go, prophesy to my people Israel'" (Amos 7:15). From this standpoint, clearly the role of the king is a *calling* that closely resembles a prophet's call. This is also the understanding of Isaiah in envisioning an ideal Davidic king in the future: "And the Spirit of the LORD shall rest on him" (Isa 11:2). And this anointing of the future king with the Spirit may be compared to the anointing of the prophet in Isaiah 61:1: "The Spirit of the Lord God is upon me, because the LORD has anointed me to bring good tidings to the afflicted" (RSV). Hosea, contrasting the work of Moses with the antics of Jacob, says, "By a prophet the LORD brought Israel up out of Egypt, and by a prophet he was preserved" (Hos. 12:13, RSV). In other words, Hosea depicts Moses as a prophet whose office overlaps kingly functions. It is possible that Jeremiah's calling in Jeremiah 1:4–10 expresses the prophet's understanding that the royal office of rule and sovereignty was being transferred to the prophet in his function of bearer of the LORD's word.[2]

In other words, the tradition understands, ideally at least, both the prophet and the king as singled out for a role among the people of God that represents the divine will for the people's present life or future welfare. A peculiar thing about being singled out, being chosen to prophesy or to rule, is that the structure of the process is very much like being singled out as a scapegoat. In the case of the king, a great number of people or their representatives presumably support the acclamation of a king, and even if there is a power struggle of some sort, a broad base of positive popular feeling is a necessary condition to kingship. At this point of popular support we may find the line where kingship and prophecy diverge into two different offices or roles. The king is the one singled out by the collective voice to lead and rule, and he is perforce obliged to obey this collective voice. This collective voice may be identified with God's will (*vox populi vox dei*), though in Israel the emergence of the prophets itself produces at least a tension between the two. The prophet is the one singled out by the voice of God to prophesy to his or her society, and the prophet is subject to this divine voice, which in many cases is highly critical of the monarchy. My argument is that prophecy and kingship have their origin in the same social reality. My thesis is that both roles stem from a "selection" that amounts to exclusion or expulsion from the community, whether self-imposed or not, and that comes to be understood by some in the Israelite context as *the call of YHWH to assume a special responsibility for those who are likewise expelled, excluded, or marginal.* Those who are thus oppressed or marginalized could be the people as a whole, individuals within the covenant community, groups or classes within the covenant people, or even foreigners.

The Israelite king was responsible for the needs of all his people, including the poor and victimized (Ps 72:4), a responsibility that Absalom opportunistically exploited in order to build up a following for revolt against his father David (2 Sam 15:1–6). However, the power of the office and the pull of archaic institutions that still influenced Israel prevented kingship from being the locus of the distinctively Israelite insight concerning the call of YHWH to take the side of victims.

Let us recall, before pursuing the subject further in the biblical context, that Girard's theory of sacred kingship is that the origins of kingship can only be adequately comprehended on the basis of the victimization mechanism and sacrifice (see chap. 1). To reiterate what I said in the first chapter, Girard holds that investing the king with sacred powers stems from the primitive attainment of order through selecting and executing a victim. The sacral kingship emerged as one form of sacred order because there was often a lapse of time between choosing a victim and the actual sacrifice. Because superhuman powers were ascribed to the victim, the latter could, in some instances, use the interval to gain more and more influence over the community, eventually prolonging the interval and achieving real political power. Girard says also, concerning the expression of the sacred in monarchy and in divinity, "In monarchy the interpretation accentuates the interval between the selection of the victim and the immolation; it is a matter of the victim being still alive, one that has not yet been sacrificed. In the case of divinity, by contrast, the interpretation accentuates a victim that has already been sacrificed and it is a matter of the sacred having been already expelled from the community."[3] In *Violence and the Sacred* Girard discusses the evidence gathered by anthropologists concerning an African culture in which the king goes through the ritual of committing all sorts of crimes (the "undoing" of prohibition) and is then executed in a sacrificial rite. "The parallelism between the Oedipus myth and these African observances is striking. . . . Behind the Athenian pharmakos, behind the Oedipus myth, there is real violence at work, reciprocal violence brought to an end by the unanimous slaughter of the surrogate victim."[4] Succession to the throne often triggers a ritual battle between father and sons or between sons of the dead king. In the latter instance the theme of *enemy brothers* reappears.[5]

The king as originally a victim is reflected also in many Mesopotamian texts in which a substitute for the king is put to death. Alberto Green, in a summary of the results of his research, includes the finding that human sacrifice can be traced throughout the Middle East and into the Indus Valley. Ritual killing of royal attendants and sacrifice of children was practiced; there was also a pattern of human victims as "adult substitutes for kings in India and Mesopotamia."[6] Throughout the Semitic world there is adequate evidence for this conclusion. Green is more cautious about ancient Egypt, holding that the texts concerning the Old Kingdom period are too difficult to interpret to maintain with certainty that instead of sacrificing the king, a surrogate was offered. It will be clear to the reader, given the theoretical perspective of this book and my earlier statements about Egyptian culture (chap. 3), that I have little doubt the practice of sacrificing the king, and later a king-substitute, was known also among the Egyptians.

In light of the hypothesis developed here, the selection of Marduk as king of the gods in the Babylonian epic of creation (*Enuma Elish*) may be viewed as a projection into the divine realm of the ritual process of choosing a victim who rises to the status of the ruler of the collectivity whose violence generated the structure resulting in kingship. As told in tablets two through four of the epic, Marduk is chosen by the *assembly* of the gods, who proclaim a decree for him, who fix for him an eternal destiny. The decree of fate or destiny is structurally related to and probably generated by the exclusionary or victimization process that is managed through the casting of lots, as for example in Joshua 7 (determining the transgressor of the holy war injunctions), Leviticus 16:8 (determining the scapegoat), and, as we shall see, 1 Samuel 10 (choosing the king). The casting of lots was used for apportioning the land of Canaan (Josh. 18:6). Both the word for lot, *goral*, and the word for portion or allotment, *cheleq*, could be used for God-given destiny, fate, or retribution.[7]

Concerning Marduk's rule over the gods, I read the slaying of the goddess Tiamat's consort Kingu as a substitute for the death of Marduk, who mythically represents the original sacred victim. After Marduk defeats Tiamat and splits her body, the assembly of the gods, manipulated by Marduk, decides to execute her consort Kingu (tablet six). From the blood of Kingu humankind would be formed by Marduk. As Widengren has noted, Kingu represents a side of Marduk, that of the suffering and dying god. He is, indeed, "viewed cultically, a substitute sacrifice for Marduk."[8] Human beings thus have their origin in what is presented as an act of just revenge, but that in fact is a kind of sacrifice overseen by Marduk the divine executioner. According to the Girardian hypothesis employed here, the original death of the one decreed to be victim has become further differentiated in the myth-making process, so that the victim-become-king is able to slay another in his stead. What the myth conceals is that the two, Marduk the maker and Kingu the supplier of the "stuff," the blood of human creatures, were originally one.

A confirmation of this reading of the myth of Marduk is found in the long-standing Babylonian New Year's ritual, which included the death of the divinity as symbolized by the sacrifice of a bull. The king as representative of Marduk suffers humiliations. He is struck down and must spend three days in the underworld. A "mock king" rules in his place. There is a festival of fate or destiny that foretells events of the coming year. At the end of the twelve-day festival the king is rein-stalled in his former position of authority and represents once more Marduk as victorious.[9]

Concerning the biblical texts, in their final form they represent a witness to revelation that has for the most part become distant from the primitive sacred. However, there are definite traces of a sacrificial mechanism that are enfolded into a new, distinctively Israelite context. Some of the clearest signs are to be found in descriptions of Job's status before his downfall (see Job 29). Job's prior "kingly" status will be dealt with in the next chapter.

Another clear instance of the involvement of the sacrificial mechanism in the origins of kingship is found in the story of Saul. According to 1 Samuel 10:20–24 he is *chosen by lot* as king. The process of selection moves from the tribes to the tribe of Benjamin, from Benjamin to the clan of the Matrites, and from the clan of the Matrites to Saul, son of Kish. The verb that the RSV and NRSV translate "take by lot" is quite interesting. It is the Hebrew *lakad*, whose ordinary meaning is "capture" or "seize" in both its active and passive forms. It is the verb used in Joshua 7 to determine who has transgressed the rules of holy war. The use of a word like this for selecting a king must reflect a very ancient practice of determin-ing the *pharmakos*, the sacred victim. The ritual process is a re-presentation of the situation of spontaneous violence, which is now controlled by the community with its ritual tradition.

With regard to spontaneous violence, the tale of the destruction of Sodom and Gomorrah is instructive (Gen 19). Lot offers to "bring out" his daughters for the local Sodomites. They refuse the offer, castigating him as an uppity foreigner who "would play the judge" (19:9). A judge (*shofet*), someone who "judges" (*yish-pot*) or establishes order, is a ruler. Once again we see the classical structural fea-tures that are present in the Oedipus myth and that characterize myth in general: in a community's mimetic crisis it converges upon the foreigner, particularly the foreigner who has come from without and attained success in some fashion.

The Sodomites want to "know" the men, the two angels. But they are struck with blindness and find themselves groping around for Lot's door. Their blindness is indicative of the undifferentiation of violence. In the rescue scene Lot lingered, "so the two men seized him and his wife and his two daughters by the hand, the LORD being merciful to him, and they brought him forth and set him outside the city" (Gen 19:16). This is a paradigm text of the divine concern for the innocent victim—God in his mercy brings forth the victims and sets them outside the per-secuting community. We should take special note of the verb "seize," *chazaq*. It means to be strong, to strengthen, and in the form of its occurrence in this text, to take hold of or seize. Here it really means to grasp firmly and decisively in order to lead someone somewhere. In this respect it occurs as a metaphor of the LORD leading his people out of Egypt (Jer 31:32) or leading his people in a new exodus back to Jerusalem (Isa 41:9, 13). In other contexts, it may denote violence (Deut 22:25) and be associated with mimetic paroxysm, as in Zechariah 14:13: "And on that day a great panic from the LORD shall fall on them, so that each will seize the hand of a neighbor, and the hand of the one will be raised against the hand of the other." This panic is caused by a plague that will beset both people and animals (Zech 14:12, 15). In short, although the text of Genesis 19 relates the rescue of Lot and his daughters, it retains a structural element of the "lot," or community decree, falling upon the victim. In this case, however, it is reversed and transformed into God's act of deliverance. Nonetheless, the older form of the violence lying behind the victimization mechanism may be discerned in Judges 19, which recounts a parallel situation of wicked inhabitants ranting to rape a stranger, the visiting Levite. There the verb *chazaq* is used for a violent act of throwing the victim to the mob in place of the Levite who owned her: "So the man seized his concubine, and put her out to them; and they knew her, and abused her all night until the morning. And as the dawn began to break, they let her go" (Judg 19:25).

If we keep in mind this background concerning a community or group "selection" process, with its roots in a ritual of sacrifice or scapegoating, we are not surprised that Saul hides among the baggage and has to be rousted out! This may not be simple modesty or undue humility, but a sense of the danger that becoming king will bring him. When he is fetched and brought to Samuel, Samuel presents him to the people, and the people shout, "Long live the king!" (1 Sam 10:24).

Many signs of the scapegoat phenomenon are evident in this passage. (1) *Crisis*: the social and political crisis of the time of the judges and the military threat posed by the Philistines are addressed by the selection of a "king" who is clearly a victim of converging mimetic forces. (2) *Selection by lot* has already been discussed. (3) *Saul's height*: he is "head and shoulders taller than any of [the people]" (1 Sam 10:23). Saul is *different* from the others, which is characteristic of the scapegoat, and different in a way that makes him seem imposing.[10] (4) *Sacrality of the king*: the association of the king with prophets and the gift of prophecy has already been mentioned.[11]

So the selection of Saul retains elements of the sacrificial mechanism stemming from the primitive sacred. What we find there is a procedure whose structure is that of a *game of chance*: the one chosen by lot is "it," and everyone converges on him—or runs away from him as the case may be—in order to keep every person joined together in the game. Saul was certainly concerned about everyone running away from him, about loss of popular support. He offered burnt offerings and peace offerings because Samuel delayed in coming to Gilgal and the people were scattering (1 Sam 13:8). In the conflict with the people over the execution of Jonathan because Jonathan transgressed Saul's oath, "the people ransomed Jonathan, that he did not die" (1 Sam 14:45). In the conflict with Samuel over sparing the king of the Amalekites and the best of the sheep and oxen, which were to be sacrificed to YHWH, Saul attributes his action to what the people wanted (1 Sam 15:15).

Saul's oath and its outcome in 1 Samuel 14 is instructive concerning Saul's scapegoat status. In the context of battle with the Philistines, Saul swore an oath that anyone was cursed who ate food before nightfall. Jonathan, not having heard the oath, tasted some honey. The Israelites succeeded that day largely because of Jonathan's daring leadership. Later, however, when Saul wanted to lead an expedition by night against the enemy, the priest could get no answer from the LORD. Saul, believing that his oath had indeed been broken, then ranged his troops on one side and himself and Jonathan on the other. The sacred lots were cast, and Saul and Jonathan were taken; they were cast again, and Jonathan was taken. Saul is then at the point of executing Jonathan, but the people intervene. They exclaim that Jonathan has accomplished victory for Israel and "ransom" him.

Some interpretive remarks about this narrative are in order. Jonathan is taken or "trapped" by the lot, just as his father had been. But the people ransom him, presumably with an animal sacrifice at the altar Saul had constructed (14:35). The Israelites (evidently Saul's troops), whose wishes Saul had both to read and to govern, also read and governed him. They ransom or redeem Jonathan, thus rescuing him from the execution of his own son. At the same time the end of the story finds Saul once more alone, singled out, with everyone else ranged against the scapegoat-king. The people have supported Jonathan, who had brought them victory. Moreover, sparing his life meant they would have in reserve the prince, the son of the scapegoat-king, as the new scapegoat if something happened to Saul.

That Saul consults the medium at En-Dor after having banned mediums and wizards from the land is another sign not only of Saul's difficulties but of the very nature of kingship. Prior to battling the Philistines he is afraid and he encounters divine silence: "the LORD did not answer him, not by dreams, or by Urim, or by prophets" (1 Sam 28:6). He finds a woman at En-Dor known as a medium and prevails upon her to bring Samuel up from the realm of the dead. Samuel is as "a god (elohim) coming up out of the earth" (1 Sam 28:13, RSV). Saul informs Samuel that he has sought him out and disturbed his rest as a last desperate measure, for he feels that all is lost before the Philistines. But Samuel offers him no comfort, castigating him again for his disobedience in not executing "[God's] fierce wrath against Amalek" (v. 18). David is now the LORD's chosen; the Philistines will slay Saul and Jonathan in battle.

There are some features of this account that betray a close acquaintance with local veneration of the dead. Girard has commented that where ancestors, or the dead, are worshiped, in times of crisis "the dead are displeased and visit their displeasure on the living. They bring nightmares, madness, contagious diseases. . . . The crisis assumes the form of a loss of difference between the living and the dead, a casting down of all barriers between two normally separate realms."[12] The dead incarnate violence, for death itself "is the ultimate violence that can be inflicted on a living being. It is therefore the extreme of maleficence." The survivors "have recourse to funeral rites, which (like all other rites) are dedicated to the purgation and expulsion of maleficent violence."[13]

Saul is partially caught up in this ancient Canaanite veneration of the dead. It appears that Samuel "haunts" him, so he seeks to give himself rest, peace of mind, by disturbing Samuel's rest. The text makes it quite clear that Samuel's spirit did not come to Saul: Saul sought it out; it is Saul's anxiety at work. At the same time, he has had the people's fickleness, including David's popular following, to worry about. He is caught between Samuel and the people, the voice of the prophet representing primarily a theology of wrath against the *vox populi*, whose instincts are primitive in desiring sacrifice and visible displays of power like those David seems to have offered them.

David Gunn has penetrated almost, but not quite, to the heart of the tragic story of Saul.[14] He points out quite rightly that Saul is a victim, the victim of a divinely determined fate. Saul can do nothing about this fate, which has nothing to do with his moral qualities. Gunn makes some interesting comparisons of Saul's predicament to Shakespeare's MacBeth, King Lear, and Othello (mentioning Oedipus a few times in passing), and he indicates as well some of the similarities of Saul to Job. Of course, what distinguishes Job from Saul are those luminous moments in Job's speeches when he cries out to the God of victims beyond the social god of the victimizers (see chap. 6). Saul, however, does not rise above the mimetic forces in which he is caught. As I have already said, he is continually swayed by the people, who are his mimetic mirror of power. Of course, ideally or ideologically in the narrative, it is *God* who is his source of power and authority— but the voice of God from this ideal standpoint comes through Samuel, who is another mediator whom Saul is constrained to imitate.

The conflict of mediators—the people versus Samuel—converges in the bands of prophets, who are a sort of *tertium quid* in relation to Samuel and the people. Saul gets caught up in prophetic ecstasy two times (1 Sam 10:9–14; 19:8–24). These prophets have an initiating function in Saul's rise to power, but his involvement with them later on brings to sharp expression his downfall. The activity of these ecstatic prophets was an expression of folk religion in that they did not have an official place in Israelite government and must have subsisted through donations of food and clothing. Nor did they invoke hereditary or dynastic principles to justify becoming prophets. On the other hand, it is Samuel who leads the prophetic band in one case and foretells that Saul will join a prophetic group in the other. This means that Saul's participation in prophetic ecstasy reflects Samuel's influence on him.

Saul is particularly subject to the contagion of group frenzy, both under the suggestive power of Samuel (1 Sam 10) and when Samuel is the leader of the group of prophets (1 Sam 19). Although Saul is separated from the general populace as king, he is so subject to mimetic influence that he must imitate the prophetic band. The prophetic "raving" or ecstatic behavior is probably an offshoot of a primitive ritual enactment of killing the sacred victim, which is unforgettably represented in Euripides' portrayal of the Dionysian craze of dismembering King Pentheus (see the epigraph at the beginning of this chapter). This ecstatic moment of the cultic sacrifice is likewise expressed in the dream of Caesar's wife in Shakespeare's *Julius Caesar:*

> She dreamt tonight she saw my statue,
> Which, like a fountain with an hundred spouts,
> Did run pure blood, and many lusty Romans
> Came smiling and did bathe their hands in it.[15]

This dream conveys the founding murder, which is played out in the murder of Caesar. But Caesar's interlocutor, Decius Brutus, immediately offers Caesar a reassuring interpretation that "corrects" the meaning sensed by Caesar's wife:

> This dream is all amiss interpreted;
> It was a vision fair and fortunate:
> Your statue spouting blood in many pipes,
> In which so many smiling Romans bathed,
> Signifies that from you great Rome shall suck
> Reviving blood, and that great men shall press
> For tinctures, stains, relics, and cognizance.[16]

What Decius tells Caesar to do, in other words, is to take his dream as allegorical or symbolic, having nothing to do with a real event. It is an oneiric or spiritual message concerning Caesar's leadership and greatness. And Caesar, wanting to believe this aggrandized image of his greatness, does believe him. Like modern interpreters dealing with violence and sacrifice in their texts, Caesar is easily seduced into accepting this symbolic interpretation that separates death and violence from anything real and goes off to meet his fate.

Indeed, if one compares the tragedy of Saul to any of Shakespeare's works, *Julius Caesar* is the play whose theme is closest to the fate of Saul, for the real subject of *Julius Caesar* is *the people as crowd and mob.*[17] It is the people's accolades that Marcus Brutus really desires, and in desiring them he is imitating Caesar, whom he truly loves. He loves him, but he wishes to acquire what Caesar has because Caesar has it—power and fame. This supremacy cannot be conferred by the Senate, which Caesar controls; it must come from the crowd. It is the people to whom Brutus and Antony give their interpretations of Caesar's death. And it is in order to fabricate a story acceptable to the public that Antony makes his final speech describing Brutus's nobility and virtuous aims, for Brutus did envy

Caesar, and he had to rationalize Caesar's death. Repeating what generations of ancestors have done, Brutus turns a murder into a sacrifice:

> Let's carve him as a dish fit for the gods,
> Not hew him as a carcass fit for hounds.
> And let our hearts, as subtle masters do,
> Stir up their servants to an act of rage,
> And after seem to chide 'em. This still
> Makes our purpose necessary, and not envious,
> Which so appearing to the common eyes,
> We shall be called purgers, not murderers.[18]

In eulogizing Brutus at the end of the play, Antony is obviously engaging in a cover-up that in effect encompasses both Caesar's murder and Brutus's suicide in a myth of twofold execution (that of Caesar and Brutus) on which the kingship was founded.

Saul himself wants to be seen as worthy to "the common eyes." Perhaps in this he imitates Samuel, who becomes a model-obstacle for Saul. In any case, it is no wonder that Saul is beside himself when David begins to attract popular acclaim. Saul becomes infuriated that David seems to be gaining more kudos than he as a warrior, and he begins to see David as a rival for his status as king (1 Sam 18:6–9). "And on the next day an evil spirit from God rushed upon Saul, and he raved within his house, while David was playing the lyre, as he did day by day. Saul had his spear in his hand; and Saul cast the spear, for he thought, 'I will pin David to the wall.' But David evaded him twice" (1 Sam 18:10–11). Saul's behavior when he "prophesies" and strips off his clothes (1 Sam 19) is linked to his envy of David. The verb that the RSV and NRSV translate "rave" in chapter 18 (hitnabbe) is the same as the verb rendered "prophesy" in chapter 19. It denotes prophetic activity—dancing, singing, raving, repeating the divine name, or whatever was encompassed in this form of the root word meaning to prophesy. What Saul does in the presence of David and with Samuel and the prophets shows him to be a radically mediated figure, subject to the mimetic contagion associated with prophecy. He, the king, envies David his popular acclaim. "They have ascribed to David ten thousands [of enemy slain], and to me they have ascribed thousands" (18:8). In a situation of military danger, cultural change, and the popularity of David, he is trapped in a mimetic crisis.

But is he finally a tragic figure? I think the response to this question has to be complex and ambiguous because of the nature of the tradition and the narratives with which we are dealing. In a broad sense, yes, Saul is a tragic figure, and that means he is a scapegoat. David Gunn's comment is quite perceptive: "Saul falls victim to Yahweh's resentment over an imagined insult (the 'sin') and becomes the pawn (or scapegoat) in a process (the 'expiation') whereby Yahweh vindicates his shift of attitude towards the monarchy and buttresses his shaken self-esteem."[19]

There is a sense in which *any* monarchy is purchased at the price of offering a sacrifice; the king is always already a sacrificial victim. The king, after all, is in principle the sacred mediator of divine order, justice, and bounty (Ps 72). The psalmist sings, "May his name endure forever, his fame continue as long as the sun" (Ps 72:17). But what if things go wrong? What if crises threaten his subjects? Who is the primary object to blame but that same one who is the primary object of praise? His ability to remain in office will then depend on the power to refer victimization to substitutes, and of course this ability of referral (or displacement) becomes institutionalized as integral to kingship.

So what Gunn observes is in great part the workings of the sacred social order as it routinely justifies its structure of self-legitimation and differentiation, which necessitates ritual exclusions of the "foreign" and the "marred." This process is ascribed to the gods and to fate, there being no real difference between the two.

Now the principle that the monarchy as such was not Yahweh's will, flying (as it does) in the face of the old Yahwist tribal tradition, touches on a complication in understanding Saul. On the one hand, this principle is doubtlessly a doctrinal veneer justifying the scapegoating of Saul. But on the other hand, this very doctrinal guise could be used only if it had some claim to validity. The anti-monarchic strand in ancient Israel's political theology may be placed within the context of the struggle to give witness to the plight of victims and to the God of victims who cares for them. The narratives and laws displaying a distinct tendency to assume the viewpoint of the victim and to ameliorate violence do not easily concede the necessity of a *"Führer,"* a divine leader who possesses all the sacred gifts of rule, prophecy, judgment, priestly intercession, and so on, for this figure is an illusion of the crowd of slaves who see themselves through the master's imagined object of desire; and vice versa, it is the illusion of the master who sees himself in the slaves' adoration. Although a complete break with the mimetic phenomenon could not be accomplished in a short time (and perhaps will never be completely achieved in human history), the story of Moses and Israel in the wilderness is a paradigm of Israel's tradition of struggle to articulate a distinctive revelation (see chap. 3 under "The Exodus" and chap. 4).

But in another sense, no, Saul is not a tragic figure and thus not a scapegoat—not in the full sense. The tragic hero is always a scapegoat, a victim to whom is transferred the ills of the community. Unlike the tragic hero, for which Oedipus is the paradigmatic instance, Saul does not finally acquiesce in his fate. Oedipus is subject to *moira*, fate, as affirmed by the chorus.

> Whence this madness? None can tell who did
> Cast on thee this spell (*moira*),
> Prowling all thy life around,
> Leaping with a demon bound.[20]

Moira is a word for specific fate, as contrasted with *tychos*. Its basic meaning is "lot" or "portion,"[21] and as such betrays the sacrificial origin both of the concept of fate and the role of Oedipus himself in the tragedy. That person or thing arbitrarily chosen by the falling of the lot, whose power is really rooted in the veiled world of the sacred community, will now bring misery and illness, now happiness and well-being to those associated with it. The functions of misfortune and good luck often become separated over the passage of time, but in certain symbols and figures they are reunited as in Oedipus. The plague will cease when he leaves Thebes, and in the later play *Oedipus at Colonus*, Creon and the Thebans will want him back as a kind of good luck charm. We also learn in the latter play that he suffered unjustly—or literally, "without cause" (*matan*)—but the question of the arbitrariness of his fate as tragic victim is not raised in the earlier, better-known play.

I think that Saul is right on the edge of being a tragic victim, but the teller of the story, spinning a web of intolerable circumstances as Saul is torn between prophet and people, will not quite let him become the total victim of either party. Perhaps the present text represents an attempt to camouflage an earlier, more obviously sacrificial tragic victim. Perhaps—but perhaps also the revelation of the God of victims is a constraining force in the text. Be that as it may, the present form of the text does not indicate that Saul, knowingly or not, was a great offender against the sacred social order. He disobeys Samuel's command completely to destroy the Amalekites, but he also repents and asks to be restored to the prophet's and the LORD's favor. His surreptitious consultation of the medium is clearly an offense against the Yahwist order, but ironically it is Samuel, the great Yahwist prophet and judge, whose word he seeks. Both of these instances are clearly ambiguous; they do not leave the reader with the sense of a person who committed great crimes as his divinely given fate.

Moreover, Saul's death does not provide relief or benefits for the Israelites, as would the sacrificial victim in archaic religion or in Greek tragedy. Although the media of the sacred are shut off to him, as to Oedipus, he never acknowledges guilt for the kind of transgression that would threaten the social order, and thus he never confesses himself worthy of the punishment of expulsion or lynching. The unanimous accord of the community would be broken without the victim's compliance—but in any case it appears that Saul still has a sizable following even to the last despairing moments of his life. Nor can we say that envy of David causes his downfall. David's refusal to kill him when he has opportunity (1 Sam 24; 26) emphasizes the tradition's attempt to avoid an essentially sacrificial form of kingship based on a founding murder. We experience Saul's death by suicide (1 Sam 31) as "tragic" in the common sense of sympathy with someone we consider unfortunate. But in the end, whether or not it moves us or we approve of it, Saul's suicide has to be viewed as a realistic option for someone who is losing the battle and sees himself as blocked at every turn as ruler. It is very much unlike Brutus's suicide, for Brutus was haunted by his double, Caesar, whom he had murdered. Saul was haunted by Samuel and his own desire for power, but as already noted, this was a form of haunting that Saul himself brought about in the midst of his mimetic crisis. Saul's "tragic flaws" of obsession with his model-obstacle Samuel and envy of David are patent, but not sufficient to make of him a tragic scapegoat.

On the other hand, the revealing way in which Saul is chosen by lot according to 1 Samuel 10 and the interplay of mimetic desire among Saul, Samuel, and people are definite indications of the traces of sacrificial kingship. As the Israelite tradition moves away from the victimization mechanism and sacrifice as its instrument of resolution, it manages in the perspective of the narratives of 1 and 2 Samuel to depict the problems of royal rule and the nonsacrificial basis of the Davidic dynasty while preserving strong traces of the cultural origins of the king as sacred victim.[22]

To repeat the thesis I presented at the beginning of this part of the chapter, both prophecy and kingship may have their origin in the same social reality: a "selection" that amounts to exclusion or expulsion from the group, whether self-imposed or not, which comes to be understood by some in the Israelite context as *the call of YHWH to assume a special responsibility for those who are likewise expelled, excluded, or marginal.* What is the evidence that there was a tendency at work to identify king and prophet with the victims or potential victims of the social order? First of all, it should be granted that the evidence is not always clear and direct, and in mounting a case we have to reckon with a cumulative increase in awareness of the victimization mechanism and the nature of the God of Israel rather than with one self-evident text.

Concerning the selection and function of kings, there are some interesting things to be noted concerning their background. Gideon, who rejected the opportunity to rule, tells the divine messenger, "Behold, my clan is the weakest in Manasseh, and I am the least in my family" (Judg 6:15). "Least," Hebrew *tsair,* may signify "youngest," as in the Jacob story (Gen 25:23). As we have observed in considering the enemy brothers theme, the younger brother displaces the older and becomes in that sense the representative of the whole. Of course, he too has to undergo an ordeal that has obviously sacrificial meaning; this basic structure of the brothers theme is that of the selection of a sacrificial victim, which the narrative must recognize at least formally and symbolically. Gideon's son Jephthah is the son of a harlot. Saul is of the tribe of Benjamin, the smallest and the tribe eventually absorbed into the tribe of Judah. David, of the tribe of Judah, is the youngest of eight brothers; his candidacy for kingship is disregarded by family members, but "the LORD does not see as mortals see; they look on the outward appearance, but the LORD looks on the heart" (1 Sam 16:7).

Now on the basis of the Deuteronomic history (Judges through 2 Kings) or the pertinent material in Psalms, it would be difficult to say that the Israelite tradition of kingship held kings to a higher standard of justice than did other cultures in the ancient Near East. It is true that a king was viewed as endowed with great wisdom, and the tale of Solomon's judgment in the case of the two harlots disputing who was rightful mother of an infant is a masterful instance of overcoming the victim- ization mechanism (1 Kings 3:16–28). The mother of the child desires to preserve her child's life, even though she will lose the child to the other woman, rather than triumphing in a situation of mimetic rivalry. To give another instance, Psalm 72 sings of the ideal king's character and deeds of justice, which includes delivering the poor and the needy from oppression and violence, "and precious is their blood in his sight" (Ps 72:14). Finally, we may note that the final writer or editor of the Books of Kings presents Josiah as a kind of Moses and David *redivivus*, living again and combined into the ideal mediator of the covenant and ruler of the covenant people (2 Kings 22–23). However, these instances of wisdom and justice ascribed to the ideal monarch are arguably very similar, in principle, to what we find in descriptions of the king's role and mission in old Semitic cuneiform texts such as the Codes of Hammurabi and Lipit-Ishtar. But what we do not find in these non- biblical texts is a tradition of accountability to *prophets* as agents of God who criti- cize the king's rule. And in the biblical texts we do not find the outright sacrality that makes of the king either a divine being[23] or a sacred victim who must be ritu- ally slain unless a substitute victim is provided.[24]

In the biblical tradition the prophet is, in some respects, a double of the king, assuming aspects of the monarchic role that were neglected, suppressed, or given only ideological lip service once power was centralized. It is the prophets who typi- cally stood for the victims against the king as an expression of their calling, their experience of being chosen or taken as prophets. Let us note first that specific nar- rations of calling or commissioning to function as a prophet do not occur until well into the monarchic period, according to the Books of Samuel and Kings.[25] Whether or not this tradition is completely accurate historically, it certainly repre- sents the insight that the distinctively Israelite form of prophecy emerged in rela- tion to and in reaction to the monarchy. Prior to the prophets the Spirit of the LORD came upon Gideon and Saul, and the LORD "took" David from following the flock. If a call or commission narrative is understood as one in which the indi- vidual is given the message that his or her primary task is henceforth that of serv- ing as God's messenger, then the first clear instance of prophetic calling is Elijah's "anointing" of Elisha to be prophet in his place (1 Kings 19:9–21). It is striking that the biblical historian understands this transfer as analogous to a monarchic succession.[26] I think it is likely that those who eventually came to be known as prophets were not at first clearly differentiated in that role, functioning in small groups as seers and diviners. These groups would have been either independent or part of the entourage of a king. The next step was the splitting off of those who opposed the monarchy but who maintained an organizational structure that recognized a prophetic leader. As we find in 2 Kings in the tales of Elisha and his followers, a prophetic group could easily become once more an extension of the monarchic power structure. The third stage of Israelite prophecy was the emergence of the true exception, the prophet who spoke with a lonely and independent voice on behalf of the God of Israel.

When we turn to the great prophets whose names are preserved in the books ascribed to them, we find the victimization mechanism overcome as they draw upon its structure and transform it. In his relation to the God of Israel, the prophet who stands out of the community structures of violence does so in order to stand for both the community and its victims. I have already referred to Amos, who was probably the first of these prophets chronologically (c. 750 B.C.E.). He says that "the LORD took me from following the flock, and the LORD said to me, 'Go, prophesy to my people Israel'" (Amos 7:15). In justifying his prophetic calling he uses the analogies of a lion attacking its prey, a bird snared by a trap, and a trumpet of war causing fear in a city. He likewise is "attacked," "snared," "afraid." "The lion has roared; who will not fear? The Lord God has spoken; who can but prophesy?" (Amos 3:8). As one who is singled out, who is a kind of "victim" for the sake of his calling, he announces divine judgment on Israel, on those who "sell the righteous for silver, and the needy for a pair of shoes" (Amos 2:6).

In Isaiah 6, which is commonly recognized as his call vision, Isaiah is set against his people with a message of destruction. Only a tenth of the people will remain, and even it will be burnt the way a stump is burnt after a great tree is felled. The process of selecting the prophet takes the form of sacrificial initiation and commission by God. The sacrificial initiation involves a burning coal from the altar that is touched to Isaiah's lips by one of the seraphim that he sees. The seraph says, "Behold, this has touched your lips; your guilt is taken away, and your sin forgiven" (Isa 6:7, RSV). I commented on "forgive," Hebrew *kipper*, in chapter 2. There I concurred with Gese's conclusion that the verb and its noun, *kofer*, has to do with the price of exchange, with what is given in exchange for one's life. In the temple setting of Isaiah's vision, animal sacrifice is in the background of the sacrificial ransom, but it is relegated to a distant point, for the giving over of the prophet's life is symbolized in the purifying effect of the burning coal. Then the prophet hears the divine voice speaking in council, "Whom shall I send, and who will go for us?" (6:8). Although the total experience is overwhelming, Isaiah, in contrast to Amos, puts himself forth as a volunteer. "Here am I! Send me" (6:8). Depicted here, then, is a group in the heavenly sphere, similar to the assembly of the gods in *Enuma Elish*; however, in this case the gods or angels are clearly subordinate to YHWH, and it is presumably a smaller group functioning as his advisers. The prophet, in responding positively, is not coerced but willingly gives himself to the task, on which he is *sent*. "Sending" (Hebrew *shalach*), simple word though it is, is quite interesting in uncovering the sacrificial mechanism. The intensive verbal stem in Hebrew sometimes means "to expel," as in the scapegoat sent into the wilderness (Lev 16:10). It is employed likewise of the act of the rapists in Judges 19:25: "And as the dawn began to break, they let her go." That could be translated "they dismissed her" or "they cast her out." However, the prophet, though he faces the possibility of being "cast out" of his society as a messenger of judgment, is sent from the divine community with a mission to Israel. This mission required that Isaiah proclaim judgment upon oppressors who "turn aside the needy from justice, and . . . rob the poor of my people of their right" (Isa 10:2).

Jeremiah's call takes the form of his being singled out to prophesy from his very conception in his mother's womb. Jeremiah's understanding of his prophetic calling is a paradigm of the prophet as exception, as isolated, as one who lives in loneliness apart from his community. As I have already commented, although the mission of speaking the LORD's word to the nations seems rather grandiose, it represents the sense that the obligation of standing for the divine rule that should belong to the king has not been fulfilled. In Jeremiah's "confessions" or laments, complaints, and dialogues with his God, the prophet often seems to be paranoid from a modern reader's point of view. However, we should keep in mind the strong sense of vocation, the conviction the prophet holds that he has been singled out, has been made the exception emerging from the larger community. In this respect, Jeremiah is an exemplification of the model of the exception in the process of emerging, wrestling with the difference between himself and his social order and between God and social order. He was persecuted by leaders of his hometown of Anathoth and cries out for vengeance. He understands God to say that he will punish them (Jer 11:18–23). Jeremiah continues in this vein, complaining to YHWH about the prosperity of the wicked, but YHWH tells him that he hasn't yet encountered real difficulties (12:1–6). He cries out for vengeance on his persecutors and describes God as like a deceitful brook, and God asks him to return to him (or repent; 15:15–21). Jeremiah curses the day of his birth, and God does not answer him at all (20:14–18). He leads a celibate life as a sign of judgment and exile that will come upon his people (16:1–13). As spokesman of God he is the new center of divine communication with Israel set against the Temple, priests, and prophets. Jeremiah's sense of being an exception is so accentuated and so imprinted with his own struggle for the revelation of God that it is difficult to conceive of the prophet as living in harmony with his community. The tension between prophet and community is reflected in the fact that Jeremiah's criterion of prophecy is basically a negative one, for from his standpoint the ancient prophets prophesied war, famine, and pestilence; a prophet of peace and success should be mistrusted unless and until his word comes to pass (28:9).

Jeremiah is sent to a people who, as he sees it, are living in chaos, in a complete breakdown of human community. Everyone must beware of his or her neighbor; people can put no trust even in members of their own family, for "every brother is a supplanter, and every neighbor goes about as a slanderer" (Jer. 9:4). We have already seen in chapter 2 that this verse may be an allusion to the story of Jacob and Esau. The Israel of Jeremiah's day is reliving the paradigmatic conflict of brothers.

Jeremiah's prophetic position at the margins of institutional structures that legitimated sacred violence through the Temple and the Law led him into a number of confrontations. When preaching against the Temple as an inviolable sacred precinct that would never be breached, he was taken and nearly executed by those who are described as "the priests and the prophets and all the people," who "laid hold of him, saying, 'You shall die! Why have you prophesied in the name of the LORD, saying, 'This house shall be like Shiloh, and this city shall be desolate, without inhabitant?' And all the people gathered about Jeremiah" (26:8–9). This is a prelude to a stoning such as happened to Zechariah according to 2 Chronicles 24:20–22. Fortunately, Jeremiah had some supporters, who are referred to as "the princes and all the people" over against "the priests and the prophets" (26:16). Exactly who sided with Jeremiah for what reasons is not clear from this account, for earlier on "all the people" were ready to lynch the prophet. It is clearly a situation of spontaneous hostility in which mimeticism runs rampant. Whether Jeremiah survived because of his own defense, the speech of the "elders" who appeal to the case of the prophet Micah almost a century before (26:16–19), or the intervention of a certain Ahikam, whose father, Shaphan, had supported the Deuteronomic Reform (2 Kings 22:12, 14)—we cannot sort out with certainty from the passage. The most important thing to note is that Jeremiah's chance to survive at all existed because Israelite traditions legitimated the role of the prophet in speaking out even against the most important institutions of the social order. Even though prophets were often ignored and repressed, and sometimes executed (see concerning Uriah in Jer 26:20–23), the validity of the prophet's task was too deeply embedded in Israelite traditions not to have an important effect in reminding Israel of the God of Israel who led them out of Egypt, out of the house of slavery.

Ezekiel's call to prophesy is evidently connected to his throne vision (Ezek 1). This is a vision of God coming to be with his people in exile in which the divine is revealed in likeness upon likeness: "Such was the appearance of the likeness of the glory of the LORD. And when I saw it, I fell on my face, and I heard the voice of one speaking" (Ezek 1:28). The voice of one speaking commands him to speak to a people who will resist the divine word. Ezekiel's call to prophesy includes the symbolic action of eating a scroll; on the scroll are written "words of lamentation and mourning and woe" (2:10). When he eats it, he says, "It was in my mouth as sweet as honey" (3:3). The prophetic word involves speaking of what is bitter to the community addressed but sweet to the prophet. This again indicates the prophet's sense of being an exception, of being singled out, of being unlike all the others. Ezekiel is to serve in the role of watchman for the house of Israel (3:16). Undoubtedly, the role of watchman was already well known in the prophetic tradition (see Hos 9:8). What is new here is the understanding of the responsibility of the prophet, whose blood will be required for those who have not been warned of God's judgment. The concept of exchange, the life of the prophet for the life of those in the community whom he does not warn, is quite striking. It shows that although Ezekiel, like Jeremiah, has begun to think in terms of individual moral responsibility, he is still very much immersed in the language of the sacred, which is at bottom the language of the sacred as violence. I will comment on this further in the next section of the chapter.

As for the great prophet who is commonly called the Second Isaiah (Isa 40–55), his calling is evidently related in Isaiah 40:3–8. He is to announce that the way of the LORD is to be prepared in the wilderness, "And the glory of the LORD shall be revealed, and all flesh shall see it together" (Isa. 40:5). In that poem of calling, the prophet's experience of being a marginal person on behalf of God and the covenant community is not indicated. However, insofar as the so-called Servant Songs are closely related to the prophet's vocation, then they may serve as a good indication of the prophet's exceptional status, his sense of alienation from his people. He speaks of giving his back to the smiters for the sake of the word of God, who has opened his ear, and he speaks of not hiding his face from spitting (Isa 50:5–6). And of course the fourth Servant Song, the poem that relates the suffering of the servant of God, which I will treat at length later in this chapter, clearly expresses his position as persona non grata. The Servant of YHWH is the very epitome of the prophet, of the one who is singled out to speak to his community, who has special responsibility for those who are marginal, excluded, or expelled. In this case, he prophesies to those in exile; the whole community of Israel in Babylon is in bondage and is addressed with a comforting and liberating word.

The prophet does not say whether "he was despised and rejected by others, a man of sorrows and acquainted with infirmity" (Isa 53:3) because of the call to proclaim the message of the new exodus from Babylon to Judah, or whether his exclusion, his situation as a person "from whom others hide their faces" (53:3), is due to his experience of becoming a prophet of YHWH. The prophet's problem is that his calling as the exception emerging from the collective reality and collective consciousness excludes his being favored with community approval. "Who has believed what we have heard? And to whom has the arm of the LORD been revealed?" (53:1).

In conclusion concerning prophets and kings, the origins of prophecy and kingship were closely interrelated; the relation of their respective calling and task can often

be observed. The role of the king was more or less determined by his positive relation to the mimetic enactment of popular feelings, symbols, and institutions, and
his power resided in his ability to control the mechanism that made him the primary scapegoat. Prophets remain typically closer to the structural origins of being
selected through the victimization mechanism in the sense that they are a kind of
radical "throwback," recalling and reenacting some primary aspects of the exception in the process of emerging. The transformation of this status of the scapegoat
victim into the basis of the prophet's vocation and of the prophet's understanding
of Israel is the chief dynamic of revelation and Scripture.

In some respects the prophet and the king are "twins," doubles of each other.
Their traditional functions, as Israelite culture developed, diverged and understandably came to be understood as distinct. Nonetheless, within the frame of the
interpretive model I am employing, they were part of the same configuration of
meaning from the beginning. The function of speaking the divine word and of ruling are originally of one piece. The distinctiveness of the Israelite tradition is the
new generative theme of the innocent victim who as a scapegoat or sacrifice for
the welfare of the community is translated, indeed transmuted, into a new form:
the one who is called to speak to and for the community. This one is singled out
to assume the meaning of the whole group in his individual life and activity. The
spirit or the hand of God comes mightily upon this person (cf. 2 Kings 3:15), and
this image of the "hand of God" or the "spirit of God" represents the taking, the
seizing, the falling upon the victim that is turned on its head in the Israelite context. Given the power of mimesis that works at all levels of the social order from
individual to monarchy, the king emerges eventually with a style that is "like all
the nations." The court, the attendants, the cultic sanctuary, the standing army—
all the roles, functions, and institutions that took form around the king developed
into an office that may appear far removed from that of the prophet. However,
our investigation has shown that the royal office stems from the same cultural
process as the prophet's office. It is the emergence of the prophet out of the
ancient and universal mimetic structure of human existence that represents
Israel's distinctiveness in preserving a witness to transformation of sacred violence
into divine concern for victims.

Ahab, at Jezebel's behest, has Naboth falsely accused, tried, and stoned in
order to acquire Naboth's vineyard. Elijah appears before him, and Ahab says,
"'Have you found me, O my enemy?' He answered, 'I have found you, for you
have sold yourself to do what is evil in the sight of the LORD'" (1 Kings 21:20).
Elijah is depicted as a kind of shadow of Ahab, his other, his "double." There is an
interesting symmetry between Naboth's fate and Elijah's role as prophet. Naboth
is taken, excluded, and lynched. Elijah goes outside the community as part of his
calling and is associated with the margins, with the wilderness; he comes from the
outside. Now he confronts Ahab on behalf of one who belongs to the people of

the God who oversees and protects those who are forced out of the community and scapegoated as Naboth was.

As indicated at the beginning of this part of the chapter, the king was very much subject to the mimetic influences that necessarily flowed into and out of the king's persona. In this sense, he is as much governed as he governs, for rival desires arise continually either from the people he governs or those who have office in the hierarchy of authority. In Ahab's case we see how subject he is to the suggestions of his wife Jezebel, who, as a Phoenician princess, in the narrative represents the bane of an idolatrous foreign culture. The prophet, on the other hand, is characteristically more independent of these mimetic forces. In principle the prophet has an *external* mediator, the God of Israel whose word comes to the prophet. The prophet's mediator does not interfere with the prophet's existence as a mirror of desire and an obstacle in rivalry, conflict, and violence. Jeremiah tries to make of God a rival whom he must oppose, but he comes to accept, even if he does not fully understand, that God's refusal directly to answer his questions and complaints means that God transcends the mimetic situation in which the prophet and his persecutors oppose one another (see above discussion of Jeremiah).

B. The Prophets Against Violence and Sacrifice

Amos (prophesied c. 760–750 B.C.E.) was the first of the great prophets whose names are attached to books in the Hebrew Bible. He deals with the very core of the meaning of Israel as a people. It is this core that exemplifies the model of the emerging exception and that enables us to understand prophecy and kingship. It is the basis of Israel's existence as the people of the covenant witnessing to the revelation of the God of Israel. Amos's understanding of the beginnings of Israel is the very foundation of what he has to proclaim.

YHWH has elected Israel and led it out of Egypt: that is the basis of Israel's destiny but also of the danger in which it stands. "Hear this word that the LORD has spoken against you, O people of Israel, against the whole family which I brought up out of the land of Egypt: 'You only have I known of all families of the earth; therefore will I punish you for all your iniquities'" (Amos 3:1–2). The people that is known, chosen, loved, has a heritage originally the same as the structures of sacred violence among all the peoples. The one crucial difference in Israel's case is that in its witness to the God of the oppressed it could never be at ease with sacred structures of violence. In Israel's tradition of the exodus a community does not converge upon a victim, but God guides the victim away from the collective structures that marginalize, exclude, or slay the victim. But of course the one who is "led out" is, or is expected to be, very sensitive to the way victimization works. The chosen one has a special sensitivity to violence and sacrifice. The precarious status of the chosen one is such that the temptation is great to use the instruments of former oppression for both survival and power in the world. But standing outside the circle of all the others whose existence is permeated with sacred violence means that Israel has a special responsibility to the God of Israel. If Israel forgets this in imitating other peoples, then it falls into the danger of losing its own special identity.

So if Amos proclaims God's judgment on Israel, this judgment of military defeat and exile is something Israel brings upon itself, for Israel *misunderstands its very beginnings.* "Did you bring to me sacrifices and offerings the forty years in the wilderness, O house of Israel?" (Amos 5:25). This rhetorical question concludes a well-known oracle in which YHWH says, "I hate, I despise your festivals," spurning the outpourings from the sacrificial cult (5:21–24). It was not, implies Amos, God's command to offer sacrifices in the wilderness. This is a remarkable insight. Amos is the first prophet or spokesperson of any sort in the scriptural texts who so unambiguously asserts this, although other prophets will reject sacrifice, and one, Ezekiel, sees the sacrificial cult in the wilderness as a kind of punishment of Israel (see below).

What was Israel supposed to do from the beginning? How was it to be constituted? Well, Amos is not very specific about that, although clearly from his standpoint it would have to do with letting "justice roll down like waters, and righteousness like an everflowing stream" (5:24). That is, the constitution of Israel has to do with concern for the victim. Not selling "the righteous for silver, and the needy for a pair of shoes" (2:6), avoiding indiscriminate licentious sex at the cultic shrine, and not drinking in a cultic sanctuary the wine of those who have been taxed or fined—here we see moral and cultic concerns brought together in a vision of justice. Yes, Israel is exceptional among the peoples (3:1–2) but not so exceptional that it can pretend to be the only people that God has cared for and guided to a land of its own (9:7).

It is no wonder then that the high priest expels Amos from the royal sanctuary of Bethel! Even if Amaziah had agreed with Amos's moral concerns and advocated reform, he quite rightly senses that Amos's message subverts the foundations of prevailing Israelite social order. Charity and purification of the cult were not enough for Amos; he held Israel's very foundations had been misunderstood.

Hosea prophesied about 740–720 B.C.E. His prophetic ministry begins with a strange divine command: that he marry a "wife of whoredom" and have "children of whoredom, for the land commits great whoredom by forsaking the LORD" (Hos 1:2). It is difficult to say whether chapter 1 of Hosea is a call narrative; however, since the narration begins with the notation "When the LORD first spoke to Hosea," the command to take a prostitute for a wife may have been part of his initial call, or may at least have been closely related to his call experience. In any case, the marriage to a prostitute is part of a process whereby Hosea involves himself with a marginal person in order to embody the message of God to the people

Israel. A harlot or prostitute was a person who existed as one marginalized within the social order.[27] What Hosea does in effect is to move out from the center of community life to the margins in order to indicate that Israel's exceptionality vis-à-vis God and other nations is now turning into a source of alienation from the God of Israel. In that bizarre kind of symbolic act found so often in the prophets, the children are given names that attest to the prophetic word on Israel's fate. The first child, a son, is named Jezreel, a sign of punishment for the murders that occurred at Jezreel a century before when the Omri dynasty was overturned by Jehu, who was supported by Elisha and his prophets. The second child, a girl, is named Not-pitied, a sign that the LORD will no longer rescue Israel by means of war and its instruments. The third child, a son, is named Not-my-people, a sign that is the gravest of all, for "not my people" means the covenant has been broken and Israel will lose its identity.

The naming of the children would make little sense unless it signified that the violence and murder expressed in the first name, Jezreel, continued into the present. In other words, Israel's institutions, particularly its religious institutions, are soaked in the blood of innocent victims.

Hosea implies that Israel was not constituted as a sacrificial cult in the beginning, for in his visions of the renewed "marriage" of YHWH and Israel the relationship will be a tender one of covenant love "as in the days of her youth" (Hos 2:15). This renewed "bride of YHWH" will not have king or sacrificial cult (3:4). Meanwhile, the present judgment on Israel comes on account of its fundamental misunderstanding, its gross lack of "knowledge": "For I desire steadfast love and not sacrifice, the knowledge of God rather than burnt offerings" (6:6). The knowledge God requires of Israel is that it was called out of Egypt by the LORD. Israel was taught to walk by the LORD (11:2); Israel was led out of that great civilization of oppression, kingship, sacrifice—the security of sacred violence—into the wilderness and into freedom. Israel was led out of Egypt by a prophet, according to Hosea (12:12). This is not a historical truth in the modern critical sense, of course, for as we have already seen, kingship and prophecy did not become differentiated until much later. It is, however, part of Hosea's "prophetic truth": that Israel came to existence by an election that transformed the victimization process into deliverance, and the office of the prophet has become the model of that election and that deliverance.

Hosea is somewhat clearer than Amos about the mimetic process. Israel goes after her lovers (2:5), the other gods, in imitation of the indigenous cults. The formation of desire by imitation (to reiterate) involves yearning to *acquire* the object of the desire imitated. The lack of that knowledge which is the basis of Israel's existence (4:6) leads to the absence of faithfulness, kindness, and knowledge of God (4:1–3). The people's "spirit of whoredom" (4:12), a key notion for Hosea, moves them continually to seek satisfaction in the *other* powers, those gods and their rituals who seem not only to promise pleasure and plenty but also, and more fundamentally, an explanation and expiation of sin, guilt, and the ills befalling the human community through an outpouring of sacrifices. "They sacrifice on the tops of the mountains, and make offerings upon the hills" (4:13)—sacrifice after sacrifice.

It is therefore not accidental in Hosea that the divine lament "I desire steadfast love and not sacrifice" is juxtaposed with God's judgment (6:5) directed against those who have transgressed the covenant and are implicated in murder, robbery, and idolatry (6:8–10).

Since the prophet perceives that desire is formed by imitation, he intuits also that it may be re-formed by the mimetic process. Thus his act of purchasing or redeeming an adulterous woman (perhaps Gomer, who had been his wife) and keeping her under a kind of restriction or corrective punishment until the time when the two could be truly husband and wife (Hos 3:3–5). So also Israel will be under discipline "without king or prince, without sacrifice or pillar, without ephod or teraphim" until they return to the LORD (3:4–5).

In order to understand Hosea's mimetic act it is necessary to observe that the prophets were performers who dramatically verbalized and enacted their understanding of Israel's situation in order to bring the people to the point of understanding and transformation. Amos delivers oracles suggested by a plumb line for a wall and a basket of summer fruit (Amos 7:7–9; 8:1–3). Jeremiah refers to a potter's broken vessels and two baskets of figs (Jer 18:1–11; 24). Isaiah and Hosea gave their children names that were signs of God's judgment (Isa 7:3; 8:1–4; Hos 1). As for dramatic enactments, Hosea married "a wife of whoredom" (Hos 1:2); Isaiah "walked naked and barefoot for three years" (Isa 20:3); Jeremiah buried a waistcloth, wore yoke-bars, purchased property, and invited the Rechabites to drink wine (Jer 13:1–11; 28; 32:6–15; 35); and Ezekiel swallowed a scroll, lay bound on his left side and then on his right side, and shaved his hair (Ezek 2:8–3:3; 4:1–5:12)—all as dramatic representations of Israel's situation. Usually the mimesis has to do with God's judgment on Israel, but in some instances it has to do with the promise of Israel's renewal, as in Hosea 3, where the viewers, hearers, or readers are invited to identify with the adulteress who becomes a faithful wife, or in Jeremiah 32, where the prophet's purchase of property is an invitation to live in hope and look to the future in spite of the devastation of exile.

Isaiah prophesied about 745–700 B.C.E. His vision of the new age includes a new Davidic king (Isa 9:1–7; 11:1–8), but there is no clear evidence that he knew or appealed to the Exodus-Sinai tradition. Likewise unclear is his view of how the sacrificial cult began. But there is no doubt that he condemns it in unmistakable terms. In fact, the connection of sacrifice and violence is made more explicitly than in Hosea and Amos. Those who bring "vain offerings," who think YHWH delights "in the blood of bulls," have hands "full of blood." This image, whether hyperbole or not, pictures mass violence and murder. The prophetic alternative is an ethical exhortation given in a staccato series of brief imperatives:

> Wash yourselves; make yourselves clean;
> remove the evil of your doings from before my eyes;
> cease to do evil, learn to do good;
> seek justice, rescue the oppressed,
> defend the orphan, plead for the widow.
>
> (1:16–17)

Torah, which for Isaiah is synonymous with the word of YHWH (1:10), does not make victims in cult offerings or in any sort of violence. Rather, it draws all the peoples to it in peace and leads them to "beat their swords into plowshares, and their spears into pruning hooks; nation shall not lift up sword against nation, neither shall they learn war any more" (2:4). This vision of the new age mentions "the house of the God of Jacob," undoubtedly a reference to the Temple, but quite strikingly there is no mention at all of a reconstituted sacrificial cult. The "house of Jacob" is associated with *torah*, with teaching, not with sacrifice (2:3).

In general, Micah's prophetic message (c. 730–700 B.C.E.) is very similar to that of these other prophets, particularly his fellow Judeans Amos and Isaiah. Especially representative of Micah's message is the oracle in 3:9–12, for which he was remembered even in the time of Jeremiah (Jer 26:18): "Therefore because of you Zion shall be plowed as a field; Jerusalem shall become a heap of ruins, and the mountain of the house a wooded height" (Mic 3:12). And why is it that this calamity will come about, so that the Temple will be destroyed and the city a heap of ruins? Micah's answer is that the "heads," the rulers, "build Zion with blood, and Jerusalem with wrong" (3:10). In an indictment he specifies rulers, priests, and prophets.

> Its rulers give judgment for a bribe,
> its priests teach for a price,
> its prophets give oracles for money;
> yet they lean upon the LORD and say,
> "Surely the LORD is with us!
> No harm shall come upon us."
>
> (Micah 3:11)

In other words, the perspective and the practices that are indicted are representative of a common sort of religion of the divine presence, which is centered in sacrifice. Sacrificial forms, with their inherent and partially concealed victimization mechanism, express themselves by many different avenues. As we see here, the sacrificial substitutions are supplemented with further substitutions through bribes and irregular payment for services. All three of these offices represent means of access to the sacred in the sense of the bounty and means of life given by God.

The word *ruler* is a very general term that probably encompasses king, prince, judge, and so on. Those who rule do so in the stead of the divine ruler. Money is, in origin, a means of substituting for the sacrificial act. The gift is a substitute for sacrifice; that is, it stands in place of the victim that is offered in place of the one for whom sacrifice is offered. One kind of remedy for conflict in a sacrificial system, one of whose offshoots may be a money economy, is the offering of a bribe, a payment beyond what is ordinarily required for someone's services. The bribe reflects both the power of the sacrificial system and its corruption, in that the system does not curtail rivalry, which uses the reciprocity of the system as a standard that must be exceeded or "supplemented."

The "priests teach for hire," evidently giving answers that people want. The verb meaning "teach" is from the same root, *yrh, as *torah*, "teaching," or "law." The root word means to cast or throw, and in at least one instance it denotes casting lots to determine the portions of land for Israelite tribes (Josh 18:6). Because many of the occurrences of the form of the verb meaning to instruct occur in passages where priests direct worshipers in ritual observance, I suspect that the sense of instruction is derived originally from casting of lots to obtain the divinity's answer or from some such process of divination. Just as in the case of rulers accepting bribes, this benefiting from the sacrificial system, beyond the economy established through the roles and relationships this system structures, shows that mimetic desire and mimetic rivalry are not effectively addressed through the sacrificial mechanism.

The picture that Micah draws is that of a sacrificial system gone haywire. We see this also in Isaiah's prophecies, for example, the oracle in Isaiah 1:10–17. In a developing state of undifferentiation, with the sacrificial system so blatantly ineffective, more and more substitutions, and substitutions for the substitutions, are sought and found. This may be seen in the indictment of the prophets who divine for hire—who foretell the future, locate lost objects, and so on. The sacrificial system has become so ineffective that people turn, sometimes in desperation, to prophets. The prophets, in turn, are drawn into this vortex of rivalry, for the structure that spawns so many substitutions offers many advantages for profit and power to the clever person who has good timing and few qualms about dominating others.

Much like Amos and Isaiah, Micah cries out against those who force the old free peasantry off the land and acquire enormous land holdings (Mic 2:1–4). A key passage in Micah, often quoted, is 6:6–8. It is often considered an addition to the Micah scroll stemming from the sort of postexilic piety that is expressed also in Psalm 51. A case may be made for this position. In fact, it would support the nonsacrificial reading of the Scriptures as evidence of part of a postexilic, antisacrificial perspective that stems in great part from the prophetic tradition. Let us pick up the passage halfway through:

> Shall I give my first-born for my transgression,
> the fruit of my body for the sin of my life?
> He has disclosed to you, O mortal (*adam*) what is good;
> and what does the LORD seek from you
> but to do justice, and love kindness,
> and to walk humbly with your God?
>
> (Mic 6:7–8)

It is quite striking that in this advanced perspective on the divine-human relationship and morality there is nonetheless a recollection of the archaic connection of
the offering of the firstborn and transgression. Right relationship with God and
reestablishment of order does not depend on eliminating the ills of the human
community by killing the firstborn son for the sake of the family or community. It
depends on the ancient covenant virtues of *mishpat*, or justice and right judgment,
and *chesed*, or kindness (the "steadfast love" of Hos 6:6), the kindness one does for
others who belong to the same community or family.

Jeremiah prophesied about 626–586 B.C.E., according to the editorial introduction of the Book of Jeremiah (1:1–3), although chapters 42 and 43 suggest his
prophetic activity may have continued somewhat longer. He belonged to a family
of priests in Anathoth (1:1), and many of the oracles in chapters 2–6 reflect the
sort of priestly concern with pollution and cleanness that we find also in Ezekiel
(see below). However, the evidence of the text indicates that Jeremiah's message
became decidedly anticultic and antimonarchic. The composition of the book represents more than one tradition, including a redaction of the scroll by those whose
point of view was determined by Deuteronomy and the Deuteronomic view of history that is evident in the final form of Judges through 2 Kings. In spite of the
composite character of the book, certain things about the prophet's life and message come through quite clearly.

The picture of Jeremiah is one of a prophet who attacked king and Temple.
Jerusalemites believe the Temple will save them (7:3), but it will not. Like Amos,
Jeremiah holds that God did not require burnt offerings and sacrifice when he led
the ancestors out of Egypt (7:22). The kingship, which Jeremiah evidently accepts
as a historical given, does figure in some of his visions of a new age (23:5–6; 30:9),
although it has to remain an open question whether the prophet finally reached
the point where he could not see the kingship as part of God's intention for the
future. In any event, the ethical imperative for Israelite kings is quite clear. At one
point he compares Jehoiakim unfavorably to his father, Josiah, and he asks,

> "Did not your father eat and drink
> and do justice and righteousness?
> Then it was well with him.
> He judged the cause of the poor and needy;
> then it was well.

Is not this to know me?"
says the LORD.

(Jer 22:15–16)

"Is this not to know me?" This question could be taken as the watchword of these great prophets. To know the God of Israel is to practice justice and righteousness, which means to help the poor and needy. *To know God is to know the cause of the victim.*

In the new age the Temple will not exist; the ark of the covenant will be no more (3:16). There will be a new covenant *different* from the one made with the fathers. "I will put my law within them, and I will write it on their hearts; and I will be their God, and they shall be my people. And no longer shall each man teach his neighbor and each his brother, saying, 'Know the LORD,' for they shall all know me, from the least of them to the greatest, says the LORD; for I will forgive their iniquity, and I will remember their sin no more" (31:33–34). This is a remarkable vision of the dissolution of the sacrificial mechanism and the liberation from violence. In an envisioned new era that God will bring about, an era without sacrificial cult, mimetic rivalry will be broken once and for all. The nations of Israel and Judah, so long in conflict (one that would continue after the Exile in the political and religious battle between Samaria and Jerusalem), will be reunited (31:31). The great Torah, the divine law, which prohibits individual and clan vengeance, ascribing authority and the right to punish to God, whose power and authority is mediated through the leaders who administer the legal structure of justice—this law will no longer be in the form of the divine command imposed by God.

The Torah of the Sinai covenant was unique, an attempt to abrogate the mythology of god-victims who are placated and summoned in the sacrificial cult to restore the community. A system of law involves a qualitative leap from the primitive stage of the sacrificial cult, which maintains a certain control over individual violence by channeling the all-against-one of collective violence into a ritual that normally allows social relations to continue and cohere. However, even though law is a system of rationalization that weakens and distantiates the sacrificial mechanism, it does not eliminate it entirely. Law presupposes the boundaries of responsibility that both distinguish individuals and groups from one another and connect them in a social bond. It deals with degrees of guilt and presupposes that an individual may be guilty, but that a given part of the community may be partially if not totally responsible for transgressions. It offers a structure that seeks to prevent one family, clan, or tribe from engaging in a blood feud, from taking vengeance against another kinship grouping. No longer is the principle of the offering of the innocent victim at work, because the actual guilty party is to bear the force of retribution. However, law presupposes that an external authority must hold desire in check; that is, it assumes that all members of the community will desire what the authoritative or sanctioning other—the god, the leader—desires as this desire is mediated through the social structure, through the hierarchy of surrogates for the primary person or reality. Although it controls individual and arbitrary violence, it rests on the principle that retribution is right and vengeance must be exacted. It is very difficult for a legal system to recognize in principle that its total social order may be involved in a crime or in the circumstances that lead to a crime. Law cannot, finally, recognize mutual guilt, the only solution to which is mutual forgiveness—the willingness of those in the community to forgive one another. Although law is a rational step away from sacrifice, it is still dependent on the sacrificial mechanism. Mimetic desire and rivalry are presupposed as the very basis of law, even though the sacrificial cult loses, in principle, its primitive power.

Thus it is easy to explain why sacrifice continues to coexist with law even in those spiritual traditions that develop advanced forms of law, as in Israel and Greece. However, in the vision of the new covenant this problem with the law would be overcome, because it is a "law" no longer given through the mediation of the prophet Moses within the context of a sacrificial cult that perpetuated many archaic elements of religion and culture. It would, rather, be immediate, written on the heart. To use Paul Tillich's terms, it would neither be *heteronomous* in the sense of a "strange," externally imposed law, nor *autonomous* in the sense of a law of human origin, but *theonomous*: the law of God perfectly implanted and realized as the law of the people of God. All mimetic rivalry would cease. One of the signs of the heteronomous character of law is the necessity not only of imposing and enforcing it but of having some people exhort others to obey it and to remember the authority behind the law. But now it will no longer be necessary for people to say to each other, "'Know the LORD,' for they shall all know me."

The only decisive step beyond Jeremiah among the great ancient Israelite prophets is the Second Isaiah's vision of the Servant of YHWH. Before turning to that, however, let us take into account the noteworthy work of Ezekiel, a prophet whose thinking was, paradoxically, both reactionary and advanced among the great prophets.

Ezekiel, prophesying about 592 to 570 B.C.E., during the Babylonian Exile, makes a statement about sacrifice that is simultaneously full of insight and permeated with a sense of dread concerning Israel's history. Ezekiel, like Jeremiah, addressed himself to the horrible practice of the sacrifice of children (see Ezek 16:15–21; 20:25–31; 23:36–39; Jer 7:31; 19:5; 32:35). One can only conclude that the desperate people of Jerusalem and its environs resorted to an age-old practice, child sacrifice, during the crisis of the final days of Jerusalem before the Babylonian conquest in 597 B.C.E. and the quelling of the rebellion in 586 B.C.E. when the Temple was destroyed and many more captives were deported. It is well known that in times of crisis we tend to fall back on primitive strands in our personal or social makeup. That the Judeans did this, there can be no doubt, both by the witness of Ezekiel and Jeremiah and the widely documented practice of the offering of human victims, including children, in the Middle East, Africa, and elsewhere in the world. In a time of crisis, of course, if the sacred social system does not have a pool of victims to sacrifice or scapegoat such as the Aztecs maintained, then those who are simultaneously most valuable and vulnerable must be given up to the god, namely, the children of the community.

Ezekiel depicts the periods in Egypt and the wilderness as a sin-history, not a salvation-history. The dark side of this story reaches its fullest extent in the oracle that says, "I gave them statutes that were not good and ordinances by which they could not live. And I defiled them through their very gifts by making them offer by fire all their first-born, that I might horrify them" (Ezek 20:25–26). In the very beginnings of Israel, of which Ezekiel gives his own revised account as a history of rebellion, the sacrificial cult and the law were not good. That usually nonconscious and concealed aspect of the statutes and ordinances, which is connected to ever-present threat of violence in the sacrificial mechanism, is here ascribed to the doing of the God of Israel. Ezekiel was a prophet who maintained and expressed a strong sense of cleanness and uncleanness and, in a priestly sense, the sacred and the profane. The book itself identifies him as a priest (1:3). As such, he attributes the ambiguity of the sacrificial mechanism to the God of Israel. Even the oracle promising a "new heart" and a "new spirit" (36:23), in some respects very reminiscent of Jeremiah, is permeated with the ambiguity of Ezekiel's cultic concerns. Israel in its present state of uncleanness, like "the uncleanness of a woman in her impurity" (36:17), will be restored to a state of cleanness (36:29). The people will then remember their deeds "that were not good"—a phrase reminiscent of the laws given by God in the wilderness that were "not good"; they will loathe themselves (36:31), and God will cleanse them.

Ezekiel's imagery of sexual lust and rivalry (chaps. 16 and 23) reflects an intuition of mimetic desire and mimetic rivalry, and his understanding of the original sacrificial cult reflects an intuition of the victimization required and controlled by sacrifice. In struggling with this he has little choice, given the priestly influence on his thinking, but to attribute the originating events to God. Nevertheless, he cannot accept the idea of divine approval of the sacrificial mechanism. He therefore conceives the cult as a necessary stage in a process of revelation, and as such its object is both punishment and instruction: "that I might horrify them; I did it that they might know that I am the LORD" (20:26). In sum, as a prophet Ezekiel stands very close to the Priestly perspective of Leviticus that views human victimization as calamitous and does not try to conceal or mythologize Israel's failures, even if it cannot see its way clear to liberation from mimetic rivalry and the sacrificial mechanism.

The great prophet whose oracles, sayings, and poems are found in chapters 40–55 of the Book of Isaiah, and perhaps elsewhere in the book (e.g., chap. 61), is usually called the Second Isaiah because of his place in the Isaiah scroll. He may well have been influenced by Isaiah or been understood as a latter-day follower of Isaiah. He clearly addressed himself to the exiles in Babylon, perhaps shortly before Cyrus's conquest of the city in 539 B.C.E. (see Isa 44:28; 45:1). His prophesying dates are usually given as about 545–540 B.C.E., although one could give or take a few years on either side.

Consider a few particulars of this prophet's message: he claims that Judah's exile was proclaimed in the past by YHWH's prophets (41:21–29; 44:6–8; passim); there will be a new exodus back to the homeland and a new world order. Second Isaiah's utterances about God and his prophets form a kind of implied syllogism: (1) The one true God can announce beforehand what he will bring about. (2) YHWH has done this through the prophets. (3) Therefore, YHWH is God.

> Who is like me? Let him proclaim it,
> let him declare and set it forth before me
> since I appointed an ancient people.
> And signs of things to come let them declare.
> Fear not, be not afraid;
> have I not told you in past times and declared it?
> And you are my witnesses.
> Is there a God besides me?
> There is no Rock; I know not any.
>   (Isa 44:7–8, my translation)

One of the most noted aspects of Babylonian Isaiah's prophecies is his theme of the Servant of YHWH. Whatever his own understanding of the identity of this servant, in four poems or songs he is depicted as an individual (42:1–4; 49:1–6; 50:4–9; 52:13–53:12) who is a prophet. He is called to prophesy (49:1), YHWH's spirit is upon him (49:1), and his ear is "opened" by YHWH. His calling entails speaking God's word to Israel (49:3–5). He encounters great difficulty and persecution, but God will help him and vindicate him (50:6–9; 53). This picture of the prophet is replete with allusions to the prophet tradition (Jeremiah, Moses, Isaiah, and Ezekiel).

The most remarkable passage is the fourth Servant Song, 52:13–53:12. This song or poem is a kind of antiphonal dialogue between the God of Israel and the people. God speaks in 52:13–15 and 53:11–12, and in my judgment the people speak in 53:1–10. It is important to recognize this formal organization of the passage, as we shall see. The divine voice begins with an "I-they" statement: "my servant shall prosper" in the end in spite of "their" astonishment, for the servant bears the signs of the victim: "so marred was his appearance, beyond human semblance." According to 52:15 he will startle nations and their kings. It is possible that these foreigners are those speaking in 53:1–3 rather than Israel. This is uncertain, however, and because the collective voice of 53:4–6 is so obviously Israel's, I will assume that the same holds for verses 1–3. (I think 53:7–10 is also Israel speaking, but this matter will be taken up below.)

The collective voice, which speaks in the grammatical form of "we-him," describes the servant as ugly from his youth and thus undesirable (53:2). All were against him. "He was despised and forsaken by others, a man of suffering and acquainted with infirmity," who was persona non grata because people hide their faces from him (v. 3). Verses 4–10 recount the servant's fate. First is the collective realization that he has borne the sins of the community (vv. 4–6), very much like the Greek *pharmakos.*

Girard contends that a "spontaneous historical event" is being described, an event that has both a collective and legal character, which he discerns in the further reflections of the collective voice (vv. 7–10).

> By oppression and judgment he was taken away;
> and as for his generation, who considered
> that he was cut off out of the land of the living
> stricken for the transgression of my people?
> And they made his grave with the wicked
> and with a rich man in his death,
> although he had done no violence,
> and there was no deceit in his mouth.
>
> (53:8–9, RSV)

This may be the spontaneous scapegoating of an individual that the poem relates. However, the poem should be related to known historical facts. One is that thousands of Judeans had been taken into exile; another, that the earlier prophets of the exilic period, Jeremiah and Ezekiel, saw themselves as suffering in behalf of their prophetic mission (Jer 11:18–23; 12:1–6; 16:1–13; 20:4–8; Ezek 3:24–4:17). One could validly conclude, as many biblical critics have and as Jewish readers particularly are inclined to do, that Second Isaiah presents an image of Israel in the form of the Servant of the LORD and draws on the prophetic tradition for many specifics of this image. Girard is therefore right about the insight into the sacrificial mechanism that the poem expresses but not necessarily correct in ascribing it to one specific event. By the way, Girard's comments about this in *Things Hidden Since the Foundation of the World*[28] do not explicitly indicate that this spontaneous event was either contemporaneous with Second Isaiah or part of ancient Israel's history. As a Christian reader he understands it as a prophecy, a prophetic vision or intimation of the future Christ-event. There is no reason, of course, why the Servant may not be construed both as an image of ideal Israel and an anticipation of the Christ of the Gospels.

To comment further on verses 4–10, "my people" appears in verse 8, raising the question whether God's voice enters in here or whether, perhaps, God is the speaker in verses 7–10. The latter is possible and would make a considerable difference in my interpretation of the passage. The objections to God as speaker are two. (1) The divine voice would be referring to himself in the third person in verse 10a ("it was the will of the LORD to bruise him," RSV). (2) And in 10b the Hebrew text reads a second person singular: "thou makest his life an offering for sin" (my translation). Most translations turn that into a third person singular, "when he offers his life." But if we stay with the Hebrew text, it appears to be the people persona speaking to the God persona.

In fact, inconsistency of pronoun usage and reference is quite in evidence in the Hebrew Bible, so one cannot use an occasional inconsistency as a warrant by itself. What I prefer to see in verses 7–10 is the further statement by the people persona. The "my people" could be a slip where Second Isaiah allows his voice to come in. It is well known that one voice can allow, usually unintentionally, another voice to slip in, for example, the "Qohelet says" that interrupts the first person voice of Qohelet in Ecclesiastes (in Hebrew "Qohelet") 7:27. Moreover, "my people" was a common epithet not only in oracles presenting divine speech but in the repertory of phrases ascribed to the prophets themselves.

I would therefore read verses 7–10 as the continuation of the collective voice, although in a different mode from verses 4–6—it is descriptive-reflective rather than primarily confessional. The importance of this for interpretation is that the inconsistency concerning divine agency in the Servant's suffering is not ascribed to the divine voice. In verse 4 the people avow, "We thought him stricken, smitten by God, and afflicted," and verse 10 says,

> Yet is was the will of YHWH to bruise him;
> he has made him sick.
> When you appoint him as an offering for sin,
> he shall see his offspring, he shall prolong his days.
> (Isa. 53:10, my translation)

If verse 10 belongs to the people persona, then there is a consistency in the people's apprehension of the sacrificial mechanism, a consistency of which the prophetic composer may be well aware. Just as Ezekiel uncovers the horror of sacrifice while feeling compelled to ascribe it somehow to God, so also the people's statement in Isaiah 53:1–10 reflects the tradition of ambiguous preservation of the sacrificial mechanism and perspective.

But it is a different matter with verses 11 and 12:

> Out of his anguish he shall see light;
> he shall find satisfaction through his knowledge.
> The righteous one, my servant,
> shall make many righteous,
> and he shall bear their iniquities.
> Therefore I will allot him a portion with the great,

> and he shall divide the spoil with the strong;
> because he poured out himself to death,
> and was numbered with the transgressors;
> yet he bore the sin of many,
> and made intercession for the transgressors.

"Because he poured out his soul [or life, *nefesh*] to death": this is the key, as I construe the passage. The Servant willingly gave himself for his people. It wasn't God who caused his suffering, it was oppressors. As the divine voice says in an oracle found in chapter 54:

> If any one stirs up strife,
> it is not from me;
> whoever stirs up strife with you
> shall fall because of you.
>
> (54:15)

"Strife"—the conflict of mimetic rivalry that results in violence—does not come from God. The two lines seem to indicate strife within the Israelite community (15a) and strife in the form of attacks upon Israel (15b). In my reading I see the Servant as the object of oppression resulting from this strife. He does not intend to become a "sacrifice," and God does not subject him to suffering, although Second Isaiah perceives that the people continue in the ambiguity of the tradition still rooted in the sacrificial cult.

This reading would fit Israel, ideally conceived as the covenant community producing the prophets and suffering for the sake of a new Israel and a new world of the future. The poem could also be a dramatic way of talking about Second Isaiah, some other contemporary figure, or someone in the future. This latter point of view is the interpretation held by the New Testament texts, and it is the one toward which this book moves.

Jeremiah envisioned a new covenant and a new Torah that would be present and real in Israel apart from the sacrificial cult and the operation of retribution. The fourth Servant Song of the Second Isaiah poem, which is a dramatic representation of the Servant's healing suffering, discloses the power of the sacrificial mechanism in the scapegoat ritual, its foundation in contempt for the victim, its operation through oppression, the human predicament of those who have benefited from the suffering of the scapegoat, and God's approval of the one who is not simply an arbitrarily chosen victim but who offers himself when necessary as part of his calling in order to overcome the strife and violence stemming from rivalry.

The Servant of the LORD depicted by the Second Isaiah is a paradigm of the victim whose expulsion is coterminous with his calling. "By oppression and judgment he was taken away . . . he was cut off out of the land of the living." But in this role he stands for the whole, the entire community. From the standpoint of the community whose theology is still rooted in the principle of god's wrath and still has not quite attained a theology of the innocent victim, it appears that this suffering has been imposed by the God of Israel on his servant, yet it is a condition the Servant has accepted voluntarily. It is very ambiguous from the standpoint of the collective voice of the social order, and thus it must always be. The suffering of the innocent victim will always be ambiguous from the standpoint of any society, which always has at the core of its structure a victimization mechanism and its sacrificial outlets. The victimization mechanism may be qualified, and there may be substitutions upon substitutions whose use seems to deny the effectiveness of sacrificial violence. Even if sacrificial violence seems to be a thing of the remote past, nonetheless culture and language are permeated with strong traces of that which brought about hominization in the first place: mimetic desire and rivalry, collective violence, prohibition, and sacrifice.

However, the prophetic author of the Servant poem has insight that transcends the point of view of the collective chorus that comments on the Servant and his work. He sees that it is not the will of God to bruise him, but it is the will of God to use him—to speak through the excluded one, who suffers on behalf of others. In understanding his suffering, in standing with him and not with the persecutors, those who are taught by him begin to transform the structures of sacred violence.

6

Job Versus the "Friends":
The Failed Scapegoat

Hasten, lead me from the land, friends, lead me hence, the utterly lost,
the thrice accursed, yes, the mortal man most abhorred of heaven!
Sophocles, *Oedipus the King*

Though I am innocent, my own mouth would condemn me;
though I am blameless, [God] would prove me perverse.
Job 9:20

My friends scorn me;
my eyes pour out tears to God,
that he would maintain the right of a mortal with God,
and that of a human with a neighbor.
Job 16:20–21

In the chapter on prophets and kings I attempted to demonstrate that the
Israelite prophet's calling, as best exemplified by the Servant of the LORD in
Isaiah 52–53, represents the characteristic Israelite inversion and transformation
of victimization and the sacrificial mechanism: the structure of exclusion or
expulsion becomes the call of YHWH to assume a special responsibility for the
community. This community, in its own history, maintains the core identity of a
marginal and expelled people whose God leads it into freedom and a new sense of
identity.

If there is a single work in the Hebrew Bible that wrestles both dramatically
and reflectively with the problem of the innocent victim as the chosen of God, it
is the Book of Job. Of course, the staging of the drama presupposes that Job is
already chosen, the servant of YHWH. However, the attacks of the "Friends" and
Job's obviously desolate, fallen state as one diseased and shunned by family and
community (Job 19:13–22) raises the question, Will this once wealthy and powerful person who is now attacked and despised by his community become the one
God "chooses" or "calls" to be the bearer of divine favor, to be the point of divine
revelation of justice and love? If so, God must be other than the community
thinks, enacts, symbolizes. It remains to be seen, however, whether the writer or
writers of Job finally succeed in this apparent intention of uncovering the victimization mechanism and its sacrificial expressions.

A. Job, Friends, and God

1. The Dialogues and Job's Final Speech (Job 3–27, 29–31)

The ambiguity of Job's protest resides in his own ambivalence: God is the divine Enemy who persecutes him yet also the Witness who will defend him.

Job had been respected, even venerated. The text presents him as a kind of idol. Others waited for him to speak as they wait for the autumn rain. They even watched his face for a reading of his emotions. "I smiled on them when they had no confidence; and the light of my countenance they did not extinguish" (29:24). He has been, in other words, a model for others—wealthy, influential, respected for his piety. Others desired what he desired, for as one who "sat as chief," who "lived like a king" (29:25), what he wanted and intended was what others wanted and intended.

Now everything is changed. Job is like a king, and his fate is comparable to that of sacred kings in tribal settings and in various royal rites.[1] His fortunes have been reversed, and he sits on the ash heap as an object of the community's derision and scorn. Who or what has brought about this disastrous change? In an apparent cause and effect statement, Job attributes his condition to God's action and then speaks of his outcast status.

> Because God has loosed my bowstring
> and humbled me,
> they have cast off restraint in my presence.
> On my right hand the rabble rise,
> they send me sprawling,
> and build roads for my ruin.
>   (30:11–12)

Likewise in chapter 19 there is an apparent causal connection between divine action (vv. 6–12) and the response of his family and community (vv. 13–22).

The assumption that there is a divinely established network of retributive violence separating the righteous and the wicked is one Job shares with the Friends. Eliphaz contends that the evildoer perishes by the breath of God (4:9), and he suffers continual pain (15:20), with "terrifying sounds" in his ears (15:21). Indeed, the wicked "wander abroad for bread" (15:23), for "they have stretched out their hands against God" (15:25). Bildad offers a graphic description of the terrors that beset the wicked, who "are torn from the tent in which they trusted, and brought to the king of terrors" (18:14), that is, the lord of the underworld. This is the fate of "the dwellings of the ungodly, such is the place of those who do not know God" (18:21).

Job, through the mimetic process, begins by assuming that the Friends (that is, his community, the tradition) are right about the way the world actually operates.

And insofar as it operates in this way, God is responsible for it and must be unjust, for he, Job, is innocent. In other words, Job agrees with the Friends concerning the world but disagrees in his own individual case. He is therefore led to a negative conclusion about divine justice. And he holds that even if he could have a trial, or at least a hearing, he doesn't believe it would proceed fairly. God, the judge, "would crush me with a tempest" (9:17, my translation).

> Though I am innocent, my own mouth would condemn me;
> though I am blameless, he would prove me perverse.
> I am blameless; I do not know myself;
> I loathe my life.

> (9:20–21)

With this sort of protest Job separates himself from the social unanimity that the social order demands (and that is never far below the surface, even in supposedly enlightened democratic societies). Girard quotes a passage from Aeschylus's *Eumenides* in which the Erinyes say, "May joy be exchanged for joy in a common love and may we hate with a single soul; for this is man's great remedy"[2]—the common human remedy: that we join "in a common love" and especially that "we hate with a single soul." The distinctive traditions of the Bible do not accept accommodation to the order of generative violence, but the Friends, even though they speak for an advanced wisdom tradition, reflect an uneasiness that shows the principle of sacrificial violence is not far below the surface. Does Job possess the divine wisdom of Adam (15:7–8)? No, he does away with the piety, the fear of God (15:4) that undergirds the sacred order of things. He keeps "to the old way which the wicked have trod" (22:15).

Job, like Oedipus, is seen by his social order as taking the ancient way of the wicked that leads to death. Oedipus, however, "is a *successful* scapegoat because he is never recognized as such."[3] And he concurs in the judgment upon himself. This is what the social order seeks to inculcate, for the unanimity of the generative mechanism will ideally include even the victim's own complicity in the judgment made. If the sacrificial pattern is submerged and rationalized in totalitarian ideology, as in the modern period, then victims will not only concur with the judgment but confess their sin publicly.[4] In this regard, Oedipus is an ancient mythopoetic archetype of the confession in a modern totalitarian trial. But Job, as a *failed* scapegoat, maintains his own point of view rather than acceding to the mythologically required unanimity that the Friends wish to impose upon him.

The theology of the Friends, whose assumptions Job initially accepts and whose conclusions he deplores, is a projection of the social order that is maintained through the generative process of the sacrificial mechanism and its operations. That is to say, the God of the Friends and the God Job accuses of injustice is really the socially transcendent symbol of the generative structure that operates in the dynamics of mimesis, victimization, sacrifice, and scapegoating. We would not expect the text to spell out such a generative structure in our own terms, but there are some definite signs of the connection of God and social order.

One sign is Job's sarcastic reply after Zophar has spoken for the first time, "No doubt you are the people, and wisdom will die with you" (12:2). This is clearly a statement of the principle *vox populi, vox dei*. Continuing in an ironic vein, Job conflates in two sentences the rationalization by which the Friends support their arguments:

> Wisdom is with the aged,
> and understanding in length of days.
> With God are wisdom and might;
> he has counsel and understanding.
> (12:12–13, RSV)

The elders and God, the elders—including undoubtedly the sages—representing God: this is the bulwark of the social order. Job then goes on to describe the putative wisdom of God as really arbitrary, tyrannical power that is just as prone to create disorder as order (12:14–25). This is the dark side of the generative order—perpetual conflict and violence. The way of controlling it is also, of course, given by this God, given through the wisdom of the elders.

The second sign concerning God and social order has to do with the kind of metaphors used for the enemies that Job says God has sent against him, enemies that from the Friends' standpoint are cohorts that torment the wicked. When Eliphaz asserts that "the destroyer will come upon" the wicked person (15:21), he probably has in mind a human agent, another unscrupulous one who follows the ancient path of the wicked. When Zophar speaks of God's fierce anger whose result is that "the possessions of [the wicked one's] house will be carried away" (20:28), attacks by human groups or armies are meant. This is probably an allusion to what happened to Job when the Sabeans and Chaldeans attacked (in the prologue, 1:13–18). In other instances, mythical allusions are made to celestial armies of God. Job speaks of being struck by the "arrows of the Almighty" (6:4) and cries out that "his archers surround me. . . . He bursts upon me again and again; he rushes at me like a warrior" (16:13a, 14). In chapter 16 the imagery of the divine armies is intermingled with attacks by his own people.

> They have gaped at me with their mouth,
> they have struck me insolently upon the cheek,
> they mass themselves together against me.
> God gives me up to the ungodly,
> and casts me into the hands of the wicked.
> (16:10–11)

"They mass themselves together against me": this is what is happening to Job. He is the object of collective violence, and the rather fluid movement between the image of human mobs and divine gendarmes—thugs from Job's point of view—is a tip-off that the movement of the social order against the scapegoat and God's action against the wicked are two ways of talking about the same thing. The God persona of the Theophany seems to confirm this connection in sarcastically instructing Job, if he is up to it, to deal with the wicked as God does, namely, humble, trample, and bury them (40:11–13; see below, "The God-Speeches").

In considering these passages depicting attacks on Job, attacks that come only upon evildoers, according to the Friends, I concur with Girard: "The multiplicity of enemies is always based on the same model, the human crowd. . . ." As he says further, "The seething crowd is the perfect vehicle for the divine vengeance. It hurls itself at the victim and tears him to pieces; all the participants share the same terrible appetite for violence."[5] An example of this appetite for violence is the Dionysiac *diasparagmos*, or ritual dismemberment, as seen, for example, in the murder of Pentheus in *The Bacchae* of Euripides. As quoted in one of the epigraphs to chapter 5, "and the whole rabid pack were on him. There was a single, universal howl: the moans of Pentheus (so long as he had breath) mixed with their impassioned yells. One woman carried off an arm, another a foot, boot and all; they shredded his ribs—clawed them clean. . . . His body lies in pieces."[6]

The model of a crowd lynching a victim, portrayed so starkly in *The Bacchae* and avoided in Sophocles' *Oedipus Rex* by Oedipus's own complicity in his victimization, may also inform the speeches of the Friends. In the Dialogues their so-called comfort takes the form of instruction and dispute that erupts increasingly into sarcastic attacks, until finally, in the third cycle of speeches, Eliphaz makes the accusation that has been in their minds all along: "Is not your wickedness great?" (22:5). He follows this charge with a list of specific iniquities (22:6–9).

Having already recognized this verbal equivalent of lynching, Job cries out, "How long will you torment me, and break me in pieces with words?" (19:2). "Break me in pieces" (*tedakkunani*) is a form of a verb used a number of times in Job. In fact, Eliphaz will use it later in accusing Job of crushing the arms of the fatherless (22:9), and he employed it earlier in an impersonal plural form as he described the short, miserable, ignorant existence of human beings who "are crushed before the moth" (4:19, RSV). And although a different verb is used at 9:17, the same metaphorical configuration is evidently involved in Job's contention that God "would crush me in a tempest." In any case, with their speeches the Friends justify the violence—they sacralize it.

God as the social order, the sacred community, is what Job presupposes but cannot accept. He protests against it, and in some lucid moments he extricates himself from the assumptions of the Friends in distinguishing God from society and affirming the God of victims who will vindicate him. At one point Job remembers the God of creation and reminds him, "You have granted me life and steadfast love, and your care has preserved my spirit" (10:12), but then he immediately falls into an accusatory complaint, "Bold as a lion you hunt me . . . you renew your witnesses against me" (10:16a, 17a). In keeping with the judicial metaphors of chapter 9, he wishes for an arbiter (9:33). Later, in one of his most bitter and graphic descriptions of the way God and man attack him, he pours out a cry for vengeance that really turns into a momentary affirmation of faith.

> O earth, do not cover my blood,
> and let my outcry find no resting place.
> Even now, in fact, my witness is in heaven,
> and he that vouches for me is on high.
> My friends scorn me;
> my eye pours out tears to God,
> that he would maintain the right of a mortal with God,
> and that of a human with a neighbor.
> For when a few years have come
> I shall go the way from which I shall not return.
> (16:18–22, my translation of 21b)

Verse 21 has posed difficulties for translators, but the sense of the Hebrew text seems clear enough to me. "The right of a mortal [Hebrew 'man'] with God" and "(of) a human ['man'] (with respect) to his neighbor" simply refers to the totality of relationships in which God maintains compassionate justice and stands on the side of the victim.

The passage nonetheless betrays a certain duality of God. Job's blood on the earth is a sign that his divine and human persecutors have done their work. Now the God of victims is ranged against the God of the persecutors. However, a second text does not bear the same ambiguity about God's duality.

> But as for me, I know that my Vindicator (*goali*) lives,
> and afterwards he will arise upon the earth.
> And after my skin is thus destroyed,
> then (even) without my flesh I shall see God.
> And the one whom I myself see taking my part,
> my eyes will see not as an alien.
> My heart fails within me!
> (19:25–27, my translation)

My own view is that verses 26 and 27 have been difficult for commentators because of theological controversies, not because of the condition of the text. Without one word, *zot* in verse 26a, everything else would be intelligible and grammatically correct. I have resorted to the old solution of Buttenweiser in changing the garbled *weachar ori niqqefu-zot* ("after my skin they destroy-this") to *niqqaf kazzot*, "and after my skin is destroyed in this manner" (or thus). As problematic as that might be, I would simply emphasize that everything else falls into place nicely—*unless* one feels compelled to deny any hint of resurrection from the dead (so many Jewish and Christian biblical critics) or to deny any christological import of the passage (so most Jewish and many Christian critics). Although other translations than mine are certainly possible, I would prefer to leave these other doctrinal and ideological issues open and note Job's note of hope in looking to the God who is *goel*, vindicator or avenger of the rights of the oppressed.

There is a third passage where he reaches a similar level of insight. In his longing to find God and make his case before him, Job again affirms the justice of the God of victims.

> I would learn what he would answer me,
> and understand what he would say to me.
> Would he contend with me in the greatness of his power?
> No; but he would give heed to me .
> There an upright person could reason with him,
> and I should be acquitted for ever by my judge.
>
> (23:5–7)

This third passage is particularly important for its indication of the "good mimesis" of the God of victims. Acquisitive mimesis involves a network of power relations in which the subject, imitating the imagined desire of the model of authority, seeks to possess what the model-rival has. The ultimate result, if carried to its conclusion, is the elimination of the model-rival or the subject's self-identity—or *both* if the conflict takes the form of savage revolt or revolution. In this moment of lucidity Job turns momentarily from bitter complaint to envisage how God would not be concerned with exercising his power but would listen to his case and give heed to him.

So these three texts, 16:18–22 and 19:25–27 and 23:5–7, go beyond Job's protestations of suffering and innocence to give a glimpse of a God of victims. As such, these brief tableaus hold the potential of subverting the mimetic certainties of the scapegoat mechanism, but they are not sustained.

2. The God-Speeches (Job 38–41)

The God of the God-speeches does not deal with the question of Job's innocence or Job's relations with his community—"the best way of neutralizing the subversive force of Job's speech." The God of chapters 38–41 avoids the dilemma of human and divine-human relationships by taking refuge in the natural world, lecturing Job at length on the wonders of the cosmos. "This God demonstrates his strength so as not to have to use it. He is no longer the God of the friends, who was openly exercising his terror against scapegoats [this clause is my translation of the French]. He no longer brandishes the celestial armies against the rebel. He resorts to cunning and wins his case."[7]

In two respects the God of the Theophany is different from the God dominating the Dialogue, who is the Friends or community writ large. One is that his concern with the cosmos shows that humankind is not "originally" in the picture. Job (humankind) sees and identifies himself through hearing and responding to God, and to that extent there is an ancient Israelite dialogical element in the God-speeches that could become the basis of a new revelation, a disclosure of a new being of God, human beings, and language. However, this dialogical element is undercut by the *rivalry* of God with Job. Job had better get the message: "Whoever confronts me I requite, For everything under the heavens is mine" (41:11, my trans.). Let him who is able draw near to Behemoth with his sword (40:19)—for of course only God is able!

The second way in which the God speaking to Job is different from the God of the Friends is that he does not condemn Job and account him one of the wicked—*though wicked there are, who must be eliminated.* Thus the poem takes away with one hand what it gives with the other. God does not exonerate Job and does demand confession of his ignorance, but he allows him to be exonerated and confirms him in the end. Nonetheless, God demands of Job that he eliminate the wicked.

In a passage often cited as proof that the Theophany does not omit questions of justice and morality, God actually reverts to the old sacred that the Friends represent.[8]

> Deck yourself with majesty and dignity;
> clothe yourself with glory and splendor.
> Pour forth the overflowings of your anger,
> and look on every one that is proud, and abase him,
> Look on every one that is proud, and bring him low;
> and crush the wicked where they stand.
> Hide them all in the dust together,
> bind their faces in concealment.
>
> (40:10–13)

Habel has commented that "Yahweh's second speech opens with a challenge for Job to demonstrate that he has the power to govern the earth with an arm as glorious and mighty as El's (40:7–14)." He goes on to say that "Job is to exhibit the capacities of El by unleashing his wrath (*ap*), abasing the proud and crushing the wicked." He points out that "the 'furies' . . . and 'wrath-anger' . . . of God are associated with his day of judgment on the wicked (Job 20:28; 21:30)." Job is called upon to "demonstrate his capacity to complete the punitive process and deliver the wicked as captives to the underworld according to the principles Job was advocating."[9]

Now the question I would ask is this: What is it that really distinguishes God in this passage from the Friends and their God in the Dialogue? Zophar has already described "the portion of the wicked from God":

> To fill their belly to the full
> God will send his fierce anger into them,
> and rain it upon them into their flesh.
> They will flee from an iron weapon;
> a bronze arrow will strike them through.
> It is drawn forth and comes out of their body,
> the glittering point comes out of their gall;
> terrors come upon them.
>
> (20:23–25, my trans. of 23c)

The God of justice who judges the righteous and the wicked, dividing them into those to be rewarded and those to be punished, is a belief that may be seen as an advance on more primitive notions of the sacred, especially if it validates a tradition of law and wisdom. However, it was easy to turn that very belief against Job by making him one of those who "keep to the old way that the wicked have trod." Moreover, the God of the Theophany exhibits a certain relish in describing what the one to be identified as El does to the wicked. The literary style is a good example of what Robert Alter has described as "intensification" in poetic parallelism.[10] Intensification in this sense is an increment or sharpening of the image or idea in succeeding lines. Not only will the El figure look on the proud and abase them, he will crush them where they stand. And not only will he crush them where they stand, he will hide their bodies in the ground where they cannot be found. A good job, done with great gusto!

A good job, but beside the point. The God who is willing to acknowledge to Job that if he really were able to perform as the great divine Judge and Warrior, "your own right hand will give you victory" (40:14)—this God does not hear Job's cry for the God of victims, the God of compassionate justice, the God who vindicates the rights of the oppressed, the God who listens to the petitioner. This is instead the God who delights in describing what he will do to the wicked.

So I read the theology of the God-speeches as poor theology. It is a definite but very ambiguous attempt to respond to the good sociology and anthropology of the Dialogue—to the awareness of the human condition that Job articulates and to the few occasions of insight when Job cries out to a God who is not identical with the sacred, is not the social order as transcendent reality. Openness to a new disclosure, a new reality of God, human beings, and language, is undercut by the rampant rivalry with which God confronts Job. God does not declare Job guilty, but it is as though he wishes to convince Job and make him a kind of human partner in crushing and eliminating the wicked. The God of the Theophany loves the animals, who are beautiful in their wildness, but his underlying savagery is great.

Whether it was the author of the Dialogues or some other writer in the subsequent tradition who composed the God-speeches, I do not know. Girard holds that the style and content of the speeches of God have nothing to do with the Dialogues, and he may be right. Or it may be that the Job poet attempted a kind of compromise between Job's cry for the divine Witness and Redeemer and the conventional wisdom of the sacred social order. Either way, the distinctiveness of the ancient Israelite tradition of revelation is lost. Even if the Voice from the whirlwind is not exactly the same as the God of the Friends (see the two differences noted above), it is hardly more than a variation on the divinization of the power of the social order that was discussed in the treatment of the Dialogues.

B. Issues in Interpreting Job

1. Job and the Canon

In my approach to Job I have neither cut the text of Job into fragments or putative redactions nor agreed completely with the text, which I assume represents the Job poet's work and point of view. Nonetheless, I have argued strenuously to save not the text but the Job of the text, the victim who has cried out to God and his friends. This Job now needs defenders, in my estimation. The first obligation of the interpreter who stands in service to the biblical tradition of the disclosure of the innocent victim and the God of victims is not to the text as such but to the victim and to the God of love and justice. As Girard has argued, this obligation is a moral demand requiring a "transformative reading,"[11] which is in effect a deliberate misreading. Faced with certain choices—for example, the denial of persecution of victims as a text's reference—"one must either do violence to the text or let the text forever do violence to innocent victims."[12]

But can this enterprise, which receives its impulse from the work of Girard, really affirm the biblical canon? In the arena of "postmodern critical theory" the very concept of canon is besieged from every side (see below, "The Book of Job as Scapegoat"). My own intention, however, is to take it very seriously. We must also take seriously, even if we cannot accept as normative, the questions and concerns arising out of diverse intellectual and sociohistorical settings: (1) The charge by women and minorities that dominant religious and literary canons have functioned to exclude them, that is, to justify their victimization intellectually, spiritually, economically, and in other ways. (2) A "postmodern" intellectual and cultural situation that, whether or not it is partially an artificial construct of intellectuals, is widely validated and employed as justification for philosophical and theological positions. An extreme side of this development in theology has moved from the "death of God" to the radicalization of the consequences of this divine demise in thinking about every kind of authority, including canonical texts. (3)

The conservative, as well as evangelical and fundamentalist, reaction in American religious life—which is very much a part of certain political currents—to the voiding of canon, authority, and conventional moral standards (criteria of differentiation), a state of affairs that is perceived as chaotic. The total state of affairs represented in this interpretive situation could be called, in Girardian terms, a "mimetic crisis."

In this interpretive situation characterized by extreme reactions that are symptoms of a mimetic crisis, I prefer to find a way that has been excluded. With respect to the biblical canon (and here I'm referring to the Protestant and Roman Catholic canons) this means to view it as an integral whole, to look to it as the touchstone of theology and religious life, but at the same time to view it as a treasury of questions that "authorize" us to question the canon itself and argue with it. In taking this standpoint I have been influenced by the Jewish tradition. This tradition includes the "Promethean element in biblical prayer" (e.g., the intercessory debates of Abraham, Moses, Jeremiah, Job, and some of the psalmists with God). The phrase was used by my late teacher, Sheldon Blank of Hebrew Union College–Jewish Institute of Religion. Also important for me are the tradition of rabbinic debate on the meaning of Scripture passages and the ongoing contest with God in the writings of Elie Wiesel.

I see the Book of Job as the paradigm instance of the canonical basis for raising questions, a basis that cannot shield the Book of Job or the canon itself. Another one of my teachers, Matitiahu Tsevat, cites at the end of his thought-provoking essay on Job the words of *Pesiqta Rabbati*, "Had he [Job] not clamored so—as it is now the practice to say in prayer 'God of Abraham, God of Isaac, and God of Jacob,' so one would say 'and God of Job.'"[13] But this position in the Midrash is one that must finally save text, canon, and tradition at the price of Job's challenge, which is his cry to and for the God of victims. And so in articulating a positive view of canon I think we should always have in mind "God of Job," the God and the Job of that challenge, even if "God of Job" does not appear in the canonical text or in our prayers.

2. Job and Christology

I think that my reading of the Book of Job and its place in a view of the canon offers a new and positive linkage of Job's cry for a vindicator and the Jesus of the New Testament Gospels. The Jesus of the Gospels becomes, for the Christian tradition, the *decisive* event revealing the reality and meaning of the God of victims, of the God, the Logos, by which the world is created and constituted and who takes the side of the poor, the needy, the oppressed. What Job calls for, the Gospels focus on. What Job expresses in a few moments of anguished lucidity, the Gospels illuminate in the story of the Passion. In this sense, I think Christian theology should look firmly and unashamedly at Job as an adumbration of Jesus as the crucified.

Girard devotes a chapter of his book on Job to the relation of Job to the Gospels. His position has determined my own, but mine is not identical with his. Allow me to quote at length two of his key statements:

> In a world of violence, divinity purified of every act of violence must be revealed by means of the event that already provides the sacrificial religion with its generative mechanism. The epiphany of the God of victims follows the same "ancient trail" and goes through the exact same phases as all the epiphanies of the sacred of the persecutors. As a result, *from the perspective of violence, there is absolutely no distinction between the God of victims and the God of persecutors.* Our pseudoscience of religions is based entirely on the conviction that there is no essential difference between the different religions. . . .
>
> This central event [of the sacrifice or scapegoating of a victim] . . . . is also present in the Gospels, but on this occasion it does not just appear in transit: it is not only clearly described, but named. It is called the Passion. Jesus is the perfect victim, because he has always spoken and behaved in accordance with the Logos of the God of victims. He provides the only perfect image of the event which is at the root of all our myths and religions.[14]

It is probably accurate to say that most historians of religion and investigators of comparative mythology would avow that in principle one should not pronounce on the soundness of the various traditions' truth claims or on the religious and moral values they espouse. This latter "impartiality" or "disinterestedness" is, I take it, what Girard is talking about, and he has certainly put his finger on a problem. When this point of view "goes to seed," becoming a sort of pan-religiosity or pan-mythology that eschews questions of morality and value (except to justify pan-religiosity), then it has a great public reception because such a view makes it easy to relegate human problems and differences to a transcendent private sphere removed from historical situations and social and political crises. Witness the popularity of Joseph Campbell's mythography via the Bill Moyers interviews on public television. In the interviews Campbell even stated in one anecdote that violence and misery occurring before one's very eyes should be affirmed as an expression of ultimate reality, a position similar to Heidegger's affirmation of the violence of the Logos. Again, "From the perspective of violence, there is absolutely no distinction between the God of victims and the God of persecutors."

With respect to Girard's biblical hermeneutics, two questions of great consequence are, How does he approach the Gospels? and Does he believe that Christianity supersedes the Jewish tradition?

As to the Jewish tradition, some of Girard's statements seem to assert an absolute truth that only the Christian tradition—and note well, for Girard, this means above all the Gospels—knows with certainty. It should be noted, however, that Girard doesn't claim this "only perfect image of the event" that demythologizes the scapegoat mechanism is a *Christian* event. No, it is an event that fulfills the Jewish tradition of revelation, and its personal bearer is the Jew Jesus. It is true that the subsequent Christian tradition has transmitted the meaning of this event through the Gospels—sometimes contradicting itself in that Christianity became, by and large, another sacrificial religion and, among other things, did violence to its own texts by persecuting the Jews.

I do think that any language implying the inherent superiority of Christianity or the "Christian" Gospels should be avoided. The argument to be made in the next two chapters is that a full disclosure of the victimization mechanism and sacred violence is attested in the Gospels. There we find a complete recognition of the God who is expelled or lynched because he is not subservient to the differences established in social structure by means of the sacred. "Not subservient" means, in effect, *subversive* of culture in all its manifestations. But I do not view the Gospels as "Christian" texts that are superior to Jewish texts. These texts have been just as misunderstood in the Christian tradition and by Christians as they have been by those in other traditions. Furthermore, the very basis and structure of these texts is fundamentally Jewish from a historical standpoint. To say this is not to deny, of course, that the Gospels have been elaborated literarily and theologically in ways that may be termed "Hellenistic."

3. The Book of Job as Scapegoat

Scapegoating and victimization is a difficult subject, in great part because it is easy to see it in enemies or outsiders or historical predecessors but not in ourselves. The problem is exacerbated by the popularity of the idea of claiming to be a victim as a way of victimizing one's enemies. This tendency arises out of the Judeo-Christian influence on Western thought and institutions, but of course, like any way of seeing things, it can be vulgarized and used for crass ideological purposes.

Thus, the theory of the victimization mechanism operative in human societies is simple at one level, but it is a very complex matter to unravel its workings and to be sufficiently aware of one's own motives.

With respect to Job, that complexity may be seen in the fact that my own argument may be turned against me in this way: You take the Girardian path of locating the core of Job in the text's insights into persecution of the scapegoat and Job's occasional lucid affirmations of a God of victims, but you execute your hermeneutics at the expense of the God-speeches and the Epilogue. Aren't you simply pitting one view against another and seeking to detract from interpreters whose hermeneutical discourse is quite different from yours?

My response is that undoubtedly I have sinned, probably in more ways than I could be aware of. I ask first for forgiveness. Then I would ask to be allowed to impose just two strictures concerning the problem of scapegoating the text and those who hold different positions. One is that the approach to the text shall not disregard any part of it, even if one does not like it. In this context I have not had opportunity to deal with the Prologue, the Epilogue, Elihu's Speeches, or the Poem to Wisdom. One would have to deal with all of them and take them seriously—not exclude them or scapegoat them. This serious treatment is what I have undertaken to achieve with the Dialogue and the God-speeches, which I think are the most important parts of Job but must certainly be related to the rest of the book, just as the book must be related to the rest of the canon. Engagement with the canonical text, questioning it and being questioned by it, is the necessary condition of an adequate doctrine of canon, as I have indicated in "Job and the Canon." Yes, maybe I missed something in the Theophany. Maybe I haven't done the writer (or writers) justice. Well, the canon will still be there tomorrow for new questions and new comprehension. It is much more important than we are as critics.

Girard views all other parts of Job as additions to the Dialogue and "additions to the additions."[15] Whether or not they are additions, they offer us a challenge, a set of voices from the tradition that must be heard. If nothing else, they may enable us to highlight what is truly distinctive about Job. Girard holds, of course, that in some cases it is necessary to "do violence" to a text (see "Job and the Canon" and the second stricture immediately below). However, I don't think he means by that to "scapegoat" it by expelling it, in effect, from the canon because it is secondary or tertiary to some original text or event. Such, at least, is not my intention.

So the first stricture is that no part of the text is to be disregarded. The other is that Job the victim and the God he discloses shall not be sacrificed to any God or to any interpretation, whether it be the sacred social order of the Friends, with their God of violence, or to some transcendental "amorality" that Job the New Man in his enlightened state is supposed to understand and represent.

Most of the students and colleagues with whom I converse and consort don't wish to take the side of the Friends, nor do they espouse a conservative or fundamentalist point of view. Therefore I will take up the other tendency to victimize Job, which poses at least as great a threat as a conservative or reactionary position affirming the God of the sacred social order. The transcendental amorality or new "higher morality" is a powerful current in modern intellectual history, and it has had, I think, quite an effect on Job interpretation. Nietzsche's theme of *ressentiment*, which he views as the detestable slave morality of Judaism and Christianity, is countered by his vision of the *Uebermensch*, whose god is Dionysus and who affirms the eternal return of all things. What Nietzsche did not understand was that his archetype of the authoritarian imposer of slave morality, the Christian God, was really his model-obstacle, and that in trying to eliminate and transcend resentment in the idea of the Overman he was really enthroning resentment in a new mode. The eternal return is the eternal cycle of violence, of revenge. "Life itself," he says in *The Will to Power*, "its eternal fruitfulness and recurrence, creates torment, destruction, the will to annihilation."[16]

Heidegger was much influenced by Nietzsche in understanding the *logos* as that structure of being that violently brings together opposites. In the tradition of Hegel, Marx, Nietzsche, and Freud, he sees the biblical concept of the relation of God and human beings as that of master and slave (although Hegel did not extend this image to the New Testament). He argues that the tradition of the Logos represented in the Gospel of John is a form of combat and violence visited upon humans understood as slaves, whereas the Logos of the Greek tradition is a violence perceived and committed by free men. Girard points out what Heidegger fails to see: that a structure of violent mastery always requires slavery, for it depends on the model-rival or the model as obstacle.[17] When the model of reality and of human existence is conceived in this way, you will simply get Nietzsche's eternal return all over again—and it's a very dull round of things. Nietzsche's eternal return appears to be an attempt to overcome repetition-compulsion by radicalizing it. The anxiety to repeat an event, to go over it again and again in one's own mind, is an attempt to remedy a disquieting episode in one's life by experiencing once again the pain of the episode's disorder (defeat, embarrassment, or whatever it is) and bringing it this time to a satisfactory solution; thus one may view oneself as the master of the situation and of one's life. Girard uses the example of the general who is so humiliated in battle that henceforth he cannot engage in any other battle for any purpose except to make up for the one defeat. "It is not a question of losing yet again, but of winning the only battle that is really worth the trouble—the battle he has already lost. So he puts all his efforts into encountering his old antagonists once again and reproducing the circumstances of his earlier defeat. The triumph he is aiming for can no longer be imagined outside the framework of this defeat and everything that goes with it."[18] The eternal return is an attempt to affirm, "Let it be as it will be, with all the pain, anxiety, embarrassment, and frustration that I have already suffered." It is an affirmation of undifferentiation as well as differentiation. What Nietzsche failed to see was that this sort of affirmation is a desperate ploy, especially as joined to the master-slave model presupposed in the vision of the *Uebermensch*, the superior human being of the future.

With this model, then, the options are basically four: submit slavishly to the master (model); get rid of the master; break away in revolt (which may also result in the elimination of the master); or get rid of yourself—suicide. So it's the same old thing over and over again: submit, submit, submit . . . or kill, kill, kill . . . or rebel, rebel, rebel . . . or kill yourself, kill yourself, kill yourself. Another way to put it is that all this is *revenge*: with the second and third options, murder and rebellion, the revenge is directed against the other; with the first and last, submission and suicide, it is internalized and directed against oneself.

So it is that when I read or hear interpretations of Job that contend Job is to see that justice is not rooted in the divine order of things, or that the divine presence, itself, is enough, or that creation is a grand mystery, or that suffering is simply a perspective on things, or that God and world are a mystery beyond good and evil, I would ask some questions in return.

1. Granted that God and the world are wonderfully and beautifully mysterious, are all understandings of truth and justice equally meritorious or unmeritorious?
2. Is the round of human violence to be justified by divine violence—that is, by the sacred, by the transcendent social order?
3. Is what happens to the victim unimportant?

A positive response to any one of these questions means that Job is being scapegoated again.

Jewish theology, in the name of the God of Abraham, the God of Isaac, and the God of Jacob, must answer resoundingly to all these questions, "No!"

Christian theology, in the name of the God of Jesus Christ, must answer resoundingly to all these questions, "No!"

And if Jewish and Christian theology say no, then the God of Job will be in no danger of an imminent demise. Nietzsche, of course, in aphorism 125 of *The Gay Science,* has his Madman announce not just that God is dead, but that "We have killed him"—a textual fact widely ignored or suppressed. The so-called death of God, if taken from a Nietzschean standpoint, is really the murder of God. But the God of Job is not a God that must slay or be slain.

C. Modern Psychological Mythology: Jung's Answer to Job

In the third chapter I discussed Moses and the exodus from the standpoint of "Egyptian" mythology. What would be a modern mythology of the Friends? In fact, there have been many modern "friends" responding to Job in a multitude of ways. One of the most important of these is C. G. Jung.

Jung's *Answer to Job* is an excellent example of one sort of modern mythology at work, supposedly examining ancient sources by means of a new mode of inquiry but actually engaging in mythical or sacrificial thinking that, in fact, is a massive denial of the text being interpreted. It is for that reason that I wish to review Jung's book on Job. I am aware that many academics influenced by Jung have been quite critical of his "monomythic" view of the self, as well as of his "Christian" presuppositions and concerns.[19] However, there is no doubt that Jung's work is representative of one important strand of modern intellectual history, and for this reason his reading of Job cannot be ignored.

Jung's interpretation of Job is a justification of evil as necessary to reality itself, which is understood in terms of psychic processes and the archetypes emerging from the unconscious. (An "archetype" in Jung's sense is a primary form or image emerging from the unconscious. Archetypes are "collective," occurring all over the world, and are constituent elements of myths.)[20] Jung's view of evil and the unconscious might be acceptable if it were simply a matter of recognizing the dark and chaotic side of human nature and arguing that it is necessary to deal with both "sides" of the human condition. However, Jung's psychological mythology amounts to a justification of this dark side as inherent in reality itself, at least as known psychically and psychologically. Jung's work is finally a justification of the victimization mechanism in human culture and its sacrificial outlets. In other words, once again, "from the perspective of violence, there is absolutely no distinction between the God of victims and the God of the persecutors." Jung's position is that of a modern Friend of Job.

Jung's statement in his preface to the reader indicates one of the main reasons the Jungian approach has appealed to so many intellectuals and nonacademic seekers of spiritual wisdom. His approach is a kind of shadow side of science and technology that does not interfere with their perspective and methods. He says, for example, "The psyche is an autonomous factor, and religious statements are psychic confessions which in the last resort are based on unconscious, i.e., on transcendental, processes. These processes are not accessible to physical perception but demonstrate their existence through the confessions of the psyche."[21] A domain of esoteric knowledge is thus opened up with which science and technology cannot interfere, but by the same token science and technology are left to go their own way.

Job's laments, complaints, and accusations that God is unjust "clearly show that . . . in spite of [Job's] doubt as to whether man can be just before God, [he] still finds it difficult to relinquish the idea of meeting God on the basis of justice and therefore of morality." Job does not doubt the unity of God—"He clearly sees that God is at odds with himself." Job's Yahweh "is not split but is an *antinomy*— a totality of inner opposites—and this is the indispensable condition for his tremendous dynamism, his omniscience and omnipotence." Unfortunately for Israel, however, Yahweh broke his own oath. He violated his own covenant; his people have gone into exile, as David asserts in Psalm 89. The problem is, Yahweh "is too unconscious to be moral."[22] Because he encompasses everything in its totality, he includes both total justice and its opposite.

What we see to this point, then, is that, for Jung, YHWH is both the God of victims and the God of victimizers; he is the God of the oppressed Hebrews and of the Egyptian oppressors. Once again the victim is expelled; once again "harsh bondage" is laid upon the slaves. For Jung, the victim is real only within the network of a psychic code in which the victim is necessary to the unconscious and conscious processes that lead to the differentiation of the self, whose real basis or

being is the Self or the God-archetype. In other words, in the beginning is undifferentiation. A theology of divine arbitrariness, of divine anger, and of the innocent victim are all bound together in one mythological theology, whose objective is
the differentiation of the Self archetype in the individual self.

Job, with his insistence on his own integrity and on bringing his case before
God, has forced God to reveal his true nature. It is YHWH himself who darkens
his own counsel. "Job is no more than the outward occasion for an inward process
of dialectic in God." YHWH sees Job as his chief rival. He "sees something in Job
which we would not ascribe to him but to God, that is, an equal power which causes him to bring out his whole power apparatus and parade it before his opponent."
That Jung sees this dynamic of a power struggle between YHWH and Job in the
Theophany is very insightful on his part. I think, however, that Jung's approach is
very close to the master-slave model of Nietzsche's view of reality, except that with
Jung it is introjected into the psychic process. In the psychic rivalry of God and
Job, Job wins; "without knowing it or wanting it, a mortal man is raised by his
moral behaviour above the stars in heaven, from which position of advantage he
can behold the back of Yahweh, the abysmal world of 'shards.'"[23] Job has won, in a
sense, but in keeping with his new understanding of the totality of God, he submits as if he were the defeated opponent.

In this record of a spiritual process of differentiation the friends of Job play
hardly any part at all. Jung scarcely mentions them, thinking more highly of the
fourth friend, Elihu, the only one he names. Jung notes that after Job has repented
YHWH is nervous about Job's friends. He has such a doubt complex that he is
anxious, in a kind of comic manner, about "these respectable and slightly pedantic
old gentlemen, as though God-knows-what depended on what they thought."[24]
That Jung considers them really insignificant and harmless is an ironic aspect of
his interpretation of the book. For Jung himself, not unlike the Friends, mounts an
attack on Job's cry for a God who will stand on his side in his suffering and defend
him: in Jung's interpretation, the most important thing to learn about the God of
Job is that he is a dark, all-embracing totality who will not, who cannot, stand for
Job and with Job.

The book is about answering Job, and that leads to the Christian doctrine of
Incarnation. Jung says quite clearly that he is reading Job and the Scriptures as a
Christian. In following the trail of Job as a kind of history of the psyche, he discusses wisdom texts, drawing particularly upon Egyptian mythology regarding incarnation of divine reality in human being. Incarnation in the Christian sense "means
nothing less than a world-shaking transformation of God. It means more or less
what Creation meant in the beginning, namely an objectivation of God." At this
point Jung's "pan-psychism" comes out. The various prefigurations and anticipations of the Incarnation, as in Israel's Scriptures and in Egyptian myth, "must
strike one as either completely incomprehensible or superfluous, since all creation

ex nihilo is God's and consists of nothing but God, with the result that man, like the rest of creation, is simply God become concrete." These prefigurations, however, are but "stages in the process of becoming conscious."[25]

Job achieved a great triumph, and the consciousness of YHWH was raised, though the full consequences were not realized immediately by YHWH. He did not at first become conscious of Job's moral victory. Sophia (Wisdom) enables God to engage in self-reflection and "thus makes possible Yahweh's decision to become man." YHWH, having done man a wrong, must become man. Wisdom teaches him, "Because his creature has surpassed him he must regenerate himself."[26]

The full articulation of the Incarnation occurs in the despairing cry of Christ from the cross, "My God, my God, why hast thou forsaken me?" Here "God experiences what it means to be a mortal man and drinks to the dregs what he made his faithful servant Job suffer. Here is given the answer to Job." The Incarnation is a *symbolum*, "a bringing together of heterogeneous natures. . . . Yahweh's intention to become man, which resulted from his collision with Job, is fulfilled in Christ's life and suffering."[27]

Jung understands the Incarnation in terms of a psychological variation on the medieval ransom theory of the atonement. Because "God" must grow into differentiated consciousness, his unconscious wishes to become conscious, but at the same time it wants to remain unconscious. "That is to say, God wants to become man, but not quite. The conflict in his nature is so great that the incarnation can only be bought by an expiatory self-sacrifice offered up to the wrath of God's dark side." Since it is impossible to "tell whether God and the unconscious are two different entities," redemption or wholeness for the individual psyche necessarily depends on a kind of "death" of resistance to unconscious processes, which must flow into consciousness. However, God himself must suffer what Job—human being—has suffered.[28] Consciousness must die to the unconscious; the unconscious must suffer for consciousness.

In the ensuing treatment, Jung deals with the Lord's Prayer (especially the petition "lead us not into temptation") and apocalyptic. In apocalyptic he is especially concerned with the feminine archetype as a coincidence of opposites. His focus in much of the latter part of the book is on the "other side" of God. He says, for example, that one would expect understanding and forgiveness from God as loving father, "So it comes as a nasty shock when this supremely good God only allows the purchase of such an act of grace through a human sacrifice and, what is worse, through the killing of his own son." The upshot of this doctrine in Jung's most important summary statement is that the seer of the Apocalypse, "Like Job . . . saw the fierce and terrible side of Yahweh. For this reason he felt his gospel of love to be one-sided, and he supplemented it with the gospel of fear: *God can be loved but he must be feared.*" The necessary fear of God is the "eternal gospel" as distinct from the temporal gospel of love.[29]

To deal adequately with the last part of the treatise would take too long and is not necessary for our purposes. In it, Jung treats at length the dogma of the Assumption of the Virgin with regard to its implications for modern Protestant Christianity and for all those concerned with a moral humanity in a new age. Jung interprets the Assumption mythico-psychologically as sacred marriage in the divine reality and the implied future birth of the divine child from this union of God and the Virgin. The divine child "will choose as his birthplace the empirical man."[30]

Now a summary of my critical comments.

1. Jung makes a radical distinction between the physical and the psychic. The "physical" seems to include everything pertaining to social and historical reality. This saves the sphere of religion and investigation of the psyche on the basis of a kind of "Platonian mystic contemplation of the archetypes."[31] Jung's methodological framework could never gain social scientific validity in a technological world, but it allows one to participate in this world without interfering with larger technological myths and symbols. A person inclined in the Jungian direction may decry technology, but that is a surface phenomenon, for there is nothing in the Jungian outlook that would work to reshape technology.

2. Although Jung accepts the religious and cultural importance of the Hebrew Bible and shows his interpretive power in making Job his focus and point of departure, he smothers Job with a blanket of mythical archetypes in which God is the supreme archetype of wholeness, the Self with a capital s. So, closely related to the first comment, Job and the other figures of the Old Testament do not represent any reality beyond the archetypal code. Israel and various individuals who are innocent victims and the God of victims are incorporated into a psychological mythology that banishes them once again and could have no social and historical effect except on the side of the oppressors.

3. Change and growth can take place only through a process of psychic violence. Sacrifice is built into the very structure of human existence. The self as consciousness must be offered up to the unconscious, and the unconscious must suffer (see discussion of atonement above). On the other hand, Jung does not relate violence to historical existence except in cursory references.

4. Mimetic process in human relationship plays no role in Jung's interpretation of Job. Therefore the Friends have an absolutely inconsequential role in his reading. The concept of mimetic rivalry that breaks out into violence plays no part in Jung's theory. As Girard says, "In Jung, the element of rivalry is totally expelled."[32] Girard's statement must be qualified, for Jung expels rivalry only to introject it into psychic processes where it is apparently cut off from actual human relations. Or to put it in another way, if we act out rivalries in different settings, it is because the Platonic essences in the form of archetypes from the unconscious are willy-nilly being realized through our attitudes and actions.

5. Although Jung speaks of morality and appeals to Christian virtues, nonetheless anything and everything can be justified by an appeal to the opposites of the divine totality. "God" and "man" are really slaves to an eternal process of differentiation in which God wants to become human and human beings strive to attain to the archetype of wholeness (i.e., "God"). But finally, for Jung, reality is undifferentiation. In this respect his thought participates in a basic theme of modern Western intellectual history according to which reality is the undifferentiated, and social science and text criticism consists in a process of deciphering and deconstructing structures of differentiation.[33]

It is surprising that Jung did not make more of Elihu's speeches, for Elihu elaborates Eliphaz's statement about a terrifying vision in the night (4:12–21) by asserting that nightmares are a warning from God to turn human beings from evil (33:14–18). Elihu's claim would fit perfectly into Jung's schema, for the warnings could be construed as the signals—the archetypes arising out of the unconscious—that establish and communicate the basis of the self. God terrifies the sleeper with these warnings, but after all—"*God can be loved but he must be feared.*"

Job often seems to share the Friends' assumptions concerning retribution and the God of the social order, and at one point he talks about nightmares.

> When I say, "My bed will comfort me,
> my couch will ease my complaint,"
> then you scare me with dreams
> and terrify me with visions.
>
> (7:13–14)

He, too, believes that God terrifies him, but for Job this terror is not a warning; it is rather an attempt to push him toward choosing death (7:15), as all good scapegoats are supposed to do. This God of Job's despair is like a mountain lion: "he seized me by the neck and dashed me to pieces" (16:12). The Friends, representing this God, are the front line of the mob attacking him: "they have gaped at me with their mouths; they have struck me insolently on the cheek; they mass themselves together against me" (16:10). But there are moments when Job appeals to the God who will defend him against the mob, which means against the God of scapegoats.

The scapegoat is not a social and historical reality for Jung and all his ilk—it cannot exist, for if it did, one would have to deal with it as if it mattered and had consequences. Those for whom desire, rivalry, victimization, and sacrifice can exist only as a kind of expression of Platonic forms within the psyche are, in effect, defending the sacred social order against the consequences of its murders and expulsions.

Jung's onetime mentor Freud turned out to be an "Egyptian" who banished the Israelites once more, while Jung turns out to be a "Friend" who comes to dismiss the earlier Friends in bringing his psychoanalytic weapons against Job and the God of victims. He does not want to slay them—just banish them from history into the psyche. The effect is to turn the "answer to Job," the Christ and the Incarnation, into an un-Jewish if not an anti-Jewish event: if the Cross represents the sacrifice of consciousness to unconsciousness and the suffering of the divine unconscious coming into consciousness, then the revelation of the Innocent Victim as a historical Jewish person is irrelevant. It is not surprising that Freud the Jew and Jung the Christian became rivals, but of course, *"plus ça change, plus c'est le même chose"*—the more something changes, the more it's the same thing. The rivals who appear to be poles apart have this most basic effort in common: they both attempted to expel their religious origins—Freud into "Egypt," Jung into the psyche; at the same time, each was acutely aware of the other's religious identity as a barrier.

7

The Gospels and the
Innocent Victim

It was to fulfill the word that is written in their law, "They hated me without cause."
When the Advocate (*Parakletos*) comes, whom I will send to you from the Father,
he will testify on my behalf. You also are to testify because you have been with me
from the beginning.

John 15:25–26

. . . but whoever wishes to become great among you must be your servant, and
whoever wishes to be first among you must be slave of all. For the Son of Man
came not to be served but to serve, and to give his life as a ransom for many.

Mark 10:43–45

And he said to them, "I am deeply grieved, even to death; remain here,
and keep awake."

Mark 14:34

And they began saluting him, "Hail, King of the Jews!" They struck his head with
a reed, spat upon him, and knelt down in homage to him. . . . Then they led
him out to crucify him.

Mark 15:18–19, 20b

The sign of Cain is the sign of civilization. It is the sign of the murderer who is
protected by God. Since Cain does not have a proper mode of sacrifice to protect
him against violence or to protect him from acting violently against the other,
against Abel his brother, God intervenes with a sign. It is with this sign that civilization begins, for under its protection Cain finally settles—in the land of
Wandering!—and builds the first city.

The story of Cain is thus similar to other myths of human beginnings in which
culture and tradition begin with a murder. The difference here is that the murder
is not camouflaged in myth and ritual that retell and reenact the crisis and resolution from the standpoint of the mythic community, which is the persecuting community in relation to the victim. It is as though the Israelite writers were thinking,
in effect, "We know that we, like all people, come from Adam and Eve through
Cain, but we know that Abel was innocent and there was no reason, saving his
envy and anger, for Cain to kill Abel." This Israelite perspective would be like
telling other stories from the standpoint of the victim: from the standpoint of
Oedipus, rather than Thebes, or of Remus, rather than Romulus or Rome. In

Greek tragedy we find plays approaching this point of view, such as the critique of the Dionysus cult in Euripides' *The Bacchae*, where the sympathy one finally feels for Pentheus implies a sympathy for the "original Dionysus." That is, Pentheus becomes a copy of Dionysus and represents at a very primitive level the fate of the one or those whose deaths gave rise to the Dionysus cult.[1] Likewise in Aeschylus's *Prometheus Bound* there is recognition that the victim, Prometheus, who takes the side of humans against the father god Zeus, acts out of tragic necessity. The divine victim is the source of fire from the Father (very much like Dionysus, whose wine is associated with fire);[2] he is also the giver of "blind hopes." The blind hopes are the fulfillment of desire and relief of conflict resulting from the execution of the victim, an act that is camouflaged by being projected as supernatural in origin.

But Greek tragedy does not have the resources, the tradition, the revelation, to attain to the narration of God taking the side of the murdered Abel, of the messengers leading Lot and his daughters out of Sodom, of God (or his angel) allowing Jacob to "defeat" him, of Joseph bringing peace and bounty to Egypt and his brothers without being deified, of God through Moses leading out the oppressed people who were perceived as a threat by the Egyptian authorities, of Saul who is entrapped between prophet and people without dying as a tragic victim. It does not have the basis for the kind of prophet whose calling is an inversion and transformation of the victimization mechanism, so that the structure of the one singled out for scapegoating becomes the structure of the one who is God's exception, proclaiming to the community the meaning of its history and covenant life.

The history of Israel is a history of revelation, of disclosure of the God whose intention is to strip off mythic camouflage, to unmask the persecuting community, and this revelation comes through the community that bears the memory of its own marginal, often victimized situation through the centuries. I have not attempted an argument for the truth of divine revelation. It is quite clear that the present situation in biblical studies, particularly as they take place within the context of the academic study of religion, obviates revelation and detests "theology."[3] It is not clear, however, what such antirevelation and antitheology values serve. Not only do they expel the basis for understanding the other in Western culture, a basis that has been precisely revelatory and theological, but they contribute to the degeneration of the current intellectual situation into a mimetic pluralism in which everyone tries to outdo everyone else in being against victimization and oppression of every sort, against ethnocentrism, and finally, basically, against Christianity. But where has this intellectual legacy brought us in standing against victimization and for understanding the other as neighbor in our day? The dominant intellectual tradition of the last century, from Nietzsche through Heidegger to Sartre and Derrida, has cast out the old sacred at the price of the new sacreds of fascism and communism and atheology and amorality. Cain's sign is a curse turned to blessing for many of these thinkers. One cannot read Heidegger's

Introduction to Metaphysics without concluding that, for Heidegger, the Cains of the world are the *Führer*, the leaders, the poets, the thinkers who must be strong and fulfill the destiny of their being even if it involves violence, for after all the Logos itself is the truth of being whose gathering together of opposites cannot take place without violence (see chapter 3, "An Egyptian Point of View").

Concerning the reality of revelation, the starting point for understanding the claim made here is the reality of mimetic desire and its outworkings. If one accepts that the human condition is founded on desiring the object desired by the model-rival, and if one accepts that this desire is acquisitive, so that conflict and violence are inevitable and must be controlled by human communities through sacrifice and scapegoating and their substitutes, then this sociological-anthropological starting point is the basis for saying what revelation is. Since we are involved in the mimetic predicament of language and culture, and since our attempts at extricating ourselves only reinforce victimization and sacrificial mechanisms, a totally different point of view that undoes the mechanisms must come from outside ourselves—that is, from outside our own resources or projections, whether these be religious, psychic, social, literary, or some other. The revelation of God is the disclosure of (1) the standpoint of the victim, who is always either innocent or arbitrarily chosen, and (2) the divine-human community of nonviolence. The incarnation of God is the disclosure of God in a life (or lives) that both takes the standpoint of the victim and is able to forgive all persecutors.

This revelation did not occur apart from a long history of struggle to realize it and to receive it ever anew. Much of the tradition and its texts continued to be structured by an older theology of the sacred, a theology of the sacred social order in which all parties involved are entrapped in the sin and guilt that arouses the divine anger until the restabilizing differentiation occurs with the punishment of the guilty or the execution of the victim. The Priestly narrative of the Torah conveys a grand and powerful vision of nonviolent community among human beings and between humankind and God. But this vision was purchased with a twofold ransom: (1) warfare with the animals, which are used as substitutes for human sacrifices, and (2) failure to account for the human predicament, as we see, for example, in the substituting of Seth for Cain and Abel.

We see likewise a struggle over mimetic rivalry, violence, and sacrifice in the Exodus story, which issues in the covenant, commandments, and law. The covenant is a model of existence that protects Israel and each member of the community within the bounds of the commands and prohibitions established in the Ten Words. Covenant so understood is a big step forward, but its outworking in law and scripture is still based on an exclusionary principle (the offender must be excluded, punished), which in turn is still tied to a theology of divine anger. The words of the covenant in Exodus 24 are a substitute for the blood of sacrifice, but the latter continues to structure religious thinking. We see this clearly in the revealing glimpses of the origin of the Levites as priests in Exodus 32, Leviticus 10, Numbers 16–17, and related passages. The substitutionary system is installed at the heart of the covenant tradition yet at the same time made known for what it is. The final Priestly vision of nonviolence enfolds it but does not radically question the substitutionary system.

With the great prophets and the Job of the Dialogues in the Book of Job we come to a high point of insight concerning the connection of sacrifice to the violence of the persecuting community. But these fragments of revelation are still shrouded with ambiguity. We now arrive at the culmination of the Israelite-Jewish tradition of revelation in the narrative witness to Jesus in the New Testament Gospels. Even here, departing from Girard, I would say that sacrificial language still has a strong hold—and how would it be possible to gain complete liberation from it, from culture, unless one were truly God? But I do agree with him that a core of revelatory insight spreads to and illuminates all the Gospels with a sustained disclosure of the innocent victim and of divine-human community that is not continually on the edge of conflict and violence because of internal mediation (see definition in chapter 1, "Girard's Explanatory Model").

In this chapter I will present a survey of the canonical Gospels, highlighting those aspects of each that are particularly important for the further treatment of the Gospel revelation of the sacrificial core of the sacred, with its ever present structures that both manage and engender violence. The next chapter will then be devoted to a sharpening of the argument with a focus on the mimetic condition of human beings and the "remedy" that is not also a "poison," the Passion of the Christ, which is the truth of the innocent victim.

A. The Gospel of Mark

The Gospel of Mark is commonly accepted in biblical criticism as the first of the Gospels chronologically and as one of the sources for Matthew and Luke, who follow its narrative outline for the most part. I have nothing in particular at stake in arguing for the chronological priority of Mark, but I see no reason at present to object to this scholarly consensus. It is, moreover, very interesting to read Matthew and Luke as readings of Mark.

Jesus is identified as God's son when he is baptized by John the Baptist. A divine voice speaks, evidently to him only, "You are my Son, the Beloved; with you I am well pleased" (Mark 1:11). The secrecy of Jesus' identity as the Son of God is one of the themes of the Gospel of Mark. He tries to conceal his identity and the secret of the kingdom of God from "outsiders," from those who are not disciples (4:11), until he acknowledges it openly before the high priest after his arrest (14:61–62). Even in the latter passage he immediately begins to speak of the Son of Man. The meaning of Son of God, or "Christ," has something to do with the title "Son of Man." Christ, from the Greek *christos*, which translates the Hebrew *mashiach*, "Messiah," occurs only six times in Mark (8:29; 12:35; 14:61; 15:32; 1:1; 9:41). "Lord" and "teacher" are more common titles.

A key to understanding the identity of Jesus in Mark is found in 8:27–33. Jesus and the disciples are in Gentile territory in the region of Caesarea Philippi. When he asks them who people say he is, they mention John the Baptist and Elijah. Peter finally calls him the Christ. Jesus accepts this response as correct as far as it goes, but he then begins to teach them that the Son of Man will have to suffer greatly "and be rejected by the elders, the chief priests, and the scribes, and be killed, and after three days rise again" (8:31). Mark notes Jesus said this *plainly*, as though he had never made it any clearer. But Peter, upset at the talk of suffering and death, rebukes him. Jesus in turn rebukes Peter and says, "Get behind me, Satan [i.e., unfriendly or persecuting adversary]![4] For you are setting your mind not on divine things but on human things" (8:33). What the secret involves is evidently not simply that Jesus is the Christ or the Messiah (which in the Jewish tradition would normally mean the new king sent by God to restore Israel's national sovereignty and rule in a new era). Peter's distress at the mention of Jesus' suffering and death indicates he has precisely this usual royal meaning of Messiah in mind. But Jesus discloses to the disciples that the Messiah is really the Son of Man who suffers, dies, and rises again.

"Son of Man" is a title commonly thought to have its provenance in the Jewish apocalyptic tradition. However, to my mind the argument of Mahlon Smith is convincing.[5] He holds that the Son of Man sayings are all generated by the saying in Q (German *Quelle*, "source," the hypothetical source of sayings used by Luke and Matthew): "Foxes have holes, and birds of the air have nests; but the Son of Man has nowhere to lay his head" (Luke 9:58). Smith argues that the saying is an ironic use of the Targum to Psalm 8:4.[6] Whereas the Hebrew text has "man" and "son of man" in the parallel lines, the Aramaic of the Targum has "son of man," *bar nasha*, in both lines. Since man, humankind, is the ruler of the earth according to Psalm 8 (and Gen 1), the saying, Smith argues, goes back to Jesus' ironic comment on the itinerant ministry in which he and his followers are engaged, and at the same time it makes aphoristic allusion to the true human situation. According to Psalm 8, human beings rule over all the animals, but even the animals have their "homes"; in Jesus' aphorism "man" or human beings may be "homeless" in the world. The saying was thus memorable enough to be preserved by the disciples, and in the process of transmission "son of man" picked up other, sometimes apocalyptic connotations.[7]

The origin of the title thus has nothing to do with the apocalyptic figure who is "like a son of man" in Daniel 7:13–14, nor does it come from the Son of Man in 1 Enoch or the heavenly Man in 4 Ezra (2 Esdras). Of course, by the time Mark makes use of the term it has become a title for Jesus, and it is associated with the apocalypse. It is, however, interesting to look at the actual occurrences in Mark and note that the apocalyptic context is apparent in only *three* out of fourteen instances in the Gospel text (8:38; 13:26; 14:62). The other eleven are as follows:

2:10: Son of Man has authority to heal.

2:28: Son of Man lord of the Sabbath. Here there is an obvious connection between the "man" or "humankind" of 2:27 (*anthropos*) and the Son of Man of 2:28.

8:31: Son of Man's suffering, death, resurrection.

9:9: Son of Man's resurrection.

9:12: Son of Man's sufferings.

9:31: Son of Man's suffering and resurrection.

10:33–34: Son of Man's suffering and resurrection.

10:45: Son of Man's mission "not to be served but to serve, and to give his life a ransom for many."

14:21a: Son of Man is betrayed and dies according to Scripture.

14:21b: "Woe to that one by whom the Son of Man is betrayed."

It seems then that even though Mark has lost the irony of the original son of man saying as applied to all human beings as well as to Jesus, he has still preserved the nonapocalyptic sense of "human one." The key text in this regard is Mark 2:27–28, which shows the synonymous parallelism of *anthropos*, in the sense of all human beings, and *ho huios tou anthropou*, "the son of man." The "humankind" for which the Sabbath was made (2:27) is represented by the "Son of Man" who rules the Sabbath (2:28). Jesus as the Human One, as the one embodying the vocation of humankind to rule the earth as in Psalm 8 and Genesis 1, has authority on earth to forgive sins (2:10). He will be betrayed, suffer, die, and rise again. He is really the ruler in the stead of all humans, and this theme makes a connection with the Son of Man's future rule after the apocalypse; but the paradox of his rule is both his submission to live as a servant, a model for his disciples (10:43–45), and his suffering and death.

So the Gospel of Mark does not eliminate all the apocalyptic associations of the activity of the Son of Man, but the interpretive center shifts; the Son of Man is a ruler of a different sort, a ruler who *suffers* for others, who "came not to be served but to serve, and to give his life a ransom for many" (Mark 10:45). In order to comprehend Jesus' ministry, death, and resurrection, the author of Mark probably used the model of the suffering Servant of the Lord in Second Isaiah (see chapter 5, "The Prophets Against Violence and Sacrifice"). The author of Mark was quite familiar with that part of the Isaiah scroll we call the Second Isaiah (Isa 40–55).[8]

There are two specific references to the Servant in Mark: 9:12 and 10:45 (quoted just above). In another episode, when Jesus is brought before the high priest, his silence, 14:61, is probably intended as a realization of the silence of the Servant before his tormenters (Isa 53:7). The reference to the Servant poem is quite clear in 9:12: "He said to them, 'Elijah is indeed coming first to restore all things. How then is it written about the Son of Man, that he is to go through many sufferings and be treated with contempt?'" What is "written" about a saving figure who suffers could only refer to Isaiah 52:13–53:12, and specifically to Isaiah 53:3b: "being a man in suffering and acquainted with the bearing of sickness, for his face is turned away; he was dishonored, and not esteemed" (Septuagint).[9]

Mark 10:45 concludes the pronouncement of Jesus on the request of James and John to be his chief lieutenants when he gains full power, which had unleashed mimetic conflict among the disciples. The saying does not refer explicitly to Scripture. However, given the clear reference to the Servant in 9:12 and Mark's obvious familiarity with the Second Isaiah portion of the Book of Isaiah, there is little doubt that the Son of Man is understood as the Servant of the Lord. Giving his life "on behalf of many" probably reflects the wording of Isaiah 53:11–12, where "many" occurs three times in the Septuagint: the Servant serves many well, will inherit many (?), and bore the sins of many.[10]

In other words, the meaning of Jesus as the Christ in Mark 8:27–33 involves a shift in the meaning of three figures representing three distinguishable strands of the Jewish tradition: Messiah, the Davidic or David-like king, is qualified by Son of Man and the implicit allusion to the Servant of Second Isaiah; the Son of Man as embodying human rule now and in the age to come is centered in, and changed into, Jesus as Messiah and Servant; and the Servant, who is a suffering prophet (or prophet-people), becomes ruler. It is not as though one of these titles is the constant around which the other two revolve. Each one affects the others and effects a shift in meaning. Although the Servant prophecy of Second Isaiah does not provide one of the titles of Jesus, it is all the more important as *the heart of the secret meaning of his vocation.*

But why is the identity of the Son of Man a secret? Clearly the way Mark portrays the secret is influenced by the Servant in Isaiah, but even so one wonders why the latter is not recognized as God's servant who bears the sin of many? The answer (which will be further developed in chapter 8) has to do with the character of people who not only form a "public" but who in many instances become a "crowd" and occasionally a "mob." As the Gospel of Mark indicates, people have mixed or shallow motives for seeking out Jesus, are easily astonished, and make it difficult for Jesus by pressing in upon him. The crowd is the locus of unfaith, is uncomprehending, and in concert with the rulers finally executes Jesus (15:6–15, 29–30). Therefore I think that Robert Hamerton-Kelly is right that the role of the "messianic secret" in the narrative is to show how Jesus tried to separate himself from the mimetic instability of the crowd.[11] Hamerton-Kelly's point may be extended to the whole problem of mimetic rivalry: the differentiations that are expected and supported by the *vox populi* require rivalry, demonstration of mastery of the world, of things divine, of competing authorities.[12]

Even though the disciples, especially the Twelve, are to be separated from the crowd, they share largely in its presuppositions, its obtuseness, and yes, even its propensity to find scapegoats. After teaching from a boat, Jesus asks the intimate disciples to go with him to the other side of the lake. "And leaving the crowd behind, they took him with them in the boat, just as he was. Other boats were with him" (4:36). This reads like a number of disciples, "those who were around him along with the twelve" (4:10), who crossed over in a number of boats. Elizabeth Malbon has shown the importance of spatial metaphors in Mark.[13] The Sea of Galilee is the space of separation of homeland from foreign land, of Jesus and the disciples from the crowd, and thus of faith from unfaith. There is a symmetry of the sea and boat passages in chapters 4–8 with the journey to Jerusalem, passion, and resurrection in chapters 9–16. As I said in an earlier study of Mark, "As Jesus crosses the deep and troubled water to non-Jewish territory and returns then to Galilee, so also he endures suffering and death on the cross to rise and return to Galilee. The boat in which he travels is the vessel of faith that transports the fellowship of the faithful."[14]

But the disciples are not up to the challenge. They become frightened on the stormy sea, and when Jesus rebukes the wind and brings peace, they are filled with awe (4:37–41). But the awe is much like the astonishment of the crowd when a miracle is performed.

Like the people or crowds, they want something concrete and substantial. James and John want a large piece of the Lord's prestige and power, which probably implies also possessions, when he comes into his full reign (10:35–45). One of them, Judas, betrays him for money (14:10–11), and another, Peter, not only deserts him along with the others but denies him three times lest, like his master, he become a scapegoat of the crowd (14:66–72). Peter's denials take place in the context of three potentially threatening situations: a servant girl identifies him as a companion of Jesus, an implicit accusation; the same girl makes the same statement to bystanders; finally the bystanders themselves say, "Certainly you are one of them." On the one hand, Peter's ordeal is a miniature version of what Jesus undergoes; on the other, he is shown to be unable to resist the crowd and stand with Jesus, who meanwhile has stayed faithfully with the disciples to the end.

For understanding Mark, the Temple passages are crucial. Jesus drives traders in animals and money from the Temple (11:15–19), and the sayings concerning the fig tree in 11:12–14 and 11:20–25 frame this episode, evidently in order to connect the withered tree to the passing of the Temple as the center of God's presence. Jesus also teaches in the Temple (12:41–44) and predicts its destruction

(13:1–2). In the hearing before the high priest and the council, this latter saying is changed into the false accusation that he claimed he would destroy the Temple himself, "and in three days I will build another not made with hands" (14:58).

The Temple was the center of the sacred in Judaism, and inasmuch as it was the place of sacrifice, it was the center of sacred violence (see chapter 4, "The Struggle over Sacrifice"). Of course, the Pharisaic movement, which began about two centuries before, represented a partial shift away from the Temple, for it focused on study of the Torah led by the sage in the synagogue. But the Jesus movement, certainly as attested by the Gospel of Mark, was revolutionary, calling the Temple radically into question in the light of a new vision of God as love and Jesus as the Servant-Son. In this regard the expulsion of the Temple traders is a crucial episode. As Hamerton-Kelly has pointed out, this attack, probably a historical event, was not simply the cleansing of an institution that was to be affirmed in its pristine or ideal form; it represented rather *an attack on the entire sacrificial system.*[15] For after all, the Temple was an institution sheltering and supporting a system of substitutions whose end was the offering of animal victims to God in the place of the human offerer. Any worshiper, foreign, Judean, or Galilean, who did not have money that had been minted in accordance with Jewish Law and religious sensibilities had to change coins, as did those who had to exchange small coins for the required half-shekel tax.[16] Profane money was exchanged for sacred (or at least acceptable) currency, this currency was used to purchase sacrificial victims, and they were offered to God in the stead of the offerers. The priests also were surrogates of the offerers and as such were in turn redeemed to serve as sacrificers for the sacrifiers.[17] The Temple, for the Jewish people, was the great sacred center of substitutions, of exchanges, the center of sacred consumption. In this respect it probably retained strong traces of the function of older temple centers in various parts of the world, centers that were typically the center of economic life. As such the temple complexes represented the still older, primitive stage of sharing the victim, the "designated object," among the participants.[18]

The destruction of the Temple as the passing of the old order of sacred violence sets off the betrayal of Jesus by Judas. He is the betrayer, the one who delivers over (*paradidous*, 14:44) the victim to the chief priests (14:10). The priests promise Judas money for the betrayal (14:11), so there is an analogy between the money changers and merchants of pigeons, who were allowed a profit margin in their transactions, and Judas, who "hands over" the Son of Man to the priests. The one who attacked the Temple is now himself delivered to the chief representatives of the sacrificial process.

Though from the standpoint of the religious authorities he was arrested, "delivered over" for trial and execution, from the standpoint of the Gospel narrative he was already "giving himself over," so to say. Before he was seized by the crowd sent by the authorities, he had already announced, at the last meal with his disciples, not only that one of them would betray him, but that he was giving himself. As he had fed the crowds in the wilderness, now he blessed and broke the bread and gave it to them, and he said, "Take, this is my body" (14:22). He gave them also the cup of wine, saying, "This is my blood of the covenant, which is poured out for many" (14:24). Again, this is by contrast with the institution of sacrifice in which individuals and communities offer victims in their stead to the god or gods of the sacred social order. Now the "Son," the one who is "God," so to speak, standing in God's stead, offers himself as victim to the worshipers. Even before the crowd seizes him, he gives his body and blood. In human culture, originating in victimization and maintained through sacrifice, this is the fate of the one "who serves many to their good" (Isa 53:11, Septuagint).

The chief irony of the Gospel of Mark occurs when Jesus is interrogated by the high priest, the representative of the sacrificial system: "But he was silent and did not answer. Again the high priest asked him, 'Are you the Messiah, the Son of the Blessed One?' Jesus said, 'I am; and you will see the Son of Man seated at the right hand of the Power, and coming with the clouds of heaven'" (14:61–62).

To conclude, I quote a paragraph from my book *Gospel Against Parable:*

> The disclosure of the Son's identity and advent, made before the high priest and "the chief priests and the elders and the scribes" (14:53) signals the end of the sacrificial and legal system of Judaism (and by implication of "Christianity" [insofar as it is a sacrificial religion] from Mark's point of view). The decisive moment from present adumbration to future realization is about to occur: the death of the suffering Son of man. The tearing of the curtain of the holy of holies and the centurion's sudden insight [15:39] indicate that the hinge-event has reached its climax. The next stage, the resurrection, is not narrated but announced by the youth in white. Suspended between narration and the story of the future, the rising of Jesus is the preface to the disciples' coming to see ("there you will see him" [in Galilee]) and the Presence to come.[19]

B. The Gospel of Matthew

The Gospel of Matthew uses Mark's basic narrative, but introduces a great deal of material that reflects the author's interpretive standpoint. In some instances, when a given passage is taken from Mark, the variations are minor, but in others the differences are highly significant. And of course Matthew includes narratives and sayings that are peculiar to the Gospel of Matthew.

Matthew begins by linking Jesus directly to the Jewish messianic tradition, by means both of genealogy (Matt 1:1–17) and Mary's conception of him by the Holy Spirit (1:18–25). With the tale of the virgin conception the Evangelist begins a constant repetition of showing that the life, death, resurrection, and teachings of

Jesus represent the fulfillment of prophecy. The typological structure of prophecy and fulfillment is not only indicated explicitly in the quotation of Scripture, particularly from the prophets, it is also suggested in the way the Gospel is arranged, particularly numerical patterns in it. For example, three sets of fourteen generations leading up to the birth of Jesus. There are actually only thirteen names in the last set. Whether this is intended to mean that the messianic age is the completion of the set or is simply an error is difficult to determine. My conjecture is that three sets of fourteen were intended, with Jesus Messiah as the climax, after the pattern of the Torah, which in its final form spans four sets of generations: Adam to Noah, Noah to Abraham, Abraham to Moses, and Moses and Covenant to the present. The pattern in Matthew suggests a perfect number of some sort, perhaps three times fourteen equals six times seven. In that case, the Messiah would be the seventh, the capstone, a sort of Sabbath figure surpassing Adam, created on the sixth day according to Genesis 1. This reading, or one like it, is bolstered by the well-known observation that the consonants of David in Hebrew, when added together (four plus six plus four), equal fourteen. The genealogy would thus be a way of repeating the name of David, the founder of the dynasty whose downfall gave rise to the hope for the restoration of the LORD's king or anointed one (*mashiach*, messiah) ruling over Israel in a new era.

Another sign of this numerically coded message in Matthew is the arrangement of the teachings for followers in five discourses: chapters 5–7, the Sermon on the Mount; chapter 10, the preaching mission of the disciples; chapter 13, the parables discourse; chapter 18, relations in the church; chapters 24–25, discourse about destruction of the Temple and final things. The number five is probably not an accident. There is no way finally to prove that Matthew is adopting the pattern of the Torah, as if the Gospel itself is another kind of Torah, but given the author's point of view on the relation of the Hebrew Scriptures to the Gospel, it is likely.

One of the key passages for understanding the perspective of Matthew's Gospel concerning the previous Jewish tradition, Jesus, and the church is found in the Sermon on the Mount, 5:17–20. It is distinctively Matthean; only one verse, 5:18, is found elsewhere in the tradition of Jesus' sayings.[20]

> Do not think that I have to abolish the law or the prophets; I have come not to abolish but to fulfill. For truly I tell you, until heaven and earth pass away, not one letter, not one stroke of a letter, will pass from the law until all is accomplished. Therefore, whoever breaks one of the least of these commandments, and teaches others to do the same, will be called least in the kingdom of heaven; but whoever does them and teaches them will be called great in the kingdom of heaven. For I tell you, unless your righteousness exceeds that of the scribes and Pharisees, you will never enter the kingdom of heaven. (5:17–20)

Here we see the theme of a dialectic of continuity and discontinuity with the Jewish tradition. The law and the prophets are not to be destroyed, but fulfilled; what the scribes and Pharisees do, the disciples are to do and to be even more radically. It becomes quite clear from the teachings that follow in 5:21–48 that the disciples' very intentions as well as their deeds are to be judged against the model of their loving heavenly Father. We find also in this passage the strong stamp of Jesus' authority as teacher and fulfiller of the end time. This authority is radically articulated in 5:21–48, a series of six antitheses, which generally take the form, "You have heard that it was said (in Scripture) . . . But I say to you . . . "

There are many passages in Matthew that are informed by apocalyptic thinking and language. That is, they speak of a "revealing" or "unveiling" (Greek *apocalypsis*) in which the present age is ended and God's reign is consummated after destruction of the present order and divine judgment. For passages with apocalyptic elements, see 7:21–23; 10:26–33; 13:36–43; and much of chapters 24–25.

There are other places where Jesus seems to be the embodiment of divine Wisdom. In one of the most important of these, a statement found only in Matthew, Jesus says, "Come to me, all who labor and are carrying heavy burdens, and I will give you rest. Take my yoke upon you, and learn from me; for I am gentle and humble in heart, and you will find rest for your souls. For my yoke is easy, and my burden is light" (11:28–30). This invitation is remarkably similar to a passage in Sirach 51:23–27, where the teacher of wisdom extends an invitation to "put your neck under the yoke, and let your souls receive instruction." However, here in Matthew, the Teacher himself seems to be identified with the voice of Wisdom. Confirmation may be found in Matthew 23:34–35 and its parallel, Luke 11:49, parallels derived from Q. Luke has the Wisdom of God saying, "I will send them prophets and apostles," and so on. Matthew changes this to Jesus as the subject: he himself is the one who sends prophets; he himself is the Wisdom of God (see also Matt. 11:19). Matthew identifies Jesus, the very voice of divine Wisdom, as the one who proclaims in parables "what has been hidden from the foundation of the world" (13:35; see Ps 78:2–3).

Matthew brings Jesus as Wisdom and Jesus as Apocalyptic Judge together in a startlingly radical way. Wisdom and Apocalyptic are played off each other and centered in the revelation of the innocent victim. Matthew builds on Mark's presentation of the suffering and death of the Son of Man, which he takes over practically without change (although changes in the larger context shift the meaning in some cases): see 16:21; 17:9, 12, 22; 20:18–19, 28; 26:24, all of which parallel the Mark passages (see above, "The Gospel of Mark"). Wisdom, then, is the Son of Man: both are vindicated by their deeds (11:19), invite the wearied and heavy-laden to them, seek to gather their children under their wings (23:37–39), send prophets— but their blood is shed. Those who persecute and kill the prophets sent by Wisdom bring catastrophe upon themselves: "that upon you may come all the righteous blood shed upon the earth, from the blood of righteous Abel to the blood of Zechariah son of Barachiah, whom you murdered between the sanctuary and the altar" (23:35). And of course, the same thing will happen to the Son of Man.

In other words, for Matthew, Wisdom is the Son of Man who is murdered, and the Son of Man is the Wisdom who would gather Jerusalem under her wings. The "things hidden from the foundation of the world" that Wisdom proclaims include above all the murder of the innocent victims. It is those (perhaps Christians) who suffer and exist in dire need in whom the righteous encounter the Son of Man (25:31–46). It is no accident that the kingdom the righteous inherit has been prepared for them "from the foundation of the world" (25:34). The hidden innocent ones who represent the Son of Man have been hidden, camouflaged, since the beginning of humankind as such. The Son of Man as Wisdom comes to reveal that and to restore humankind to the state God intended in creation, a condition of life in community without victimization.

As for Apocalyptic, its core meaning for Matthew is indicated in the parable of final judgment, already cited, 25:31–46. There Jesus uses traditional apocalyptic language in order to talk about encountering the Son of Man, which means to meet God in the world here and now. The righteous, those who "inherit the kingdom prepared for [them] from the foundation of the world" (25:34), are those who fed the Son of Man, gave him to drink, welcomed him when he was a stranger, gave him clothing when he was naked, cared for him when he was sick, visited him in prison. How, they ask, did we do these things for you? The answer: "just as you did it to one of the least of these who are members of my family [Greek 'these my brothers'], you did it to me" (25:40). Those who did not help the needy are rejected, for they did not do these things for the least of these.

Matthew thus employs apocalyptic imagery in order to present the Son of Man as the point of differentiation here and now. We should pause, though, to take note of the debate whether these "least," these poor ones, are also members of the Jesus community or are outside it.[21] It is possible that "brothers" is intended in the exclusively sectarian sense of poor, weak, struggling Christians, perhaps missionaries who have fallen on hard times. Much has been made of other occurrences of "little ones" and "least" in Matthew. These terms occur in Matthew 5:19; 10:42; 11:11; 18:6, 10, 14. "Least," *elachistos*, in 5:19 carries a very negative sense: those who teach others to relax the commandments. "Little ones," from *mikros*, refers to children in chapter 18, and the "smallest ones" of 11:11 (from the superlative case of *mikros*) is in a context derived from Q that may not be pertinent to our parable. Only 10:42 is really relevant to the parable; there "little ones" are identified as disciples.

More relevant is Matthew's use of "brother," *adelphos*, in the sense of some relationship other than blood kinship. The instances of this usage are found in

5:47; 12:49; 18:15; 23:8; 28:10. In every case the word signifies a disciple or member of the Jesus community. So if one bases the interpretation solely on the actual usage of "brother" in Matthew, the "least of the brothers" must refer to disciples or members of the Jesus community. It may be that the final form of the parable in Matthew intends this sense.

However, the passage in question is a parable, and there is no evidence in the parables preceding it in chapters 24 and 25 that a decidedly intra-Christian sense is intended. That is, there is no evidence of the hardened doctrine that only those who bear the name of Jesus are exclusively those who do the will of God. Indeed, the occurrences of the "will" of God the Father in Matthew belie such a conclusion:

6:10: "Thy will be done" in the Our Father or Lord's Prayer.

7:21: Those entering the kingdom of heaven are those who do the Father's will.

12:50: Jesus' true "relatives" are those who do the will of his Father.

18:14: The will of the Father is that no children be lost.

21:31: In the parable of two sons, the one who refused to obey but changes his mind does his father's will.

26:42: "Your will be done," in Jesus' second prayer in Gethsemane.

An exclusively Christian doctrinal or sectarian sense does not attach to any of these occurrences. In fact, that meaning seems to be called into question by the pronouncement in 7:21–23, that those who do the will of the Father are not necessarily the ones who call on the name of the Lord (Jesus), who perform exorcisms, who work miracles in his name. One other thing to bear in mind is the teaching in 5:43–48: ideally members of the Jesus community are to recognize their community with others whatever their identity. This community, the sharing of a common being, comes from "God," the "Father," not from Jesus. The standard of reference is the character of God and the care of God for his creatures.

We may infer, therefore, that those who do the will of the Father are not necessarily "Christians" in some sectarian sense. Of course, even if the "least of the brothers" carries the sense of "Christian" in the parable, that still does not mean that the sheep, those who help them, are so named. There are those who have faith who are not Israelites and who do not join those gathered around Jesus (8:5–10); encounter with the Son of Man is possible in the world, apart from names, doctrines, and party lines.

This judgment "parable" or "allegory," set in Matthew immediately before the Passion narrative, is a kind of introduction to the meaning of the Christ's suffering, death, and resurrection. God is always and everywhere calling his children to do his will by standing on the side of the marginal, the needy, the oppressed, the incarcerated. He is calling them to believe in "mercy, and not sacrifice" (9:13 and 12:7), thus not to stand with the sacrificers and scapegoaters.

The reality of this God, the love of this God, is now about to be revealed in the Passion of Jesus, the Son. The wrathful judgment of apocalypse, its rage to differentiate the righteous and the wicked, is a carryover from a tradition of apocalyptic language that was already two centuries old when Matthew was written. What is truly "apocalyptic," what is revealed as past, present, and future, is the new being, the Suffering Servant (8:17; 12:15–21), who is present and resurrected in the kingdom of sharing and healing.

C. The Gospel of Luke

The Gospel of Luke is above all the Gospel of tradition. It is the gospel of the way of Jesus to Jerusalem, and from there the way of the apostles from Jerusalem to the world. It is the gospel centered in the conversation of the disciples with one who meets them on the way and opens up to them the meaning of the Scriptures (Luke 24:13–27). The Gospel of Luke, the first part of a two-part work, Luke and the Acts of the Apostles, is the first Christian interpretation of history that takes the future as history fully into account. Matthew's principle of prophecy and fulfillment, which necessarily includes the concept of the age of Scripture, of the Law and the Prophets, is broadened to a universal history that comprises three eras:

1. The Law and the Prophets extends back to the beginnings of humankind with Adam. Luke's genealogy of Jesus, quite different from Matthew's, traces his lineage back from Joseph through the sons to "Seth, the son of Adam, the son of God" (3:38). As in the final Priestly form of the Torah, whose point of view has influenced his own theology of history, Luke passes over Cain and Abel in seeing a unbroken chain of sonship continuing the image of God to Jesus.

Jesus' predecessor is John the Baptist, who represents the former era of the Law and the Prophets (16:16). Luke has John already in prison when Jesus is baptized (3:18–22), evidently wishing to indicate that John, important as he is, belongs to a prior age, the age of preparation for the Son of God and the Church.

2. The time of Jesus is the era of full revelation of the pattern or model of the kingdom of God, the divine-human community. It is not that the content of the disclosure through Jesus is essentially different from that through the Law and the Prophets. For example, part of the teaching ascribed to John, concerning bearing fruits of repentance and sharing one's garments and food (3:8, 10) is remarkably similar to what Jesus teaches (6:30, 43–44). The parable of the rich man and Lazarus concludes, "If they [the rich man's surviving brothers] do not listen to Moses and the prophets, neither will they be convinced even if someone rises from the dead" (16:31). In other words, what is required for eternal life is already

to be found in the Scriptures of the Jews, which is precisely what Jesus says to the lawyer before telling the parable of the Samaritan. The lawyer had asked what he must do to inherit eternal life. Jesus replies, "What is written in the law?" The lawyer, giving an answer based on Deuteronomy 6:5 and Leviticus 19:18, replies, "You shall love the Lord your God with all your heart, and with all your soul, and with all your strength, and with all your mind; and your neighbor as yourself" (10:27). And Jesus responds, "You have given the right answer; do this, and you will live" (10:28). The lawyer's further question (10:29) indicates he still did not understand what Jesus was teaching, but the point is that the way to eternal life is already in the Law.

What difference, then, does Jesus make? What do the titles Son of God, Son of Man, Christ, and Lord mean for Luke? For Luke, the difference Jesus makes is as the embodiment of the revelatory patterns given by God from the beginning of creation; he lives them, he actualizes them, in a way no other human has. In this respect he is the person, the "divine man," that Adam was intended to be. Luke's depiction of Jesus is thus the beginning of the Christian tradition of *imitatio Christi*, the imitation of Christ. In the narration of the three temptations in the wilderness, the temptation to cast himself from the pinnacle of the Temple occurs last; in Matthew, it is the second temptation (see Luke 4:1–13/Matt 4:1–11; cf. Mark 1:12–13). The answer of Jesus, "You shall not tempt [i.e., test] the Lord your God," derived from Deuteronomy 6:16, serves to show his self-mastery in the inspiration of the Holy Spirit. That is, as the true Son of Adam–Son of God he is not subject to anger or depression and is not motivated to make God prove his care for him.

He begins his ministry in Nazareth by going to the synagogue "as was his custom" (4:16). Participation in the institutions and rituals that transmit the salvation history and are validated by it is an aspect of the "modeling" that Jesus does. After reading Isaiah 61:1–2 concerning the one anointed to bring good news to the poor, he announces to the congregation, "Today this scripture has been fulfilled in your hearing" (4:21). In other words: not in the future, not at some end of time appointed by God, but here and now the meaning of this text is coming to pass in my ministry. What you see is, so to say, the model of God at work in the world.

The people in attendance like what he has to say to that point. But then he begins to talk about how a prophet is not accepted in his own hometown, about how aliens, foreigners like the Sidonian widow who helped Elijah and Naaman the Syrian who was healed by Elisha, are the ones who understand and respond authentically to the prophet. The people present then become an enraged mob, driving him out of town and attempting to hurl him off a cliff. That is, they attempt to engage in the classic ritual of the *pharmakos*, the scapegoat. The whole passage, Luke 4:16–30, is a micro-pattern of Jesus' identity and ministry. He as revelatory model finds and proclaims the truth of God from the Hebrew prophets and informs his audience, in effect, that their own assumptions prevent them from receiving the prophet. They then prove his words by driving him away and seeking to lynch him, a victimization process that is at the very core of the structures blinding them.

In keeping with attendance at the synagogue, Jesus is a model of *prayer* for his followers. There are seven occasions on which Jesus is presented as praying. This is, I believe, a significant number, suggesting a model that is perfect.[22] These instances and their contexts in Luke are baptism (3:21), retreat after healing the crowds of diseases (5:16), choosing the disciples (6:12), the question of Jesus' identity (9:18), the transfiguration (9:28–29), before giving his disciples the Our Father prayer (11:1), on the Mount of Olives prior to his arrest (22:39–46). In other words, Jesus is shown to be praying in connection with decisive moments in his ministry. His act of praying is both a model to disciples and a signal that the associated event is occurring by God's intention. Jesus' baptism and anointing with the spirit is a response to prayer. The healing of diseases cannot be authentically done except through withdrawing from the crowds and praying. His identity as the Christ of God has to be understood in relation to his character, his "ethos" as a pray-er. The transfiguration occurs in and through prayer. The Lord's Prayer is a *divine pattern of prayer:* in Luke, by contrast to Matthew, the prayer is not the kind of model whose petitions give one the *pattern* of proper petitioning but one to be repeated in precisely this form. This is because it is taught by the Divine Pray-er. His praying on the Mount of Olives is both an agonizing struggle with temptation (the devil had previously departed from him "until an opportune time," 4:13) and an anticipation of the crucifixion. "In his anguish he prayed more earnestly, and his sweat became like great drops of blood falling down on the ground" (22:44)[23]

These examples of Jesus as the human embodiment of the divine model to be imitated could be multiplied. One of the most interesting instances is the way that Jesus is represented as a source of peace, so that conflict is avoided or remedied in situations of conflict based on Mark's narrative or taken from some other source . The crowd about to crush him in Mark 3:9 simply comes to him and seeks to touch him in Luke 6:17–19 (see also Matt 12:15–21). Jesus does not need to establish a distance from the crowd, as in Mark. Because of the crush of the crowd he gets into a boat to teach (Mark 4:1/Matt 14:1–2), but this is not necessary in Luke 8:1, where both sea and boat are dropped from the narrative. The controversy with the Pharisees over eating with defiled hands (Mark 7:1–13/Matt 15:1–9) does not even appear in Luke. Matthew uses a Q passage, the healing of the centurion's servant, to denounce the Pharisees (8:5–13), but the parallel in Luke 7:1–10 makes no reference to the Pharisees. Jesus acknowledges that the Pharisees, in fact, already have the key to life in the Scriptures (10:25–28), as already indicated.

Likewise, Jesus says nothing derogatory about the Twelve and the other disciples. Conflict in which the distance between the actual obtuseness and blindness of the disciples and their ideal comprehension is accentuated in Mark is modified if not minimized in Luke (e.g., Mark 9:33–37 and 10:35–45/Luke 9:46–50 and 22:24–27). The argument between Jesus and Peter is omitted altogether (Mark 8:27–33/Luke 9:18–22; note also the parallel Matt 16:13–23, where Jesus assigns to Peter the "keys of the kingdom of heaven").

Even when crucified, Jesus enacts the pattern of divine revelation. He forgives his crucifiers (23:34) and promises one of the criminals hanged with him that he will join him this day in Paradise (23:43). For Luke, Jesus as Son of God is thus the Perfect Human or the Divine Human, both continuing and making immediate the image of God in Adam. Luke does not understand the death of Jesus as a sacrifice God ordains in order to prevent the just punishment of humans but as what happens, what necessarily happens, to the Son in enacting the divine model of existence. Of course, neither do Matthew and Mark present a sacrificial doctrine of the atonement such as emerged in Christianity, which definitely became a sacrificial religion in its dominant institutional forms. But Luke tries to avoid all connotations of such an understanding, as, for example, in the episode of the dispute among the disciples, where Mark (followed by Matthew) has Jesus say the Son of Man gives his life as a *ransom* for many (see Luke 22:24–27/Mark 20:35–45/Matt 20:20–28). The word "ransom" (Greek *lutron*, a "freeing"), the "price of release" of the hostage, is deeply rooted in the substitutionary language of sacrifice. Mark probably intends to say, in effect, "The human condition is such that only the price of the Son of Man's suffering and death will have the effect of loosening the bonds of the sacred social structure, enabling humans to see what the human predicament is and the kind of faith and action that will bring liberation." In this sense, the Son of Man as "a ransom for many" is the Son of Man as a revelatory way, a means of access to community and nonviolence. Luke wants to make doubly sure that this nonsacrificial sense is understood. He thus avoids not only the "ransom" of Mark 10:45 but the language of the Master's blood "poured out for many" (Mark 14:24/Matt 26:28). The words of the last meal, "This cup which is poured out for you is the new covenant in my blood" (Luke 22:20), imply that the drinking of the cup together seals the community of Teacher and disciples. The cup is indeed a sign of the Lord's death, as is the bread a sign of the body broken for the disciples, but these are to be remembered and reenacted in the Eucharist as the reality of his bond with them, not as a death of sacrificial atonement. The resurrection, in turn, is the seal on this bond.

The time of Jesus concludes with the resurrection appearances in Jerusalem and vicinity, and these resurrection appearances form an interim between the time of Jesus and the era of the Church, which is the age of the mission to the Gentiles. These three appearances, reported in chapter 24 (including the report of an appearance to Simon, 24:34), include the final instructions of Jesus to his followers. It is then that he opens up the Scriptures to them (24:32, 45). The disciples recognize him in the sharing of bread, as in the last supper with them (24:31).

Chapter 24 of Luke is remarkable in that the resurrection appearances of Jesus are narrated as the core reality of the *tradition*, the way, that reaches back through the Scriptures and forward into the future when the disciples will be clothed with "power from on high" (24:49). "Were not our hearts burning within us while he was talking to us on the road [Greek *hodos*, 'way,' 'path,' 'road'], while he was opening the scriptures to us?" (24:32).

3. The era of the Church, with its mission to the Gentiles, begins properly with Pentecost, Acts 2; it could thus be named also the age of the Spirit. The disciples are told to stay in Jerusalem until the Spirit comes upon them (24:49), a promise reiterated in Jesus' final appearance before his ascension (Acts 1:5, 6–8). The time of the Church is the time of mission to the Gentiles (see Luke 21:24), which is prefigured at the beginning of Jesus' ministry when his ancestry is given (3:23–38).

The mission of the Church radiates out from Jerusalem. The destiny of Jesus had been to go to Jerusalem, and the so-called travel narrative of Luke could be characterized as the "way of the Lord" to Jerusalem. For occurrences of the word itself, *hodos*, see 9:57; 10:38; 11:6; 13:22; the verb *hodeuo*, "journey," occurs in the Samaritan parable, 10:33. The transition to the way of the Church takes place during the postresurrection appearances of the risen Lord to the disciples on the way when he impassioned their hearts and opened to them the Scriptures (24:32, 35). But they recognized him only *at table*, in the breaking of bread (24:30–31). They are already beginning to eat with him in his "kingdom" (22:28–29), the kingdom of the king who is not like a Gentile king (i.e., the king in the sacred social order) but who is "among you as one who serves" (22:27). According to Luke-Acts, the home congregation of Jerusalem tries to live in this society of sharing and service, having all things in common, selling their goods and possessions to distribute for the common welfare, spending time in the Temple and praising God (Acts 2:44–47). As for common meals, they are one of the four prerequisites for the Christian life, beyond endowment with the Spirit, listed in the formulaic statement of Acts 2:42: "They devoted themselves to the apostles' teaching and fellowship [*koinonia*, 'sharing,' 'common life'], to the breaking of bread and the prayers." The Church, in other words, is a new society based not on victimization and sacrifice but on the Spirit of the "king" who is among his people as one who serves.

The mission of the Church moves out from Jerusalem to "Judea and Samaria, and to the ends of the earth" (Acts 1:8). It is an expression of the way of God through history, and those who participate in it belong to the "Way" (see Acts 9:2 and 22:4, *inter alia*). This way may be long; the journey may be hard. The parousia, or second coming of the Lord, is indefinitely delayed—long enough for "the times of the Gentiles" to be fulfilled (Luke 21:24), which evidently corresponds to the climax of the Church's mission. Luke thus revises passages from Mark and Q that indicate, or could be construed as intimating, an imminent final judgment.

The Roman destruction of the Temple, which in Mark may be a sign of the eschaton, is for Luke clearly a sign of Jerusalem's subjection until the age is completed (Mark 13:14–24/Luke 21:20–24). Mark has Jesus beginning his ministry with the announcement of the approaching kingdom of God (Mark 1:14–15), but Luke, as we have seen, marks its commencement with Jesus reading Isaiah 61:1–2 in the synagogue at Nazareth and announcing the fulfillment of the scripture in their hearing (Luke 4:16–21). Mark's version of the interpretation of the parable of the sower concludes with the wonderful, evidently eschatological harvest (Mark 4:20), but Luke's version concludes, "And as for that in the good soil, these are the ones who, when they hear the word, hold it fast in an honest and good heart, and bear fruit with patient endurance" (Luke 8:20). Patience is required in the long journey of faith, for the kingdom of God, in its full form, will not appear immediately. The parable of the pounds, taken from Q, is addressed to those who believe its appearance is imminent, but in Luke's form of the parable the king goes into a far country and so presumably will not return for a long while (Luke 19:11–12; compare Matt 25:14). The way of the Lord is a long way; the way of the Spirit involves a long journey.

D. The Gospel of John

The Gospel of John is the Gospel of the Word, the Christ-event; that is, it is the Gospel that seeks to express a threefold inner unity: God, Jesus as the Christ, and the disciples of Christ.

The Gospel of John shares little with the synoptic Gospels in terms of literary formation or redaction. Its theological outlook is quite different, although it can be argued that at a deeper level it brings to radical articulation basic features of the testimony of the synoptics. It may have been written toward the end of the first century of the common era when the conflict of the church with Jewish synagogues had intensified in some areas (John 16:2). However, the now widespread bias that John is anti-Semitic, seeing the Jews as enemies of mythical proportions, is not accurate. The textual basis of this charge is the argument of Jesus with Jews in John 8 and specifically his pronouncement, "You are from your father the devil, and you choose to do your father's desires" (8:44). Two things are not commonly noted about this passage. (1) Jesus was arguing with Jews "who had believed in him" (8:31). He is not talking to all Jews. The use of the perfect participle (*pepisteukotas*) seems to indicate a temporal reference to those who had believed in him until that moment or context. The sense in context seems to be that among many Jewish followers, some had just fallen away because he foretold his death (8:21–30) and would be among those who murdered him (8:40). (2) The devil is not uniquely the father of the Jews, or of these particular Jews; he is the father of *all*, which includes these opponents who are entrapped by his deceit, his lies. "He was a murderer from the beginning, and does not stand in the truth" (8:44). As the murderer from the beginning, he is the ruler of all human beings; he is the power and empowerment of Cain's murder of Abel, a paradigm of the violent substructure of civilization. The Devil, like the serpent in Genesis 3, is a metaphorical embodiment of mimetic desire (see chapter 2, "Once More Cain and Abel").

What is it about the Christ in the Gospel of John that separates those who are entrapped in the ancient mimesis of the Devil from those who know the truth? To begin to answer this question, it is necessary to stress that the Gospel of John is centered in the central paradox of Christian faith, whose traditional term is *incarnation:* God has become human (1:1–14). In this, John radicalizes what is implicit in the synoptics. For Mark, Jesus becomes the Son of God and Son of Man from his baptism by John; his suffering, death, and resurrection are the "ransom" or price of release from sin and death for those who accept him as the access to the new community of God. Matthew understands Jesus' life as divinely conceived, from the virgin's womb, and in his text wisdom and apocalyptic are centered in Jesus as the Suffering Servant who is present and resurrected in the new community of sharing and healing. For Luke, Jesus' life is not only divinely conceived and virgin born(e) but a recovering and recapitulation of the image of God in which Adam was created. He is God's Son as the Divine Human whose teachings and actions offer to humanity the revealed pattern of life in divine-human community. The Gospel of John is not in conflict with the other three Gospels, but confronts the divine origin of the human Jesus more directly. John says, in effect, "Here in this man Jesus God has entered into human existence, and his fate must necessarily be that of expulsion and death, for human darkness and deceit cannot tolerate the presence of One who does not distinguish people and values according to structures of violence and sacrifice."

I will need to support this characterization of John's doctrine of incarnation, but first some comments about the symbolic language in which he expresses it. In the prologue, 1:1–14, Jesus is identified as the Logos or Word. Many commentators now think the author of the Fourth Gospel took this passage over from some anterior source, but whether or not that is the case, the poem to the Logos says what he wants to say. God, as the source and end of all things, is in a sense the *ultimate difference,* the "wholly other." All philosophies and religions that have abstracted deity and being from strict identification with the sacred social order have had to deal with the problem of the relation of "ultimate difference" to the world and human society. Plato, for example, resorted to the myth of the Demiurge in order to bring together the unchangeable being of the Good and the realm of perishing. The Demiurge (Greek *demiourgos,* "worker for the people") is a divine artisan that shapes resistant matter according to patterns of the Good.

The Hebrew Bible witnesses to God's word and presence with the covenant people, but its tendency is to establish the utter difference in kind between Spirit and the realm of creatures (see Isa 31:3). The people of Israel, ideally conceived as covenant community, are still a sacred social order to the extent that the Law and the sacrificial system preserve and accentuate *difference*—the difference between those in the community and those outside it, between the clean and unclean within and without the community, between priesthood and laity, between man and woman, and so forth. All of these differentiations are grounded in the difference between God and the human being. The Essenes at Qumran engaged in reformation by withdrawing in order to maintain the purity of difference—the true Israel against the world, the children of darkness. The Scribes or Pharisees reformed the tradition by developing study and leadership at the local level, thus qualifying but not undercutting the authority of the Temple, the primary symbol of sacred difference. But the witness of the Gospel of John is, in effect, that the differences established in the tradition, which both bring the covenant community to God and keep God and human community separated, are not differences that God observes. Even God, as the "ultimate difference," is not different after all, at least not in the way we humans had imagined. In Jesus "the Word (*logos*) became flesh and lived among us, and we have seen his glory, the glory as of a father's only son, full of grace and truth" (1:14). This is the Word that says, "Before Abraham was, I am" (8:58).

One cannot adequately speak of this presence of God in human being without symbols that seek to cross the bridge between the difference and nondifference between divine and human in Jesus Christ. It is truly and finally known only through the experience of the divine-human oneness for which Jesus prays in his final hours (17:21). The author, recognizing that one cannot approach the meaning of the God-Man directly, uses instead indirection, which expresses itself in an ironic style, the use of multiple metaphors, and an emphasis on signs. He draws upon mythic motifs, such as the heavenly stranger.[24] But the most important thing to note about John's language is the many "I am" statements attributed to Jesus, which indicate the multiple ways in which the presence of God may be viewed: as the bread of life (6:35, 48), as the light of the world (8:12), as the gate of the sheepfold (10:7), as the good shepherd (10:11), as the resurrection and the life (11:25), as the way, the truth, and the life (14:6). The primary departure from the approach of indirection and multiplicity occurs in Jesus' recurring self-affirmation "I am" where it is not qualified in any way (see 6:20; 8:58; 13:19; 18:5). The informed reader is presumably supposed to perceive the great irony of these occurrences of *ego eimi*, especially the last one, where Judas leads the mob of soldiers and police to arrest Jesus. When Jesus asks them, "Whom are you looking for?" and they answer, "Jesus of Nazareth," he replies, *ego eimi*—"I am [he]."

Thus we see many "I am" statements in the predicate nominative, suggesting the multiple reality of the Word become flesh (Logos, Bread, Light, Good Shepherd, Gate, etc.), and absolute self-affirmations, in which the many names are reduced to his being. This relation of multiplicity to singularity is probably related to what Werner Kelber has noted as "a distinct tendency in John's narra-

tive to refocus attention from the plural to the singular."[25] The examples he gives
are plural commandments and the "new commandment" (13:34); Jesus' many
works fulfilled in his work of glorifying the Father (17:4); the sign of the loaves of
bread and Jesus as the Bread (6:48); the disciples ideally represented in the
Beloved Disciple (19:26); the sheep becoming one flock under one shepherd
(10:16); and finally the many sayings or *logoi* that are expressed in the *Logos*.[26]
The many signs that Jesus performs could also be refocused in Logos; although
these signs are events understood at one level as miracles (e.g., 2:1–11 and
4:46–54), the word for sign, *semeion*, conveys a special sense of communication.
Something is made known that leads to belief. There is thus a close relationship of
Jesus' signs, *semeia*, and his sayings or words, *logoi*.

The Fourth Gospel tries to indicate that everything distinctively human—culture, community, regulations or differentiations, and above all, language—is rooted in and manifests one reality: God the Father, who encompasses truth and
being. But this truth, this reality, this being, this Word of God is expelled and crucified. I will return to this and to Kelber's essay shortly.

The meaning of the Logos, of the God-Man, comes to concrete focus in Jesus'
final meeting with his disciples at Passover. In John there is no eucharistic institution at the last supper; rather, Jesus washes the feet of the disciples. The import is
much the same as the treatment of the "least of the brothers" in Matthew and the
Son of Man as servant in all three synoptic Gospels: the disciples should also wash
one another's feet; they should also be servants. "Very truly, I tell you, whoever
receives one whom I send receives me; and whoever receives me receives him who
sent me" (13:20).

After foretelling his betrayal, Jesus gives the disciples a new commandment,
"that you love one another. Just as I have loved you, you also should love one
another" (13:34). Thus the relation between commandments and commandment,
between sayings and the one Word, is made manifest in the community of love.
"By this everyone will know that you are my disciples, if you have love for one
another" (13:35).

Jesus tells the disciples he is the way to the Father (14:1–14), a significant passage for understanding the christology of the Fourth Gospel. That Jesus is in the
Father and the Father in him (14:10; cf. 17:21) expresses the relationship, yet a
distinction between the two. This could, of course, be understood as the relation
of God the Father and God the Son who are one and the same, but even so, God
the Son is "human," as evidenced in the subsequent words, "The words I say to
you I do not speak on my own; but the Father who dwells in me does his works"
(14:10). The Gospel recognizes in Jesus a human I, a "from me," that is distinct
from God's words and works; this is the self that says "the Father is greater than I"
(14:28). Nonetheless, this distinction is not God's intention but a concession to
the human rage for differentiation. Thomas wants to know the way, as though

God's way could be different from seeing the human Jesus, and Philip wants to be shown the Father, as though seeing the Father could be different from the human Jesus. They want distinctions; they want differences. The notion that God could be present in such a way that human differences, above all the old differences of the sacred, are not determinative is something they cannot comprehend.

Whoever believes in Jesus will do his works and even greater works "because I am going to the Father" (14:13). In other words, his suffering and death are necessary for the disciples to understand the work of God and to receive the Holy Spirit.

Whoever loves him will keep his commandments and be given the *parakletos*, the spirit of truth (14:16–17). The Paraclete is the Advocate, the Defender,[27] the God who cares for those who would otherwise be "orphaned" (14:18), who stands on the side of victims. The coming of the Spirit-Paraclete is the (second) coming of Jesus (14:18). The Spirit-Paraclete will teach the disciples; it will be the reality of the peace that Jesus leaves with them (14:27). The "peace of the world" is a security bought at the price of troubled and fearful hearts, the security of success in continual mimetic rivalry, sacred differentiation, and violence. It is the peace of the "ruler of this world" (14:30), who has no power over the Son.

Jesus subsequently repeats his commandment, that they love one another "as I have loved you" (15:12). The commandment is grounded in what the Logos-Paraclete must undergo in order to become known in the world: "No one has greater love than this, to lay down one's life for one's friends" (15:13). The death of Jesus is therefore revealed, at its deepest and most intimate level, as what the Son does for his friends, who are united through him with the Father. One can be a "friend" (*philos*) only with an equal; one might consider the meaning too radical or too sacrilegious to have been intended by the author. But again, in the Fourth Gospel's witness, an attempt is made, futile though it may finally be in human language, to overcome the difference between God and humans that humans establish in the mimetic order, in the order of the *ruler* of this world.

There is no reason for hating the Innocent Victim. "They hated me without a cause" (15:25; cf. Ps 35:19). Or to put it differently, there *is* a reason, but the reason is the maintenance of *differentiation* in the sacred social order. When rivalries threaten to dissolve all differences in the chaos of violence, it is necessary to have a victim from whatever available pool there may be: those who are foreign or those who are weak and vulnerable within the social order. As Caiaphas the high priest said, "it is better for you to have one man die for the people than to have the whole nation destroyed" (11:50). It is necessary to have *a* victim, any victim, an innocent or at least arbitrarily chosen victim; how much more so, then, that the Logos, coming to "his own" (or "his own home"), will not be accepted (1:11), will be taken out to the place of execution and put to death! But his death is not the end; it is the prelude to the giving of peace and the Holy Spirit (20:21–22).

Finally, a further word, as promised, on Kelber's essay. In its concluding segment, "The Logocentric Circle," he points out that contrary to what Derrida says about Christianity and a Logos-theology of presence, in John "The *Logos* is installed *en arche* [in the beginning] only to be dislodged from *arche*." The Logos surrenders "a privileged position in the interest of the human condition." Therefore, "readers are invited to understand themselves in relation not to absolute, transcendent presence, but rather to the incarnation and crucifixion of the *Logos*."[28]

Kelber's interpretation of the Fourth Gospel, in dialogue with Derrida, is remarkably full of insight. He has taken the lead in bridging a hermeneutical gap. He does not simply report what critical theorists are saying and try to apply it; rather, he wrestles with it in order to disengage the distinctiveness of one of the key texts in the Western tradition of religion and metaphysics. I regret to say, however, that in my opinion he allows the model-obstacle of Derrida and deconstruction to skew, if not overwhelm, his argument, for he writes and thinks using the rival's rules. He does this by positing difference as the basis of John, that is, as that which really generates the text. This difference is the distance, the play, the tension between logocentrism and "rupture with the logocentric origin." He states, "The very narrative which thrives on the erasure of the transcendental *arche* cultivates a signs language which aspires to pleromatic presence." The narrative "is dramatically motivated by this logocentric gesturing"; it is "deeply informed by the double gesture of decentering and logocentrism." John, therefore, "suffers the problem of language and metaphysics in search of central presence."[29]

Kelber's essay borders on a breakthrough in Gospel interpretation, but in accepting Derrida's field of discourse he shows how one can continue indefinitely in the cycle of differentiation and always come around to the same thing—difference, Derrida's *différance*, which in denying the primacy of origin and presence is but another substitute for them. One stays on this merry-go-round by two refusals. First is the refusal to deal with *undifferentiation*, chaos, confusion, which is the medium, the reality, the stuff, the very context out of which differentiation—the trace, the writing, the *pharmakon*, the scapegoat—emerges. This refusal, built into the deconstructionist project, does not encompass everything Kelber has to say, but it seems to have a certain hold on him. This is probably why he focuses on the Logos in John as a problem that is linguistic (signifiers versus transcendental signified) and theological (Logos becoming flesh and forgoing glory or reflecting glory and denying the flesh).[30] But it is not fundamentally a linguistic or theological problem; it is a matter of testifying to divine revelation and divine being in the human condition of mimesis, victimization, and sacrifice. Second is the refusal to admit into the sphere of thought the reality of One whose difference is that his reality does not conform to human differences. And above all the One who is different does not conform to the principle of difference, which is one of the strongest of those traces in contemporary thought that have been carried over from the myth of the sacred social order.

E. The Unity of the New Testament Gospels

The tendency in Gospel criticism is to show differences, and not only to show differences but to accord them a "reality status" that amounts to undercutting the truth and authority of the distinctive testimony of the Gospels. This may take the form of demonstrating the redactional differences of the Gospels from one another, or the differences in the oral and written traditions that emerge from different life-settings, or—the supreme act of critical differentiating—showing how Jesus was not at all the way he is represented in the Gospels. No matter how valiantly some of the believing critics struggle to justify this critical approach theologically and religiously, the result is to deny the authority of the Gospels and to elevate the critic to the status of high priest controlling the knowledge of text and tradition. In this respect, postmodern and deconstructionist thought is simply the logical continuation of the trend that began with the Enlightenment and modernism: once the influence of religion is discounted and the authority of the individual interpreter is exalted, there is no "origin" (even if finding it is admitted in principle) that can be satisfying; there is no archetype or presence that can ground and "authorize" (i.e., "originate") one's enterprise, so the multiplication of critical differentiations is crucial for intellectuals to maintain their "authority." Alternatives to this chaotic and atomistic situation have been proposed, of course. Prominent among these in the modern intellectual tradition are Nietzsche's *Uebermensch*, Heidegger's German people enacting the destiny of Being, and Derrida's reign of *différance* which must be managed by the priestly philosopher who commands esoteric knowledge.

I do not wish to deny, of course, differences among the Gospels. If Mark is viewed as the earliest, then it can be interesting and fruitful to read Matthew and Luke as revisionary readings of Mark. In general Matthew uses Mark's narrative and adds and changes according to his own religious vision and theological assumptions. He links the gospel story to Scripture and the Jewish tradition in a number of ways, providing continuity where Mark often represents abruptness and discontinuity. Matthew's view of the disciples is much more positive. He radically intensifies the elements of wisdom and apocalyptic in Jesus sayings and deeds. In the end, however Jesus as Apocalyptic Judge and Wisdom is a language demythologized and rooted to the revelation of the Son of Man in the innocent victim.

Luke also adds continuity with the past to Mark's narrative, but extends it into the future, so that Luke-Acts is Christianity's first "history," a history of salvation.

He eliminates conflict where it is found in Mark (and in Matthew with the Pharisees), describing the disciples and usually the crowds very positively. Jesus is the Servant from God as in Mark, but any connotation of his death as sacrifice is eliminated.

As for the Gospel of John, it is so different from the other three that it is difficult to compare them. At the same time, to repeat what was said in the earlier discussion, it radicalizes what is implicit in the synoptics. And here we find the unity of the Gospel witness. To quote the summary from the discussion of John, in Mark's witness Jesus becomes the Son of God and Son of Man from his baptism by John; his suffering, death, and resurrection are the "ransom" or price of release from sin and death for those who accept him as the access to the new community of God. Matthew understands Jesus' life as divinely conceived, as from the virgin's womb, and in his text wisdom and apocalyptic are centered in Jesus as the Suffering Servant who is present and resurrected in the new community of sharing and healing. For Luke, Jesus' life is not only divinely conceived and virgin born(e), but a recovering and recapitulation of the image of God in which Adam was created. He is God's Son as the Divine Human whose teachings and actions offer to humanity the revealed pattern of life in divine-human community. John's language and perspective say the same thing, that God, the divine reality, the source and end of all things, encounters us in a particular life, in a concrete setting, as the Innocent Victim whose life is not destroyed by sin and death. The difference is that John's language confronts the divine origin of the human Jesus more directly. It is an "origin" that is simultaneously transcendent and with us and in us. It is paradoxical from the standpoint of human differences, but the Word of God is not "different" in the way we expected it to be. The meaning of John's witness is that, in this man Jesus, God has entered into human existence, and his fate must necessarily be that of expulsion and death, for human darkness and deceit, the prevalence of mimetic desire and rivalry, cannot tolerate the presence of One who does not distinguish people and values according to structures that control and validate violence. But his fate is not the same as that of the tragic hero or the dying and rising god, for his death on the cross is not a necessary sacrifice of man to God but God's self-giving gift of love to his creatures. It reveals the violent origins of sacrifice and the complicity of us all in victimization, which makes our world go round. It is the secret hidden since the foundation of the world.

8

Desire, Violence, and the Truth of the Victim

Because [Oedipus's] sufferings were great, unmerited, and untold,
Let some just god relieve him from distress!
                              Sophocles, *Oedipus at Colonus*

You alone are at pains for this city—you alone.
A triumph you deserve is in store for you.
                              Euripides, *The Bacchae*

And sleep [from wine], the oblivion of our daily ills,
[Dionysus] gives—there is none other balm (pharmakon) for toils.
                              Euripides, *The Bacchae*

Chorus: What sort of cure (pharmakon) did you find for this affliction
        [of mortals foreseeing their doom]?
Prometheus: I caused blind hopes to dwell within them.
                              Aeschylus, *Prometheus Bound*

Surely he has borne our infirmities
and carried our diseases.
                              Isaiah 53:4

It is more beneficial for you that one man die for the people
than that the entire nation be destroyed.
                              John 11:50

The Word that states itself to be absolutely true never speaks except from
the position of a victim in the process of being expelled.
                              René Girard, *Things Hidden Since the Foundation of the World*

I concluded the last chapter by stating that the paradox of the Word of God, the speaking, the "presentation" of God to human beings, is that it is not different in the way we expect it to be different. Neither I nor anyone else is a high priest controlling what it means and what its effects are, but the witness of the Gospels is that all power structures and social classifications, which are based on mimetic rivalry, domination, and exclusion, are subverted by this Word. It is a Word revealed finally only in the expulsion and death of the Word, which cannot be separated from its bearer and speaker but encompasses the human being who reveals it. The revelation, the disclosure, the unmasking of the mimetic world, occurs in his death on the cross, the sign whose signification and significance is that the prevalence of mimetic desire and rivalry, which are actuated and controlled through social structures of substitution or sacrifice, cannot tolerate the presence of the One who does not distinguish people and values according to these structures that control and validate violence.

This unity of the Gospel witness now becomes my point of departure for an analysis of mimesis and the testimony of the Passion accounts in the Gospels. For the sake of economy in a discussion that could and should be treated in a book of its own, my text of reference will be Mark, with the other three compared or contrasted as appropriate.

A. Mimesis

1. Desire, Rivalry, and Conflict

The initial calling of disciples in Mark 1:16–20 is strange and abrupt, in keeping with Mark's style. The reader or hearer gets the impression that Jesus has not met them before. Simon and Andrew and James and John simply leave their fishing boats "immediately" when Jesus passes by and summons them to "fish for people." Matthew follows Mark's account closely (Matt 4:18–22). Luke presents a more realistic narrative, for Jesus already knows at least Simon (Luke 4:38–41) prior to the astonishing catch of fish that leads to the commitment of the four to follow Jesus (5:1–11). John knows part of this tradition, but his depiction of the beginnings of the community of disciples is quite different. Two disciples of John the Baptist become followers of Jesus. One of them is Andrew, who tells his brother Simon Peter they have found the Messiah, and so Simon, whom Jesus names Cephas, becomes a follower (John 1:35–42). Subsequently Philip and Nathaniel, rather than James and John as two of the first four, become disciples (1:43–51).

The dramatic abruptness of the call of the first four followers in Mark is integral to the whole secrecy theme in Mark. As indicated in chapter 7, the reason for secrecy is essentially the problem of popular expectations concerning differentiation—the establishing or using of differences. Popular differences always depend on rivalry, which is generally quite open, and scapegoating, which is usually partially if not completely camouflaged. Mark's account of the initial call is not realistic at all; Luke moves it closer to accepted literary forms of the first-century C.E. Greco-Roman world. No doubt none of the Gospels presents this "historically" in the commonplace empirical sense; what they strive to render is "historicity": the human reality of the early disciples' care for Jesus and his for them.[1] At the core of this historicity is the witness to discipleship, seen from a "divine" point of view, as not constituted by mimetic desire and rivalry. How does one express this? Mark, characteristically, attempts to say it by using a combination of urgency and enigmatic abruptness. The links of continuity with the ordinary world are literarily severed by saying, in effect, "It just happened, suddenly, like that. He came, he called them, they followed him."

Matthew either understands this or agrees with it. Luke is more constrained by "world" in a sense, that is, by the conventions of some imagined audience, for he typically presents a period of acquaintanceship (at least for Jesus and Simon) and then a miracle that astounds the fishermen in the boat. Insofar as "astounding" implies "overwhelming," the hierarchical structure of rivalry (master-slave, ruler-subject, etc.) is at work in Luke's narrative. However, the effect of this is mitigated in Luke by Peter's humble outcry ("Go away from me, Lord, for I am a sinful man!") and Jesus' reassuring reply, "Do not be afraid." As for the Gospel of John, the first disciples are presented as coming to Jesus as a matter of course, so to say. That is, John the Baptist testifies that Jesus is the Son of God, and the next day, watching Jesus walk past, exclaims that he is the Lamb of God (John 1:34–35). Hearing this, two of John's followers begin to follow Jesus. There is thus no mimetic conflict between John and Jesus. All of the Gospels stress this (see below on John and Jesus in Mark). Luke and John, in their respective ways, relate this lack of conflict by drawing clear lines of differentiation: Luke places the Baptizer as the end of the old era, the age of the law and the prophets (16:16), and the Fourth Gospel narrates John's witness to Jesus as Lamb of God, Son of God, and baptizer with the Spirit. In fact, neither John nor anyone else baptizes Jesus in the Gospel of John.[2]

The appointing of the Twelve is quite strategically placed in Mark and has an important bearing on the Markan understanding of mimesis. Jesus withdraws to a mountain and calls to himself those whom he wishes, from whom he chooses twelve to preach and have authority over demons (3:13–14). There is apparently no special significance to the use of the Greek thelo, which may mean "wish," "would," "like," and, as here, often has the connotation of "choose." It is distributed pretty evenly through the Gospels and is used by a variety of speakers.[3] What is significant here in context is the withdrawal to a mountain where the Twelve are appointed; it comes in between two episodes of the "crush of the crowd," 3:7–12, 20–22. The relation of all the disciples to Jesus, and particularly of the Twelve, is that of differentiation from the crowd with its mimetic contagion that poses a danger even to its object of admiration.

Mark 3:7–12 is a beautiful text for illustrating the mimetic role of the leader as scapegoat-victim. Of course, there is ostensibly no popular hostility toward Jesus, but three details should be noted. First is the function of Jesus as a kind of "magnet": "for he had cured many, so that all who had diseases pressed upon him to touch him" (3:10). This could be understood as a transference process, the ills of the multitude imputed to the victim-qua-god. Second is the menacing underside of the polarity of healer and crowd, as indicated in the preceding verse: "He told his disciples to get a boat ready for him because of the crowd, so that they would not crush (*thlibosin*) him" (3:9). The verb, *thlibo*, occurs only here in the New Testament in the sense of "crush." The closely related *sunthlibo*, "press about or around," also occurs only in Mark (5:24, 31). *Thlibo* usually means oppressing and afflicting someone and is associated with the persecution of believers (2 Cor 1:6; 1 Thess. 3:4; 2 Thess 1:7), as is its noun *thlipsis*, which Mark uses in the sense of pre-apocalypse tribulations (13:19, 24; cf. 4:17). Therefore *thlibo* is a strong word for expressing Jesus' reaction to what the crowd might do to him. It is as though he is beset on every side. Following the appointment of the Twelve, his family, hearing about the crowd around Jesus, came to *seize* Jesus, "for people were saying, 'He is beside himself (*exeste*)'" (3:21, RSV)—that is, he is "ecstatic" or "crazy," there being a fine line between the two. The convergence of the crowd, with their diseases and conflicts, leads Jesus' family to ascribe the crowd's transference of maladies to Jesus to the actual state of Jesus' mind and spirit. This too is a mimetic process; in this case the family imitates the crowd and misunderstands exactly how Jesus is ecstatic, "standing outside."

Third and finally, the diseases are attributed to unclean spirits, who identify Jesus as the Son of God (3:11). It is a crucial fact that the presence of demons and the exorcising of demons and unclean spirits is characteristically associated with a people, crowd, or mob. In Mark there is only one exception to this, and the exception proves the rule.[4] This one passage is 7:24–30, where the Syrophoenician woman beseeches Jesus to cast a demon out of her daughter. She is rewarded for her faith, which is associated with not a little wit. The interesting thing about this pericope is that Jesus has again withdrawn from the crowds into the gentile region of Tyre, wanting to remain anonymous for a while. The gentile woman seeks him out. The situation is thus of someone *coming out of the crowd* and, apart from its mimetic effect, pleading for her child's well-being. This structure of separation from the crowd is similar to what happens in Mark 5:24–34. There a great crowd throngs or presses (*sunthlibo*) about Jesus, and a women suffering from continual bleeding comes up behind him and touches his garment. Immediately she is healed. When Jesus turns about in the crowd and asks, "Who touched my garments?," the disciples react as if the question is nonsensical: "You see the crowd pressing in (*sunthlibonta*) on you; how can you say, 'Who touched me?'" (5:31). But Jesus begins to try to single out the person, and the woman comes and falls before him in fear and trembling, telling him what happened. "He said to her, 'Daughter, your faith has made you well [*sesoken se*, literally "saved you"]; go in peace, and be healed of your disease'" (5:34). In some respects both passages are a reversal and transformation of the scapegoat mechanism. Faith is associated with separation from the crowd—either someone within the crowd situation, as here, or someone going to Jesus in his solitude, as the Syrophoenician woman does. Healing comes when rivalry is not the motivation. The Syrophoenician woman does not argue with Jesus' provocative assertion of the prior rights of the Jews, and the bleeding women, once healed, does not withdraw because she has "won" something for herself. Going to the healer to get healing for oneself could be and typically is a kind of competition in and with the crowd, both in the sense of trying to get to him ahead of others and of getting something from him rather than giving something to him. Perhaps this is why the bleeding woman's response to Jesus' question looks like a confession of sin: she has recognized her complicity with the crowd. Why else would the text say that "she told him the whole truth" (*pasan ten aletheian*, 5:33)? This awareness of complicity with the crowd is a true coming out of it and clarifies why Jesus pronounces the word of healing even though she has evidently already been healed. The "second healing"—the real healing, so to speak, the healing associated with faith—is to come out of the crowd.

To return to an earlier point about demons as a reality of the multitude, of the crowd that can easily become a mob, demons or unclean spirits must be the mimetic contagion of a community on the edge of dissolving into mimetic crisis, with its potential for violence. They are an objectified projection of the reciprocal imitation whereby objects of desire and models to emulate have become confused to the point that all must turn against one another or against their own bodies. The latter, the suffering of disease, of foreign bodies, is a defense that works only up to a point. Somehow liberation of the body, of the self, must occur. The disease, the mal-aise, the mimetic conflict must be expelled. Two further incidents in Mark confirm this association of demons with the mimesis of the crowd in mimetic conflict and offer good contexts for enhancing this discussion of mimesis. One has been touched on already, 3:20–22; the other is 5:1–20.

In 3:20–22 the scribes from Jerusalem accuse Jesus of being possessed by Beelzebul and of casting out demons by the prince of demons. Beelzebul is one of the names for Satan, the Devil, the prince of darkness, the prince of this world, and so on.[5] He is the symbolic embodiment of the many—the demons, the unclean spirits, the wildly running contagion of human conflict, which is always mimetic and thus dangerously reciprocal. The crowd has pressed about Jesus and the disciples to the point that they are unable to eat. Jesus' family wishes to get him out of there; in the Greek it is not clear whether the family members or some in the crowd were saying, "He is beside himself." If the latter, then the text gives us already an inkling of what a crowd can do to its hero. Then the scribes get into the act with their accusation that he is the agent of Beelzebul. At one level the issue between Jesus and the scribes seems apparent. They, as interpreters of the Law (and I assume they are really identical with the Pharisees), lay claim to be the authoritative interpreters of the tradition, and the issue of traditional practices comes up a number of times in Mark (e.g., 2:23–28; 7:1–23; 10:2–9). An additional matter, closely related to interpretation of the tradition, is that of political authority, both in the sense of authority over the populace and alignment with the Romans. Maintaining smooth relationships with the Romans was probably more of a concern of the priests, and in any case when Jesus goes to Jerusalem he seems to be even more embroiled with the priests than with the scribes. But what the conflict comes down to is a rivalry in which the object of desire, from the standpoint of Jesus' enemies, is *the favor of the people*. This is quite clearly indicated in one of the Temple episodes, 11:27–33. The "chief priests and the scribes and the elders" ask Jesus by what authority he did certain things—presumably teaching in the temple precinct and expelling the money changers. "Authority" (in Greek *exousia*) has various connotations, but they all have to do with the right of disposal over other people or over property. (The noun *ousia*, which Derrida associates with "presence" and "origin" in "Plato's Pharmacy,"[6] means "substance" or "property" in the Koine Greek of the New Testament.) Jesus in turn asks them whether the baptism practiced by John came from heaven or from humans. This put the opponents in a quandary. If they said from heaven, then this would be a confirmation of John's ministry (and by implication, of Jesus' ministry). If they said it was of human origin the people would not like it—"they were afraid of the crowd, for all regarded John as truly a prophet" (11:32). This is the crux: "they were afraid of the crowd." Their authority really comes from the people, even if they seem to have them under tight control. This same is true of Pilate later on. Even the Roman governor, agent of the mighty Roman Empire, could only accede to the crowd that the chief priests stirred up (15:11). "For [Pilate] perceived that it was out of envy that the chief priests had delivered him up" (15:10, RSV).

So this is what underlies the attack of the scribes on Jesus: fear of the people, fear they were losing control of the crowd. And, of course, in the situation of rivalry in which the object is the crowd's favor, envy is the motivating emotion. In ascribing Jesus' power—closely related to authority—to Beelzebul, the scribes are imitating the all-pervading desire of each person to be and have what the other is and has. When this desire becomes all-pervading, when a community becomes a crowd at the edge of becoming a mob, then *panic* is not far away. This is the work of the all-god, the mimesis that is so powerful that it seems to come from a transcendent source. Beelzebul or Satan is the true Pan ("All"), and under his sway it appears that the only way to defeat him is to imitate him—to fight Satan with Satan, like fighting fire with fire or poison with poison (as in allergy desensitization, or in using modified or dead bacteria to combat an illness). Like imitates like.

There is a certain similarity in the reactions of crowd, family, and scribes. The crowd press upon the healer in a way that could be construed as menacing. Family members either think he is crazy or feel dishonored because others think so. And scribes find their authority is being swallowed in the mimesis of the crowd, that is, by Beelzebul. This is all the more the case if, as Horsley has argued, one of the significations of demon possession is rule by a foreign imperial power. (The other two are struggle between God and Satan at the cosmic level and possession of individuals at the local or personal level.)[7] Insofar as the scribes are perceived, at least from the standpoint of Mark's narrative, to be implicated with religious and political "powers that be," the demons could also be their mimetic correlates.

The episode of the Gerasene demoniac, Mark 5:1–20, has already been touched on in chapter 1 and has been beautifully elucidated by Girard in *The Scapegoat*. Here I would simply emphasize that the demoniac, who appears to be so isolated, and thus ostensibly removed from mimetic processes, is actually the object and magnet of these very processes. He is the differentiation that allows the people of the city and region to manage their mimetic rivalry. As long as he dwells in the tombs, the realm of the dead, the community may remain in the realm of life. As long as he cries out against himself and injures himself with stones, the others will not have to cry out against one another and throw stones. He is a perpetual scapegoat, being lynched continually outside the border of community life.

There is a certain symmetry between the plea of the demons not to be expelled from the country and the plea of the Gerasenes that Jesus leave their region. It is as if the demons are a correlate of the people in their mimetic conflict. Therefore the logic of the situation is that if Jesus did not depart, they themselves, like the swine, would have to "leave." The scene depicts what humans do to one another. They either "drown" in the chaos of mimetic conflict, or they substitute animal victims for one another.

So the Gerasenes are not primarily concerned with the local economy, unless economy is construed in a very broad sense that encompasses its sacrificial underpinnings. What they have lost is the primary resource that allows them to continue in a world governed by victimization and the sacrificial mechanism. Their potential doubles, the Legion of demons gathered into the demoniac, have been "drowned" with the swine, as if the latter have been sacrificed as a substitute for the man who is a surrogate for the community; but in a mimetic, sacrificial world who knows how soon the demons will "come to life" again (see below on Mark 6:14–29)?

Concerning the name "Legion," Greek *legion*, it was the Roman name of an infantry brigade. The demons are thus the metaphorical correlates of the townspeople as foot soldiers, the (armed) crowd attacking the demoniac on behalf of the people of the area. To lose the demons, then, is to lose the "army" that defends Gerasa.

To have the man "clothed and in his right mind" seems like the worst thing that could happen, for now the community descends again into a vortex of sameness, without its primary basis of differentiation. I do not wish to be condemnatory or condescending in thus commenting on the situation of the Gerasenes, for the text is misunderstood if we do not see ourselves in it. Is it not typical for communities to have some ritualized or routinized form of victimization that functions to maintain the line of differentiation between order and disorder, good and evil, sane and insane, law-abiding and criminal, clean and unclean, and so on?

Could the Gerasenes be liberated from their mimetic condition? Their hope for release from the mimetic cycle would be the gift of a good mimesis, a mimesis that Jesus seeks to impart to the disciples, a mimesis of love, service, and exorcism of demons. But how are they to learn this? They see in Jesus only another healer and exorcist, amazing perhaps, but a destructive stranger nonetheless. He is something like a "one-man army" who is amazingly more powerful than their army of demons. The one element of hope is Jesus' command to the restored man, who begged to remain with Jesus, but Jesus refused him. He tells him instead, "Go home to your friends, and tell them how much the Lord has done for you, and what mercy he has shown you" (5:19).

A text that does not deal directly with demons as a mimetic phenomenon, but that is closely related to it, is the pericope concerning the death of John the Baptist, 6:14–29. It is closely related to demon possession because the demon is a way of dealing with the *double* by objectifying it; a demon is subject to exorcism, whereas the actual human double is more difficult to cope with. John the Baptist is a double for Herod (Herod Antipas).

When word about Jesus and his powers spread about, Herod was one of those who believed he was John risen from the dead. Herod had imprisoned John because the Baptizer condemned his marriage to Herodias, who had been married to Herod's brother (see Lev 18:16). Herodias wanted to execute John for the public shame he had brought upon her, but Herod's attitude toward John was complex. He admired him as a righteous man and protected him from Herodias, and evidently he sent for him often to hear his preaching and instruction. Yet: "When he heard him, he was greatly perplexed; and yet he liked to listen to him" (6:20). John has become Herod's *alter*, the other from whom he cannot adequately differentiate himself. What John says perplexes him because it brings judgment upon him and causes him discomfort, yet John is clearly an authority figure whom Herod admires.

All these matters have been treated at length by Girard in *The Scapegoat*, so it would be superfluous for me to dwell on them. Of particular acuity is his insight into the function of desire in the passage, the desire of the persecutor to have what his victim possesses, authority over the people and favor with God, and the desire that the young girl (Greek *korasion*) must learn from her mother in asking for John's head. Herod the persecutor, caught between the cunning of Herodias and the presence of all his guests before whom he has sworn an oath, "does not have the courage to say no to his guests, whose number and prestige intimidate him. In other words he is controlled by mimesis. . . . By yielding to this pressure he loses himself in the crowd; he is no more than the least of its members." But then, in keeping with the phenomenon of the double, Herod is haunted by the other whom he has murdered: "Persecutors cannot believe in the definitive death of their victims. The resurrection and consecration of the victims are above all phenomena of persecution, the perspective of the persecutors themselves on the violence in which they have participated."[8]

Of particular interest is the fact that the mimetic preoccupation of Herod with John is completely absent from Mark's portrayal of the relation of Jesus and John. In spite of the similarities between them—proclaimers of repentance, arrested, subjected to humiliation, executed—they are not subject to mimetic rivalry. When John announces that "one mightier than I" will come who will baptize with the Holy Spirit rather than with water (1:7–8), the author doubtless has Jesus in mind as the referent of what John says. However, the narrative itself does not make the connection except by juxtaposition of John's announcement and Jesus' coming to be baptized. Even at his baptism the message of the heavenly voice, "Thou art my beloved Son," could be construed as "heard" only by Jesus. In other words, Mark does not present overlapping spheres of concern and potential competition for Jesus and John. Those who identify Jesus as John raised from the dead (6:14), like Herod, suffer mimetic illusion.

From Mark's standpoint the disciples themselves, unfortunately, do not rise above this mimetic illusion. The feeding of the crowd in a wilderness or "lonely place," 6:34–44, following almost immediately on the Herod-John pericope, is intended as part of the teaching process on the mystery of the kingdom about which the disciples are so puzzled (4:10–13). Another way to put it is that the disciples are supposed to be learning the *good mimesis* of the Son of God–Son of Man. The account centers in the mode of sharing the little food available, and the sharing itself takes on eucharistic dimensions. "Taking the five loaves and the two fish, he looked up to heaven, and blessed and broke the loaves, and was giving them to his disciples to set before the people; and he divided the two fish among them all" (6:41). Here I have departed from the NRSV only in translating the imperfect *edidou* literally as "was giving": "he was giving" the loaves of bread to his disciples for distribution. The use of the imperfect, indicating continual and habitual action in the past, seems to be quite deliberate on Mark's part; it is surrounded by aorists (for action completed at a point in time), and the aorist is used at the Last Supper for giving the bread (14:22). There are mistakes and infelicities in the Greek text of Mark, indicating that Greek was not the author's native language. It is clear, nonetheless, that Mark knew how to use the Greek aorist, but here he deliberately employs the imperfect. It is used in the same fashion in the parallel account of feeding in the wilderness, 8:1–10. It must indicate the continual giving of God, the abundance of the kingdom of God.

Both the feedings in the wilderness are anticipations of the Last Supper, 14:22–25. The giving of the bread is the giving of the divine life and the expression of the divine compassion. In context, the difference between the disciples and the *ochlos*, "the throng," is that the disciples are challenged to understand the good mimesis, the abundance of the Kingdom. But they do not. This is apparent in the parallel feeding account and the subsequent discussion of bread in the boat (8:14–21); it is immediately clear from the incident on the sea, 6:47–52. Straining to make headway against a storm wind, the disciples are terrified when Jesus appears on the water, thinking they see a *phantasma*, "phantasm" or "ghost." Hence their way of seeing Jesus was really not so different from Herod's perception of John the Baptist: in both instances the authority figure is a kind of ghost that haunts those who are obsessed with the model-obstacle. So it is that the narrator's enigmatic comment, "for they did not understand about the loaves, but their hearts were hardened" (6:52), does not refer to the miraculous power of Jesus in multiplying the small amount of food available. If that were the case, it would only reinforce the position of Jesus as model-obstacle on the verge of being a double to the disciples. It refers rather to the good mimesis that calms human fear and conflict. But the disciples do not understand.

The core of what they do not fathom is why the Son of Man must suffer and die and rise again (8:27–33). One way to express the Son of Man's suffering and death is that within the structures of language and culture, that is, within structures of mimetic desire and rivalry, victimization, and the sacrificial mechanism, the only way to reveal the good mimesis is subversive and invariably fatal; the human community, like the Gerasenes with their demoniac, must have their sacrificial commodity (or commodities) lest everything fall apart and they be at one another's throats. But the radical enactment of good mimesis will point to another power, the reign of God, and will open up something new for the world. The key episode in this regard is the request of James and John, 10:35–45.

The request of James and John to be Jesus' chief officials when he becomes honored as king of the new age was perceived as a troubling, negative reflection upon these two disciples. This is attested by the fact that Matthew has their *mother* make the request, thus transferring blame from members of the apostolic circle to someone outside the circle. Luke deals with the problem by omitting the passage altogether.[9]

Jesus initially responds to the desire of James and John by asking whether they are able to share his cup and baptism. The wording of his question may arise out of the liturgical practices of the early church, but the import here in narrative context is whether they are able to share in his suffering and death. At this point the narrative seems to move toward a decisive disclosure, for if the mystery of the Kingdom is the suffering, death, and resurrection of the Son of Man as God's servant-messiah, then the positive answer of James and John, "We are able," would, on the face of it, indicate their comprehension of what he has been trying to reveal to them. The problem is that the very nature of their question already reveals that they do not understood and cannot as long as their view of Jesus is determined by mimetic desire and rivalry. Their concept of the Kingdom, very much like Peter's concept of the Messiah, is that of a realm and people ruled by Jesus after God leads him in triumph over all his foes and establishes him as dispenser of power, prestige, and property.

Since this sort of assertion of power (and thus of violence) is the import of their question, it evokes the imitation of the other ten, who "began to be angry with James and John" (10:41). Though not stated, the anger is clearly directed at the attempt of James and John to obtain what they themselves think they want, the approval of their master, which they associate with prestige and power, and probably also with property (cf. 10:30).[10] The disciples then are little different from the crowd, although the distinctive thing about them is that they are supposed to be called out of the crowd into a relationship of trust and faith with their teacher and with one another.

The pronouncement of Jesus in 10:42–45 makes it quite clear that the ordinary model of human order, as represented by variants on kingship, is not to be the basis of the mimesis at work among them. Among the Gentiles rulers "lord it over" (*katakurieuousin*) their subjects, and their great ones "exercise authority" (*katexousiazousin*, "act according to *exousia*") over them. But among the disciples the great one is to be a *diakonos*, "deacon" or servant, and one accounted as first must be the *doulos*, slave of all. "For the Son of Man came not to be served (*diakonethenai*) but to serve (*diakonesai*), and to give his life a ransom for many (10:45). The imitation of the divine model of the Son of Man must replace the ancient religiocultural model of kingship, with its tyranny and scapegoating.

But the new model necessarily has contact with the old one; anything new in human culture can only emerge, grow out of, and change prior structures of language and culture. Therefore the new model of good mimesis depends on paradoxical reversal of the institution that, stemming from sacrifice, is the paradigmatic case of power and rivalry: kingship (see discussion in chapter 5). And at one point the saying appropriates a straightforwardly sacrificial word in an apparently literal sense: *ransom*.

As I pointed out in chapter 7, the word *ransom* (Greek *lutron*, a "freeing"), the "price of release" of the hostage, is deeply rooted in the substitutionary language of sacrifice. In the Septuagint the noun occurs twenty times. (The verb, *lutroo*, occurs many more times than that and translates either *gaal*, "redeem," "act as kinsman," or *padah*, "ransom," from the Hebrew text.) It denotes a redemption by purchase, the giving of money or other goods in order to gain release from punishment (Exod 21:30) or servitude (Lev 19:20; 25:51–52). Proverbs 6:35 speaks of the impossibility of *lutron* for the revenge of the cuckolded husband. It is the purchase price that releases land from ownership by one family and appropriation by another (Lev 25:24, 26). It may be used metonymically with "rewards" or "gifts" (Isa 45:13). It is a metaphor for wealth that preserves and enhances life in

Proverbs 13:8, undoubtedly because it is associated with redeeming someone from death, as in Exodus 21:30 and 30:12. Most of these occurrences of *lutron* render the Hebrew *geulah*, "redemption," or *kofer*, "ransom" (see discussion of the Hebrew root *kpr*, meaning "atone," "ransom," or "redeem," in chapter 2, under "Jacob and Esau"). All of these uses, even (or above all) the most metaphorical, do not stray far from a substitutional meaning rooted in sacrifice. The primary and generating context of the exchange indicated by *lutron* is seen in the offering of money to avert plague when a census of Israelites occurs (Exod 30:12) and in the role of the Levites as a ransom for Israel's firstborn males (Num 3:12, 46, 48, 49, 51; see 18:15).[11]

There is no gainsaying, then, *lutron* as an unmistakably sacrificial word that would be readily understood as such. However, as I asserted in the last chapter, I think Mark probably intends to say, in effect, "The human condition is such that only the price of the Son of Man's suffering and death will have the effect of loosening the bonds of the sacred social structure, enabling human beings to see what their predicament is and the kind of faith and action that will bring liberation." In other words, sacrificial language is used, necessarily, in order to break out of a sacrificial view of the world. In this sense, the Son of Man as "a ransom for many" is the Son of Man as a revelatory way, a means of access to community and nonviolence. Further argument for this understanding of Mark 10:42–45 will be given in the ensuing section on violence and sacrifice.

The disclosure of the good mimesis of God's reign is capped off in the Last Supper, 14:22–25. As the one who comes not to be served as a king or tyrant but to serve, Jesus acts out his willingness to give the full *lutron*, the release or liberation, in the form of his very life, his body and blood. Whatever the historical facts concerning a betrayal of Jesus, Judas' betrayal of Jesus is a perfect counterpoint to Jesus' enactment of the divine self-giving. We have no way of knowing whether or not Judas, moved by considerations of power, prestige, and property, as were all of the Twelve according to 10:35–45, became disappointed in Jesus' prospects and decided to get what he could, namely, property—here in the form of money. Any such conjectures aside, the mimetic contrast is perfect. Whereas Jesus declares he is willing to give himself, which would be an act of great value for the disciples, Judas, the betrayer (*paradidous*, literally "giver over"), gives him over for a substitutionary value, money. In doing this he pleases the chief priests (14:11), the officials in charge of redemptive substitution, that is, sacrifice; he thus mimetically confirms his own sense of value (i.e., "exchange") by giving over the valuable person to the priests. He has, indeed, a *perfect sacrificial understanding* of Jesus' value, of what Jesus means. Judas resorts to dominant sacrificial structures and imitates the desires of those with prestige and power over the sacrificial cult. In the world of the latter, the "ransom," the exchange price given in order to obtain the life of Jesus, functions in the same fashion as the quite legitimate payment for animals to be offered in the Temple. The leader of a subversive movement will be executed, and any further danger from the movement will be avoided. There is an immediate sense, then, in which the arrest (in Greek "giving over") of Jesus releases the disciples from danger. When one looks at the sacrificial situation in this way, it is easy to see why there was a tendency in the history of Christianity to validate Judas as betrayer and even view him positively.[12]

Even after the last meal and prayer in Gethsemane, the disciples are not able to imitate Jesus, but only one another. Jesus takes Peter, James, and John aside with him and asks them to watch, to stay awake (cf. 13:33–37) while he prays. They all three fall asleep. Yawning itself is a particularly mimetic activity. As in previous disputes, so now in Gethsemane, they do the same thing as the others. Then when Judas arrives with an armed crowd, "all of them deserted him and fled" (14:50). What one does, the other does.

As noted in the previous chapter, Peter not only deserts him along with the others but denies him three times lest he become a scapegoat of the crowd like his master (14:66–72). Judas betrays his master to the authorities that fear the people and brings an armed crowd to arrest him. The disciples flee from the armed crowd. Peter is unable to resist the mimetic constraints of the "bystanders," even "anathematizing" or cursing himself in order to assure them that he does not know the man of whom they speak (14:71). The question implied at the end of the Gospel narrative is whether the disciples who deserted Jesus will come back and rejoin their risen lord in Galilee. We know that they will, of course; the Gospel of Mark, by its very existence, presupposes the link of the Twelve and the others to Jesus. Meanwhile, however, the question is raised as to whether they are ready and willing to share in and enhance the good mimesis of the Son of Man. It is only the three women, Mary Magdalene, Mary mother of Joses, and Salome, clearly understood as disciples, who do not abandon him.

The mimetic desire and rivalry of the disciples and their corresponding inability to comprehend the call of Jesus as the Christ, Son of Man, and Suffering Servant is the most difficult aspect of Mark for the Christian tradition to understand and assimilate. Surely this depiction of the disciples was a scandal and a primary factor occasioning the writing of the Gospels of Matthew and Luke. Kelber hypothesizes that the written Gospel wrenched authority away from the oral tradition stemming from the apostles and relocated it in the written text controlled by the evangelist-author.[13] Whether or not he is right, I would stress that if the author's insight into the mimetic condition of the disciples is as acute as I have presented, then one of his primary intentions was to make sure that any hearers or readers of the narrative text would see themselves in the disciples. The disciples act exactly like the crowds and everyone else in Mark: they see themselves through one another's eyes; they view Jesus ambivalently as one who will give them power, prestige, and property but who also brings disaster upon them; and the contagion of sleep and abandonment spreads among them as readily as among all the others. As those close to Jesus, they offer simply a sharpened, highly focused view of the human condition. Mark's message is, in effect, "If there was hope for them even after their monumental mimetic mess-up—if their master is still faithful and still awaits them—well, there is hope for all the rest of us, too."

2. Violence and Sacrifice

According to Mark, the acts and teachings of Jesus overturn many distinctions of the Jewish Law and tradition. The Son of Man is the lord of the sabbath (2:28). Healing on the Sabbath is good even when it is not essential for saving life (3:1–6). Doing the will of God is more important than family or blood relationships (3:34). What comes out of a person—what one says and does—is more important than laws of purity and diet (7:1–23). The Temple should not be a place of sacrificial substitution but of prayer (11:15–19; more on the Temple below). Jesus' exousia— what he does out of his "substance" or "presence"—is not as that of the scribes (1:22). For the Gospel of Mark, this means his authority does not come from the people or from a tradition validated by popular consent but from God.

Those who follow Jesus leave the crowd and go to "the other side" (4:35–41). They are to beware of the leaven of Herod and the leaven of the Pharisees (8:15). They are to understand Jesus as the *new point of differentiation*, as the new occasion of God's revelation and God's rule, for the Messiah–Son of God is the Son of Man as Suffering Servant (8:31–33).

It is difficult to tell whether Mark preserves a strong historical core from the actual lifetime of Jesus, with its attendant conflicts due to the colonial rule of Rome, burdensome taxation, and loss of land and heavy unemployment.[14] Some of the sayings in Q, better represented in Matthew and Luke, probably reflect the situation closer to Jesus' own time. It is more likely that Mark reflects the turmoil surrounding the period just prior to, during, and perhaps shortly after the Jewish-Roman War, 66–70 C.E. Both the Sicarii ("dagger-men") and Zealots had claimed messianic leaders. The Temple was destroyed, never to be rebuilt, and many members of the Jesus movement probably fled from Judea and perhaps from every part of Palestine. In this cauldron of disaster and change, there were undoubtedly charismatic preachers and prophets who were more troublesome than ever in their rivalry with each other, which simultaneously would have pitted individuals and groups against one another. Such must have been the prevailing conditions for Mark to have had Jesus warn the four disciples against following anyone who claims, *ego eimi*, "I am the one!" (13:6). Eschatological proclaimers announcing that the Christ has come are not to be believed (13:21). False Christs and false prophets will work miracles and try to lead astray the chosen ones (13:22).

The Gospel of Mark intimates that the turmoil and violence of the events Jesus prophesies are already adumbrated in his encounters with human foes and demons. Dispute over what is permissible on the Sabbath leads to a conspiracy of Pharisees and Herodians to destroy him (3:6). As already pointed out, the battle with demons was simultaneously a struggle with the scribes (or Pharisees). The expulsion of demons is reason for the people of Gerasa to ask Jesus to depart from their area (5:1–20). In spite of the difference maintained in the narrative between Jesus and John the Baptist, Herod insists on viewing them as the same; John's fate, played out in Herod's mimetic obsession both with John as an authoritative prophet and with the approval of the banquet crowd, is a foreshadowing of Jesus' death due to the preoccupation of religious and political authorities with maintaining popular order and their own status.

Jesus himself performs an act that may be viewed as "violent," the attack on the Temple. Bruce Chilton, in a forthcoming work, describes it as Jesus' "occupation of the Temple" in order to purify it. This occupation and purification is part of his program of proclaiming forgiveness as the condition of sacrifice, rather than vice versa.[15] Jesus did not reject sacrifice (e.g., Matt 5:23–24; Mark 1:40–45) but required its purification based, first of all, as stated above, on the condition of the forgiveness of sins.

Chilton's purpose is to give a plausible historical reconstruction of Jesus' attitude toward the Temple and sacrifice. Such a historical reconstruction is a feasible and worthwhile project. It is not my intention here to engage in historical reconstruction, but to focus on the Jesus tradition as it has come to the Gospel stage. I would simply make two comments on historical reconstruction as it relates to my task.

First, it is important in this study not to concede the "world without reference" of structuralism and poststructuralism—a world utterly made up of signifiers referring to other signifiers, ad infinitum. What is wrong with this contemporary "metalanguage" is not the notion that nothing is known and communicated apart from interpretation, but that there is no beginning or point of departure that can be focused, defined, and discussed (except for some principle like Derrida's "différance," which involves starting from a discussion of a concept that is a nonconcept that cannot be discussed or debated). Thus, just as I stated in chapter 3 concerning the Exodus, reference to a historical core, no matter how transmitted, embellished, and overdetermined, is crucial for my reading of Scripture. And indeed, the Gospel texts are analogous to the Book of Exodus in that both stem from a group viewed as subversive by political and religious authorities and both revolve around an innocent victim, collective in Exodus (the Hebrews) and an individual in the Gospels (Jesus). Therefore it is important to note the trend, if not consensus, in current Gospel criticism that the protest in the Temple, however labeled, was a historical event. E. P. Sanders goes so far as to identify it as the best starting point for understanding the historical Jesus and his relation to the Jewish context of his time.[16]

Second, in placing Jesus in the context of his time, the intention of those like Sanders and Chilton is to counter the influence of prejudice in New Testament scholarship, especially in Germany, which has unduly separated Jesus from the Jewish matrix. The problem is to identify what distinguishes Jesus and the early Jesus movement within this matrix. The Pharisees, who were probably the forerunners of rabbinic Judaism, were not "Judaism" in the first century of the common era; they were one very important grouping within it. The Essenes were not "Judaism"; they were one important grouping. The Sadducees made up the priestly class, whose authority was threatened by the Pharisees and the emergence of the synagogue. There were various apocalyptic and communal movements, such as those gathered around Judas the Galilean, Simon bar Giora, and others. In other words, one cannot take a normative concept of "Judaism," such as doctrines and practices associated with the Pharisees, and say "This is Judaism in the first century C.E." These considerations lead me to the observation that not only the early Jesus movement but the Gospel themselves are "Jewish." They undoubtedly employ Hellenistic forms, and the gospel form itself is, arguably, a literary expression representing an encounter of the early movement with Hellenistic culture. But that does not mean they are any less Jewish, either in the appropriation of non-Jewish forms[17] or in terms of the historical and literary core that generated them. Even those aspects that Chilton calls "Christian *haggadah*" (homiletical exposition in rabbinic texts), such as the overturning of the money changers' tables, have a certain logic stemming from the Jewish core tradition, whether or not they have a historical referent.

I will therefore deal with the Temple incident in Mark's account as centrally significant for understanding Jesus and the Gospels, with full recognition that aspects of it may amount to "Christian *haggadah*."

First, then, back to the observation that it is reported as a "violent" act. Part of the reported action, blocking the way of traffic, perhaps involving the obtaining of animals for sacrifice, is more in the mode of nonviolent protest. Overturning the tables of the money changers may be viewed as "violent," but it should be noted that the entire protest is of very short duration. It is not narrated as though there is any intent to harm anyone, to maintain a long occupation, or to assert Jesus' power over the Temple and its dealings. It is clearly in the tradition of the prophets' dramatic representations of Israel's situation and God's word of judgment (see the second part of chapter 5). In a situation of oppression and a brewing mimetic crisis, it is impossible to avoid the taint of violence if one is to act decisively. The word *decision* itself, a "cutting off" or "cutting from," already suggests that the harmonious reconciliation of all persons and elements in a situation will not take place. This is the human condition in the world of differences, especially when these differences no longer manage the mimetic desire and rivalry that are ever present and effective.

As stated in chapter 7, I think Hamerton-Kelly is right in inferring that this attack was not simply in the form of a cleansing of an institution that was to be affirmed in its pristine or ideal form; it represented instead *an attack on the entire sacrificial system.* Moreover, in the Gospel of Mark it appears quite clear that Jesus was not simply purifying an institution of which he basically approved.[18] The framing incidents of the fig tree, 11:12–14 and 11:20–25, as well as the pronouncement in 13:1–2, indicate a more radical view, a denial of the Temple's *raison d'être* in the dawning new age. What the author of Mark perceives (or receives from the earlier tradition, as the case may be) is that the changing of money was directly tied to a system of substitutions that is rooted in sacrifice. The Temple was an institution sheltering and supporting a system of substitutions whose end was the offering of animal victims to God in the place of the human offerer. (See again the discussion on the Gospel of Mark in chapter 7.)

What is crucial to grasp in the Temple pericope, and what at the same time provides a link both to the Gospel's understanding of sacrifice and the historical reason for Jesus' notoriety and death, is the combination of popular response and the reaction of the priestly authorities. "When the chief priests and the scribes heard it, they kept looking for a way to kill him; for they were afraid of him, because the whole crowd was spellbound by his teaching" (11:18). The crowd is the ever present factor, clamoring for "more of" Jesus, more of both his teaching and his healing power. Those identified as "chief priests and elders and scribes" (11:27) wanted to arrest him, "but they feared the crowd" (12:12). Later on they plot to arrest and kill him secretly, but not during the festival "or there may be a riot among the people" (14:2). But the crowd, those people whom the chief priests manipulated and stirred up, later shouted for his crucifixion; so Pilate, "wishing to satisfy the crowd, released Barabbas for them; and after flogging Jesus, he handed him over to be crucified" (15:15).

The Jerusalem Temple was not simply a "religious" institution in some restricted sense; it was the basis of a system simultaneously religious, political, and economic.[19] From the priests who appropriated the offered meat and the animal skins to the officials who administered monetary exchange, acquired animals ritually clean, and distributed funds for communal use, it can surely be characterized as a socioeconomic center. As such, it was undoubtedly like other great temples in various parts of the world. The Temple was the site of *exchange* par excellence, and this exchange stemmed from and was centered in the offering of sacrifices.

The Temple is supervised by the priests under the chief priest, but their power and authority depends on the management of the *people* who come to fulfill their socioreligious duties. As stated at a number of points in earlier chapters, sacrificial ritual is the dividing point between order and confusion. The altar is the primary point of sacred space that defends the prohibitions of the community and grounds its myth. The altar and the prohibition are the spatial and verbal safeguards against the crisis that is reenacted and resolved in sacrifice. Without altar and prohibition, people "go wild" in the sameness of mimetic undifferentiation. So Moses observes when he comes down from the mountain: he "saw that the people were running wild (for Aaron had let them run wild, to the derision of their enemies)"(Exod 32:25). The source of the Temple's power is the obedience of the people, but if a sizable number of the latter should begin to protest in any way against the authority of the priesthood, and above all against the validity of sacrificial offerings, the situation would be understandably perceived as a real threat to the ancient order of things, to the whole system of differences that has been established between orderly and disorderly, clean and unclean, inside and outside, superior and inferior—a threat, in short, to the total language of signs and gestures and marks that make up a culture.

It is no wonder, then, that the opponents of Jesus feared him, for in fact they feared the people who listened to him (12:12), who seemed to be ready to "run wild" under his spell.

My own surmise about the historical core of this narrated incident is that Jesus engaged in a prophetic symbolic action, a basically nonviolent protest or witness at the Temple that aroused many people and sealed his fate with both Roman and Jewish authorities. His disciples, who went underground when the authorities arrested Jesus, perceived him both as steadfast in announcing God's rule that transcended the Temple and what it stood for and as steadfast in his loyalty to them. He was one who betrayed neither his message nor his followers, and this was surely one of the main factors in their concentration on him as the center of a new community. In fact, their guilt over their betrayal in the face of his steadfast love reinforced their sense of his importance.

The author of Mark, taking up a tradition that had already filtered and expanded the meaning of Jesus for the new community, juxtaposes Jesus to the Temple as the new point of differentiation not only for the Jews but also for the Gentiles. That is, he is God's difference, the exception, the stone that has "become the head of the corner" (12:10), which offers a different kind of *lutron* for many. It is a "ransom" or "redemption" that releases in the way the Suffering Servant of the Lord releases those who understand him: by providing an objective, historical model that evokes a sympathetic identification with his willingness to take upon himself the consequences of our transgressions. It is liberation from the principle of punishment or vengeance that underlies any sacrificial or substitutionary system. The *lutron* of the Son of Man is given to end the cycle of mimetic desire and mimetic rivalry and victimization and sacrifice, for with the God revealed in the Son of Man there is no punishment; there is no violence; there is no need for exclusivistic differentiation into those who are superior and those who are inferior, those who are inside and those who are outside. Therefore when Jesus says, "The Son of Man came not to be served but to serve, and to give his life a ransom for many," the Temple and all it stands for is brought proleptically to an end. The "sacrifice" offered by those who take the Son of Man for their model is not in the offering of a victim, whether a human, an animal, or even themselves as "victims," but in the willingness to commit themselves to the Son of Man and his community as formed and informed by this divine self-giving. If this commitment necessitates giving one's life in a literal sense, it is not because "martyrdom" in that sense is sought. To be authentically a martyr or witness is to seek not to be served but to serve, whatever that may entail.

"But," one may object, "if this was the intention of Jesus, or at least of Mark's Jesus, why was it necessary to use such an obviously sacrificial word as *lutron?*" There is no denying the force of the question, for using such a word and the concept that lies behind it seems somewhat like fighting fire with fire or poison with poison—the strategy itself is sacrificial, based on an exchange that brings the disease or destruction to an end with a "remedy" that is just as dangerous as the problem or malady. Indeed, it may in turn have to be "managed" or "controlled" just as carefully as what precipitated its use in the first place. My response to this question has to take the form of agreeing with the thrust of the question to this extent: within a given system of language and culture (and I think probably within *any* system), in order to break out into new insight, new paths of discovery, new ways of forming human community, it is necessary to employ and be determined by what the system offers. If transformation of anything—such as the principle of sacrifice—actually occurs, then those involved must wrestle with its reality and be influenced by it. Otherwise, the result is abstract and abstruse and serves only as an ideological overlay. For example, the Priestly narrative of the Torah presents a grand vision of nonviolence in the human sphere—as such, worthy of meditation and respect. But this vision is impaired to a great extent by its inability to account for the human condition as it actually is (see chapter 1, under "Brothers in Conflict"). And hidden behind the vision is the displacement of the problem of desire and violence to the use of animals for sacrifice.

Finally, of course, it has to be acknowledged that given language and culture as they are, one can never be absolutely certain of the "ransom," of "liberation" from the outworkings of mimetic desire. The Gospels are not an island of absolute certainty available apart from all the contaminations of the human yen for a source of uncontested power and authority. Here is where faith enters in—faith that what is revealed there through human language and culture comes from beyond this setting where differences rage in combat with confusion, disclosing One who is different from us only in not establishing differences between God and human beings.

B. The Truth of the Victim

Girard has stated concerning the truth of the Christ and the Incarnation, "Since the truth about violence will not abide in the community, but must inevitably be driven out, its only chance of being heard is when it is in the process of being driven out, in the brief moment that precedes its destruction as the victim. The victim therefore has to reach out at the very moment when his mouth is being shut by violence."[20] He says also, in response to the question whether there is a privileged position in language from which the absolute truth can become known, "I agree that no such stance exists. That is why the Word that is affirmed as absolutely true never speaks except from the position of a victim in the process of being expelled. Its presence among us is not humanly explicable."[21]

Girard did not intend this to be understood literally in the Gospel accounts, that is, to postulate the necessity of attending primarily to what Jesus says at some chronological point just before he is executed. Nor do I take it that Girard has in mind exclusively what Jesus is reported to have said in his last moments on the cross. That sort of literal approach would be neither literarily nor theologically fruitful, given that important sayings and deeds relating to his suffering and death are scattered throughout the Gospels. Nonetheless, it would be interesting to consider how the Gospels dramatically focus the response of the Innocent Victim as he faces ultimate expulsion from the prevailing human community. Therefore I will include the Gospels' narration of some of his sayings during the crucifixion. I will take Mark's text as point of departure but comment also on the other Gospel accounts. From the standpoint of the Gospel witnesses, what is the truth of the victim being revealed in expulsion (execution) of the Innocent Victim?

1. Silence

The first thing that strikes the reader of Mark's narrative of the Passion is how *little* Jesus says from the time of his arrest to the moment of his death. His *silence* is the overriding theme that has to be taken into account. According to Mark, there are only four occasions when Jesus responds verbally to his arrest, hearings, and execution: at the time of the arrest (14:48–49), before the council and the high priest (14:62), before Pilate (15:2), and on the cross (15:34). All four are very brief. It is worth reviewing the first three in order to put his outcry from the cross in context.

First the crowd, which is something like a loosely organized posse, comes with Judas, who identifies him. The betrayer kisses him, saying, "Master!" The crowd seizes him; there is a skirmish in which someone cuts off the ear of the high priest's slave. Jesus then says, "Have you come out with swords and clubs to arrest me as though I were a bandit? Day after day I was with you in the temple teaching, and you did not arrest me. But let the scriptures be fulfilled" (14:48–49). At this point, "All of [the disciples] deserted him and fled" (14:50).

Two comments on this passage. First, the evangelist orders it around the fulfillment of Scripture, specifically the Servant in Second Isaiah. Jesus is treated as though he is a robber or a bandit ("he was numbered with the transgressors," Isa 53:12), and all his followers deserted him ("all we like sheep have gone astray," Isa 53:6). Second, the crowd or mob arresting him comes by stealth at night rather than taking him openly at the Temple. At the Temple, as we have seen, there was the danger that others of the people, other "crowds," would have defended him and turned against the authorities. Jesus is thus caught and "seized" between the crowds of the Temple who posed a threat to the authorities and the crowd manipulated by the authorities.

The next time that Jesus speaks is in the hearing before "the chief priests and the whole council" (Luke adds "assembly of the elders"). In Mark, Jesus breaks his characteristic silence about his identity and vocation. After Jesus remains silent during the testimony of false witnesses, the high priest asks Jesus, "Are you the Messiah, the Son of the Blessed One?" (14:61). Jesus said, "I am; and you will see the Son of Man seated at the right hand of the Power, and coming with the clouds of heaven" (14:62). In Matthew and Luke, who are concerned only peripherally with Mark's secrecy motif, Jesus is more reticent. Matthew presents him as making the Son of Man pronouncement, perhaps drawn from Psalm 110:1 and Daniel 7:13–14. However, in Matthew his initial response to the high priest's question is, in effect, "That's what *you* say" (Matt 26:64, "you have said"). Luke has Jesus say, as it were, "You wouldn't believe me whatever I told you." The pronouncement that follows, which is decidedly apocalyptic in Mark and Matthew, is shorn of its apocalyptic motif in Luke, whose text does not speak of "coming with the clouds of heaven" (Luke 22:69). Then they *all* ask him whether he is the Son of God, and he replies, "You say that I am" (22:70).

My own reading of the synoptic parallels is that Mark's account is ironic and paradoxical. At the very moment that Jesus is in the power of his foes, particularly the priestly authorities, he responds to the chief priest, the official supervising all sacrifices in the Temple, with a revelation formula, "I am (the one)." The revelation formula is then connected to the Son of Man's ultimate triumph. What the chief priest cannot know, but what the hearer or reader of Mark is supposed to understand, is the secret of the loaves (6:52): as the bread was broken in the wilderness and satisfied the people, with many pieces left over, so also would the suffering and death of the Son of Man be the liberation—the *lutron*—of many from sin and violence, even the sin and violence both redeemed and perpetuated in the Temple. The resurrection and final reign of the Son of Man in a divine-human community is affirmed in apocalyptic language.

Matthew and Luke portray Jesus as refusing or deflecting the high priest's question, because they do not perceive it as ironic, only paradoxical, that Jesus would stand as he does before any human authorities. Matthew and Luke both have what could be called ironic paradoxes, but they are not part of a literary style that the reader has to decode, and they lie elsewhere than in the events leading up to the crucifixion. For Matthew, the great paradox, in the sense of what is surprising or unexpected, is the discovery that the Son of Man is encountered when one assists the "least" of the members of God's family (25:31–46). For Luke, it is the discovery of the Lord "on the way" (in experience, in tradition), above all in the common meals (Luke 24).

Pilate's interrogation and condemnation of Jesus is one of the most interesting scenes in the canonical Gospels. One of the striking facets thereof is the unanimity of the synoptics that Jesus does not answer Pilate's question. Pilate asks him, "Are you the King of the Jews?" And Jesus replies, "You have said so" (Mark 15:2/Matt 27:11/Luke 23:3). In Mark and Matthew the accusers then bring further charges, and Pilate asks Jesus to respond, but he remains silent.

This response, "you have said," is a kind of "yes" but involves throwing the question back to the questioner; it is basically the same as Jesus' reply to the chief priest in Matthew 26:64; it is similar, but in slightly extended form, to what he says to all those at the hearing, according to Luke 22:70. Pilate's question is an obvious trap, just as the chief priest's question was, for to identify oneself as the Messiah would be viewed as both blasphemous and seditious. There is no way that Jesus can answer the question in such a way as to satisfy the Temple authorities, Roman authorities, crowds, and disciples. With his intimate followers he had sought to redefine "messiah" in terms of the Son of Man who suffers and dies and is raised again like the Servant of the Lord in Isaiah, but even the disciples had not understood, according to Mark. To be true to his companions, even though they deserted him, and to be true to his mission, he remains silent.

Pilate perceives that the real issue in Jesus' arrest is *envy* (Mark 15:10)—the religious authorities' envy of his popularity with the crowds. But now the crowd appearing before Pilate is one stirred up by the chief priests, and Pilate shows himself in the same light as the priests. "So Pilate, wishing to satisfy the crowd, released Barabbas for them; and after flogging Jesus, he handed him over to be crucified" (15:15). Through this episode and the mock coronation by the soldiers (Mark 15:16–20/Matt 27:27–31/John 19:1–3; see also Gospel of Peter 2:5b–3:9; Acts of Pilate 10:1a), Jesus remains silent. The mock ceremony ascribed to the Roman soldiers fits the well-known ritual pattern of taking a prisoner or otherwise marginal person as a mock king.[22] In some instances this person is executed. The mock ritual is thus based on a very serious substitutionary process: the mock king for the real king, and the real king for the people (see discussion in first part of chapter 5). But in the Gospel witness to Jesus' Passion, not only the obvious mock ritual but the whole persecution process is revealed as "mockery," as the persecution of the innocent victim.

Behind the king is always the people, who in the form of a "crowd" become volatile, both to themselves and the government; without the king and his surrogates they become a mob. From the standpoint of mythical, sacrificial thinking, the king holds office by virtue of what the "others" say. This is the ironic meaning of Jesus' reply to Pilate in John, when Pilate asks him, "'Are you the King of the Jews?' Jesus answered, 'Do you ask this on your own, or did others (*alloi*) tell you about me?'" (John 18:33–34). Since all the "*alloi*," the "others," are rivals who gauge themselves through one another's eyes in desiring the other's object of desire, the scapegoat is necessary so that the mimetic process will be managed; the king, as the scapegoat become ruler, is the magnet and director of these mimetic forces. His power and authority are created by "others." In John's drama of salvation, Pilate is predetermined to play out the scene in ironic ignorance, for he has no basis for understanding the king—the truth, the logos—that comes from outside the cycle of the mimetic process, that comes from beyond the others, that transcends the realm of differences.

2. God-Forsakenness

According to Mark, Jesus says nothing further through the whole process of humiliation and pain on the cross until midafternoon, when he cries out, "My God, my God, why have you forsaken me?" (15:34). This saying is transcribed by Mark from Aramaic; the preservation of a few Aramaic words and phrases in the Greek-speaking church (e.g., Abba, "father"; Maranatha, "our Lord, come!") is probably because of their significance. There is no doubt that Jesus' cry is an Aramaic version of Psalm 22:1:

> My God, my God, why have you forsaken me?
> Why are you so far from helping me, from the words of my groaning?

Psalm 22 is one of the many descriptions of persecution in the Book of Psalms. It is one of the "seminal" sources that Mark uses in shaping his narrative about Jesus.[23]

The psalm begins with the petitioner's sense of abandonment and moves on to affirm the holiness of the God who can be trusted, who delivered the ancestors (vv. 3–5). The public mockery (vv. 6–8) and distribution of the victim's clothing by casting lots (v. 18; cf. Job 6:27) are obviously in the mind of the author of Mark as he tells the story. The use of lots to divide up the clothing is a metonym (or image by association) of the entire scapegoating process. The choosing of the victim must not produce discord, so two conditions must be met: the selection must be by chance (or by "fate") and the victim must be one who is defenseless, without means of retaliation. The dividing of the clothing is a suggestive trace of the more primitive *diasparagmos* associated with the Dionysus cult and known in some form from many accounts of sacrificial practices (see epigraphs to chapter 5). In other words, the distribution of the clothing is a metonym of the tearing and eating of the victim's body—except, of course, the use of lots imposes a ritual control.

The psalm, however, does not quite succeed in disentangling the god of the sacred social order from the true God who delivers the oppressed and whose Spirit is one of advocacy and comfort for the innocent victim. The God who abandons the victim is the God of the crowd, the *vox populi*. Of course, the speaker in the psalm does appear to affirm his ultimate restitution, even if the scapegoat mechanism is not clarified. God will bring benefits to those afflicted (v. 26), God will rule, and future generations will serve him.

That the Son of Man is not ultimately delivered over, betrayed, abandoned to the voice of the people is affirmed in the witness of the Gospels to the resurrection. The Innocent Victim, experiencing and revealing what all arbitrarily chosen victims feel, expresses the despair of being *cast out* of the social order in every way: re-jection, e-jection, de-jection, ab-jection. The divine nature of the victim is not *created* by his death; that sequence belongs to the ancient mode of sacrifice and myth. In this case, divinity is *confirmed* by the drama of his "life after death."

3. The Implications of Silence and Abjection

In one sense the silence of Jesus in Mark and his cry to God may seem like a void or an immense darkness that threatens to overwhelm the story. On the other hand, informed hearers and readers will know this is not the case if they attend to the full narrative of Mark, whose specific narrative time is demonstrably connected to a broader *story time*. The narrative time is the scope of events plotted and narrated within the text itself. The story time is the totality of past and future events stated or implied in the plotted narrative time. The story time of Mark includes the Scriptures from the Jewish past and the fulfillment of God's reign in the future.[24] There are two things about the seminal parts of the scriptural heritage that stand out in Mark's witness to the crucifixion of Jesus: (1) As already discussed, Jesus as the Servant of the Lord who is *silent* in the face of persecution (Isa 53:7), and (2) the identification of the Victim with the persecuted (Ps 22; cf. Ps 41:5–10). In all these passages the one who is persecuted will be vindicated and restored (Isa 53:11–12; Ps 22:21–24; 41:11–12).

> For [the LORD] did not despise or abhor
> the affliction of the afflicted;
> he did not hide his face from me,
> but heard when I cried to him.
> (Ps 22:24)

The one who "poured himself out to death, and was numbered with the transgressors," who "bore the sin of many, and made intercession for the transgressors," this one—"out of his anguish he shall see light" (Isa 53:12, 11a).[25]

However, in the Christian *hagaddic* process the author of Luke-Acts and John filled out the crucifixion scene using what was implied in the specific story time, the scriptural seeds of the gospel. In some instances the writers may have been privy to something transmitted in an earlier tradition of the crucifixion. Be that as it may, four of the remaining six sayings from the cross are clearly understood as the fulfillment of Scripture. These I will comment on briefly.

a. As Jesus and the other two condemned men are brought to Golgotha, Luke reports that Jesus says, "Father, forgive them; for they do not know what they are doing" (Luke 23:34). Some of the important ancient manuscripts omit this quotation. However, practically the same understanding is attributed in Acts to Peter in the context of a speech to a crowd at the Temple: "And now, friends [Greek 'brothers'], I know that you acted in ignorance [in crucifying Jesus], as did also your rulers" (Acts 3:17; cf. 7:60). The point of forgiving those who do not know what they are doing is not to picture Jesus as a really nice Christian who *overlooks* the bad things some evil people are doing to him. The people responsible for executing Jesus were probably no better and no worse than the great majority of us human beings at any given time in a particular culture, especially if we take into account that rulers must maintain order, which means concretely controlling conflicts, eliminating subversion, and generally doing what is necessary to ensure *survival.*

No, the persecutors are to be forgiven because *they do not know* what they are doing. As Girard has said, "In this passage we are given the first definition of the unconscious in human history, that from which all the others originate and develop in weaker form: the Freudians will push the dimension of persecution into the background and the Jungians will eliminate it altogether."[26] In other words, what is unique about the Passion is not that evil is done to an innocent victim. The uniqueness lies in the revelation of the scapegoat mechanism. The Gospel witness to Jesus as the Christ is centered in the way his death brings it to light. Luke wishes to spell out quite clearly this disclosure that generates the core of the tradition: Jesus as the revelation of what God has already revealed through the Law and the Prophets, as the perfect revelation, as the Innocent Victim, teaches and *enacts* that the persecutors *do not know what they are doing.* As Girard has rightly stated, "That is why they must be pardoned."[27] And those that are disciples, whose eyes are opened (Luke 24:31), will likewise teach and enact this understanding, as Peter does (Acts 3:17) and Stephen (Acts 7:60).

Luke's representation of Jesus' forgiveness of his executioners involves a creative reshaping and extension of Isaiah 53:12, he "made intercession for the transgressors." It is not completely clear in the prophetic text that the Servant-Prophet intercedes even for those who lynch him, but Luke makes that explicit. He also adds, as discussed immediately above, that this pardon is based not only on divine compassion but also on the ignorance—of social structures and language camouflaging victimization—in which the persecutors are entrapped.

b. In Luke Jesus cries out in the moment just before he dies, "Father, into thy hands I commit my spirit!" (23:46, RSV). This sentence is obviously based on Psalm 31:5, "Into your hand I commit my spirit; you have redeemed me, O LORD, faithful God." The Redeemer is the one who reveals, first of all, that God has redeemed him. This psalm is another psalm combining lament and complaint over persecution with affirmation of God's faithfulness and compassion. The speaker's description of his state (vv. 11–13) sounds like a composite portrait of Job and Jeremiah. The main thrust of the psalm is to affirm trust in the God of victims.

c. Mark and Matthew report that immediately prior to crucifixion the soldiers offered Jesus wine mixed with bitters of some sort (Matt 27:34; Mark 15:23), evidently as a sedative. This he refused. Subsequently, according to these two Gospels, bystanders offered him a sponge filled with vinegar, which he evidently drinks (Matt 27:48; Mark 15:36). The purpose of the latter in the context of the Gospel accounts seems to have been to assuage his pain just enough to enable him to last a little longer—whether simply in order that the bystanders might enjoy his continued suffering or that they might see whether Elijah would come, it is not clear. The offering of vinegar is an allusion to Psalm 69:21, "They gave me poison for food, and for my thirst they gave me vinegar to drink." The setting is once again persecution of the speaker (vv. 19–21), who has expressed his distress and implored God, "Draw near to me, redeem me, set me free because of my enemies" (v. 18).

The Fourth Gospel makes it a point to call attention to the vinegar as fulfillment of Scripture (John 19:28–29; note 19:30, to be discussed below). But in keeping with John's portrayal of the Savior who constantly takes the initiative in a preordained drama, Jesus himself says, "I thirst." It is the "world's" last chance to recognize the Victim, the Logos that comes into his own world and his own place but is not accepted (1:10–11). But rather than water, the soldiers give him vinegar.

In the thirst of Jesus the Gospel of John alludes ironically to two interrelated themes. One is the persecution of the Innocent Victim. Jesus had told his disciples that the hatred of the persecutors fulfills what is written in the "law": "They hated me without a cause" (15:25, quoting Ps 35:19). There is no reason for scapegoating a victim—except for the most basic reason in a sacrificial culture, which is that "it is better ... to have one man die for the people than to have the whole nation destroyed" (11:50).

The other theme is the living water. Just as the Samaritan woman at Jacob's well did not know that the one who asked for a drink was the fountain of water "gushing up to eternal life" (4:14), so the executioners do not understand the request for water. Jesus is the human form of the Word, the Spirit that witnesses to the truth and defends and comforts, as the *parakletos*, those who need an advocate (14:15–31; 15:25–27). The implication, then, of the request for water is that those who have come to know and believe in the Son-Spirit will recognize him and his presence wherever and whenever they are victims or are in the situation of aiding a victim.

d. The final saying to be considered cannot be separated from the drinking of the vinegar. "When Jesus had received the [sour] wine, he said, 'It is finished.' Then he bowed his head and gave up his spirit" (John 19:30). This final act of the persecutors, that of giving vinegar or sour wine to their victim rather than a drink of water to assuage his thirst, completes the drama of the Truth crucified in the Innocent Victim. The will of the Father has been done, his work completed (cf. 4:34). With the completion of this work, the spirit given up in death will be breathed on the disciples as the Holy Spirit (20:22). The fulfillment of the Father's will, which includes the unmasking of the structures whose generative heart is violence, ends in the expulsion from life of "the only agent who is capable of escaping from these structures and freeing us from their dominance…. A nonviolent deity can only signal his existence to mankind by having himself driven out by violence—by demonstrating that he is not able to establish himself in the Kingdom of Violence."[28] Or, in the words of Jesus in the Fourth Gospel, "Nevertheless I tell you the truth: it is to your advantage that I go away, for if I do not go away, the Advocate (*parakletos*) will not come to you; but if I go, I will send him to you" (John 16:7).

C. Conclusion

The truth of the human condition is the truth of a mimesis that both gives rise to and structures desire, the wish to acquire what the other has and is imagined to desire and of being what the other is. This leads inevitably to conflict and rivalry and will issue in violence unless averted or overcome by a differentiation process that requires that in the event of crisis, a victim be found "by chance" (even if many reasons be given) in order to regain the stable order of differences that supposedly reigned before the crisis began.

There is another mimesis—or another side to mimesis, for in and of itself it is a neutral capability of the brain and of every aspect of systems that can be considered "human." But the point of our study from Genesis to the Gospels has been to show that the "good mimesis" can only really be known from the standpoint of the victim. And the victim has to gain—or be given—a voice. To repeat part of the quotation of Girard given at the beginning of part B of this chapter, "Since the truth about violence will not abide in the community, but must inevitably be driven out, its only chance of being heard is when it is in the process of being driven out, in the brief moment that precedes its destruction as the victim."

The voice of the victim is heard fragmentarily in many texts and other witnesses from the past, and in the Greek tragedians it begins to arrive at a thematic coherence that is powerful, although not sustained by the ongoing Greek cultural tradition. It is first in ancient Israel that narrator-thinkers and prophets begin to view their past, their seminal stories and figures, and their hope for the future from the victim's standpoint—from the standpoint not of the sacred social order and generative principle of exclusionary violence, but from the perspective of those who are oppressed and who are aided and defended by a power and a presence not associated with the sacred social order as such, but with a new covenant community: YHWH, God of Israel.

The truth of the victim and the potential of the innocent victim to uncover our structures of desire and violence is articulated in the Servant of the Lord (Isa 52:13–53:12) but is expressed in its most sustained form in the Gospel witness to Jesus as Christ–Son of God–Son of Man–Lord. These titles mean "the only agent who is capable of escaping from these structures [of violence] and freeing us from their dominance." The only agent is a human being, because we are capable of comprehending only the human that meets us within the structures and conditions of our human existence. But this only agent must be God, or we must meet God in this agent, for only God can be subject to the structures of desire and violence, overcome them, and show us the way of liberation. "Very God of very God and very man of very man": that is the truth of the innocent victim that can heal us.

The Gospel witness to the truth of the victim as expressed in the good mimesis of the Innocent Victim may be epitomized in the voice of the latter during those moments immediately preceding his destruction as a victim. The word of this voice is revealed above all in silence before the accusations and conflicting desires of the persecutors and in a cry of anguish, of utter abjection, over the casting out, the rejection and ejection perpetrated by the sacred social order, for which the word *god* typically stands.

But since the witness of silence and god-forsakenness that gives voice to the victim is grounded in and surrounded by the testimonies of Scripture, which is the text of faith's story, then this twofold witness is further unfolded as the power and authority of divine love in revealing and forgiving violence, whose cultural foundations are perpetuated out of ignorance or "unconsciousness." It is explicated as the trust of the victim in the God who redeems or releases the victim. It is clarified as the call of the victim to the persecutors to learn the truth through coming to his aid. And it is made known as the victim's departure, allowing himself to be murdered, so that the truth may be known—that is, so that the Spirit may be with the witnesses to this truth.

9

Conclusion:
"A Citty upon a Hill"

A. The Two Traditions

John Winthrop could not have known all the implications or foreseen all the consequences of his allusion to the metaphor of the messianic community, the new *ekklesia*, from the Sermon on the Mount. The United States of America has become historically what the faith and hermeneutics of the Puritan forebears dictated: "a city built on a hill [that] cannot be hid" (Matt 5:14). I don't mean to imply that the United States as we know it today is the fulfillment of Jesus' words according to Matthew or as the Puritans understood it. I do believe, however, that the destiny of the United States is part of a Spirit-guided historical process that is decisively centered in the disclosure of the Innocent Victim and is moving toward God's good end of judgment and restoration of all things. I do not have a map or timetable of America's place in all of this, and I certainly think that witness to the God of the Scriptures is misguided if it seeks to assert the *chosenness, the special destiny* of a people as *superiority,* as inevitable triumph culturally and militarily over other nations. This is precisely the mistake Heidegger made with respect to German culture and the aims of National Socialism.

America is a city upon a hill through a combination of its own pretensions to be the new chosen people and its transmission of a Judeo-Christian heritage that exists through and in spite of pervasive secularism, "separation of church and state," and an ostensibly strict division of private from public spheres in dealing with morals and religion. This distinctive combination of historical patterns and convictions involves American culture, society, and government in many contradictions that will not be easily resolved: Are we responsible for the rest of the world or primarily for ourselves? If responsible for the rest of the world, should we serve as peacemakers by policing militarily or by pursuing reconciliation through diplomacy? Should we develop markets and various business enterprises at home and abroad as free expressions of capitalism or control economic exploitation for the good of our nation and other peoples? Should we affirm and legislate the right of private enterprise, private property, personal achievement, and so on, or assure that the "underdog," the victim of exploitation, the person who is poor, aged, or infirm has an equal opportunity to participate in the good and enjoy the goods of the human community? Is our national unity something like a "church" or an "assembly of the Lord," or is it more like an athletic league whose teams and individuals compete to best one another under a set of common rules?

Quite clearly American national life is rooted in a dialectical tension between rivalry and community. The two do not exclude each other; in fact, part of the thesis of this book has been predicated on the inevitability of rivalry in all cultures. But it is fair to say, as Alexis de Tocqueville pointed out over 150 years ago, that the drive to outdo other individuals, groups, and peoples combined with a strong gregariousness and desire to be like others are uniquely mixed in the American character. Capitalism is an economic and ideological projection of mimetic desire and rivalry onto the scheme of things, and, as Thorstein Veblen argued so insightfully around the turn of the century, it simply extends and sharpens the common economic motive of "conspicuous consumption." In other words, our primary reason for trading and acquiring goods is not in order to survive but to *display* our acquisitions to others. Of the three P's, power, prestige, and property, it is power and prestige that are the motivators for obtaining property of any sort (land, buildings, movable goods, money, etc.). Property is a means of exchange in order to gain power and prestige, although to a great extent each of the three is a means of exchange for the other two.

If my remarks so far are even approximately correct, it means that American culture is not only subject to mimetic forces, which all cultures would be but is *supremely exemplary* of these forces. That is to say, there is a twofold dynamic at work in American history and institutions. One is an ideology of election, of superiority to others, that brings with it a tendency to punish or exclude those who do not appear to belong to or accept this worldview. This part of the dynamic entails acquisitive desire and rivalry with other nations and between different social groupings within the country. The other part of the dynamic is awareness of the plight of the oppressed, which comes about through a mixture of factors and motives, but the biblical heritage has certainly had an important role to play in it. Many of our ancestors left the "Egypts" of England and Europe and Asia, especially in the seventeenth and nineteenth centuries. "You shall also love the stranger [or resident alien], for you were strangers in the land of Egypt" (Deut 10:19). Many have been taught and believed that "just as you did it to one of the least of these who are members of my family [Greek 'brothers'], you did it to me" (Matt 25:40). In this regard, then, there is tension between humanitarian social concerns and the drive to maintain and express superiority over others. The situation is complicated by the political manipulation of concern for those who are needy and those who are victims in the interest of gaining and maintaining political power and property and prestige.

I would mention one other complicating factor, one that stems from international perceptions of America but affects domestic life in a number of ways: whether loved or hated (it is almost always both), America is a "city upon on hill" in the sense of its power, visibility, influence. Even apart from an attempt to distinguish enlightened from unenlightened aspects of our foreign policy and economic involvements, the situation of the United States is comparable to that of the king-scapegoat: at the level of foreign relations and perceptions we are the primary differentiating symbol; the ills of the world are transferred to our doing, to our *reality*, whether we have any connection with them or not. America is automatically the chief rival and candidate for blame because it is the chief model. The Iranian tendency, even after Khomeini, to impute every misfortune to the "Great Satan" America is simply a radicalization of what others feel and perceive.

In a way, we are the most mythical of nations and the supreme scapegoat nation. That is inevitable in the present world situation, though it is partly a function of the sacrificial stream of thought in our own tradition that asserts American superiority and hegemony.

The primary objective of this study has been to shed further light on structures of violence as grounded in sacred social order and to show how the biblical witness to the innocent victim and the God of victims demystifies and demythologizes this sacred social order—even the supreme sacred community of the "chosen" people, for their calling is really a liberation or "release" (Mark 10:45) to be servants of one another and those whom they encounter on the way (Luke 10:30–35). These two currents, the sacred social order and the unmasking of desire, violence, and sacrifice on behalf of the victims, intermingle in American traditions and in every aspect of American public and private life. I would not make any pretense of "solving" the problems this poses. I am uncertain, for example, to what extent American policing and military readiness should be maintained in the world. The current crisis in the Persian Gulf is a case in point. On the negative side, it is easy to see that the crisis is being used politically to pull attention away from national domestic conflicts. It is interesting that in the wake of a new working relationship with the Soviet Union and the changes occurring in Eastern Europe we have a new enemy, Saddam Hussein, who is portrayed in demonic terms. It is almost as if the new demon-enemy is a substitute for the old one. Perhaps Saddam Hussein is "demonic," that is, destructively power-hungry, but the political manipulation of hostility toward Hussein arises partly from the superiority ideology of American traditions and draws not a little upon anti-Arab, anti-Muslim feelings. The demonic image of Hussein could easily expand to encompass the functions of a scapegoat for American ills and anxieties.

On the other hand, is it not right to stop someone like Hussein from further attempts at conquest and, in light of the carnage he has caused his own people and the people of Iran, additional loss of human life? Moreover, whatever one thinks about modern industry and technology, the requirement for oil is so all-pervasive that we probably, most of us, have little comprehension of how the entire Western world would be affected if someone like Hussein controlled not only Kuwait but also Saudi Arabia and perhaps other parts of the Middle East. If oil became scarce or the prices were increased fourfold, one could envisage an economic collapse that would make the Great Depression pale in comparison. Economics is fundamentally a mimetic process, that is, a process of watching what others are doing (how else to explain stock market fluctuations?) and of displaying to others what one has or can acquire. In such a crisis, the ordinary management of mimesis would not suffice, people would be faced with the frustration and even desperation of others; in the worst scenario there would be violence and scapegoating. Short of moral leadership stirring up the spread of good mimesis, which would have to be combined with a national commitment to development of alternative sources of energy, the mimetic effects are scary to contemplate. And this best scenario would entail long-range goals, wholesale public commitment, and daring political leadership.

Of course, such a crisis might never come about if Saddam Hussein controlled Saudi Arabia and other parts of the Middle East. After all, he would have to sell the oil and build up his own technology, would he not? The point is, it is also possible to imagine a scenario in which Hussein is as much controlled by economic forces as he controls them. So the argument about control of oil is not entirely convincing. But in fact, *no* argument about the situation is entirely convincing. The best reason for stopping Hussein, if common American and Western perceptions of him are more or less correct, is to prevent further murder and savage exploitation in his quest for power and acclaim in the Arab world.

However, stated political and religious reasons function typically to elicit popular support and to justify policies in the best light possible. Most of this manuscript was completed prior to the conclusion of the war with Iraq. To insert just a very brief comment here, it has become clear since the overwhelming military victory of the United Nations forces that the mimetic model has been demonstrated once again in the outcome of the hostilities. Hussein still rules a diminished Iraq, and who knows where his power-hungry, sacrificial leadership will lead in the future? He needs continual crises and victims as surrogates for himself.

If the U.S. and other forces had moved on to crush the country and capture him, what would the political consequences have been in light of the United Nations mandate and the ambivalent attitude toward American power already present in the Middle East and elsewhere? Would a replacement for Hussein and another government have been that much better? And how about the Kurds? Their independence could be viewed as desirable, but it could also lead simply to an increase of tensions and eventual violence in the region. As it was, the initial decision not to pursue Hussein and bring his government down allowed an Iraqi retaliation against the Kurds that resulted in enormous death and injury. So eventually the U.S. and the U.N. intervened in a modified way.

As for Kuwait, its government has shown itself unable to act effectively and the trials of "war criminals" have been, until foreign outcries had some impact, simply a pretext for the scapegoating that is typical of the dominant social order that seeks to avoid coming apart at the seams by turning the desire for revenge against foreigners and outsiders. In this fashion, the Kuwaiti regime is mitigating a mimetic crisis in which, without foreign scapegoats, their own citizens might turn against on another or even against the government itself.

Violence begets violence. Violence is the supreme chaos of reciprocity in which everyone imitates everyone else.

So I have no easy answers of a world-historical sort for current social, political, and economic problems. At the international level we should, it seems to me, be as nonviolent as possible while defending national interests. As individuals and in our respective religious communities there are many valid positions, ranging from pacifism to "just war," but even the just war position should argue that short of defensive action if one's nation-state comes under immediate attack, every attempt at peacemaking should be exhausted before military action is taken.

B. The American Pharmacy

1. Cultural Crisis

The tensions and conflicts riddling American culture are enormous. Everyone can name them: the use of drugs, both legal and illegal; uncertainty about sexual identities; mistreatment or ignoring of women, which is related to the syndrome of uncertainty about sexual identities; the mistreatment or ignoring of minorities, which is related to the all-pervasive lack of clarity about differences (about who is "in" and who "out" of some normative boundaries of human community); the plight of families and particularly of children in the context of increasing economic inequality; closely related to the plight of families is the problem of adequate housing; and deficiencies in education, both in terms of preparation for productive work and moral training for commitment to human community and self-discipline.

In all these problems, and many others that could be named, the mimetic structure is the key. The use of drugs is determined by who of the "others" is using them and what object or "reality" is gained therefrom. The "reality" is a matter of substitution, which will be discussed below.

Uncertainty about sexual identity is a twofold social question: (1) How may any given individual or grouping affirm and feel comfortable with their own sexual tendencies? (2) How may the overarching social order establish a consensus of differentiation, so that the acceptable and unacceptable is fairly distinguished without injury to the well-being of the whole? (It seems impossible on the face of it that a society would view every form of sexual activity as unacceptable, and just as improbable, for the sake of order, would be to embrace *all* forms as acceptable. There is no *order* without differentiation.) The two parts of the question are interrelated. The increasing variety of individual and group sexual identity is simultaneously a function of reaction against models in the overarching social order and of imitation of those who are engaging in the minority form of activity. The consensus in the overarching social order depends upon dominant models of behavior and the conception of activity that is "other"—that is different, unacceptable, or bad. So in a way the two categories create each other. Short of the eschatological or heavenly community in which sexual differentiation is no longer an issue,[1] any society must maintain some sort of balance between the opposing tendencies. Part of our present problem is that in the *sameness* that prevails with the loss of traditional models, there arises a rage to differentiate, but the multiplicity of differences in turn arouses the anxiety of those in the majority or, if there is no real "majority," of those holding primary social and economic power, to engage in the ultimate form of differentiation, which is *scapegoating*. In this case, those who are different in an unacceptable way (e.g., homosexuals) and who seem justly afflicted with the plague of confusion of differences (e.g., those who suffer with AIDS) become the object of exclusionary tactics.

The mistreatment and ignoring of women and minorities obviously depends on the perpetuation of old models of authority that command and commend lines of differentiation that say, in effect, "A female person is like this or does that," or "An African-American person is like this or does that." Persons in this category may traditionally be viewed as objects of desire but not as acting, initiating subjects in their own right. Moreover, in a transitional period such as the present in which there is growing sensitivity to this problem and increasing recognition of legal and political rights, there is at the same time an increase in confusion because new, more all-embracing forms of community and ways of relating are not in place. Furthermore, in this interim women and minorities and others, in spite of increasing legal, political, and economic power, still do not control the full means of support to establish themselves firmly.

All the other problems mentioned above, the plight of families and of children, inadequate housing, poor education, revolve around two interrelated mimetic phenomena. One phenomenon is a continuation of strong traces of the old master-slave dialectic (see the discussion in chapter 3). Those of a dominant class, due to their color, status, or income, continue to regard others as inferior. This is often perpetuated in the very government agencies created to improve the welfare of the poor and disenfranchised. This continuation of a relation of superiority-inferiority has two mimetic reinforcements. One is that many agency employees look with disdain upon their clients. But the master-slave relationship and its derivatives will not work unless the "slave" or "inferior" party returns to the "master" the superiority he is seeking. Most of the ways in which this is done are not obvious, and neither party may be conscious that it is happening.

The second mimetic phenomenon is that of people learning who they are and what they must do to cope in the world from the people around them. When clusters of people live isolated from the mainstream and see around them only models of welfare dependence, they maintain that dependence, they maintain that dependence in each generation.

In this situation of mimetic crisis, *violence* is a threat to the entire social order. It is easy enough, of course, to resort to mythical reflexes that are part of the archaic heritage of the human race by ascribing problems to an external enemy or to *plague*, namely, the "infection" of false ideas (communism, integration, sexism), or "mixing" (racial intermarriage, different gender roles, homosexuality, religion in public life), or actual disease (AIDS). There is a partial truth in the mythical reflex, namely, that old patterns of differentiation have broken down, with the result that desire and rivalry are not kept within former boundaries. However, mythic reactions are ignorant or self-deceived to the extent that they do not recognize that *we are all involved in the mimetic crisis*. We have all, by omission or commission, participated in the development of a drug culture. We have all, by omission or commission, had a part in the confusion about sexual identity, in the perpetuation of racial and gender stereotypes, in maintaining lines of superiority and inferiority in income, housing, education, in posing as victims in order to gain power over others.

We participate, every one of us, in a culture in which the ancient religious forms, with their systems of sacrificial substitution, have been called radically into question. The demise of sacrificial religion could be a good thing if it were replaced with the good mimesis of the God of victims. Otherwise, we face what is described in the parable of the unclean spirit: "When the unclean spirit has gone out of a person, it wanders through waterless regions looking for a resting place, but not finding any, it says, 'I will return to my house from which I came.' When it comes, it finds it swept and put in order. Then it goes and brings seven other spirits more evil than itself, and they enter and live there; and the last state of that person is worse than the first" (Luke 11:24–26). Sometimes getting rid of a demon not only leads to its return, but to the arrival of others even worse than the first one.

The authority of the Roman Catholic church, with its representation of sacrifice in the Mass, has less and less hold on a majority of Catholics. The rejection of priestly and prophetic authority in the mainline Protestant denominations has turned ministers into some combination of pastors and business managers. Obviously sacrificial religion, with a doctrine of the sacrifice of Christ at the center, is repugnant to most of these Protestant groups, while other modes of sacrificial substitution are left unexamined. Only the fundamentalist churches have

continued to adhere to a sacrificial doctrine of atonement and a highly differentiated religious community, but this sort of religious identity is often purchased at
the price of strong exclusionary tendencies that result in self-righteous separation
from "the others" and justification of divine and human violence. As for the black
church, the various black denominations are still important and numerous, but
they have largely lost their place as the dominant, catalyzing social agent in urban
black communities. All these institutions, so significant in American history, have
resources to offer in the mimetic crisis of our culture, but at the moment they are
overwhelmed or irrelevant.

2. Addictive Culture and Culture as Addiction

The specific problems we can educe from this crisis are in truth a form of *substitutionary activity* that represents an attempt to cope with the crisis. Our cultural
predicament *revolves around a continual series of substitutions* for some power,
some "reality," some form of satisfaction that is never articulated. Rivalry in the
quest for economic power and prestige has recently been in the news, particularly
stock manipulators and dealings that led to the savings and loan failures. Readers
have avidly followed the rise and fall (?) of Donald Trump. (The American public
does have its idols, but it is even more fascinated with its fallen idols.) It seems that
players in the money game are out for the money, but money is like its ancestral
prototype, the sacred victim: it is a means of exchange for the community, being
viewed simultaneously as evil ("filthy lucre") and the source of power ("money
talks"). In other words, as in the case of those who exercise authority *ex-ousia*, "out
of substance or property," the "substance" is really the insubstantial sentiment of
the people, who confer on their victims the blessing of signifier (god, savior, hero,
great man, tycoon) and signified (becoming a disguised symbol of the community).

   The use of drugs is one of the most obvious instances of substitutionary activity. I prefer to use the word *pharmacy* to describe American culture, which is a
"drug culture" in an obvious sense, but the use and abuse of drugs is simply a
symptom of a broader culture of *addiction*. The dictionary I keep beside my desk
gives as the first entry for the word *pharmacy* "the act or practice of preparing and
dispensing drugs and medicines."[2] If culture is viewed from the standpoint of a
"supplement" to nature, as suggested by Rousseau and explicated in recent years
by Derrida, then the *pharmakon*, which in Greek means both remedy and poison,
may be taken as a metaphor of culture. As such, its function is structurally the
same as that of the scapegoat: in Greek, *pharmakos*.[3] But the notion of an addition, supplement, trace, or pharmakon should not be allowed to obscure the expo-
sure of concealment that is achieved in a Girardian analysis of culture and religion.
That is, human beings unconsciously conceal their own violence through a series
of substitutions that can be deciphered in sacrifice and myth.

American culture has become a pharmacy; I argue this assertion as a twofold thesis: (1) American culture has produced a plethora, a veritable cornucopia of medicines, remedies, drugs, which in numerous cases are also poisons. (2) The pharmacy itself has become a substitute for the culture that produced it and a way of understanding this very culture. As has been often remarked in the last two decades, the problem of "drugs" does not begin in the ghettos but in the culture at large. The production of medicines for every ailment under the sun has become a hallmark of modern technology. Many elderly people take so many medicines prescribed by physicians that it becomes a matter of no little organizational effort for them to work out what to take at a given time of the day. I have seen ten to twenty bottles lined up on a table or in a medicine cabinet. But it is not only the elderly; younger people are now using all sorts of medicines, particularly pain relievers. When I was in my teens and early twenties I cannot remember that the question of using aspirin, for example, came up except in the case of a severe cold or some kind of painful injury. Acetaminophen and ibuprofen had not come onto the market. Now it is rather commonplace for younger people to use these analgesics, and certainly not uncommon for them to drink alcoholic beverages and use various controlled substances.

While I was growing up in the 1940s and 1950s there was, of course, the drug alcohol. Alcohol is the most commonly used "drug," and alcoholism is a tremendous problem in America. The substitutionary effect of alcohol is quite evident. It relieves minor pain; it makes one "feel good"; it enables one to escape from "reality" or participate in "reality," as the case may be. This "reality" is as often as not the social world. For one thing, a very high percentage of drinking is associated with social occasions and group activities. It is a commonplace that drinking helps people relax in the tension of a social gathering. This very fact is an indication of mimetic conflict, which is ritually resolved with the agreement to take a drink with the others. It is not difficult to see, then, that the drink is an object of social confluence and harmony in much the same structural way that the scapegoat is. Indeed, drinking of this sort probably originated in scapegoating. One supporting fact in perceiving it in this fashion is that people who do not participate in the drinking activity are viewed, sometimes mildly, sometimes with great annoyance, as breaking the conviviality of the group. One can imagine drinking the blood of the victim, a common practice in primitive sacrificial rites, in which refusal to participate would be as blameworthy as the offenses imputed to the victim in the first place.

With the widespread employment of various and sundry drugs in order to gain healing or at least relief from pain, and with the practice of drinking alcoholic spirits at every level of society, we can observe the workings of mimesis in two respects: parental models, cultural heroes, and peers cast up a continual series of models, and group process reinforces doing what the others are doing. The replacement of tension, anxiety, or pain with a sense of well-being (or of feeling better) and the substitution of a substance for the group in conflict: these substitutionary effects are the outcome of the mimetic process. The use of the illegal substances, ranging from marijuana to cocaine, are simply based on this all-pervading model of the culture as pharmacy. Aside from the question of whether these substances are physically more dangerous than alcohol, for example, the same dynamic structure applies to the social dimension of their use. They would not become part of a pharmacy culture without authoritative models and the reality of mimetic tendencies that lead to scapegoating and violence.

For those without a strong sense of identity, the power of a tradition, and the sense of their worth beyond the immediacy of the individual and the individual lifetime, old forms of differentiation and traditional forms of sacrifice or substitutional rituals are no longer effective. This is not necessarily bad if a new "clean spirit," a "new being," is moving in to replace the "unclean spirit" that was exorcised. But if the unclean spirits move in, those demons of undifferentiation and mimesis gone wild, what necessarily occurs is a series of eruptions of spontaneous violence or of extreme substitutionary measures, which may allay the violence, but only for a very short time before further such measures must be taken. The drug must be taken again more and more frequently; the community called a "gang" must attack or kill others lest it fall apart from its internal violence. This community without tradition and direction not only must fight against other such communities, but it may find itself selecting victims at random, arbitrarily. The victim must be "innocent," or at least arbitrarily chosen from those who are outsiders and deficient and vulnerable.

Addiction is an expression of the cultural pharmacy, but not simply in the sense of a result, what is produced in a society undergoing a crisis. There is a deeper sense in which *culture itself is addiction,* and American culture, as exemplary of mimetic forces, is likewise an exemplar of what addiction is.[4] "Addiction" is from the Latin *addictus* (root *addicere*), "adjudged," "pledged." The common Latin meaning seems to have been "bound" or "pledged." In keeping with the Girardian model, I surmise that behind it lies the judgment of the crowd or the lottery that selects a victim. The "addicted" in this sense is the victim who is condemned to be expelled or sacrificed, and of course this victim-god is a substitute for the whole community as well as for given individuals who bind themselves in some way (by an oath of devotion, for example) to the victim-god. At the basic level of survival, the exchange is simple: I am addicted, bound or pledged, to the one sacrificed in place of my life. But beyond bare survival, the scapegoat-addiction purportedly confers various benefits, ranging from fertility to access to the higher realms of spirituality in religious experience.

As for that aspect of addiction associated with physical dependence, I am not competent to comment as a biologist or a medical scientist. Rather, I would make two remarks, one indicating what I would hypothesize and one indicating where I think the emphasis should be placed in dealing with addiction. The hypothesis is the conjecture that our brains and total mental makeup are rooted in mimetic capacities, as Girard has argued.[5] These capacities are present in all forms of life and particularly in higher mammals. There must be patterns or networks in our physiology that require repetition when triggered in a certain way, and this phenomenon is probably related to the very base of our genetic endowment, which probably has been produced by some form of differentiation and acquisitive imitation.

Second, and crucial for this discussion, physical dependence must be seen as part of the larger framework of culture as addiction. Addiction, in other words, is first and foremost a social phenomenon related to all aspects of human culture. For one thing, the pleasure and relief gained from resolving mimetic crises by the scapegoating actions of the group may have entered into our genetic inheritance at some point. However conjectural that may be, a profile of addiction in any form will show it to be substitutional behavior that can easily be traced to scapegoating. I would characterize addiction in this sense as *behavior revolving around some person, thing, or mode of action that is repeated over and over again, that has the purported effect of alleviating cares or ills, and that has such an overriding hold on the lives of individuals or communities that they believe themselves "necessitated" or "fated" to continue the repetition no matter what the consequences.*

Addiction viewed in this way is how culture began and, by and large, how it is maintained. American culture brings the phenomenon of addiction to extremely sharp expression because of its mythology of superiority, its practical success in the world, and the technology that both reflects and enhances its own mythology. The use of drugs is simply one of the most dramatic symptoms of this pharmacy, this pharmacopoeia, that American culture is. Gambling in its various forms would be another dramatic symptom, related as it is to the attempt to "beat the odds," that is, to obtain the *different*, what is selected by chance, by the falling of the lot. To the degree that many persons may be described as addicted to it, it could be characterized as an ongoing attempt to reenact the sacrifice of the scapegoat.

All of the problems mentioned so far in this discussion, along with many others that could be noted, are an outpouring from the pharmacy. Drugs of all sorts are among the wonders of technology; they are also poisons that can kill us unless we use them with real art and skill (both meanings of the Greek *techne*) and with real understanding. Making money is a way of "getting a piece of the action," as we say—a way of gaining property, prestige, and power (somewhat like getting a piece of the sacrificed victim; cf. the epigraphs to chapter 5); it may also be an addiction, a binding to an endless process that requires further substitutions, because desire is never satisfied as long as there are "others," those who likewise desire what their rivals desire. Collective violence and scapegoating seems to be a way in which a given collectivity, from a local gang to a mighty nation, can come together against an enemy, but the sacrifice offered up to Violence, the ancient and still mighty Sacred, cannot be ended; it must go on and on as long as there are others who desire what their model-rivals have, just as we do.

I would mention one more expression of the American pharmacy: guns, the use of various firearms, especially rifles and hand guns. Much of the increased danger of death or injury, particularly in urban areas, is due to random violence, and of course the availability of firearms, especially hand guns, increases the danger, which in some cities must be described as a crisis. After all, not many people in their own homes or apartments, not many children playing on the street or in schoolyards, are struck down by a random knife-thrower or someone running amok with a baseball bat. Schoolchildren were mowed down with a semiautomatic rifle in Stockton, California; such mass slaughter of the innocents could not have occurred except with an automatic weapon.

The gun, too, is an addiction, a creation of the "pharmacy." We know, of course, that the gun is a weapon whose ammunition can kill or maim, but the point is that its function is much like that of the amulet that wards off diseases and evil powers or the medicine that will prevent sickness and maintain one's health. In a world of rivalry run amok where people do not trust one another and where real dangers lurk, the gun is doubtless a kind of *pharmakon*, a remedy that is also a poison. It is an extension of the human being—all tools are—that gives added power, and perhaps in some instances also property and prestige (especially the latter). The gun is a metonym of the conglomerate model of the soldier-hunter-cowboy that emerged in American history and that had, of course, very old prototypes. The manipulation of this model by politicians and groups like the National Rifle Association has led even to the absurdity of interpreting the constitutional right to bear arms (a provision for military defense against hostile forces) as the right of private citizens to own firearms, even without testing, investigation, and licensing!

It is a difficult issue because the dangers are real. The dangers of attack on person and property are real because of the uncontrolled mimetic forces in American culture. But substitutes for substitutes, limited sacrificial supplements more poisonous than remedial, will only pull us down deeper into the vortex of violence. To the extent that the ownership and use of guns in this country has reached the point that the firearm is a sign of behavior that brings supposed benefits and that is felt to be necessary or fated no matter what the consequences, it is an addiction that must be healed.

But healing addiction, healing violence, how is that done? As I have already indicated in commenting on the Persian Gulf crisis, I have no easy answers. I propose, however, that any healing, whether for individuals, for small intentional communities, or for the nation (if that is possible), must be based on recognizing what is real and true in the nonmythical, nonsacrificial side of the American tradition. That side is rooted in the biblical heritage of the God of victims, and attending to it involves listening to the voice of the victim.

C. The Truth of the Victim

> A voice was heard in Ramah,
> wailing and loud lamentation,
> Rachel weeping for her children;
> she refused to be consoled,
> because they are no more.
> (Matt 2:18, quoting Jer 31:15)

To listen and look for the truth of the victim we must begin with recognition of the victim's *silence*. The victim who protests has already reached an advanced stage of complicating the victimization mechanism by breaking its unanimity. This more advanced stage is given voice in much of the world's great literature and has become a cultural datum in our appropriation of the biblical heritage. It is a sign of the work of the Spirit, the Paraclete.

But the deepest predicament lies where there is yet no voice, where there is perhaps even no knowledge of alternatives to exclusion from the human community and its benefits. The perfect victim, the revealer of victimization, has reenacted this.

> He was oppressed, and he was afflicted,
> yet he did not open his mouth;
> like a lamb that is led to the slaughter,
> and like a sheep that before its hearers is dumb,
> so he did not open his mouth.
> (Isa 53:7)

The perfect example of the innocent victim without knowledge, with no awareness and no resources for defense, is the child, particularly the infant and the fetus in the womb. That is why Matthew's narration of the slaying of the infants (Matt 2:16–18) is such a powerful dramatic backdrop to the work of Jesus, Yeshua, the new Joshua, who "will save his people from their sins" (Matt 1:21). The Savior comes precisely to overturn the order in which the Pharaohs and the Herods of the world can offer up children as substitutes for their own immolation.

Children and the yet unborn are made to suffer all the productions of the pharmacy, of the culture of addiction. They are most available as the "odds," those whose number comes up in the scapegoating process. Conflict is temporarily abated by elimination of the one who is made to bear the sign of conflict and is abolished in the ultimate manner: by death.

The issue of abortion is a radical instance of the voiceless victim who needs a defender, a comforter, a Paraclete. The victim as the substitute for the disordered desire and rivalry of the human world is nowhere more apparent than in the killing of infants, those who cannot speak.

But the issue is very complex, in that the mother of the infant may be a victim practically without voice and caught up in intolerable circumstances. Another facet of the complexity of the problem is that to advocate bringing children into the world morally entails that advocates of the innocents' "right to life" also concern themselves with the social well-being of individuals. That in turn would entail greater public support of parents and children and increased commitment of time, money, and effort. Otherwise, we are bringing children into the world to feed them into the victimization machine at some later stage. The arms of this machine are many: poverty, disease, incarceration, addiction in its more obvious forms. To advocate a right to life without recognition of the victimization mechanism can further a cruel illusion. Surely we do not want to be in the business of bringing more children into the world in order to create a bigger sacrificial pool!

Most victims are silent because they have no voice, they are voiceless and without vote. The silence of the *perfect* victim is deliberate. The Suffering Servant is silent before his persecutors because he knows there is no way he can satisfy or mediate the conflicting desires of friends and foes except through pouring out his soul to death, by allowing himself to be expelled and murdered (from the standpoint of the governing authorities, it is, of course, a legitimate execution). The perfect victim, the revealer of the God of victims, discloses the nature of our tragic conflicts in which someone has to be given up, delivered over to the executioner's hand—given over to that mighty god of the social order, that reality that in ancient times was revered as the Sacred. Will it be the foreigner, or ourselves? Will it be our military troops at risk, or our own safety? Will it be the "criminal" and the "insane," or our domestic tranquillity? Will it be the mother or the child?

Of course, to the extent any of us are victims of structures of violence, we have legal recourse—or we like to think we do. A system of law has in principle replaced the substitutionary processes of victimization and sacrifice. However, what has already been stated in the discussion of Jeremiah's vision of the new covenant (see the second part of chapter 5) would apply *mutatis mutandis* to any legal system: it is based ultimately on a sacrificial principle of vengeance or retribution. In any case, our system of law and other social structures are not working to the extent that so many turn to the "remedies" or "addictions" that are pale substitutes for love and community.

These remedies and addictions are, in their own way, an outcry of *god-forsakenness*. That is, from the standpoint of revelation of the truth of the victim, we are summoned to listen and look not merely for verbal expressions and outcries but for those signs of the victim seeking substitutionary redress of disrespect, despair, and pain. There have been many discussions of illegitimate children as substitutes, especially those borne by very young women who, lacking other role models and short of any real hope for future education and career, find becoming a mother a way to be creative, to have life, to perform a recognized function. This is addiction, the work of the *pharmakon* that is both remedy and poison. Gambling, alcoholism, and dependence on drugs are all, in their respective ways, means of coming to terms with the world by getting a piece of the *pharmakon* given by fate, given by the other—which always goes back to the sacred social order. The behavior that may fairly be designated as "addictive" is always not only a means of reaching out for a substitute for the "real"—for the three P's of power, prestige, and property—but also a cry for help. Its verbal and other symbols are disguised displacements, but it is always fundamentally a way of saying, "Why do you turn against me? Why do you forsake me? Why do you cast me out in my moment of need?" This is the cry of Job, of the psalms, of Jesus from the cross.

What those listening and looking for the truth of the victim must be able to affirm is that the silence and abjection or god-forsakenness of the victim has already been revealed through the witnesses of Scripture, to the end that faith may see this condition as known, suffered, and redeemed by the God of Israel and the God of Jesus Christ. Those who give heed will not only seek to express this faith verbally but reenact it in their lives, in their bodies.

Because none of us is in the position of the utterly Innocent Victim, who must be very God of very God and very human of very human, we must recognize our complicity with the persecutors. The power of the parable of the Samaritan in Luke 10:30–35 is precisely that the hearers are invited to see themselves in all the characters. Luke's rendition of the conclusion of Jesus' dialogue with the lawyer, 10:36–37, emphasizes imitation of the Samaritan: "Go and do likewise" (as the Samaritan did). That is surely one fundamental aspect of the parable's point, and it fits Luke's own theology perfectly. The Samaritan for Luke is probably an image of the Christ who is to be imitated. Doing as the Samaritan did is *imitatio Christi*. But the parable is more powerfully polyvalent than that. Am I or are we the robbers who in some fashion or the other have extracted all of someone's wealth or other resources and left her half-dead? Am I or are we the priest or Levite who has some position of authority, which in the pharmacy of culture is construed as good in and of itself, but who *precisely because of this good role or office*, passes by on the other side of the victim? Am I or are we the victim? Have we in some way been beaten and robbed, left half-dead? Or perhaps our cultural indoctrination tells us we are not victims at all but possessors of power and wealth and prestige—thus perfect candidates for being victimizers rather than victims. But that cultural assumption is deceptive, for the victimizers can be victims of their own system of victimization. Or am I or are we the Samaritan, going out into some foreign, hostile territory and binding the wounds of the victim?

Now everyone intuits in reading or hearing the parable that the position of the Samaritan cannot be an excuse for self-righteousness. We are impelled to confess that even in our best moments we have assumed the roles of all these characters. We are thieves and priests and victims even when we are truly Samaritans. If we *start from that very confession and humble acknowledgment before God and one another*, we can begin to actualize the full truth of the innocent victim.

From this standpoint of confession of sin, and only from this standpoint, can we realize and reenact *forgiveness of those who don't know what they are doing.* "Father, forgive them; for they do not know what they are doing." The precondition of forgiveness is the humility that recognizes and acknowledges one's own complicity in structures of mimetic desire and violence. We are therefore not superior to our ancestors who shed the blood of the prophets (Matt 23:30), for if we are blind to our own complicity, we are probably doomed to repeat what our ancestors did. Forgiveness of one another is the only possible way we can live together and begin to address the immense problems that face us.

The foundation of forgiveness is not knowledge of the unconsciousness of mimetic cultural processes, important as that is. Rather, the knowledge itself is based on *trust* in the God who defends and delivers victims. "Father, into your hands I commend my spirit." This defense and deliverance is not done apart from our own agency. The problem with a simplistic view of God as "supernatural" is that it imagines God as the utterly different being whose acts are somehow separable from the world and human beings. If one were, by contrast, to imagine the world and particularly its human inhabitants as something like God's "body," as in process thought,[6] this image would enable us to see the key role we have in providence and the work of the Paraclete. We are not simply subject to what the Other, the Divine Outsider does, but in some sense we are part of it and contribute to it.

Heeding the silence and the cries of abandonment, forgiving the persecutors who act unconsciously, trusting in the God of victims: these facets of hearing and doing the truth enable us to *hear* the one who calls out, "I am thirsty." Then we are able to hear the plea of those hungry and sick and in prison. But there is a sense too in which we relearn the truth each time we come to someone's aid and realize simultaneously our own needy condition.

Finally, we do not seek martyrdom, for to *seek* martyrdom is to do untruth, to belong to the "father of lies." Seeking martyrdom is a pretext for self-righteousness; it is another form of addiction, one that seeks benefits through making oneself the scapegoat—through various behaviors ranging from what we commonly call addictions to suicide. No, true martyrdom is based on the role of *witness*, Greek *martyr.* Witness is absolutely necessary to realize and reenact the truth of the innocent victim. Whether or not it requires the surrender of one's life depends on the situation, on the "friends," the *philoi* for which one is responsible (John 15:12–17). There is only One who, not belonging to the world of mimetic desire and differences, had to be put to death that we might see and do the truth. If we sometimes run away, like the disciples, when we should have watched with our Master, well, we do not always know what we are doing, and we stand in need of forgiveness from one another. But it is clear that the good mimesis of the innocent victim requires realization and reenactment of that sort of commitment to the members of the community of the faithful and to all members of the human family of which Jesus spoke, according to the witness of Mark, "For the Son of Man came not to be served but to serve, and to give his life a ransom for many" (10:45).

And there we are back to "ransom" again: the substitution, the price of exchange, the freeing, the liberation that is without money and without price and without need for repayment, for it does not come from the world of differences but from the God who gives himself in his Son Jesus. It is this ransom that ends sacrifice and adumbrates the end of violence that we, if we wish to be Samaritans, must humbly reenact. This is the good mimesis.

In the presidential campaign of 1988 George Bush exulted in the "thousand points of light" that Americans in their goodwill and through their voluntary activities and local governments could provide. It was effective rhetoric, appealing at the same time to the American sense of being a "light to the nations," of aspiring to be "stars" in our own individual ways, and of privileging individual initiative and local and state government rather than federal control of political and economic affairs. It was effective partly because it dipped into the heritage of concern for the other, including the innocent victim. But the background and assumptions of the rhetoric were one-sided, for it was calculated to appeal most strongly to the tradition of rivalry that is ontologically projected as the capitalistic principle of world history, which is reconciled with the humanitarian thrust of American traditions only through the good will of individuals. The "thousand points of light" is really a phrase that exalts voluntarism or seeing things in terms of will, initiative, and individual commitment. This view of the world has its own truth, but as proposed by the President it offers no critique of the American pharmacy, the culture of addiction. It comes out of a worldview that recognizes Christianity and the Judeo-Christian heritage but seeks to incorporate it into the world of mimetic desire and rivalry that goes under the name of some sort of capitalism. The result is that the god of the system decrees that some—more and more it seems in the last several years—will bear the lot falling on them, the lot of differentiation that says, "You are excluded." Of course, there is always a rationalization of exclusion. There are few appeals nowadays to "bad blood" or the inherent inferiority of non-whites, although such ideas have by no means died out. The most common explanation is that certain people are inherently lazy or lack motivation to take advantage of the opportunities that our system affords them. This is a veneer, sometimes very thin, justifying the perpetuation of an underclass that provides a pool of sacrificial victims for the system. I am reminded of the account by Captain Cook (1728–1779) of his observations of sacrifice in Polynesia. In one instance the man immolated was termed a *towtow*, someone from the lowest class of people. Evidently Cook was given to understand that he had committed some crime, for he noted, "But after all my inquiries, I could not learn, that he had been pitched upon, on account of any particular crime . . . meriting death." He goes on to say, "It is certain, however, that they generally make choice of such guilty persons for their sacrifices; or else of common, low fellows."[7] Cook believed the indigenous people's story about the choice of victims, he accepted their myth, and they undoubtedly believed it themselves: it is generally "guilty persons" or "common, low fellows" who are sacrificed. It is generally the guilty and the debased who do not succeed in a capitalist world. So the myth goes. But the Judeo-Christian witness to the innocent victim exposes the myth as a camouflage for a theology of fate that requires expulsion and scapegoating.

To be sure that I am not misunderstood, I want to emphasize that the element of voluntarism is necessary to democracy. The radical concept of democracy is to presuppose the participation of all citizens who have reached maturity; they all have a *voice* to be heard, a *vote* to cast. The restrictions on individual freedom and voluntary associations are undoubtedly one of the primary factors in the economic and political failure of the Soviet Union and the Eastern European bloc of nations. But before we congratulate ourselves too much, we should consider whether our own crisis, our own time of judgment (Greek *krisis*), is imminent because of our lack of a vision that binds all members of American society together in common concern and common assistance.

The truth of voluntarism is that the true Spirit of history works first of all through individuals and voluntary or intentional communities who come out of the crowd, who stand apart from the inevitable popular mythicizing of the social order. The metaphor of "a city upon a hill" was directed first to the community of disciples who are addressed in the Sermon on the Mount as the ideal community that lives out of the Passion, which is reenacted in love of neighbor and love of the enemy.[8] Grounded first of all in individual commitment and participation in some sort of intentional or voluntary community, those who heed the voice of the victim through whom God is calling us will think, trust, and act on the premise that a good mimesis, the work of the Spirit, is expanding like leaven and will bring us to some good end, whether in this world or in the world to come.

Notes

Chapter 1. A New Approach to Biblical Texts

1. Seldom stated so baldly as by Jonathan Z. Smith in *Violent Origins: Walter Burkert, René Girard, and Jonathan Z. Smith on Ritual Killing and Cultural Formation,* ed. Robert Hamerton-Kelly (Stanford, CA: Stanford University Press, 1987), 222.

2. See David Chidester, "Rituals of Exclusion and the Jonestown Dead," *Journal of the American Academy of Religion* 56 (1988): 698–700.

3. W. Hudson, *Religion in America,* 4th ed. (New York: Macmillan, 1987), 102–103.

4. Alexis de Tocqueville, *Democracy in America,* 2 vols., ed. Phillips Bradley (New York: Random House, 1967).

5. Conrad Cherry, ed., *God's New Israel* (Englewood Cliffs, NJ: Prentice-Hall, 1971).

6. See Wolfgang Palaver, "Gleichheit als Sprengkraft? Zum Einfluss des Christentums auf die Entwicklung der Demokratie," in *Verweigerte Mündigkeit: Politische Kultur und die Kirche,* ed. J. Niewiadomski (Thaur: Osterreichischer Kulturverlag, 1989), 203–209.

7. Girard is avowedly Christian, but there is a certain openness and complexity in his understanding of the Jewish tradition and Jesus as the Christ that is sympathetic toward Judaism and offers Jewish interpreters considerable scope in the appropriation of his theory. I will deal briefly with the role of the Jewish tradition in Girard's thinking in chap. 6.

8. Raymund Schwager, S.J., *Must There Be Scapegoats?* trans. Maria L. Assad (San Francisco: Harper & Row, 1987). Schwager's book appeared in German in 1978: *Brauchen Wir Einen Sündenbock?* (Munich: Kösel-Verlag GmbH).

   More recently, Robert Hamerton-Kelly has written introductions to Girard's work for *Curing Violence,* ed. Theophus Smith and Mark Wallace (Minneapolis: Fortress, 1992), and his own book, *Sacred Violence: The Hermeneutics of the Cross in the Theology of Paul* (forthcoming; hereafter *Paul*). For a brief overview, see James G. Williams, "The Innocent Victim: René Girard on Violence, Sacrifice, and the Sacred," *Religious Studies Review* 14 (1988): 320–326.

9. Stated in a seminar at Stanford University, winter quarter, 1990.

10. See James G. Williams, *Those Who Ponder Proverbs: Aphoristic Thinking and Biblical Literature* (Sheffield: Almond, 1981), chap. 1. Retribution is also the basic principle of legal systems.

11. In addition to many articles and contributions to anthologies, Girard has written or edited the following books. Abbreviations will be given for titles I use frequently.

    Mensonge romantique et vérité romanesque (Paris: Grasset, 1961, 1973; Livre de Poche, 1978). Translated by Yvonne Freccero under the title *Deceit, Desire, and the Novel* (Baltimore: Johns Hopkins, 1966, 1969, 1976). Hereafter *Deceit.*

    Editor of *Proust: A Collection of Critical Essays* (New York: Prentice-Hall, 1962).

Dostoievski: du double à l'unité (Paris: Plon, 1963; reprint, Sainte-Pierre de Salerne, Brionne: Gérard Montfort, 1979).

La violence et le sacré (Paris: Grasset, 1972, 1974, 1977; Livre de Poche, 1980). Translated by Patrick Gregory under the title *Violence and the Sacred* (Baltimore: The Johns Hopkins University Press, 1977; paperback, 1979, 1986). Hereafter *Violence.*

Critiques dans un souterrain (Lausanne: L'Age d'Homme, 1976; Livre de Poche, 1983).

Des choses cachées depuis la fondation du monde, with Jean-Michel Oughourlian and Guy Lefort (Paris: Grasset, 1978). Translated by S. Bann and M. Metteer under the title *Things Hidden Since the Foundation of the World* (London: Athlone, 1987; Stanford: Stanford University Press, 1987). Hereafter *Things Hidden.*

"To Double Business Bound": Essays on Literature, Mimesis, and Anthropology (Baltimore: Johns Hopkins, 1978). Hereafter *Double Business.*

Le bouc émissaire (Paris: Grasset, 1982). Translated by Yvonne Frecerro under the title *The Scapegoat* (Baltimore: The Johns Hopkins University Press, 1986; paperback, 1989). Hereafter *Scapegoat.*

La route antique des hommes pervers (Paris: Grasset, 1985; Livre de Ponche, 1988). Translated by Yvonne Freccero as *Job: The Victim of His People,* (London: Athlone, 1987; Stanford, CA: Stanford University Press, 1987). Hereafter *Job.*

Shakespeare: les feux de l'envie, trans. Bernard Vincent (Paris: Grasset, 1990). Winner of the Prix Medicis de l'essai. This book on Shakespeare was written first in English but published first in French translation. The English original is *A Theatre of Envy: William Shakespeare* (New York and Oxford: Oxford University Press, 1991). Hereafter *Shakespeare.*

12. Robert Hamerton-Kelly, "Sacrificial Violence and the Messiah: A Hermeneutical Meditation on the Marcan Passion Narrative," unpublished paper presented to the Bible, Narrative, and American Culture Seminar and the Jesus Seminar, October 15–18, 1987, 6–7. See references to Hamerton-Kelly's works in note 8. His study of Mark from a Girardian perspective has recently appeared: *The Gospel and the Sacred: Poetics of Violence in Mark* (Minneapolis: Fortress, 1994). I have modified Hamerton-Kelly's text somewhat, as indicated by the brackets. It should be noted that Girard himself prefers not to call the basis of his approach a theory, hypothesis, or even model. He believes that the patterns he has adduced amount to a kind of proof, so that the scapegoating part of his argument is fact, not theory. My use of the phrase *explanatory model* is meant as a compromise between his position and current academic discourse.

13. As often noted, Girard's concept of desire and rivalry is influenced by Hegel, particularly through Alexandre Kojève, whose lectures have been brought together in *Introduction to the Reading of Hegel,* assembled by Raymond Queneau, ed. Allan Bloom, trans. James H. Nichols, Jr. (Ithaca and London: Cornell University Press, 1980). Girard differs from Hegel and Kojève in not construing consciousness as metaphysical and in emphasizing the subject's desire for the *object* of the model-rival's desire (or the imagined object of the model-rival's desire) rather than simply the desiring of the other's desire. Thus the dynamic social character of mimesis comes out more clearly in Girard's analysis.

14. Girard, *Violence,* 159.

15. *The Bacchae,* in *Three Plays of Euripides,* trans. Paul Roche (New York: Norton, 1974), lines 917–920, p. 108.

16. Girard, *Violence*, 162.
17. In a recent unpublished lecture Girard also spoke of "good mimesis" as the social bond established by the "scapegoat effect." In that case it is necessary to have "external mediation" (see next paragraph of the chapter) that keeps mimetic rivalry in check. In using "good mimesis" in this sense Girard really means "effective mimesis," mimesis that works, that keeps culture going with adequate differentiations even though it is maintained through an underlying sacrificial mechanism. If that were Girard's only sense of good mimesis, his position would be little different from that of Thomas Hobbes (see reference to Palaver's study, chap. 5, n. 2). However, good mimesis can also mean the revelation of the divine model that is not merely external to a given set of cultural differences, but is not part of the differential system that requires exclusion, victimization, and the latter's ritualization in sacrifice or its subsequent traces. This is the mimesis of which he speaks, for example, in referring to Jesus' enterprise of "starting the good contagion originating in good reciprocity" (*et amorcer la bonne contagion de la bonne réciprocité*; my trans. of the French text, *Des choses cachées depuis la fondation du monde* [Livre de Poche,], 297; *Things Hidden*, 203). Here "good contagion" is the response of revelation to mimetic crisis and panic, and "good reciprocity" is exchange on the basis of the divine model, not on the basis of retribution and the possibility of revenge.
18. Girard, *Deceit*, 9.
19. Girard, *Deceit*, 9.
20. Girard refers to the "unconscious" motives in rivalry, acquisitive desire, and scapegoating, but he views Freud's concept of the "unconscious" as a modern psychoanalytic myth. It is a reflection of residual "Platonism" in Western culture, an appeal to essences or essential drives, whereas the theory of mimetic desire and rivalry much more elegantly clarifies the problems that Freud tried to unravel in terms of the "Oedipus complex," "latent homosexuality," "narcissism," etc. See *Things Hidden*, 352–392.
21. The structure of the scapegoat mechanism is thus similar to games in which someone is "it," selected for exclusion and some ordeal; it is likely that these games are patterned after scapegoating.
22. Girard holds that the sacral kingship emerged as one form of sacred political order because there must often have been a lapse of time between choosing the victim and actual sacrifice. Since superhuman powers were ascribed to the victim, the latter could use an interval between selection and execution to gain more and more influence over the community, eventually prolonging the interval and achieving real political power (*Things Hidden*, 53). He says also, "In monarchy the interpretation accentuates the interval between the selection of the victim and the immolation; it is a matter of the victim being still alive, one that has not yet been sacrificed. In the case of divinity, by contrast, the interpretation accentuates a victim that has already been sacrificed and it is a matter of the sacred having been already expelled from the community" (*Things Hidden*, 55–56).
23. R. Otto, *The Idea of the Holy* (New York: Oxford University Press, 1958).
24. "Sacrifice" = "make sacred" or "render sacred," from the Latin *sacrificare* through the French *sacrifier*.
25. Livy, *The Early History of Rome*, trans. A. de Sélincourt (London and New York: Penguin, 1960, 1971), I.3–6, pp. 37–40. Livy reports two versions of Romulus's slaying of Remus. One is in a controversy over supremacy in which bird augury was used, the other occurring when Remus jeeringly jumped over the unfinished wall of the

settlement that was to be Rome. It is interesting that Livy also reports two versions of Romulus's death. One has it that while reviewing troops a storm struck; a cloud enveloped him and he disappeared. (Cf. the disappearance of Oedipus in *Oedipus at Colonus*.) The other has it (according to "a few dissentients," says Livy) that he was torn to pieces by the senators (I.6, pp. 50–51). Girard notes that Plutarch's versions of Romulus's death include three that are forms of collective murder (*Scapegoat*, 89).

26. Menahem Stern; see note 41, chap. 2.
27. Girard, *Things Hidden*, 219.
28. See Mark 5:1–20, and Girard, "The Demons of Gerasa," in *Scapegoat*.
29. Girard, *Scapegoat*, 182–183.
30. Hamerton-Kelly, *Paul*.
31. Karl Popper, *The Logic of Scientific Discovery* (1959; New York: Harper Torchbooks, 1968).
32. Hamerton-Kelly, *Paul*.
33. Edward Burnett Tylor, *Primitive Culture* (New York: Harper, 1958; first published 1871).
34. W. Robertson Smith, *Lectures on the Religion of the Semites* (1889). Later published as *The Religion of the Semites*. I have used the Meridian paperback edition, 1956.
35. James George Frazer, *The Golden Bough* (1890).
36. See further my comments on Frazer in chap. 2.
37. Henri Hubert and Marcel Mauss, "Essai sur la nature et la fonction du sacrifice," which appeared first in *L'Année sociologique* (1898). Translated by W. D. Halls under the title *Sacrifice: Its Nature and Function* (Chicago and London: University of Chicago Press; 1968).
38. Émile Durkheim, *Les formes élémentaires de la vie religieuse* (1912). Translated by J. W. Swain under the title *The Elementary Forms of Religious Life*. I have used the Free Press paperback, 1965.
39. E. E. Evans-Pritchard, *Nuer Religion* (Oxford: Clarendon, 1956).
40. Jean-Pierre Vernant (with Marcel Detienne), *The Cuisine of Sacrifice Among the Greeks* (Chicago: Chicago University Press, 1989). Also recently translated into English is Vernant's *Myth and Tragedy in Ancient Greece*, trans. J. Lloyd (New York: Zone Books, 1988).

    Marcel Detienne has written some significant books on Greek religion and culture, including *The Gardens of Adonis*, trans. J. Lloyd (Atlantic Highlands, NJ: Hassocks, 1977), and *Dionysos at Large*, trans. A. Goldhammer (Cambridge: Harvard University Press, 1989).
41. Jean-Pierre Vernant, *Religion grecque, religions antiques*, inaugural lecture at Collège de France, Paris, 1976, 30–31.
42. L. de Heusch, *Sacrifice in Africa: A Structuralist Approach*, trans. Linda O'Brien and Alice Morton (Manchester: Manchester University Press, 1985).
43. *Sacrifier* is a term introduced by Hubert and Mauss to desgnate the one on whose behalf the sacrifice is performed.
44. De Heusch, *Sacrifice in Africa*, 205.
45. De Heusch, *Sacrifice in Africa*, 215.
46. Hamerton-Kelly's criticism of Lévi-Strauss in *Paul*: "Lévi-Strauss' topological interpretation leaves some critical points unaccounted for. Firstly, one might ask why the generation of something as antiseptic as his immaculately conceived differential thought should so frequently be represented by a violent expulsion. Secondly, if the

expulsion is for the purpose of disencumbering a field, the expelled must come from within that field; in the myths the victim comes both from within and from without. Thirdly, his topology cannot account for the conjunction of the chief elements in the structure. Fourthly, it cannot account for the fact that the eliminated fragment at first bears a negative connotation and then a positive connotation. Only the surrogate victim mechanism accounts for all the important phenomena"(37).

47. Shakespeare, *The History of Troilus and Cressida*, ed. D. Seltzer (New York: Signet, 1963), I.i.94–95, p. 50.

48. Stated in a lecture at Stanford University, winter quarter of 1990.

49. De Heusch, *Sacrifice in Africa*, 16.

50. De Heusch, *Sacrifice in Africa*, 17.

51. De Heusch, *Sacrifice in Africa*, 17.

52. See Girard, "The Founding Murder," in Paul Dumouchel, ed., *Violence and Truth* (Stanford, CA: Stanford University Press, 1988).

53. De Heusch, *Sacrifice in Africa*, 17.

54. See note 46.

55. Girard, *Things Hidden*, 100–101.

56. See Jacques Derrida, "Structure, Sign, and Play in the Discourse of the Human Sciences" and other essays in *Writing and Difference*, trans. Alan Bass (Chicago: University of Chicago Press, 1978), and "Plato's Pharmacy" in *Dissemination*, trans. Barbara Johnson (Chicago: University of Chicago Press, 1981). Derrida coined the neologism "différance" in order to call attention to his view of the many functions of difference and deferral in texts and culture.

57. See Derrida, "Structure, Sign, and Play," 292–293.

58. One must say concept or image of the object, since modern linguistics, influenced by the dichotomies of Kant's philosophy, does not understand signifiers as representing the thing "in itself." I agree that nothing is represented purely and absolutely in and of itself, but one of the functions of the Girardian model is to call into question the dogma of antireferentiality in modern intellectual history.

59. Girard, *Things Hidden*, 103.

60. Girard, *Things Hidden*, 103.

61. *Webster's Third New International Dictionary of the English Language*, s.v. "metaphor," "metonym," "synecdoche."

62. This application of the emergence of tropes in language to a theory of generative scapegoating was inspired by the seminar session at Stanford University with Girard on March 12, 1990, and in particular by the contributions of Robert Hamerton-Kelly and Jorgen Jorgensen.

63. In biblical criticism since the nineteenth century, the Pentateuch or Torah has been analyzed into different parts that were composed at different times in the history of ancient Israel. Originally viewed as "documents" by Julius Wellhausen and his predecessors, they are now construed on a spectrum ranging from "sources" to "layers" and "traditions of interpretation." Since Wellhausen's time, P, or the Priestly Source, is seen as really the completion of the Torah sometime in the exilic or postexilic period. J, or the Yahwist Source (for the divine name Yahweh, Jahweh in German), is commonly accounted to be the oldest, going back in some form perhaps to the tenth century B.C.E. It is the only account of Israel's past that is often viewed as the work of a creative writer. The other two main sources or traditions of interpretation (there are many variations on these) are E, for the Elohist (from Elohim,

God), ninth–eighth century B.C.E., and D, for Deuteronomy, the core of which was written by 621 B.C.E. (see 2 Kings 22–23), but which may have been completed as we know it much later. It is very difficult to distinquish the J source from E, and in fact redaction critics are now inclined to focus on the "Jehowist," a hypothetical redaction of J and E that dates to the late pre-exilic period.

64. Girard, *Things Hidden*, 146.
65. Livy, *Early History*, 40. Girard, referring to information given by Michel Serres, states that *in turba* should be translated "in the crowd" (*Scapegoat*, 92).
66. Girard, *Violence*, 4.
67. Girard, "Differentiation and Reciprocity in Lévi-Strauss and Contemporary Theory,"in *Double Business*.
68. The Hebrew *tehom* is a cognate of the Babylonian *tiamat*. The *-at* is a feminine ending in old Babylonian, which has no *h* sound. Tiamat is the mother goddess of the ocean waters who is defeated and slain by Marduk in the Babylonian cosmogony, *Enuma Elish*.
69. Norbert Lohfink, "Die Schichten des Pentateuch und der Krieg," in Lohfink, ed., *Gewalt und Gewaltlosigkeit im Alten Testament* (Freiburg im Breisgau: Herder, 1983), 89, 86, 110, my translation.
70. Girard, *Things Hidden*, 143.
71. James B. Pritchard, *Ancient Near Eastern Texts*, 2d ed. (Princeton, NJ: Princeton University Press, 1955), 3–6.
72. John 15:25 citing Ps. 35:19; Luke 22:37 citing Isa 53:10.

Chapter 2. Enemy Brothers

1. See S. H. Hooke, *Middle Eastern Mythology* (Middlesex and New York: Penguin, 1963), 123–126. This interpretation is opposed by Theodor H. Gaster, *Myth, Legend and Custom in the Old Testament*, a comparative study with chapters from Sir James G. Frazer's *Folklore in the Old Testament* (New York: Harper & Row, 1969), 74.
2. *Dialectical* is a word that stems from formal argumentation in logic. As I am using it here it has another, common meaning derived from its usage in modern theology: the play, the movement back and forth between two ideas or phenomena that stand in tension or opposition to each other, but that require each other, e.g., the particular and the general, the present and the absent, or here prohibition (which interdicts killing) and sacrifice (which requires killing).
3. Gaster, *Myth, Legend and Custom*, 55.
4. Hamerton-Kelly, *Paul*, 92–93.
5. See entries 1 and 2 under *"chata"* in Francis Brown, S. R. Driver, C. A. Briggs, *Hebrew and English Lexicon of the Old Testament*, based on the lexicon of William Gesenius (Oxford: Clarendon, 1959), 306–307.
6. Girard, *Violence*, 127.
7. See Girard, *Job*, chap. 6.
8. See Girard, *Scapegoat*, chap. 13.
9. See Hyam Maccoby, *The Sacred Executioner: Human Sacrifice and the Legacy of Guilt* (New York: Thames & Hudson, 1982). This is an interesting book whose thesis overlaps my own. However, Maccoby's argument is finally vitiated by the lack of a consistent theoretical model by which to judge his use of data and his conclusions. Insofar as he has a model it is Freudian. For example, his view of the ancient Israelite and

the early Christian traditions reads like an adaptation of Freud's thesis in *Moses and Monotheism* (see discussion of Freud in chap. 3 of this book): "One of the most important ways in which this process of transformation and sublimation [of pagan myths and rituals of sacrifice] can be traced is in the Biblical myths and stories, which are often basically pagan myths of sacrifice elaborated and essentially transformed to accommodate the new Hebraic insights about moral responsibility and the undesirability of shifting blame by splitting-off devices and excuses of various kinds. Nevertheless, in the basic myth of the New Testament, we shall note a regression to earlier modes of atonement, and, inevitably, a revival of the idea of shifting blame by vicarious atonement, both in the form of a sacrificial victim and in the less understood form of the Sacred Executioner . . . who vicariously undergoes the guilt felt by mankind because of its desperate recourse to sacrificial modes of atonement for its sins" (10).

10. Gaster, *Myth, Legend and Custom*, 55–56.
11. Gaster, *Myth, Legend and Custom*, 57.
12. Gaster, *Myth, Legend and Custom*, 65.
13. Ruth Mellinkoff, *The Mark of Cain* (Berkeley and Los Angeles: University of California Press, 1981), 98.
14. David Daube, *Studies in Biblical Law* (New York: Ktav, 1969), 193–194, 199–200.
15. Daube, *Studies in Biblical Law*, 199.
16. See Daube, *Studies in Biblical Law*, 195.
17. Daube, *Studies in Biblical Law*.
18. See entries 1b and 2 under *"avur"* in Brown, Driver, and Briggs, *Hebrew and English Lexicon*, 721.
19. Frazer, in Gaster, *Myth, Legend and Custom*, 175, 181–182.
20. Girard, *Violence*, 5.
21. Girard, *Violence*, 6.
22. For instance, as the sacrificial victim in Gen 22 and in getting (receiving) Rebecca as his wife in Gen 24.
23. Hartmut Gese, "Die Sühne," *Zur Biblischen Theologie* (Munich: Kaiser Verlag, 1977), 90 (my trans.). The passages discussed include Exod 21:30; 32:30–32; 2 Sam 21:1–14; Deut 32:43; Isa 6:7; Deut 21:1–9; 1 Sam 3:14.
24. See James G. Williams, "The Comedy of Jacob," *Journal of the American Academy of Religion* Supplement 46 (1978), 241–266, where I treat in some detail wordplays, sound plays (e.g., on the consonants in Jacob's name), and repetitions.
25. For example, "angel of the LORD " in Exod 3:3, 7.
26. See Williams, "Comedy of Jacob."
27. See Stanley Gevirtz, "Of Patriarchs and Puns: Joseph at the Fountain, Jacob at the Ford," *Hebrew Union College Annual* 46 (1975), 51–53.
28. See Vladimir Propp, *Morphology of the Folktale*, ed. S. Pirkova-Jacobson, trans. L. Scott (Bloomington: Indiana University Press, 1958), function 17.
29. R. Barthes, in Barthes, et al., "La lutte avec l'ange," *Analyse Structurale et Exégèse Biblique: Essais d'interprétation* (Paris: Delachaus et Niestlé, 1971), 28, 33, 34 (my trans.).
30. Barthes, "La lutte avec l'ange," 35, 36.
31. Barthes, "La lutte avec l'ange," 39.
32. Michael Fishbane, *Text and Texture* (New York: Schocken, 1979), 52.
33. Fishbane, *Text and Texture*, 52–53.

34. See in particular Girard's comment on the concept of the unconscious as a kind of *deus ex machina* that intervenes from the past in neurotic episodes. *Critiques dans un souterain*, 33–34.

35. Fishbane certainly comes close to this recognition with his statement that the Jacob cycle "opens as a tale of barrenness and birth, of deception and strife, of rights and priorities, and of blessing and power. As intimated, these issues recur throughout the narrative" (Fishbane, *Text and Texture*, 46).

36. Jacob's final words in Gen 49 are actually identified more as prophecy than blessing (49:1). Only the pronouncement on Joseph is completely favorable. Reuben committed near incest with Bilhah, Jacob's concubine and mother of his half-brothers Dan and Naphtali (Gen 49:4; 35:22; 30:1–6). Simeon and Levi are denounced for their violence (49:5–7; 34; see discussion in chap. 4). The words about Judah contain an allusion both to the betrayal of Joseph (49:9) and to the unsavory incident involving Tamar (49:10; 38). There is a reference to Dan as like a "snake" and Benjamin as like a "ravenous wolf" (49:17, 27).

37. See "The 'Emerging Exception,' Language, and Culture" in chap. 1 for the discussion of synecdoche, metonym, and metaphor.

38. I owe this schema to Hans J. L. Jensen, who presented it to a seminar at Stanford University in the winter quarter of 1990. It is found also in Jensen's introduction to Girard, which is written in Danish: *René Girard* (Frederiksberg: ANIS, 1991), 51.

39. Because Potiphar is like a father to Joseph, the accusation is comparable to the charge of incest.

40. See also the same phrase in Jacob's mouth in Gen 30:2, where it has the same meaning of denying divine power but without the same dramatic force in the story.

41. Menahem Stern, ed., *From Herodotus to Plutarch*, vol. 1 in *Greek and Latin Authors on Jews and Judaism*, 3 vols. (Jerusalem: Israel Academy of Sciences and Humanities, 1972–1984), 337. Stern observes that Pompeius's remark about Joseph seeming like a god "should be related to the tradition, prevalent in literature from the second century C.E. onwards, which derives from a syncretistic Graeco-Egyptian environment. . . . According to this tradition, Joseph was considered worthy of divine worship under the name of Serapis. The same tradition prevails in the talmudic sources" (240).

42. Stern, ed., *From Herodotus to Plutarch*, 419. Stern remarks, "There may be some justification for discerning here an Egyptian tradition that knew the leaders of the defiled people as the priests Tisithen and Peteseph, who were supposedly identified with Moses and Joseph at a later stage" (421).

43. See James G. Williams, *Women Recounted: Narrative Thinking and the God of Israel* (Sheffield: Almond, 1982), chap. 2, on such typical elements in the stories of the matriarchs.

44. See, e.g., the genealogical order in Gen 25:12–18 and the sequence of the names in the Blessing of Jacob, Genesis 49.

45. Undifferentiation is also signaled in the birth of the twins Jacob and Esau, in that Esau is the elder but just barely. The plot of the story then revolves around the proper differentiation of the twins. See Jacob and Esau section in this chapter.

46. Stith Thompson, *Motif-Index of Folk-Literature*, rev. and enlarged ed. (Bloomington: Indiana University Press, 1956). H1242, youngest brother alone succeeds in quest. *Type 402, 471, 550, 551, 577; BP 260, 503; Irish myth, etc. L10, victorious youngest son (under Reversal of Fortune).

47. Hans J. L. Jensen, in a paper written for a seminar with René Girard at Stanford University, winter quarter of 1990. See Propp, *Morphology*. See analysis of stories 79

and 92 on pp. 115–116, 118–119. Note also stories 195 and 77 on pp. 44–45. See the excursus at the end of this chapter for a note on folkloristic approaches to the Bible.

48. See the summary of stories 195 and 77 in Propp, *Morphology*, 44–45. "A dying father requests his sons to spend three nights beside his grave. The youngest son fulfills the request and receives a horse." "Brothers find a large stone. 'Should it not be moved?' (trial without a tester). The elder brothers cannot manage to move it. The youngest moves it, revealing below it a vault in which there are three horses."

49. There are some problems with the text, which is translated quite differently in the Septuagint (Greek translation of the Hebrew Scriptures). A note in the critical text that I use (*Biblica Hebraica Stuttgartensia*. Stuttgart: Deutsche Bibelstiftung, 1977), suggests that the phrase is a gloss that uses the wording of Gen 3:16: "To you (sin) is his desire and you (sin) will master him." The problem is that this form of the word *sin, chattat,* is feminine, whereas *crouching* in Hebrew is an active masculine participle (*croucher*) and the possessive suffix with *desire* is masculine. However, I read the sentence as shifting the subject from *sin* (feminine) to the beast or demon crouching, which is masculine ("sin is a croucher" or "crouching beast"); see the discussion of the verse in the Cain and Abel section of this chapter: the beast or demon crouches in ambush for Cain.

50. Brown, Driver, and Briggs, *Hebrew and English Lexicon*, 306.

51. See the discussion of this tale in the next chapter.

52. See the section in chap. 3 on Manetho, Apion, and Freud as promulgators of an "Egyptian" myth of the Exodus.

53. As indicated in John R. Donahue, S.J., *The Gospel in Parable* (Philadephia: Fortress, 1988), 152.

54. This aspect of the parable became paradigmatic both religously and literarily in Western culture. See Gabriel Josipovici, *The Book of God: A Response to the Bible* (New Haven, CT: Yale University Press, 1988).

55. Note that the emotional if not always the factual connection of disappointment and deception is captured in the French *decevoir*, whose basic meaning is "trick" or "deceive," but which is the verb commonly employed to express disappointment: *je suis déçu* = "I am disappointed."

56. See the work of W. Robertson Smith, discussed in chap. 1, and Girard's thesis concerning hunting and meat eating in *Things Hidden*, 72–73. Girard says, "Specialists tell us that the human digestive tract has remained that of the mainly vegetarian omnivore, the kind of system that preceded ours in the course of evolution. . . . To understand what might have impelled human beings to set off in pursuit of the largest and most dangerous animals or to devise the strategies necessary for prehistoric hunting, it is necessary and sufficient to recognize that hunting, at first, was actively linked to sacrifice. . . . What impelled men to hunt was the search for a reconciliatory victim" (73).

57. William F. Arndt and F. Wilbur Gingrich, *A Greek-English Lexicon of the New Testament and Other Early Christian Literature*, based on Walter Bauer's *Griechisch-Deutsches Wörterbuch*, 4th rev. ed. (Chicago and Cambridge: University of Chicago and University Press, 1957), 525.

58. See the critique of various approaches to sacrifice in chap. 1, "Theories of Sacrifice," under "Girard's Explanatory Model."

59. Susan Niditch, *Underdogs and Tricksters: A Prelude to Biblical Folklore* (San Francisco: Harper & Row, 1987).

60. Robert Pelton, quoted in Niditch, *Underdogs and Tricksters*, 45.

61. Niditch, *Underdogs and Tricksters*, referring in particular to the work of Paul Radin.
62. Niditch, *Underdogs and Tricksters*, xi.
63. Girard, *Scapegoat*, 84.
64. Girard, *Scapegoat*, 84–85.
65. Niditch, *Underdogs and Tricksters*, 146–147.
66. The work of Hans J. L. Jensen of the University of Aarhus is very promising in this regard. So far only one of his writings is available in English, "The Fall of the King," *Scandanavian Journal of the Old Testament* 1991 volume, issue 1, 121–147. For those who read Danish, a good sampling of his approach may be found in "Den strukturelle myteanalyse-og Det gamle Testamente," in B. Otzen, H. Gottlieb, K. Jeppesen, and H. J. L. Jensen, *Myter in Det gamle Testamente* (Frederiksberg: ANIS, 1990). He has also written an introduction in Danish to Girard, *René Girard* (Fredericksberg: ANIS, 1991).
67. Niditch, *Underdogs and Tricksters*, 147.
68. Niditch, *Underdogs and Tricksters*, 152.
69. See the discussion of Derrida's *différence* as continual mimetic crisis in chap. 1, "The Emerging Exception, Language, and Culture," under "Girard's Explanatory Model."

Chapter 3. Moses and the Exodus

1. John A. Wilson, in *Ancient Near Eastern Texts Relating to the Old Testament*, 2d ed., ed. James B. Pritchard (Princeton, NJ: Princeton University Press, 1955), 230.
2. See Girard, "The Plague in Literature and Myth," in *Double Business*, 136–155.
3. See Francis Brown, S. R. Driver, C. A. Briggs, *Hebrew and English Lexicon of the Old Testament*, based on the lexicon of William Gesenius (Oxford: Clarendon, 1959), 68–69.
4. See chap. 7 of Girard, *Job*. In chap. 26 of his book on Shakespeare he notes that the name of Achilles' underlings, the Myrmidons, meant "ant" in Greek. The image suggested is that of many killers attacking their victim in a swarm.
5. Martin Buber, *The Prophetic Faith* (New York: Harper & Brothers, 1949), 52. See also his chapter "Divine Demonism" in *Moses: The Revelation and the Covenant* (New York: Harper & Brothers, Torchbook, 1958), 56–59.
6. This is also the way I would view Genesis 22, the Binding of Isaac. Whatever the specifics of one's interpretation of the passage, it should be placed within this context, whose structure and dynamics are those of *ritual*. The promises are undone in order to reaffirm them.
7. Gaster's explanation is that the Hebrew *chatan* is cognate to the Arabic *hatana*, "circumcise." On this explanation, Zipporah would be understood to say, "Surely you [the deity] are a circumcision of blood to me." A proper translation of 4:26b would then be, "She said, 'A circumcision of blood' with respect to circumcision." By this act she establishes kinship with the deity. Theodor H. Gaster, *Myth, Legend and Custom in the Old Testament*, a comparative study with chapters from Sir James G. Frazer's *Folklore in the Old Testament* (New York: Harper & Row, 1969), 234. Gaster's reading is interesting, though it does not finally matter for our purposes in this context. What is essential is the sacrificial act whereby the relationship with deity is established or regained.
8. See Brevard Childs, who concludes this is the redactor's perspective. Childs, *The Book of Exodus: A Critical, Theological Commentary*, Old Testament Library (Philadelphia: Westminster, 1974), 101.
9. Eric Voegelin, *Order and History*, vol. 1, *Israel and Revelation* (Baton Rouge: Louisiana State University Press, 1956), 401. In this statement Voegelin presupposes his discussion of Exod 4:22–23, which will be taken up below.

10. Voegelin, *Israel and Revelation*, 390.

11. Von Rad, *Old Testament Theology*, vol. 1, trans. D. M. G. Stalker (New York: Harper & Brothers, 1962).

12. Childs, *Book of Exodus*, 15.

13. Voegelin, *Israel and Revelation*, 391.

14. The Christian response, based on the Gospels, is that Jesus as the Christ succeeds. The basis of this affirmation will be examined in chaps. 7 and 8.

15. Girard, *Violence*, 69.

16. See Childs, *Book of Exodus*, 28–42.

17. See Girard on Ulysses' speech in Shakespeare's *Troilus and Cressida*, in *Violence*, 50–51: "O when Degree is shaked/Which is the ladder to all high designs,/The enterprise is sick!" See also chap. 18 of his *Shakespeare*.

18. The crucial character of the master-slave relationship for self-consciousness was recognized by Hegel; see chap. 4A of *Phenomenology of Spirit* trans. A. V. Miller (Oxford: Oxford University Press, 1977) and the illuminating commentary by Alexandre Kojève, chap. 1 of his *Introduction to the Reading of Hegel*, assembled by Raymond Queneau, ed. Allan Bloom, trans. James H. Nichols, Jr. (Ithaca and London: Cornell University Press, 1980).

19. See George Coats, *Rebellion in the Wilderness* (Nashville: Abingdon, 1968).

20. The Hebrew verb is *lun*, which is found only in Exod 15–17, Num 14, 16, and 17, and Josh 9:18. The standard work of reference on the murmuring traditions in contemporary biblical scholarship is Coats, *Rebellion in the Wilderness*.

21. So Bernhard Anderson: "It was believed that the leaves or bark of certain trees had magical properties for sweetening or 'healing' water," *The New Oxford Annotated Bible with the Apocrypha*, ed. Herbert G. May and Bruce M. Metzger (New York: Oxford, 1973), 87. Gaster implies that his understanding is the same in *Myth, Legend and Custom*, 241–242.

22. Childs, *Book of Exodus*, 269.

23. Jacques Derrida, "Plato's Pharmacy" in *Dissemination*, trans. Barbara Johnson (Chicago: University of Chicago Press, 1981), 61–171.

24. Derrida, "Plato's Pharmacy," 130–133.

25. For Girard's appreciation of Derrida's analysis of *pharmakon*, see *Violence*, 296–297.

26. Girard, *Scapegoat*. I owe this paragraph primarily to Hans Jensen's helpful comments on the passage in a letter of July 22, 1990.

27. See Girard, *Scapegoat*, chap. 2. I cannot resist quoting a sports columnist who wrote about Pete Rose, the baseball "star" who was accused of gambling on baseball games and betting on his own team, "If there's one thing the American public likes better than an idol, it's a fallen idol." Unfortunately, I no longer have the source for this quote.

28. It is possible that the episode of the "unholy fire" offered by Nadab and Abihu, Aaron's oldest sons (Lev 10:1–7), represents an underlying conflict between Moses and Aaron. That the narrator notes, "And Aaron held his peace" (Lev 10:3, RSV), may be a sign that Aaron was not content with Moses' leadership. This passage will be discussed in chap. 4, under "The Struggle over Sacrifice."

29. In ancient Egyptian, Moses (*mosheh* in Hebrew) is derived from a word for "son," which is found in many royal names (e.g., Thutmose). See Childs, *Book of Exodus*, 19.

30. For a helpful summary, see von Rad, *Old Testament Theology*, 289–296.

31. See von Rad, *Old Testament Theology*, 293–294.

32. Girard, *Deceit*, 9.

33. Von Rad, *Old Testament Theology*, 294.

35. Josephus referring to Manetho and Apion et al.; see Menahem Stern, ed., *From Herodotus to Plutarch*, vol. 1 of *Greek and Latin Authors on Jews and Judaism*, 3 vols. (Jerusalem: Israel Academy of Sciences and Humanities, 1972–1984): Hecataeus of Abdera, c. 300 B.C.E., no. 11; Manetho, third century B.C.E., nos. 19 and 21 concerning Exodus; Diodorus, first century B.C.E., no. 63; Pompeius Trogus, end of first century B.C.E., beginning of first century C.E., no. 137; Lysimachus, date unknown, no. 158; Apion, first half of first century C.E., nos. 164 and 165 concerning Exodus; Chaeremon, first half of first century C.E., no. 178. For a survey of Moses in these sources, see John G. Gager, *Moses in Greco-Roman Paganism*, Society of Biblical Literature Monograph Series 16 (Nashville: Abingdon, 1972), 113–133.

35. For a version of this summary and information on sources, I am indebted to Hans Jensen.

36. Gager, *Moses in Greco-Roman Paganism*, 123.

37. See Girard, "The Plague in Literature and Myth" in *Double Business*: "The distinctiveness of the plague is that it ultimately destroys all forms of distinctiveness. . . . All life, finally, is turned into death, which is the supreme undifferentiation" (137). Concerning the plagues in Exodus: "The 'ten plagues' are a worsening social breakdown, which also appears in the form of a destructive rivalry between Moses and the magicians of Egypt" (144).

38. Sophocles, *The Oedipus Cycle*, trans. D. Fitts and R. Fitzgerald (New York: Harcourt, Brace & World, 1949), 7.

39. Sir James George Frazer, *The New Golden Bough*, ed. T. H. Gaster (Garden City, NY: Doubleday Anchor Books, 1959), 192–193; see also Cornelius Loew, *Myth, Sacred History, and Philosophy* (New York: Harcourt, Brace & World, 1967), 74–78. Note an instance of routine ceremonial questioning in the Pyramid Texts:

    "Question [on the part of the court]: 'How did it come to pass that Horus, the god, died?'

    "Answer [on the part of the crown prince]: 'The death of the god could not be effected but by murder. It was only the equal of Horus, his brother Seth, who was powerful enough to kill him.'

    "Q: 'You have said that your father who thus has become Osiris is buried in the earth and at the same time lives in heaven. What does this mean?'

    "A: 'The king who was Horus and is now Osiris originated in the primeval beginning, in eternity, and he has gone back to where he originated'" (quoted in Loew, *Myth, Sacred History, and Philosophy*, 76).

40. Girard has anticipated some aspects of this discussion of Freud with a brief statement in *Scapegoat*: "Freud is the only major modern author who took these rumors [of collective murder in ancient mythology] seriously. . . . But he fails to draw the obvious conclusion from the remarkable similarity of the rumors about Moses and those about so many other religious lawgivers and founders (an unusual omission for the author of *Totem and Taboo*, one that may be explained by his overly partial critique of the Jewish religion)" (88).

41. Freud, *Moses and Monotheism* (New York: Random House Vintage Books, 1967), 33–34.

42. Freud, *Moses and Monotheism*, 58.

43. Freud, *Moses and Monotheism*, 71.

44. Totemism as a universal phenomenon has been discredited in anthropology and history of religion, but Freud's insight into the substitutionary process should be given more credit than it has been given. Freud's psychological anthropology has obviously

influenced Girard, as the latter has acknowledged. Girard believes that Freud was on the right track but became caught up in his own myth of the Unconscious, the Oedipus complex, and the death wish.

45. Freud, *Moses and Monotheism*, 158.
46. Freud, *Moses and Monotheism*, 172–173.
47. Freud, *Moses and Monotheism*, 176, 175.
48. See Emanuel Rice, *Freud and Moses: The Long Journey Home* (Albany: State University of New York Press, 1990), and William J. McGrath, *Freud's Discovery of Psychoanalysis* (Ithaca, NY: Cornell University Press, 1986). This evidence was either not known to Peter Gay or ignored by him (see n. 53 below). Religious instruction, introduction to biblical and liturgical Hebrew (despite Freud's later disclaimers), and especially the effect of some of the illustrations in the Philippsohn Bible are factors that considerably complicate the picture of Freud and his attitudes toward religion.
49. "No consideration, however, will move me to set aside truth in favour of supposed national interests" (Freud, *Moses and Monotheism*, 3).
50. Freud, *Moses and Monotheism*, 39.
51. See P. Lacoue-Labarthe, *L'imitation des modernes* (Paris: Editions Galilée, 1986).
52. See Peter Gay, *Freud: A Life for Our Time* (New York: Doubleday Anchor Books, 1988). What Freud published carried the influence of his reputation as the founder of psychoanalysis; however, he was probably very ambivalent about the status of his *Moses* as social science. In a letter to Lou Andreas-Salome of January 6, 1935, he described the work as a "historical novel" (Gay, 605, and notes, 732).
53. Gay, *Freud*, 204–205 and notes, 679.
54. McGrath, *Freud's Discovery of Psychoanalysis*, chap. 1.
55. M. Robert, *The Psychoanalytic Revolution*, trans. Kenneth Morgan (New York: Harcourt, Brace & World, 1966), 380.
56. Robert, *The Psychoanalytic Revolution*, 383.
57. S. Handelman, *The Slayers of Moses: The Emergence of Rabbinic Interpretation in Modern Literary Theory* (Albany: State University of New York Press, 1982), 132–133.
58. See William Scott Green, "Romancing the Tome: Rabbinic Hermeneutics and the Theory of Literature," *Semeia* 40 (1987), 147–168.
59. See Gay, *Freud*.
60. In a letter to me commenting on this segment of the excursus, Stuart Lasine said, "I think the great man myth really is a romantic hangover" (September 10, 1990). Concerning Mann, opposed as he was to Nazism and any sort of political fascism, Lasine observes that "Mann liked the sloppy and fascist *Demian* by Hesse. . ., the most popular book in Germany immediately after WWI. . . . The notions of having a *Doppelgänger* (internal or not), being internally alienated, being aware of being a human bridge to a new age or realm, [all stem from the romantic myth of the great man]."
61. See Victor Farias, *Heidegger and Nazism* (Philadelphia: Temple University Press, 1989), 215–228, which makes this connection clear. For a less polemical, more balanced critique of Heidegger's political involvement with National Socialism, see Hugo Ott, *Martin Heidegger: A Political Life*, tr. A. Blunden (New York: Basic Books, 1993).
62. See Farias, *Heidegger and Nazism*, 227–228, and Ott, *Martin Heidegger*, 271, 273.
63. As quoted in Farias. I have consulted the German text of 1953: *Einführung in die Metaphysik* (Tübingen: Niemeyer, 1953), 117.
64. My translation of Heidegger, *Einführung in die Metaphysik*, 47.

65. Heidegger, *Einführung in die Metaphysik*, 100–101, 101, 102.
66. As cited in Robert, *The Psychoanalytic Revolution*, 367–368.
67. Thomas Mann, *The Tables of the Law*, trans. H. T. Lowe-Porter (New York: Knopf, 1945), 62. The German text has only "*Denn das Bündig-Bindende ist es und Kurzgefasste, der Fels des Anstandes,*" p. 874 of *Das Gesetz* in Mann, *Gesammelte Werke*, 2d ed., Band 8 (Frankfort am Main: Fischer, 1974), 808–876.
68. Mann, *Tables*, 1, 2.
69. Stuart Lasine pointed this out to me. "He [Mann] . . . did so in order to depict Moses as an artist working with great toil and difficulty with resistant raw human material" (letter of September 10, 1990).
70. Mann, *Tables*, 9.

Chapter 4. Covenant and Sacrifice

1. I am using *Biblia Hebraica Stuttgartensia* (see ch.2, n.49) and the New Revised Standard Version.
2. Jewish interpreters have traditionally combined the words concerning the neighbor in 20:16–17 into one commandment.
3. See Brevard Childs, *The Book of Exodus: A Critical, Theological Commentary*, Old Testament Library (Philadelphia: Westminster, 1974), 409–412.
4. See James G. Williams, *Those Who Ponder Proverbs: Aphoristic Thinking and Biblical Literature* (Sheffield: Almond, 1981), 26–28, 40–42.
5. See Mark 3:31–35; Matt 12:46–50; Luke 8:19–21; 9:59–60.
6. See Childs, *Book of Exodus*, 419–421.
7. Childs, *Book of Exodus*, 427.
8. Martin Buber *Moses: The Revelation and the Covenant* (New York: Harper & Brothers Torchbook, 1958), 114. This reference comes from an unpublished paper by Gil Bailie.
9. Jacques Derrida,"Violence and Metaphysics," in *Writing and Difference*, trans. Alan Bass (Chicago: University of Chicago Press, 1978), 108.
10. "Edmund Jabès and the Question of the Book" in *Writing and Difference*, 64–66.
11. Mark S. Smith, *The Early History of God: Yahweh and the Other Deities in Ancient Israel* (San Francisco: Harper & Row, 1990), 132–138.
12. Explicitly only in Mic 6:6–8, mentioned below in this chapter, but implicitly in the prophetic condemnation of sacrifice. See chap. 5.
13. See Stuart Lasine, "Levite Violence, Fratricide and Sacrifice in the Bible and Later Revolutionary Rhetoric," in *Curing Violence*, ed. Theophus Smith and Mark Wallace (forthcoming).
14. Lasine, "Levite Violence, Fratricide and Sacrifice."
15. Gil Bailie, in an unpublished paper on the Levites and Israel's beginnings.
16. Lasine, "Levite Violence, Fratricide and Sacrifice."
17. Lasine, "Levite Violence, Fratricide and Sacrifice."
18. For a discussion of the possible relation of this story to the account of Jeroboam and his sons Nadab and Abijah in 1 Kings 12, 14–15, see David Damrosch, "Leviticus," in Robert Alter and Frank Kermode, eds., *The Literary Guide to the Bible* (Cambridge, MA: Harvard University Press, Belknap Press), 1987.
19. Bailie, see note 15.
20. Lasine, "Levite Violence, Fratricide and Sacrifice."
21. Bailie, see note 15.

Chapter 5. Kings and Prophets

1. See Psalm 2, where in the cultic drama of coronation the voice of God says, "I have set my king on Zion, my holy hill" (v. 4).

2. Voegelin thought Jeremiah was here appropriating the royal son of god symbolism of the ancient Near Eastern imperial myths. Eric Voegelin, *Order and History*, vol. 1, *Israel and Revelation* (Baton Rouge: Louisiana State University Press, 1956), 467–470. William Holladay has argued that Jeremiah understood himself as a prophet like Moses, *Jeremiah: Spokesman out of Time* (Philadelphia: Pilgrim, 1974). Holladay's thesis could complement Voegelin's: if they are correct, then Jeremiah understood himself as the new Moses in history, as the new bearer of order to whom God's rule had been transferred. On kings functioning as prophets, see Wolfgang Palaver, *Politik und Religion bei Thomas Hobbes: Eine Kritik aus der Sicht der Theorie René Girards*, Innsbrucker theologische Studien 33 (Innsbruck: Tyrolia-Verlag, 1991).

3. Girard, *Things Hidden*, 55–56.

4. Girard, *Violence*, 108–109.

5. Girard, *Violence*, 109.

6. Alberto R. W. Green, *The Role of Human Sacrifice in the Ancient Near East*, ASOR Dissertation Series 1 (Missoula: Scholars Press, 1975), 201. On ancient Israel, see Mark S. Smith, *The Early History of God: Yahweh and the Other Deities in Ancient Israel* (San Francisco: Harper & Row, 1990).

7. See Isa 17:14: "This is the *cheleq* of those who despoil us, and the *goral* of those who plunder us." Note also Josh 15:1: "The lot (*haggoral*) for the tribe of the people of Judah," where "lot" means the same thing as "portion."

8. Geo Widengren, *Religionsphänomenologie*, 294 (my trans.), as cited in Palaver, *Politik*, 222, n. 225. Frazer collected many instances of ritual regicide and royal surrogates in *The New Golden Bough*, ed. with notes and foreword by T. H. Gaster (Garden City, NY: Doubleday Anchor Books, 1959 [abridgment of work published in 1890]), 129–154. On this phenomenon in Mesopotamia, see Green, *Role of Human Sacrifice*, 85–95.

9. For this paragraph I am indebted to Palaver's treatment, which is richly documented (Palaver, *Politik*, 221–222). For a brief, accessible description in English, see Mircea Eliade, *Cosmos and History: The Myth of the Eternal Return* (New York: Harper Torchbooks, 1959), 55–58 (first published in English 1954). The ritual enactment of Marduk's descent into the underworld and the corresponding humiliation of his representative, the king, is another indication that the myth partially conceals that Marduk was a scapegoat and that Kingu was his surrogate and executed in his stead.

10. On the size of the king as associated with stature, see Theodor Gaster, *Thespis: Ritual, Myth, and Drama in the Ancient Near East*, 2d rev. ed. (Garden City, NY: Doubleday Anchor Books, 1961), 218–219.

11. For this paragraph, I have drawn upon Palaver, *Politik*, 219, n. 218.

12. Girard, *Violence*, 254.

13. Girard, *Violence*, 255.

14. Gunn, *The Fate of King Saul, Journal for the Study of Old Testament* Supplement Series 14 (Sheffield: JSOT Press, 1980).

15. William Shakespeare, *The Tragedy of Julius Caesar*, rev. ed., ed. W. Rosen and R. Rosen (New York: Signet, 1987), II.ii.76–81, p. 71.

16. Shakespeare, *Julius Caesar*, II.ii.83–90, p. 71.

17. See Girard, *Shakespeare:* chap. 22.

18. Shakespeare, *Julius Caesar*, II.i.173–180, p. 62.

19. Gunn, *Fate of King Saul*, 128 (emphasis mine). A study like Gunn's shows what *good* literary criticism can accomplish on the basis of sensitive examination of the text. One of the keys to this accomplishment in Gunn's case is familiarity with literature beyond the biblical and ancient Near Eastern texts. The widening of the Bible's literary context to include classical and other literature in order to gain insight into its distinctive themes and its distinctive testimony will be part of the foundation of healthy biblical criticism in the future.

20. Translation of Sophocles' *Oedipus Rex*, by F. Storr, in Loeb Classical Library (Cambridge, MA: Harvard University Press, 1962), lines 1299–1302, pp. 120–121.

21. See William Chase Green, *Moira: Fate, Good, and Evil in Greek Thought* (Gloucester: Peter Smith, 1968), 401–402.

22. The postbiblical tradition preserved a legend of Saul and Jonathan that has all the features of the scapegoat pattern. During David's reign a famine caused by drought ended when he recovered the corpses of Saul and Jonathan, placed them in a shrine or coffin, and sent it throughout the land of Israel so the people could pay homage. When this had been accomplished, the LORD had compassion and sent rain. See R. S. Kluger, *Psyche and Bible* (Zurich: Spring, 1974), 79–81.

23. See H. Frankfort, *Kingship and the Gods* (Chicago: University of Chicago Press, 1948).

24. See Green, *Role of Human Sacrifice*.

25. God's revelation to Samuel in 1 Sam 3 is not a call narrative. Samuel's mother had dedicated him to service at the sanctuary of Shiloh, and the account in 1 Sam 3 indicates both the end of the house of Eli and the future leadership of Samuel.

26. The title of the prophet leader was probably *av*, "father." See my article "The Prophetic 'Father': A Brief Explanation of the Term 'Sons of the Prophets,'" *Journal of Biblical Literature* 85 (1966), 344–348.

27. Phyllis Bird, "The Harlot as Heroine: Narrative Art and Social Presupposition in Three Old Testament Texts," *Semeia* 46 (1989), 119–139.

28. Girard, *Things Hidden*, 155–157.

Chapter 6. Job: the Failed Scapegoat

This chapter is a revised and expanded version of an essay to appear in Leo G. Perdue and W. Clark Gilpin, eds., *The Voice from the Whirlwind: Interpreting the Book of Job*. A still earlier form of the paper was presented in the Job Symposium of the Society of Biblical Literature, Anaheim, California, November 18, 1989.

1. Girard, *Job*, 86–90.

2. J. Grosjean, trans., *Eumenides*, cited in Girard, *Job*, 148.

3. Girard: *Job*, 35.

4. Girard, *Job*, 111–117.

5. Girard, *Job*, 25.

6. Euripides, *The Bacchae*, in *Three Plays of Euripides*, trans. Paul Roche (New York: Norton, 1974), lines 1130–1137, p. 115.

7. Girard, *Job*, 141–142.

8. On "crush," see Norman Habel, *The Book of Job*, Old Testament Library (Philadelphia: Westminster, 1985). On the last line, see Matitiahu Tsevat, "The Meaning of the Book of Job," *Hebrew Union College Annual* 37 (1966).

9. Habel, *The Book of Job*, 558, 563.

10. Robert Alter, *The Art of Biblical Poetry* (New York: Basic Books, 1985), 19–21 and

chap. 3; see James Kugel, *The Idea of Biblical Poetry* (New Haven, CT: Yale University Press, 1981), chap. 1.

11. Mark Wallace's term, in "Postmodern Biblicism: The Challenge of René Girard for Contemporary Theology," *Modern Theology* 5 (1989), 314.

12. Girard, *Scapegoat*, 8.

13. *Pesiqta Rabbati* (ed. M. Friedman, 190b), quoted by Tsevat, in "Meaning of the Book of Job," 106.

14. Girard, *Job*, 159, 160–161 (emphasis mine).

15. Girard, *Job*, 143.

16. No. 1052, as quoted in Girard, "The Founding Murder," in Paul Dumouchel, ed., *Violence and Truth* (Stanford: Stanford University Press, 1988).

17. See Girard, *Things Hidden*, 266; see discussion of Heidegger in chap. 3 under "An Egytian Point of View."

18. Girard, *Things Hidden*, 344.

19. See David L. Miller, *The New Polytheism* (New York: Harper & Row, 1974), 56–57. Miller, following the lead of James Hillman, offers a fragmentary "polytheistic theology." In my view this is simply a kind of double of the putative monomythic and monotheistic imperialism that is held out as a foil.

20. See C. G. Jung, *Psychology and Religion* (New Haven, CT: Yale University Press, 1938), 63–64.

21. C. G. Jung, *Answer to Job*, trans. R. F. C. Hull (Cleveland: World Meridian Books, 1960), 15. This work is part of vol. 11 of Jung's *Collected Works*.

22. Jung, *Answer to Job*, 27, 28, 33.

23. Jung, *Answer to Job*, 43, 46, 48. Jung here alludes to a motif in the kabbalistic philosophy of medieval Jewish mysticism.

24. Jung, *Answer to Job*, 51.

25. Jung, *Answer to Job*, 82, 83.

26. Jung, *Answer to Job*, 88.

27. Jung, *Answer to Job*, 94, 96.

28. Jung, *Answer to Job*, 178, 199, 94.

29. Jung, *Answer to Job*, 133, 168, 169.

30. Jung, *Answer to Job*, 197.

31. Girard, *Things Hidden*, 363.

32. Jung, *Answer to Job*, 197.

33. See chap. 8 of Girard, *Double Business*.

Chapter 7. The Innocent Victim

1. See summary of myths in James G. Frazer, *The New Golden Bough*, ed. with notes and foreword by T. H. Gaster (Garden City, NY: Doubleday Anchor Books, 1959 [abridgment of work published in 1890]), 299–302.

2. Marcel Detienne, *Dionysos at Large*, trans. A. Goldhammer (Cambridge, MA: Harvard University Press, 1989).

3. See Robert A. Oden, Jr., *The Bible Without Theology: The Theological Tradition and Alternatives to It* (San Francisco: Harper & Row, 1987).

4. See René Girard, "Job as Failed Scapegoat," in Leo G. Perdue and W. Clark Gilpin, eds., *The Voice from the Whirlwind*.

5. M. Smith, "No Place for a Son of Man," *Forum* 4,4 (1988), 83–107.

6. The "Targums," in Aramaic "translations" or "interpretations," were expansive paraphrastic translations of the Hebrew Bible.

7. In Q the Son of Man is involved in future, apocalyptically oriented activity in these

instances: Luke 17:24/Matt 24:27; Luke 17:26/Matt 24:37–39; Luke 17:28–30/Matt 24:37–39; Luke 11:30/Matt 12:40; Luke 12:40/Matt 24:4; Luke 12:8–10/Matt 10:32–33. There are three passages where the Son of Man engages in activity in the present: Luke 7:34/Matt 11:19; Luke 12:10/Matt 12:32; Luke 9:58/Matt 8:20. See Richard Edwards, A *Theology of Q: Prophecy, Eschatology, Wisdom* (Philadelphia: Fortress, 1976).

8.   See Williams, *Gospel Against Parable: Mark's Language of Mystery* (Decatur, IL, and Sheffield: Almond, 1985), 222 n. 6 (hereafter *Gospel*); and H. L. Chronis, "The Torn Veil: Cultus and Christology in Mark 15:37–39," *Journal of Biblical Literature* 101 (1982) 97–114.

9.   The Septuagint is the Greek translation of the Hebrew Bible. Most, though not all, of the New Testament citations of Scripture draw upon a Greek translation.

10. The Hebrew text says he will make many righteous, will receive a portion of the great (*rabbim*, which could mean "many" in Hebrew), and bear the sin of many.

11. Robert Hamerton-Kelly, *The Gospel and the Sacred: Poetics of Violence in the Gospel of Mark,* (forthcoming; hereafter *Mark*).

12. As the Grand Inquisitor tells the silent Christ in the famous scene narrated by Ivan in Dostoievski's *The Brothers Karamazov*, he and his institution are simply supplying what people really want: miracle, mystery, and authority.

13. Elizabeth Malbon, *Narrative Space and Mythic Meaning in Mark* (New York and San Francisco: Harper & Row, 1986).

14. Williams, *Gospel*, 137.

15. Hamerton-Kelly, *The Gospel and the Sacred*, 17–18. Mark 11:16, as many commentators have held, might seem to indicate that in Mark's view Jesus was simply purifying an institution of which he approved. However, the framing incidents of the fig tree, 11:12–14 and 11:20–25, as well as the pronouncement in 13:1–2, indicate a more radical view, a denial of the Temple's *raison d'être* in the dawning new age. Ched Myers, *Binding the Strong Man: A Political Reading of the Gospel of Mark* (Maryknoll, NY: Orbis, 1988), also reads Jesus' act in the Temple as an radical attack upon it as an institution (300–302). However, his statement that the Jerusalem temple "was *fundamentally an economic institution*" (300; emphasis his), misses a nuance that is fundamental. The Temple *was* an economic institution to the extent that the sacrificial mechanism and economic exchange were identical. But to understand the generative level of the institution and its traditions, it is imperative to begin with sacrifice.

16. See G. Buttrick, gen. ed., *Interpreter's Dictionary of the Bible*, vol. 3 (New York and Nashville: Abingdon, 1962), 423–435 and 435–436, esp. 427–429.

17. *Sacrifier* is a term used by Hubert and Mauss in their classic essay. See chap. 1, "Theories of Sacrifice" under "Girard's Explanatory Model."

18. See E. Gans, *The End of Culture* (Berkeley: University of California Press, 1985), 34.

19. Williams, *Gospel*, 139.

20. In Luke 16:17, so presumably Luke 16:17/Matt 5:18 is based on Q.

21. On the question concerning the meaning of "least of the brothers," see John Donahue, *The Gospel in Parable* (Philadephia: Fortress, 1988), 99–125; for the history of interpretation, see Sherman W. Gray, *The Least of My Brothers: Matthew 25:31–46, A History of Interpretation*, SBL Dissertation Series 114 (Atlanta: Scholars Press, 1989).

22. Just like the seven times Jesus is involved in an event on a mountain or hill in Matthew: temptation (4:8), the first long discourse (5:1), prayer (14:23), healing and

feeding the multitude (15:29), transfiguration (17:1–13), the final days and passion in Jerusalem (20:17–27:54), and the resurrection appearance in Galilee (28:16–20). To arrive at this number I have to count "going up to Jerusalem" (20:17), which is especially associated with the Temple mount, Zion, and the subsequent events as one occurrence. The number seven makes sense as part of Matthew's propensity for organizing his narrative into obvious biblical and sacred patterns. I think also that in the Apocalypse, or Book of Revelation, the function of the number seven, and more specifically the uses of four plus three in different combinations, is a sign of revelation and the perfect pattern given from on high.

23. Luke 22:43–44 is found in Sinaiticus, one of three most important manuscripts of the New Testament. These verses are not found in the other two, Vaticanus and Alexandrinus. However, even if one did not accept the verses, the connection of the episode with the suffering of Jesus and the ostracism of his followers is clear. It ends with Jesus' command to the sleeping followers, "Get up and pray that you may not come into the time of trial" (i.e., temptation or testing; 22:46).

24. See Wayne Meeks, "The Man from Heaven in Johannine Sectarianism," *Journal of Biblical Literature* 91 (1972), 44–72.

25. Werner Kelber, "In the Beginning Were the Words: The Apotheosis and Narrative Displacement of the Logos," *Journal of the American Academy of Religion* 58 (1990), 90.

26. Kelber, "In the Beginning," 90–91.

27. See *parakletos* in H. G. Liddell and R. Scott, *A Greek-English Lexicon*, rev. H. S. Jones (Oxford: Clarendon, 1968), 1313.

28. Kelber, "In the Beginning," 92.

29. Kelber, "In the Beginning," 92, 93.

30. Kelber, "In the Beginning," 93.

Chapter 8. Desire, Violence, and the Truth of the Victim

1. On historicity, see Williams, *Gospel Against Parable: Mark's Language of Mystery* (Decatur, IL, and Sheffield: Almond, 1985), 13, 17–18.

2. Nor does John baptize Jesus in Luke, though according to Luke Jesus is baptized by followers of John. See Luke 3:18–22.

3. However, the noun from the same root, *thelema*, "will," is a key word in Matthew. See the discussion in chap. 7.

4. The relevant passages for demons: 1:32, 34, 39; 3:15, 22 (Beelzebul); 5:15, 16, 18; 6:13; 7:26, 29, 30; 9:38; for unclean spirits: 1:23, 26, 27; 3:11, 30; 5:2, 8, 13; 6:7; 7:25; 9:17, 20, 25 (these latter three occurrences are a "dumb" and "deaf" spirit). Whatever the origin of the terms, *demon* and *unclean spirit* mean the same in these passages.

5. See Walter Wink, *Naming the Powers* (Philadelphia: Fortress, 1984); *Unmasking the Powers* (Philadelphia: Fortress, 1986).

6. In Derrida, *Dissemination*, trans. Barbara Johnson (Chicago: University of Chicago Press, 1981).

7. Richard Horsley, *Jesus and the Spiral of Violence* (San Francisco: Harper & Row, 1987), 186.

8. Girard, *Scapegoat*, 144–145, 147.

9. A similar way of handling something negative about the apostles is encountered also in Mark 8:31–33/Matt 16:21–23/Luke 9:18–22. Jesus' rebuke of Peter in Mark is narrated also in Matthew but mitigated by Jesus' prior assignment of apostolic authority to Peter, Matt 16:13–20. Luke does not report the rebuke of Peter at all.

10. Mark's attribution of the promise of eventual possession of houses and lands to Jesus (10:30) is a contradiction and sensed as a problem by Matthew and Luke. Matthew revises the saying so that an unambiguous promise of houses and lands is not stated but simply receiving a "hundredfold" and inheriting "eternal life" (Matt 19:29). Luke likewise directs the saying toward spiritual reward in Luke 18:29–30.

11. In these last instances the root *pdh*, "ransom," is used.

12. See Frank Kermode, *The Genesis of Secrecy* (Cambridge, MA: Harvard University Press, 1979), 94–95.

13. Werner Kelber, *The Oral and the Written Gospel* (Philadelphia: Fortress, 1983).

14. See Horsley, *Jesus and the Spiral of Violence*.

15. Chilton, *The Temple of Jesus: His Sacrificial Program* (University Park: Pennsylvania State University, 1992), ch. 7.

16. E. P. Sanders, *Jesus and Judaism* (Philadelphia: Fortress, 1985). However, I disagree with Sanders's hypothesis that Jesus' announcement of the Temple's destruction presupposed, in keeping with a number of contemporary texts, that God would create a new temple in the age to come. He discounts the Apocalypse's vision of the heavenly Jerusalem without a temple (Rev 21:22): "This is clearly polemic against the normal expectation in Judaism" (86). Sanders in his own way develops a concept of "normative" Judaism. But why would every sort of charismatic leader have to fit into a normative concept? For one thing, the texts available give us little sense of popular movements. (See Richard A. Horsley and John S. Hanson, *Bandits, Prophets, and Messiahs: Popular Movements at the Time of Jesus* [San Francisco: Harper and Row, 1985].) For another thing, there was a biblical prophetic tradition of opposition to sacrifice (see chap. 5, "The Prophets Against Violence and Sacrifice"); in Jeremiah's case, this probably extended to the very existence of the Temple, which did not belong to his vision of a new age (see Jer 3:16; 7:1–15 [Jer 7:11 is cited in Mark 11:18 and parallels]; 26; 31:27–34). Had this tradition completely died out? See further Horsley's refutation of Sanders's argument concerning a restored Temple in the eschaton, *Jesus and the Spiral of Violence*, 289–296.

17. See James G. Williams, "Paraenesis, Excess, and Ethics: Matthew's Rhetoric in the Sermon on the Mount," *Semeia* 50 (1990): 163–187.

18. Mark 11:16 might seem to say the latter, namely, that Jesus was engaged in purifying an institution of which he basically approved. However, not allowing "any one to carry anything (*skeuos*) through the temple" is reminiscent of Mark 3:27: "But no one can enter a strong man's house and plunder his property (*ta skeua*) without first tying up the strong man; then indeed the house can be plundered." The binding of Satan, as expressed in the parabolic image, and the overcoming of the sacrificial cult are understood in Mark as analogous actions. See Ched Myers, *Binding the Strong Man* (Maryknoll, NY: Orbis, 1988), 164–167, 299–302.

19. See Horsley, *Jesus and the Spiral of Violence*, 286–287.

20. Girard, *Things Hidden*, 218.

21. Girard, *Things Hidden*, 435; my trans. of the last sentence.

22. See Vernon Robbins, *Jesus the Teacher* (Philadelphia: Fortress, 1984), 187–191. On the mock king and king-substitutes, see the material gathered by Frazer, *The New Golden Bough*, ed. with notes and foreword by T. H. Gaster (Garden City, NY: Doubleday Anchor Books, 1959 [abridgment of work published in 1890]), 133–140.

23. See Williams, *Gospel Against Parable*, 60, 182–183.

24. See Norman Petersen, *Literary Criticism for New Testament Critics* (Philadelphia: Fortress, 1978).

25. In Isa 53:11a "light" is not in the Masoretic Text, but is found in the Isaiah Scroll of Qumran and in the Septuagint.
26. Girard, *Scapegoat*, 111.
27. Girard, *Scapegoat*.
28. Girard, *Things Hidden*, 219.

Chapter 9. Conclusion

1. "For in the resurrection they neither marry nor are given in marriage, but are like angels in heaven" (Matt 22:30).
2. *The American College Dictionary*, C. L. Barnhart, editor in chief (New York: Random House, 1958), 909.
3. See discussion of Derrida's suggestive explication in the first part of chap. 3, in the section "Sacrifice" under "Sacrificial Crisis in the Wilderness." See further the epigraphs in chap. 8 regarding Dionysus and Prometheus. Prometheus brings the remedy of blind hope to mortals so they will not be preoccupied with their mortality. The gift of Dionysus is the remedy of wine. Wine is analogous to the scapegoat: it dissolves order (ordinary prohibitions and inhibitions), but it also enables humans to forget the pain both of order and of disorder. It is both baneful and beneficial, and as such, its cultivated use may be construed as a kind of ritualization of sacrificial functions.
4. Both "society as culturally addictive" and the addictive character of American culture are recognized by Michael H. Crosby, *House of Disciples: Church, Economics, and Justice in Matthew* (Maryknoll: Orbis, 1988), 251–262; he cites a number of writers on the problem. Although he touches on addiction as a surrogate or subtitutionary phenomenon, he does not penetrate to an analysis of the sacrificial character of addiction, whose structure is that of victimization and sacrifice.
5. Girard, *Things Hidden*, 88–91.
6. See Schubert M. Ogden, *The Reality of God* (New York: Harper & Row, 1966), 58–60, 177–180.
7. As quoted in Joseph Campbell, *The Mythic Image* (Princeton, NJ: Princeton University Press, 1974), 445.
8. See James G. Williams, "Paraenesis, Excess, and Ethics: Matthew's Rhetoric in the Sermon on the Mount," *Semeia* 50 (1990), 163–187.

Index

Abraham, Karl, 95
Addiction, 248–52; the addicted person bound to victim-god, 250; culture as, 248–52; definition of, 251; gambling as, 251; making money as, 251–52; firearms, 252; and mimetic capacities, 251; rooted in selection of victim by lottery or crowd, 250; truth of the victim, 253–57
Advocate. *See* Paraclete
Aeschylus, 165, 186, 213, 274 n.2
Ahab, 147–48
Alcohol: and mimesis, 250; substitutionary effect of, 249
Altar: as dividing point between prohibition and confusion, 34; as representation of covenant mountain, 113
Alter, Robert, 274 n.10
America, United States of (culture of): as city upon a hill, 241; contradictions of, 241; cultural crisis, 245–48; cultural predicament revolves around substitutions, 248; election, ideology of, 242; master-slave dialectic, 246; mimetic structure of crisis, 245–47; oppressed, awareness of plight of, 248; as pharmacy, 248; rivalry and community, 242; status in world comparable to king-scapegoat, 243; two traditions—mythical and humanitarian, 241–45; voluntarism, 257
Amos, 148–49; calling of 143; sacrifices not offered in wilderness, 149; tradition begins with liberation of victim, 148–49
Anderson, Bernhard, 269 n.21
Andreas-Salome, Lou, 271 n.52
Apion, 89–90
Arndt, William F., 267 n.57
Atonement: Hebrew *kipper, kofer,* price of exchange, 46; Greek *lutron,* ransom, 223–24; Jesus as new *lutron,* 230–31;

Jung's understanding of, 181; sacrifical doctrine of, 1
Authority *(exousia):* people as source of, 218

Bailie, Gil, 122, 272 n.8, 272 n.15, 272 n.19, 272 n.21
Barthes, Roland, 48–50, 265 nn. 29–31; metonymy, 49–50; symbol as displacement, 49; trace, 49
Bauer, Walter, 267 n.57
Beelzebul, 217; Jesus accused of being agent of, 217
Bellah, Robert, 3
Bible, vi; anthropological and literary approaches to, 68; and Western institutions, 4
Bird, Phyllis, 274 n.27
Blank, Sheldon, 173
Blood, 33; broth, 41; as sign of victim, 34; and water from the rock, 82
Briggs, C. A., 264 n.5, 265 n.18, 267 n.50, 268 n.3
Brother stories, patterns in, 60–66: in myth and folklore, 62; younger brother displaces the older, 62; younger brother is favored, 61; younger brother is shepherd, 60; younger son and scapegoating ordeal, 64
Brown, Francis, 264 n.5, 265 n.18, 267 n.50, 268 n.3
Brutus, Decius (in Shakespeare's *Julius Caesar*); interprets Caesar's dream, 137
Brutus, Marcus (in Shakespeare's *Julius Caesar*), 33; envy of Caesar, 137–38; haunted by Caesar, 140–41
Buber, Martin, 268 n.5, 272 n.8; on Exodus 4:24–26, 74–75
Bush, George, 257
Buttrick, George, 276 n.16

Calling, prophetic: structural similarity to victimization, 143–44

Caesar, Julius (in Shakespeare's *Julius Caesar*), 33; assassination according to Plutarch, 129; death as sacrifice, 138; real subject of play: people as crowd and mob, 137

Caiaphas, 208

Cain (and Abel), 12, 26–30, 33–38, 62–63; in founding act, violence not justified, 38; knowledge and victimization, 34–35; sign of as sign of civilization, 185; sign or mark of, 36

Campbell, Joseph, 174, 279 n.7

Canon, 176

Cherry, Conrad, 4, 259 n.5

Chidester, David, 259 n.2

Childs, Brevard, 76, 83, 268 n.8, 269 n.12, 269 n.16, 269 n.22, 269 n.29, 272 n.3, 272 nn.6–7

Chilton, Bruce, 227, 228, 278 n.15; Christian "*haggadah*," 228

Christ. *See* Jesus

Christology: and the Book of Job, 173–75

Chronis, H. L., 276, n.8

Church and state, separation of, 3

"Citty upon a Hill," 4. *See also* America

Civil religion, 3–4

Civilization, beginning of, 35

Coats, George, 269 nn.19–20

Commandment(s): fifth of Decalogue, 110–11; fifth as demarcation of social authority, 110; first of Decalogue, 109; fourth of Decalogue, 110; as periphery of covenant community, 105; second of Decalogue,109; sixth through ninth of Decalogue, 111–12; tenth of Decalogue, 112; third of Decalogue, 109–10

Cook, Captain James, 258

Covenant, Sinai, 105–17; as center of covenant community, 105; ceremony, 114–15; exclusionary principle of, 187–88; Exodus 19:1–6, 106; Exodus 19:7–15, 106–7; Exodus 19:16–25, 107–8; Exodus 20:1–17 (Decalogue), 108–13; Exodus 20:18–26, 113–14; Exodus 24:1–14, 114–16; subsitute for altar, 115

Crosby, Michael H., 279 n.4

Cyclops, 43

Damrosch, David, 272 n.18

David, and brothers, 60

Daube, David, 40–41, 265 nn.14–17

Deconstruction, viii

Demons, 12, 277 n.4; correlate of the people in their mimetic conflict, 220; and crowd/mob, 216–20; legion of, in Gerasene demoniac, 219

Derrida, Jacques, 6, 218, 263 nn.56–57, 268 n.69, 269 nn.23–25, 272 nn.9–10, 277 n.6, 279 n.3; on différance, 20, 210, 227; God as Difference and Indifference, 116; on pharmakon, 83, 248; on writing and difference in relation to the Jewish tradition, 115–16

Desire, as acquisitive, 8. *See also* mimesis

Detienne, Marcel, 15, 262 n.40, 275 n.2

Deuteronomy (and Deuteronomic), 86–88, 264 n.63; and kingship, 141–42; regarding Edomite and Egyptian, 64

Différance, 263 n.56; as sacrificial, 70. *See also* Derrida, Jacques

Difference and differentiation, 53–54; as creation, 82; in Decalogue, 112–13; Jesus as new point of, 226; in law and sacrificial systems, 205–6; and the innocent victim in John, 208; without violence, 54; in wilderness, 81–82

Dionysus, 9, 186, 279 n.3

Donahue, John R., S. J., 267 n.53, 276 n.21

Dostoievski, Fyodor, 276 n.12

Double, 9; haunting and possession, 9; John as Herod's, 220–21; mark protects Cain from Abel as; prophet and king as, 147

Double transference, 10

Driver, S. R., 264 n.5, 265 n.18,; 267 n.50, 268 n.3

Durkheim, Emile, 15, 16, 262 n.38

Economics, as a mimetic process, 244

Edwards, Richard, 276 n.7

Egypt (and Egyptian): kingship, 76; myth and ritual of kingship, 91; mythical perspective on the exodus, 89–91; oppression of Hebrews, 71–72

Eliade, Mircea, 273 n.9

Elihu, speeches supporting Jung, 183

Elijah, 147–48

Elohist, 87–88, 263 n.63

Envy: and covetousness, 112; real issue in Jesus's arrest, 234

Ephraim and Manasseh, 60

Ethnocentrism, 18–19

Euripides, 9, 129, 137, 186, 213, 260 n. 15, 274 n.6

Evans, Pritchard, E. E., 15, 262 n.39

Ezekiel, 156–57; calling of 145–46; priestly influence on, 157; sacrifice of firstborn in wilderness, 157

Face of God, 46–47; Esau's face as reminder of, 53
Faith: as coming out of crowd, 216–17
Farias, Victor, 271 nn.61–63
Firstborn: offering of and child sacrifice, 117–18; redeemed by animal substitute, 118; slaying of, 117–21
Fishbane, Michael, 51–53, 265 nn.32–33, 266 n.35
Frazer, James G., 14–15, 43, 262 nn. 35–36, 264 n.1, 265 n.19, 270 n.39, 275 n.1, 278 n.22; on mark of Cain, 37–38; scapegoat, vii, 15
Freud, Sigmund, vii, 270 nn.41–44, 271 nn. 45–50, 271 n.52; and anti-Semitism, 93–95; and Aryan double, 95; Christianity, Freud's understanding of origin of, 92–93; derogatory attitude toward Jews in Moses and Mon., 94–95; elimination of Israel's uniqueness, 97–98; expulsion of Jewish origins in Moses and Mon., 95–97; on identification, 8; monotheism—ambivalence and guilt, 93; on Moses in Moses and Monotheism, 91–98; myths of, 8–9; on Oedipus complex, 8; primal horde, 92; return of the repressed, 92

Gager, John G., 270 n.35, 270 n.37
Gambling, as addiction, 251
Gans, Eric, 276 n.18
Gaster, Theodor, 37, 264 n.1, 264 n.3, 265 nn.10–12, 268 n.7, 269 n.21, 273 n.10
Gay, Peter, 270 n.48, 270 nn.52–53, 271 n.59
Gese, Hartmut, 46, 265 n.23
Gerasene Demoniac 12–13, 36, 219–20
Gevirtz, Stanley, 265 n.27
Gideon, 141
Gingrich, F. Wilbur, 267 n.57
Girard, René, 1, 5, 33, 43, 165, 213, 259 n.7, 260 nn.12–14, 261 n. 16, 261 nn.18–20, 262 nn. 27–29, 262 n.48, 262 n.52, 262 n.55, 263 nn.59–60, 264 n.64, 264 nn.66–67, 264 n.70, 264 nn.6–8, 265 nn.20–21, 266 n.34, 268 nn.63–64, 268 n.2, 268 n.4, 269 n.15, 269 n.17, 269 nn.26–27, 269 n.32, 270 nn.37, 40, 271 n.44, 273 nn.3–5, 273 nn.12–13, 274 n.17, 274 n.28, 274 nn.1–5, 274 n7, 275 n.12, 275 nn.14–18, 275 n.31, 275 n.33, 275 n.4, 277 n.8, 278 nn.20–21, 279 nn.26–28, 279 n.5; act precedes idea, 17; on additions to Job, 176; appreciation of Derrida on pharmakon, 269 n.25; bibliography (books only), 259 n.11; explanatory model of religion and culture, 13–14; on external mediation, 9, 87; on fear of the dead, 135–36; on forgiveness and the true unconscious, 237; Freud's unconscious as modern psychoanalytic myth, 261 n.20; on Gerasene demoniac, 219–20; on good mimesis and effective mimesis, 261 n. 17; on Heidegger and violent mastery, 177; on hunting and meat eating, 267 n.56; on internal mediation, 10; on John the Baptist as Herod's double, 220–21; on Jung's expulsion of rivalry, 182; on kingship, 131; on mimetic desire, 7–8; perspective of violence eliminates distinction between God of victims and God of persecutors, 174–75; on pharmakos-pharmakon, 84; on plague as destroyer of distinctions, 270 n.38; on sacral kingship, 261 n. 22; schema for mythic narrative, 90; stereotypes of persecution, 84; on "transformative reading," 172; truth about violence and the incarnation, 232
God: beyond differences, 12, 48, 50; good mimesis of God of victims, 169; versus Pharaoh in Exodus, 76–78; as projection of social order in Job, 167–68; as revealed in Son of Man: no violence or exclusivistic differentiation, 230–31; as socially transcendent symbol of generative scapegoating structure, 165–66
Good Samaritan, parable of, 255–56
Gospels (four canonical Gospels of the NT): calling of disciples in, 214–15; and Christian supersedure of the Jewish tradition, 174–75; as Jewish texts, 175, 228; unity of, 210–11
Gray, Sherman W., 276 n.21
Green, Alberto, 131–32, 273 n.6, 274 n.24
Green, William Chase, 274 n.21
Green, William Scott, 271 n.58
Gunn, David, 273 n.14; on Saul as scapegoat and tragic victim, 136, 138–39

Habel, Norman, 274 nn.8–9
Hamerton-Kelly, Robert, 14, 259 n.8, 260 n.12, 262 n.30, 262 n.32, 263 n.62, 264 n.4, 276 n.11, 276 n.15; Girard's model as "likely story," 7, 10; on Jesus' Temple

protest as attack on sacrificial system, 193, 229; Lévi-Strauss, criticism of, 262 n.46; on messianic secret and the crowd, 191–92

Handelman, Susan, 97, 271 n.57

Hanson, John S., 278 n.16

Hegel, G. W. F., 260 n.13, 269 n.18

Heidegger, Martin, vii, 6, 98–100 (*Introduction to Metaphysics*); 174, 241, 271 nn.63–64, 272 n.65; Being as the sacred, 99; biblical logos excluded, 99–100; Cains of the world as the *Führer* (leaders), 186–87; degree or rank essential to being, 99; *Führung* (leadership), 99; German people and destiny of Being, 210; logos of Heraclitus, 99; master-slave hierarchy, 177; *polemos*, 99

Heusch, Luc de, 16, 18–20, 262 n.42, 262 nn.44–45, 262 nn.49–51, 263 n.53

Hobbes, Thomas, 20, 260 n.17

Holladay, William, 273 n.2

Hooke, S. H., 264 n.1

Horsley, Richard, 218–19, 277 n.7, 278 n.14, 278 n.16, 278 n.19

Hosea, 39, 149–51; Israel not constituted as sacrificial cult, 150; knowledge of God and steadfast love, 150; on mimetic process, 150–51; names of children, 150

Hubert, Henri, 15, 16, 262 n.37, 276 n.17

Hudson, Winthrop, 259 n.3

Hussein, Saddam, 243–44

Infanticide, 73, 253–54

Isaac and Ishmael, 60

Isaiah, 151–52; calling of, 143–44

Israel (and Israelite); boundary experiences, reality of, 107; as emerging exception, 30; stories told from perspective of victim, 185

J (or Yahwist) narrative, 25, 85, 87–88, 263 n.63; "chaos-and-conflict" perspective, 30

Jabès, Edmond, 116

Jacob (and Esau), 39–54; the birthright, 40–42; differences between, 39–40; Jacob's encounter at the Jabbok, 46–50; meeting of, 50–53; unlike Oedipus, 48; the Other of Jacob, 48; theft of blessing, 42–45

James and John, request of, 22–23

Jensen, Hans J. L., 62, 266 n.38, 266 n.47, 268 n.66, 270 n.35

Jeremiah, 39, 154–56; attacked king and temple, 154–55; calling of, 144–45; knowing God is to know cause of the victim, 155; new covenant, 155–56

Jesus: as double to disciples, 222; as healer-scapegoat, 215–16; and John not subject to mimetic rivalry, 221; meaning of titles, 240; as new point of differentiation, 226; 230; offers himself as victim, 194; as perfect victim, 174; protest at Temple, 226–30; prophetic symbolic action at Temple, 230; protest nonviolent, 228; overturns distinctions of the Law, 226

Jewish-Roman War, 226

Job (and Job, Book of): affirmation of God of victims, 168–69; Book of, as scapegoat, 175–78; and the canon, 172–73; and Christology, 173–75; compared to Oedipus, 165; determined by mimetic process, 164–65; the dialogues and Job's final speech, 164–69; God as projection of social order, 167–68; the God-speeches, 169–72; God-speeches as poor theology, 171–72; God of theophany compared to God of dialogues, 170; friends, theology of, 165–66; like a king, 164; metaphors for enemies of, 166; as model for others, 164

John the Baptist: death of in Mark, 220–21; John as Herod's double, 221

John, Gospel of, 204–11; not anti-Semitic, 204–5; differentiation and the innocent victim, 208; disciples as friends of the Son, 208; footwashing replaces institution of Eucharist, 207; God as paradoxical "ultimate difference," 206; "I am" statements, 206; incarnation, 205; Jesus as way to Father, 207–8; the Paraclete, 208; radicalizes what is implicit in synoptic Gospels, 211

Jorgensen, Jorgen, 263 n.62

Joseph (and brothers), 54–60; brothers betray Joseph, 55; brothers envy Joseph, 55; conflict in family, 54; deification, nullification of, 58; Egyptian perspective on, 59–60; and Oedipus, 58; reconciliation and forgiveness, 63; and typical myth, 56

Josephus, 89, 270 n.34

Josipovici, Gabriel, 267 n.54

Jung, Carl G., viii, 95, 275 nn.20–30, 275 n.32; *Answer to Job*, 178–84; approach a shadow side of science and technology, 179; archetypes, 179; atonement, understanding of, 181; Christian doctrine of

Incarnation, 180; and Freud compared, 184; friends of Job largely irrelevant, 180; Job outward occasion of divine dialectic, 180; as modern "friend" of Job, 178; and psychic violence, 182; rivalry expelled, 182; scapegoat not a historical reality for, 183–84; YHWH as antinomy, 179; YHWH both God of victims and of victimizers, 179–80

Judas, as having perfect sacrificial understanding, 224

Kant, Immanuel, 263 n.58
Kelber, Werner, 277 nn.25–6, 277 nn.28–30, 278 n.13; on Derrida and logos, 209–10; John's narrative refocuses attention from plural to singular, 206–7; on oral and written gospel, 225
Kermode, Frank, 278 n.12
Kings (and kingship): antimonarchic strand in Israelite political theology, 139; calling of, 129–48; confronted by prophets, 142; David, dynasty of, 129–30; Jesus before Pilate, 234–35; and Marduk as scapegoat, 132; originates in same social reality as prophecy, 130–31; in Psalm 72, 131, 142; sacral, Girard's theory of, 261 n.22
Kingu, as substitute for Marduk, 132
Kluger, R. S., 274 n.22
Kojève, Alexandre, 260 n.13, 269 n.18
Korah rebellion, 125–26
Kugel, James, 275 n.10

Lacoue-Labarthe, Philippe, 270 n.51
Lamech, 32, 38
Language: and cultural origins, 20–25; and culture: sacrificial strategy, 231
Lasine, Stuart, 121, 122, 126, 271 n.60, 272 n.69, 272 nn. 13–14, 272 nn.16–17, 272 n.20
Levi, 122
Lévi-Strauss, Claude, 15, 16, 20, 28
Levites: Korah rebellion, 125–26; Levite in Judges 19, 122; origins of, 121–27; scapegoats for atonement of Israel, 123; as substitutes for the firstborn, 118–19
Liddell, H. G., 277 n.27
Livy, 264 n.65; on Romulus and Remus, 261 n.25
Loew, Cornelius, 270 n.39
Lohfink, Norbert, 28–29, 264 n.69
Lot (and casting of lots): god of the system, 257–58; metonym of scapegoating process, 235; as moira (fate), 139–40; structure of and games of chance, 134
Luke, Gospel of, 199–204; atonement: Luke avoids sacrificial connotations of, 202; conflict avoided or remedied, 201–2; Jesus as model (discloser of revelatory patterns), 200–202; Jesus as model of prayer, 201; Jesus as Perfect or Divine Human, 202; Jesus as pharmakos, 200–201; John the Baptist represents period of Law and Prophets, 199; kingship, authentic, 203; period of the church, 203–4; period of Law and Prophets, 199; resurrection appearances in Jerusalem and vicinity, 202–3; time of Jesus, 199–203; tradition and "way," 199; 203–4

Maccoby, Hyam, 264 n.9
McGrath, William J., 271 n.48; 271 n.54
Malbon, Elizabeth Struthers, 276 n.13
Manetho, 89–91
Mann, Thomas, 271 n.60; 272 nn.67–70; novella about Moses, 100–102; Moses and Michaelangelo, 101; view of Freud, 100
Marduk, 28; and kingship, 132–33
Mark, Gospel of, 188–94; boat and lake in, 192; Caesarea Philippi episode, 189; Judas as betrayer, 193; Last Supper and feedings in wilderness, 221–22; mimesis in, 214–31; Peter's denials, 192; Son of Man, 189–91; Suffering Servant, 190–91; Servant as secret meaning of Jesus's vocation, 191; Temple passages, 192–93
Mark (or sign) of Cain, 30; violence and sacrifice, 226–31
Massah and Meribah, 84
Matthew, Gospel of, 194–99; allegory of sheep and goats as introduction to Passion narrative, 198–99; apocalyptic, 196; "brother," meaning of, 197–98; messianic tradition, 194; numerical patterns, 195; prophecy and fulfillment, 195; Sermon on the Mount, 195–96; will of the Father, 198; Wisdom and apocalyptic judge revealed as innocent victim, 196–97; Wisdom, divine, 196
Mauss, Marcel, 15, 16, 262 n. 37, 276 n.17
Meeks, Wayne, 277 n.24
Mellinkoff, Ruth, 265 n.13; on badge laws, 38
Metaphor, 21–24, 56
Metonymy, 21–24, 56
Micah, 152–54; antisacrificial perspective in Micah 6:6–8, 153–54; bribe and sacrificial

system, 152–53; sacrificial system gone haywire, 153

Miller, David L., 275 n.19

Mimesis (and mimetic desire), 7–9, 75; in Cain story, 62–63; and the current intellectual situation, 186; and demons, 217; desire and rivalry among Jesus' disciples, 222–23; and the double, 35; and economics, 244; good mimesis, 63, 221; good, known only from standpoint of innocent victim, 239; illustrated in Persian Gulf crisis and its aftermath, 244–45; and kingship, 235; in parable of Prodigal Son, 67–68; prophets and king, vii; serpent as metaphor of, 35; in wilderness, 81

Miriam, 85

Mob (and crowd): authority, source of, 218; bleeding woman's complicity with, 217; demons and, 216–20; function in the Temple protest pericope, 229; Jesus' feeding of in a lonely place, 221; and insect swarms, 74; in wilderness, 81

Money changers: changing of money tied to a system of subsitutions, 229; Jesus' attack on them an attack on sacrificial system, 229

monster (and monstrous): Jacob's masquerade, 44

Moses, 39; and Aaron, 60, 61, 84–85, 123; versus court magicians, 73–74; as external mediator, 87; as non-Jew and non-Aryan for Freud, 94; versus God, 74–76; versus Israel, 79–80; killing of Egyptian, 79; offers himself as sacrificial ransom, 123; versus Pharaoh, 73

Myers, Ched, 276 n.15, 278 n.18

Myrmidons, 268 n.4

Myth, 11, 127; confirming reign of science and technology, 77; Egyptian, 29–30; National Socialist of *der Führer*, 98; great man, 96, 98–102; Mesopotamian, 28; sequential structure of narrative, 56–57, 90

Naboth, 147

Nadab and Abihu, 60, 124

Nakedness, associated with confusion, 114

Name, 47–48; God's as boundary, 110

Narrative: and ritual process, 64–65; narrative time and story time, 236

Niditch, Susan, 69–70, 267 nn.59–60, 268 nn.61–62, 268 n.65, 268 nn.67–68; on the trickster, 69

Nietzsche, Frederich, 6; on the eternal return, 177; on murder of God in *The Gay Science*, 178; options with model of eternal return, 177; resentment and the *Uebermensch*, 176–177; resentment or slave morality, vii; on Christian God, 19

Oden, Robert A., Jr., 275 n.3

Ogden, Schubert M., 279 n.6

Oedipus, 17, 71, 105, 110–11, 163, 213; compared to Egyptian myth of the exodus, 90–91; subject to *moira* (fate), 139–40

Ott, Hugo, 271 nn.61–62

Otto, Rudolph, 261 n.23

Palaver, Wolfgang, 259 n.6, 273 n.2, 273 nn.8–9, 273 n.11

Pandemonium, 35

Panic, 218

Paraclete, 185, 238–39; in Gospel of John, 208; as Spirit of history, 258

Parricide, 110–11

Pelton, Robert, 267 n.60

Pentheus, in *The Bacchae*, a copy of Dionysus, 186

Perdue, Leo G., 274 intro. note to ch. 6

Perez and Zerah, 60, 61

Petersen, Norman, 278 n.24

Pharmakos (scapegoat), 13, 83, 248; Jesus as, in Luke 4:16–30, 200–201

pharmakon (poison/remedy), 20, 83, 213, 248

Phineas, 122

Plague, and prohibition, 82

Plutarch on Romulus's death, 262 n.25

Polytheism, and rivalry among the gods, 30

Popper, Karl, 14, 262 n.31

Priestly narrative, 85, 87, 187, 263 n.63; on eating blood and shedding blood, 34; genealogy in Genesis 5, 25; human nature as nonviolent, 28; world beginnings, 25

Pritchard, James B., 264 n.71

Prodigal Son, parable of, 66–68; calf, fatted, 67; goat, 67

Prohibition, 11, 33; and plague, 82

Prometheus, 186, 279 n.3

Prophets (and prophecy): calling of, 129–48; challenged principle of sacrifice of the firstborn, 118; Israelite legitimation of role of, 145; originates in same social reality as kingship, 130–31; as performers, 151; prophet double of king, 142

Propp, Vladimir, 265 n.28, 266 n.47, 267 n.48

Pyramid Texts, 270 n.40

Q (Quelle or "[Teaching] Source"), 189

Rad, Gerhard von, 76, 86, 269 n.11, 269 nn.30–31, 269 n.33
Rank, Otto, 96
Reciprocity, 6; of violence, 79
Revelation: of the God of victims, 12; undoes mechanisms of victimization and sacrifice, 187; of scapegoat mechanism through forgiveness of persecutors, 238; Word subverts mimetic structures, 213; true Word speaks only from position of victim, 232; unmasking of mimetic world occurs through death of Word on cross, 213–14
Rice, Emanuel, 271 n.48
Ritual, 11; Babylonian New Year, 132–33; as expelling of expulsion, 59; primitive elements of, in Leviticus 9:22–24
Rivalry, 6; over favor of the people, 218
Robbins, Vernon, 278 n.22
Robert, Marthe, 96–97, 271 nn.54–56, 272 n.66
Romulus and Remus, 13; compared to story of Cain and Abel, 31
Rousseau, Jean-Jacques, 20, 248

Sabbath, as temporal boundary, 110
Sacrifice (and sacrificial), 33; blessing and, 45; of children, 118; crisis when differences dissolve, 105; crisis in the wilderness, 81–84; etymology of, 261 n.24; Judeo-Christian witness exposes myth of, 258; substitutions and, 42; substitutionary code, 120; theories of, 14–20; tree as subsitute for Moses, 83; in the wilderness, 82–84
Samuel, 130
Sanders, Ed P., 278 n.16; Jesus' Temple protest a historical event, 227–28
Saul, 130; chosen by lot as king, 133; and ecstatic prophets, 126–27; and Jonathan as scapegoats, 135; and medium at En-Dor, 135–36; as radically mediated, 138; and selection as scapegoat, 134; tragic victim, not completely, 139–40
Scapegoat: biblical disclosure of scapegoating, viii; dragon in creation myths, 28; the goat sent to Azazel, 124–25; hated without cause, 238; Jesus as healer-magnet, 215–16; leader as, 84; lot and games of chance, 134; mechanism and genesis of religion, v, vi; as mediatory overshadows

altar, 108; selection of transferred to prophecy, 131, 141; structure of mechanism similar to games, 261 n.21; theory, vii;
Schwager, Raymund, 259 n.8
Scott, R., 277 n.27
Scripture, fundamentalist-evangelical approach to, 2
Second Isaiah, 157–62; calling of, 146; new exodus, 158; Servant of the LORD, 158–62; YHWH is the only God, 157; Servant as paradigm of transformation of victimization into prophecy, 161–62; Servant not a sacrifice intended by God, 161
Seth: replacing Cain and Abel in Priestly account, 27–28
Simeon, 122
Sin, 62–63
Shakespeare, William, 263 n.47, 269 n.17, 273 nn.15–16, 274 n.18; Troilus and Cressida, 18; Julius Caesar, 137–38
Smith, Jonathan Z., 259 n.1
Smith, Mark, 118, 272 n.11, 273 n.6
Smith, Mahlon, 189, 275 n.5
Smith, Theophus, 259 n.8
Smith, W. Robertson, 14, 16, 129, 262 n.34, 267 n.56
Social order: constituted by prohibition, myth, and ritual, 11; demands unanimity, 165; sacred, and the true God, 109; as transcendent, 16
Sodom and Gomorrah, and Oedipus myth, 133
Solomon, and the case of the two harlots, 142
Son of Man, 189–91; largely nonapocalyptic in Mark, 190; origin of title not apocalyptic, 189; in Q, 275 n.7; as ransom, 223–24 (see atonement); as servant, 223; suffering, death, and resurrection, 222
Sophocles, 270 n.38, 274 n.20
Stern, Menahem, 262 n.26, 266 nn.41–42, 270 n.34
Synecdoche, 21–24, 56

Temple, Jerusalem: as center of exchange and sacred substitutions, 193, 229; and Jesus' protest, 226–30
Text, as substitution, 107
Theology: of divine anger, 69, 119–20; of divine caprice, 69
Thompson, Stith, 266 n.46

Tiamat, 28
Tillich, Paul, 156
Tocqueville, Alexis de, 4, 242, 259 n.4
Totemism, 270 n.44
Tragedy, Greek, and Israelite tradition of
    innocent victim, 186
Trickster, and victimization mechanism, 69
Tsevat, Matitiahu, 173, 274 n.8, 275 n.13
Twins, and need for differentiation, 53–54
Tylor, Edward Burnett, 14, 262 n.33

Unclean Spirit, parable of, 247
"Unconscious," 52
Undifferentiation: prohibited in Decalogue,
    112–13; signaled in birth of twins Jacob
    and Esau, 266 n.45
University, modern, viii; religious studies in
    American, 3

Veblen, Thorstein, on conspicuous con-
    sumption, 242
Victim: prayer for forgivenness of persecutors
    by innocent victim, 237; god-forsakenness
    of innocent victim, 235–36; "infant" or
    voiceless victim, 253–54; innocent vic-
tim's call to persecutors to aid him,
    238–39; innocent victim fulfills Servant
    prophecy, 232–33; innocent victim's trust
    in God, 238; role of in Girard's model, 10;
    slaying of first act of differentiation, 11;
    silence of innocent victim, 232–35; truth
    of, 232–40, 253–58; victimization, 8;
    deception concerning, 41–42
Vernant, Jean-Pierre, 15–16, 262 nn. 40–41
Voegelin, Eric, 268 n.9, 269 n.10, 269 n.13,
    273 n.2; on Exodus 4:24–26, 75–76; on
    son of god symbolism in Pyramid Texts,
    76

Wallace, Mark, 259 n.8, 275 n.11
Wellhausen, Julius, 263 n.63
Widengren, Geo, 132, 273 n.8
Wiesel, Elie, 173
Williams, James G., v, vii–viii, 194, 259 n.8,
    265 n.24, 265 n.26, 266 n.43, 272 n.4, 274
    n.26, 276 n.8, 276 n.14, 276 n.19, 277 n.1,
    278 n.17, 278 n.23, 279 n.8
Wilson, John, 72, 268 n.1
Wink, Walter, 277 n.5
Winthrop, John, 1, 5, 241